Ptolemy I Soter

Also available from Bloomsbury

Alexander the Great: Themes and Issues by Edward Anson
Philip II, the Father of Alexander the Great: Themes and Issues
by Edward Anson
The Idea of Marathon: Battle and Culture by Sonya Nevin
The Seleukid Empire 281–222 BC: War Within the Family
edited by Kyle Erickson

Ptolemy I Soter

Themes and Issues

Edward M. Anson

BLOOMSBURY ACADEMIC
LONDON • NEW YORK • OXFORD • NEW DELHI • SYDNEY

BLOOMSBURY ACADEMIC
Bloomsbury Publishing Plc
50 Bedford Square, London, WC1B 3DP, UK
1385 Broadway, New York, NY 10018, USA
29 Earlsfort Terrace, Dublin 2, Ireland

BLOOMSBURY, BLOOMSBURY ACADEMIC and the Diana logo are trademarks of
Bloomsbury Publishing Plc

First published in Great Britain 2023

Copyright © Edward M. Anson, 2023

Edward M. Anson has asserted his right under the Copyright, Designs and Patents Act, 1988, to be identified as Author of this work.

Cover image: Bust of Ptolemy I Soter (305–282 BC). Marble, 3rd century BC. The identification is based upon coin effigies. Louvre Museum, Paris

All rights reserved. No part of this publication may be reproduced or transmitted in any form or by any means, electronic or mechanical, including photocopying, recording, or any information storage or retrieval system, without prior permission in writing from the publishers.

Bloomsbury Publishing Plc does not have any control over, or responsibility for, any third-party websites referred to or in this book. All internet addresses given in this book were correct at the time of going to press. The author and publisher regret any inconvenience caused if addresses have changed or sites have ceased to exist, but can accept no responsibility for any such changes.

A catalogue record for this book is available from the British Library.

Library of Congress Cataloging-in-Publication Data
Names: Anson, Edward M., author.
Title: Ptolemy Soter I : themes and issues / Edward Anson.
Description: London ; New York : Bloomsbury Academic, 2023. | Includes bibliographical references and index.
Identifiers: LCCN 2022060164 | ISBN 9781350260801 (paperback) | ISBN 9781350260818 (hardback) | ISBN 9781350261808 (ebook) | ISBN 9781350260825 (epub)
Subjects: LCSH: Ptolemy I Soter, King of Egypt, -283 B.C. | Egypt–History–332-30 B.C.
Classification: LCC DT92 .A74 2023 | DDC 932/.01–dc23/eng/20221220
LC record available at https://lccn.loc.gov/2022060164

ISBN: HB: 978-1-3502-6081-8
PB: 978-1-3502-6080-1
ePDF: 978-1-3502-6180-8
eBook: 978-1-3502-6082-5

Typeset by RefineCatch Limited, Bungay, Suffolk
Printed and bound in Great Britain

To find out more about our authors and books visit www.bloomsbury.com and sign up for our newsletters.

It is with greatest gratitude that I dedicate this volume to Marissa Spencer and Jessica Cornelious and all those who have worked in the Interlibrary Loan Department over the years and without whom, especially during the pandemic, my research and writing would have been severely curtailed.

Contents

Preface	viii
Map of Ancient Greece	ix
Map of Asia Minor	x
Map of Ancient Macedonia	xi
Map of the Empire of Alexander the Great	xii
Map of Ptolemaic Egypt	xiii
List of Abbreviations	xiv
Chronology	xvii
1 Ptolemy: An Introduction	1
2 An Early Life Imagined	13
3 The Man with a Plan	29
4 The Destruction of an Empire	45
5 The General	67
6 The Lord of Egypt	103
7 Ptolemy and Religion	127
8 The Royal Historian	145
9 Ptolemy: A Conclusion	167
Notes	171
Bibliography	199
Index	215

Preface

This current work is not a standard biography. As with my earlier works on Alexander the Great and his father Philip, this book is organized around particular themes and examines the various debates surrounding Ptolemy and his impact on the Hellenistic world. The details of his life are examined but only as they impact these themes. In the case of Alexander and Philip, there was no question concerning their impact on future history. With Ptolemy, there is greater debate. What was his contribution to what became the Hellenistic Age? This examination with respect to Ptolemy blends into a discussion of the importance of the Hellenistic Age itself. Afterall, Ptolemy's kingdom and dynasty lasted the longest and his capital in Alexandria became the center of Hellenic culture during this period.

As with my other works, I owe a debt to my wife who critiques what I write and offers many helpful suggestions. Having a microbiologist as my editor brings a whole new perspective to my writing. With respect to this volume, I also need to thank the Ottenheimer Library Interlibrary Loan staff. While they have been important for all my research over the years, during the last few they have been critical. So, let me personally thank Marissa Spencer and Jessica Cornelious. They have made my research during these covid-ridden times not only possible but also successful. There have been times when I've requested something in the morning and had it in my possession by lunch. It is with my gratitude to their recent assistance and to that of the past as well that I wish to dedicate this volume to them personally, and also to those who have peopled the interlibrary loan department before them.

I also wish to thank Sophie Beardsworth from Bloomsbury and Merv Honeywood at RefineCatch who have shepherded this project to completion.

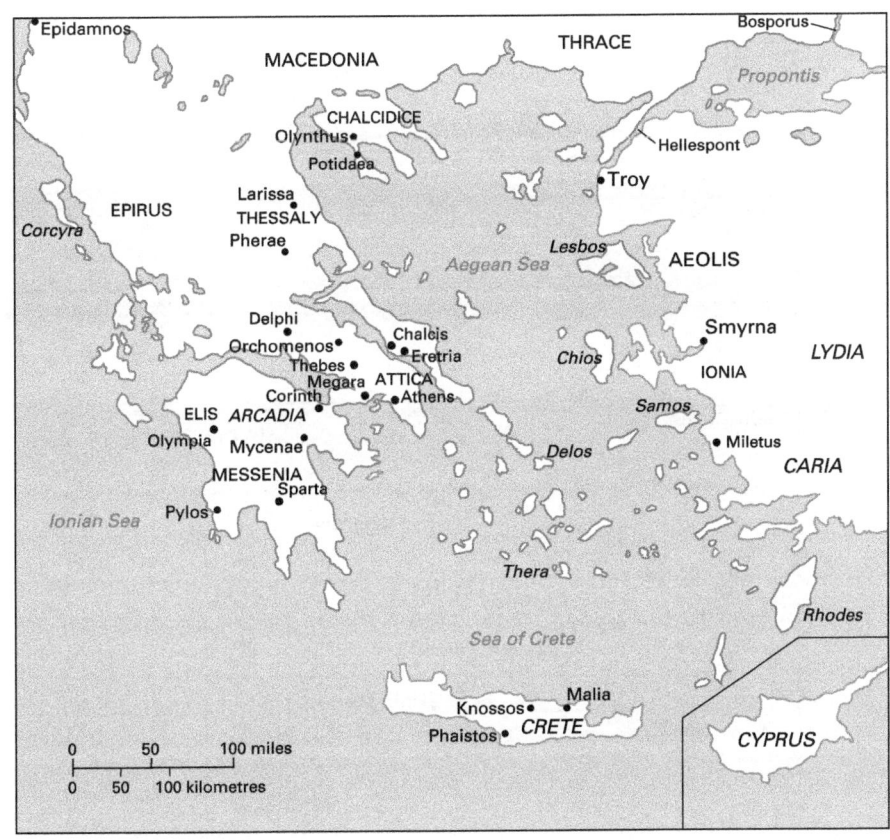

Map of Ancient Greece.

Map of Asia Minor.

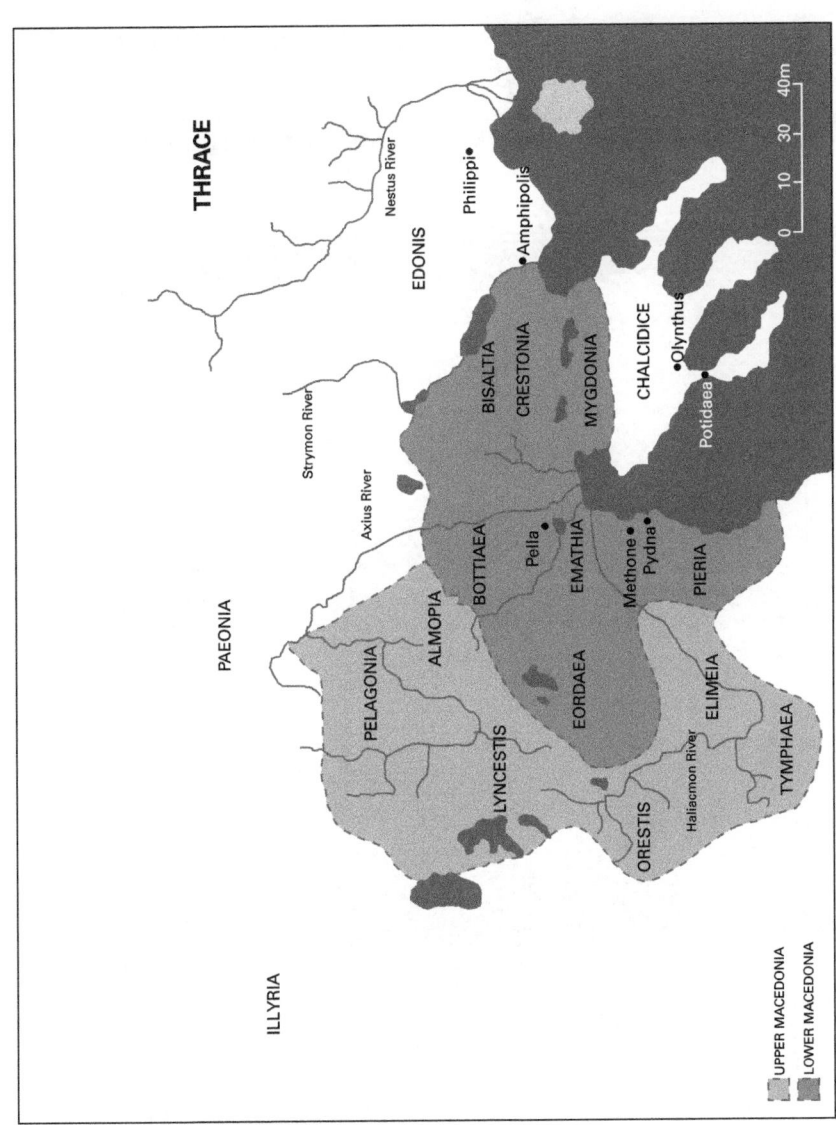

Map of Ancient Macedonia.

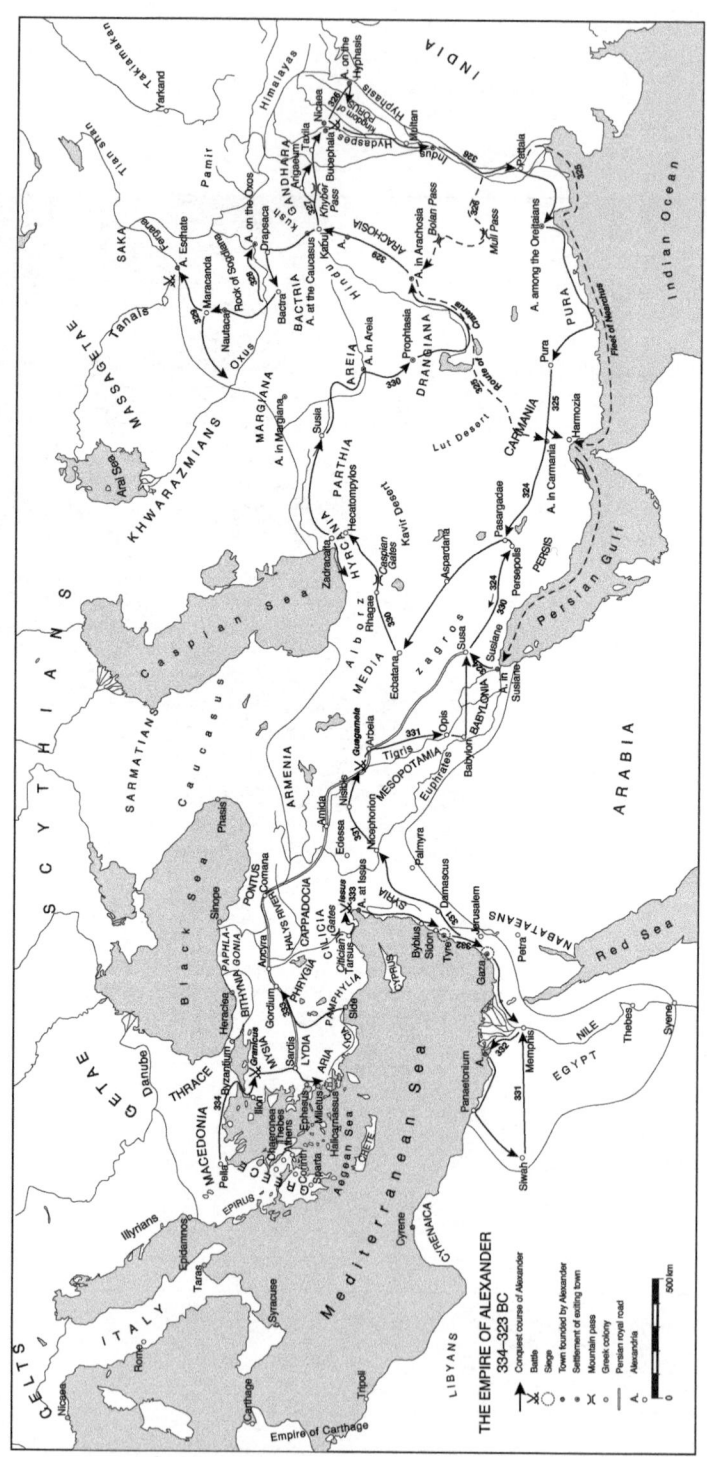

Map of the Empire of Alexander the Great.

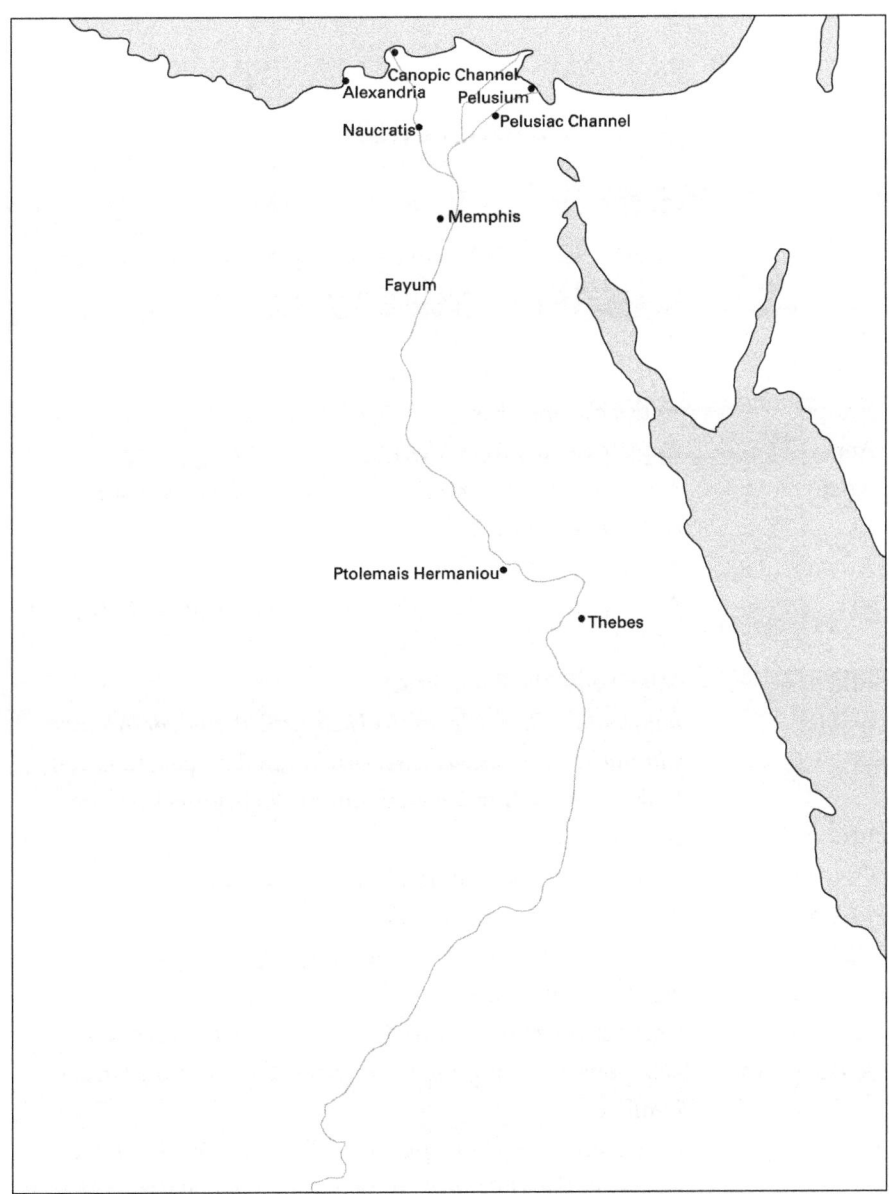

Map of Ptolemaic Egypt.

Abbreviations

ABC	*Assyrian and Babylonian Chronicles* (https://www.livius.org/sources/about/mesopotamian-chronicles/)
Ael.	Aelian, *Varia Historia* (*VH*)
Aeschin.	Aeschines, 2 (On the Embassy)
Antiph.	Antiphon, *Speeches*
App.	Appian, *Syrian Wars* (*Syr.*)
Arist.	Aristotle, *Nicomahean Ethics* (*Nic. Eth.*); *Politics* (*Pol.*); *Oeconomica* (*Oen.*)
Aristid.	Aristides, *Orations* (*Or.*)
Arr.	Arrian, *Anabasis Alexandri* (*Anab.*); *Indica* (*Ind.*); *Successors* (*Succ.*)
Athen.	Athenaeus, *The Banqueteers*
BCHP	*Babylonian Chronicles of the Hellenistic Period*, Babylonian Chronicles of the Hellenistic period, van der Spek, R. J., and Finkel, I. 2004. http://www.livius.org/babylonia.html
BNJ	*Brill's New Jacoby*
Cass. Dio	Cassius Dio Cocceianus, *Historiae Romanae*
2 Chron.	*The Second Book of Chronicles*
CPJud	*Concordance of Original Editions of Papyri* http://www.attalus.org/docs/papyri.html
Curt.	Curtius, *The History of Alexander the Great of Macedon*
Arr. Succ. 1b	Dexippus *History of the Events after Alexander the Great's Death*
Dem.	Demosthenes, 4 (*Philippic 1*); 9 (*Phiilippic 3*); 15 (*On the Liberty of the Rhodians*); 16 (*For the Megalopolitans*); 18 (*On the Crown*); 19 (*On the False Embassy*)
Didymus	*On Demosthenes* (*In Dem.*)
Din.	Dinarchus, 1 (*Against Demosthenes*)
D.L.	Dionysius Laertes, *Lives and Opinions of Eminent Philosophers*
Diod.	Diodorus, *Library of History*
Euseb.	Eusebius [Porphyry], *Chronica* (*Chron.*)

FGrH	Jacoby. *Die Fragmente der Griechischen Historiker*
Frontin.	Frontinus *Strategemata*
GHI	*Greek Historical Inscriptions 404–323 BC*. Rhodes, P. J., and Osborne, R. (eds). Oxford University Press. Oxford and New York
Hdt.	Herodotus, *Histories*
HE	*Heidelberg Epitome*. Wheatley, P. 2013. "The *Heidelberg Epitome*: A Neglected Diadoch Source." In *After Alexander: The Time of the Diadochi (323–281 BC)*. Alonso-Troncoso, V., and Anson, E. M. (eds). Oxbow Books and The David Brown Book Company. Oxford and Oakville: 17–29.
Hom.	Homer, *Iliad* (*Il.*)
Hyp.	Hyperides, 6 (*Funeral Oration*)
IG	*Inscriptiones Graecae*
Isoc.	Isocrates, 5 (*To Philip*); 11 (*Busiris*)
Jer.	*The Book of Jeremiah*
Joseph.	Josephus, *Antiquitates Iudaicae* (*AJ*); *De bello Iudaico* (*BJ*); *Contra Apionem* (*Ap.*)
Just.	Justin, *Epitome of the Philippic History of Pompeius Trogus*
2 Kings	*The Second Book of Kings*
LM	*Liber de Morte Testamentumque Alexandri Magni*
Liv.	Livy, *From the Founding of the City*
Lucian Macrob.	*Macrobii*
1 Macc.	*First Book of Maccabees*
Memnon	Memnon of Heraclea's *History of Heraclea Pontica* (*FGrH* 434 F-5. 7)
Nep.	Nepos, *Life of Eumenes* (*Eum.*); *De Regibus* (*Reg.*)
OGIS	*Orientis Graeci Inscriptiones Selectae*
P.Cairo.Zen.	*Cairo Zenon Papyri*
P.Eleph.	*Papyrus Elephantine*
P.Louvre	Louvre Papyri (https://papyri.info/ddbdp/p.louvre;2;106)
P.Oxy.	*Oxyrhynchus Papyrus*
Paus.	Pausanias, *Description of Greece*
Pl.	Plato, *Laws* (*Leg.*)
Plut.	Plutarch, *Life of Alexander* (*Alex.*), *Life of Mark Antony* (*Ant.*); *Life of Demosthenes* (*Dem.*); *Life of Demetrius* (*Demetr.*); *Life of Eumenes* (*Eum.*); *Moralia* (*Mor.*); *Life of Phocion* (*Phoc.*); *Life of Pyrrhus* (*Pyrrh.*)

Polyaen.	Polyaenus, *Stratagems*
Polyb.	Polybius, *Histories*
SB	*Sammelbuch griechischer Urkunden aus Agypten*, 1–16, 1913–88.
Schol.	*Demosthenes: Scholia Graeca ex codicibus aucta et emendata.* Arno Press. New York. 1983
SEG	*Supplementum Epigraphicum Graecum*
Steph. Byz.	Stephanus of Byzantium
Str.	Strabo, *Geography*
Suda	*Apis, Antipatros, Lagos, Demetrios Antigonou, Ophellas, Perdiccas*
Suet.	Suetonius, *Divus Augustus* (*Aug.*)
Syll.³	*Sylloge inscriptionum graecarum*, 3rd ed. 4 vols. Hildesheim. New York and Olms. 1982 [1915–24]
Tac.	Tacitus, *Annals* (*Ann.*); *Histories* (*Hist.*)
Theoc.	Theocritus *Idylls* (*Id.*)
Thuc.	Thucydides, *History of the Peloponnesian War*
Vitr.	Vitruvius, *On Architecture*
Xen.	Xenophon, *Anabasis* (*Anab.*); *Constitution of the Spartans* (*Resp. Lac.*)

Chronology

367/366	Birth of Ptolemy
359	Philip II, king
356	
July	Birth of Alexander (the Great)
338	
August	Battle of Chaeronea
336	
Spring	Pixodarus Affair; exile of Alexander's *philoi*
October	Death of Philip; Alexander III, king; return of *philoi*
335	
September	Destruction of Thebes
334	
April	Alexander crosses to Asia
May	Battle on the Granicus
September	Siege of Halicarnassus
333	
November	Battle of Issus
332	
January–July	Siege of Tyre
August–October	Siege of Gaza
October	Alexander and army enters Egypt
331	
March	Founds Alexandria; journeys to Siwah
May	Alexander and army leave Egypt
October	Battle of Gaugamela; Alexander and army in Babylon
330	
January	Battle of the Persian Gates
February–May/June	Army stays in Persepolis
July	Death of Darius III
October	Philotas plot; Ptolemy promoted to Somatophylax
329	
June	Ptolemy's capture of Bessus

July	Start of Sogdian-Bactrian Revolt
328	
October/November	Death of Cleitus
327	
March	Sogdian Rock, capture of Roxane; Rock of Chorienes
August	Pages Conspiracy
326	
February	Advance into India; campaign against the Aspasians; capture of the Rock of Aornus
May	Battle on the Hydaspes
July	"Unpleasantness" on the Hyphasis
325	
January	Campaign against the Mallians
April	Harmatelia, "the last city of the Brahmans"
September	Exits Indus; Gedrosian desert
324	Mass marriages at Susa; Hephaestion's death; campaign against the Cossaeans; arrival in Babylon
323	
June 11	Death of Alexander the Great
Summer	Philip III and Alexander IV proclaimed kings; revolt of the Greeks in the Upper Satrapies
Fall	Start of the Lamian War; Thibron attacks Cyrene
Fall/winter	Battle of Abydus; crossing of Leonnatus to Europe; death of Leonnatus
322	
Late Spring	Craterus crosses to Europe
June	Battle of Amorgos
July	Perdiccas moves to Asia Minor
Late July/August	Battle of Crannon, end of Lamian War; Antipater arranges affairs in Greece
Late summer/fall	Annexation of Cyrene by Ptolemy
Late fall/winter	Return of Antipater and Craterus to Macedonia; Craterus marries Antipater's daughter Phila
321	
Spring	Perdiccas campaigns in Pisidia; calls for Antigonus to answer charges; arrival of Nicaea and Cleopatra with marriage proposals; marriage of Perdiccas and Nicaea;

Summer	marriage of Ptolemy and Eurydice; invasion of Aetolia by Antipater and Craterus
Summer	Cynnane arrives in Asia and is murdered; marriage of Adea (Eurydice) and Philip III; Perdiccas determines to seize the monarchy; Alexander the Great's body begins its journey west
Late fall/winter	Antigonus flees to Macedonia; end of Aetolian campaign; diversion of Alexander's body to Egypt
320	
Spring	First Diadoch War begins. Perdiccas marches to Egypt; Eumenes to the Hellespont; desertion of Cleitus and the fleet to Antipater; crossing of Antipater and Craterus to Asia; Antigonus attempts to intercept Eumenes, then to Cyprus
Late spring	Eumenes defeats Neoptolemus; later Neoptolemus and Craterus; deaths of Neoptolemus and Craterus
Early summer	Death of Perdiccas; condemnation of Perdiccans by royal army; Pithon and Arrhidaeus new regents for the kings
Late summer	Triparadeisus; Antipater regent; marriage of Demetrius and Phila
Fall/winter	Failed negotiations among the surviving Perdiccan leaders
319	
Winter	Antipater crosses back to Europe with the kings; start of Second Diadoch War
Spring	Eumenes defeated by Antigonus and enters Nora
Summer	Antigonus defeats Alcetas; death of Alcetas
Late summer	Death of Antipater; Polyperchon new regent, Cassander chiliarch
Winter 319/318	Flight of Cassander to Antigonus; Polyperchon's "Freedom of the Greeks" decree
318	
Spring	Nicanor seizes Piraeus; Ptolemy occupies Phoenicia and Syria; Alexander the son of Polyperchon arrives in Athens; followed later by Polyperchon
May	Cassander arrives in Piraeus
Summer	Antigonus captures all of Lydia; Eumenes allies with Polyperchon; Polyperchon invades Peloponnesus,

	besieges Megalopolis; Eumenes moves into Cilicia,. joined by argyraspids; Menander occupies Cappadocia; Eumenes creates "Alexander Tent"
Fall	Polyperchon returns to Macedonia, orders Cleitus to the Hellespont
Fall/winter	Eumenes moves into Phoenicia;
317	
Summer	Sea battles in the Hellespont; defeat of Cleitus
July	Demetrius of Phalerum in charge of Athens
Late summer	Death of Nicanor; Cassander's first invasion of Macedonia
September	Eumenes leaves Phoenicia for the east
Fall	Eurydice claims the regency; Olympias returns to Macedonia
Fall/winter	Philip III Arrhidaeus and Eurydice murdered
316	
Spring	Cassander successfully invades Macedonia
315	
January	Death of Eumenes; death of Pithon
Spring	Death of Olympias; imprisonment of Roxane and Alexander IV; Cassander marries Thessalonice
Late spring/summer	Peucestas replaced as satrap of Persis
Summer	Cassander refounds Thebes, invades Peloponnesus; flight of Seleucus from Babylon; Cassander's army invades Asia Minor
314	
Spring	Ultimatum to Antigonus; start of the Third Diadoch War; Agesilaus to Cyprus; Polemaeus to Cappadocia; Aristodemus to Greece, forms an alliance with Polyperchon; Siege of Tyre begins
Late spring	Antigonus' capture of Joppa and Gaza
Fall	Alexander the son of Polyperchon to Tyre; Tyre Proclamation; number of Aegean islands including Samos and Lemnos revolt from Athens
Winter 314/313	Antigonus winter quarters near Tyre; alliance between Asander and Ptolemy; Athenian expedition against Samos

313

Summer	Siege of Tyre ends; creation of the "League of the Islanders"; Cassander presides over Nemean Games (August), then returns to Macedonia; Aristodemus in Aetolia; Ptolemy sends Menelaus to Cyprus
Late summer/fall	Alexander deserts Antigonus and allies with Cassander, then is slain
Early winter	Cassander sends an army to Caria; Antigonus leaves Demetrius in Syria and moves to Phrygia

312

Summer	Revolt of Cyrene
Fall	Ptolemy to Cyprus; Battle of Gaza; Ptolemy occupies Phoenicia
Winter 312/311	Demetrius defeats Cilles; Antigonus in Syria

311

April	Seleucus retakes Babylon
Fall	Seleucus occupies Media and Susiane; Demetrius' raid on Babylonia
Winter 311/310	Peace between Antigonus, Cassander, Ptolemy, and Lysimachus

310

Spring	Murders of Roxane and Alexander IV
Late spring/summer	Antigonus invades Babylonia

309

Late spring/early summer	Polemaeus revolts from Antigonus; Ptolemy's operations in Cilicia; death of Polemaeus
Late summer	Death of Heracles, son of Alexander the Great
Fall/winter	Founding of Lysimacheia

308

Spring	Ptolemy's operations in Lycia; his acquisition of Sicyon and Corinth
Summer	Ophellas' campaign in North Africa; return of Antigonus from the east; murder of Cleopatra, sister of Alexander the Great; Seleucus occupies Upper Satrapies, makes treaty with Chandragupta

307

Spring	Ptolemy's operations in the Aegean and Greece; Demetrius "frees" Athens

Fall	Pyrrhus becomes king of Epirus
306	
Spring	Demetrius' operations in Cyprus begin
June	Battle of Salamis; Antigonus and Demetrius proclaimed kings
Summer	Surrender of Cyprus to Demetrius; death of Philip, son of Antigonus
November	Antigonus' and Demetrius' failed invasion of Egypt
305	
Spring	Demetrius launches attack on Rhodes
304	
Spring	Cassander captures island of Salamis, besieging Athens; Demetrius abandons siege of Rhodes and returns to Athens; other Diadochs with exception of Cassander proclaim themselves kings
303	
Late summer/fall	Demetrius secures Achaea, all of Arcadia, except Mantinea, and Argos; marries Deidameia and forms an alliance with Epirus
Winter 303/302	Failed attempt by Cassander to make peace with Antigonus
302	
Winter	Alliance of Cassander, Lysimachus, Ptolemy, and Seleucus against Antigonus
Spring	Start of Fourth Diadoch War; formation of new League of Corinth
April/May	Lysimachus and Cassander's general Perpelaus cross to Asia
Summer	Antigonus moves into Asia Minor
Summer/fall	Demetrius campaigning in Thessaly
Fall	Antigonus and Lysimachus campaigning in Phrygia; Pyrrhus forced from the throne of Epirus and joins Demetrius
Winter 302/301	Demetrius recalled from Greece; Ptolemy seizes Phoenicia and returns to Egypt
301	
Late spring	Battle of Ipsus; death of Antigonus

300

Spring	New alliance of Ptolemy, Cassander, and Lysimachus; alliance between Seleucus and Demetrius; Demetrius takes possession of Cilicia; Lachares takes control of Athens
Late spring/summer	Alliance between Demetrius and Ptolemy; Pyrrhus to Egypt as a hostage for Demetrius' good behavior

298

	Demetrius' failed attempt to "liberate" Athens
Winter 298/297	Death of Cassander, succeeded by son Philip IV

297

Spring	Death of Philip IV, ruler of Macedonia; Macedonia divided among Cassander's surviving sons, Alexander and Antipater
Early summer	Pyrrhus returns to Epirus

296

Spring?	Demetrius begins siege of Athens

295

Spring	Demetrius "liberates" Athens

294

Summer	Civil war between the brothers in Macedonia; intervention of Pyrrhus
Late summer/early fall	Demetrius arrives in response to invitation from Alexander
Fall	Murder of Alexander IV; Demetrius I king of Macedonia

288

Spring	With Demetrius preparing to invade Asia Minor, new coalition of Ptolemy, Seleucus, Lysimachus, and Pyrrhus formed against him
Fall	Lysimachus and Pyrrhus invade Macedonia; Macedonia divided between Lysimachus and Pyrrhus; Demetrius flees to Cassandreia; death of Phila

287

Spring	Reestablishment of Athenian democracy; Ptolemy new patron of Nesiotic League
Summer	Ptolemy repudiates Eurydice and Ceraunus; Ptolemy regains Cyprus; Demetrius returns to Asia

286	Demetrius campaigning in Asia Minor
285	
Spring	Seleucus captures Demetrius; Lysimachus subverts Pyrrhus' army and becomes sole king of Macedonia
Summer?	Ptolemy Philadelphus made co-ruler of Egypt
283	
February?	Death of Demetrius
Spring?	Death of Ptolemy I; Ptolemy (II) Philadelphus, sole ruler of Egypt
Winter 283/282	Lysimachus murders his son Agathocles
282/281 Winter	Seleucus invades Lysimachus' possessions in Asia Minor
281	
February/March	Battle of Corupedium; death of Lysimachus
Summer	Seleucus crosses to Macedonia; Seleucus murdered by Ceraunus (September); Ceraunus king of Macedonia
280	Death of Ceraunus
279	Antigonus Gonatas king of Macedonia

1

Ptolemy: An Introduction

When Alexander the Great died in June of 323 BC,[1] he left behind an empire stretching from Greece to Egypt to India. Perhaps even greater than the expanse of his conquests was the growth of the myth of Alexander. He was a figure in life larger than life and in death a legend that only expanded and became more fantastic with time. Alexander, in what became known as the Romance, goes to the depths of the ocean, speaks to mermaids, journeys to the ends of the earth, and builds the gates of Gog and Magog. Whoever would follow after his mercurial career would find it hard to live up to the man let alone the legend. Those who tried, those known as his Successors or the Diodochi, were left in the dust of failure. Leonnatus, the son of Anteas, a member of the former ruling house of Lyncestas, one of Alexander's elite bodyguards, the *somatophylaces*, who at one time was considered for a share in the regency for the new kings, Alexander's half-brother and infant son, died in his attempt to become the new Alexander in 322. He was followed in death by others who dreamed of succeeding the Conqueror as the holder of his entire empire. Perdiccas, the first regent for the kings, Antigonus, Lysimachus, and Seleucus, all had such dreams, which all ended in failure and death. When the funeral games that Alexander supposedly predicted would erupt on his death finally ended, there was no unified empire even in theory. Three large kingdoms/empires emerged, the Ptolemaic, Seleucid, and Antigonid, and numbers of smaller ones and about as many city-states as had existed before in the Classical Age, although many of the latter were now organized into federations or leagues.

Those Successors who did survive the wars at least long enough to build states that would endure were faced with a problem that Alexander had left them. His life had been one of conquests not of consolidation. In a Persian analogy, Alexander was the Macedonian Cyrus, that individual who created the Persian Empire, which was now overthrown by the Macedonians. Alexander had created the empire but, like Cyrus, had not created an overall structure to rule his conquests. In the case of Persia, the creator of the administrative structure was the third Persian king, Darius. In Alexander's empire there would be no single empire and therefore no single creator of its political, economic, and social structure.

There was little uniformity in Alexander's governing structure beyond a general tendency to adopt a hybrid version of the Persian satrapal system. This was a problem left to his heirs. Perhaps, given time—after all, Alexander was not quite thirty-three years of age when he died—he might have addressed his realm's organizational diversity, but in truth Alexander was more interested in the acquisition not the ordering of his conquests. He planned, having returned from India, to turn westward in pursuit of greater glory and a wider empire. After all, he was young; even his father at some years short of age fifty did not rest on his laurels but had planned his own invasion of the Persian Empire, which only his assassination prevented. In most cases, Alexander did little to change the governmental structure he found except to put his people in charge. With respect to the Greek cities of Asia, he did not change the basic organization of the *polis*, but typically changed the governments from oligarchic to democratic. The oligarchies had been supported by the Persians. Alexander, the autocrat, thus became the founder of many new democracies in the Greek cities of Asia. These were, however, limited democracies, with local affairs left in the hands of the locals but foreign policy in particular, and whatever else Alexander wished in general, superseding these democratic assemblies. The cities often had garrisons imposed on them and provincial governors as well. In the non-Greek world of his conquests, Alexander typically left the basic Persian satrapal system intact. His chief innovation with respect to his conquests was the introduction of city-colonies of retired Macedonian veterans and Greek mercenaries, especially in the more eastern areas of his empire. These, in addition to his many garrisons, left a significant number of Macedonians and Greeks in Asia. His Successors, through their encouragement of Greek migration to these newly acquired lands, led to significant minority populations of these migrants throughout the lands of Alexander's conquest.

What becomes very clear in the aftermath of the Conqueror's death is that Alexander did not plan for what might follow his death. Here again, Alexander appeared more interested in other things. Ernst Badian (1964: 203) has declared and I believe accurately,[2] "Alexander was, essentially, not interested in a future without himself." Where Philip had prepared for what would follow his death, ultimately leaving his son Alexander and his nephew Amyntas as possible successors, he had, however, also eliminated a great many members of the Argead clan. Alexander had pruned the clan even further until at the time of his death there were but two remaining Argeads and one in the offing. The only surviving adult was Alexander's half-brother Arrihidaeus, who survived Alexander's purge only because no one saw him as able to be king because of some mental incapacity. Alexander had a son by his mistress Barsine, Heracles, who was, perhaps, as old as five years at the time of his father's death, and a pregnant wife, who did subsequently produce a son. Of course, Philip had died at around forty-seven years and Alexander at not quite thirty-three. Had he lived to be as old as his father, then, perhaps, his "legitimate" thirteen- to fourteen-year-old-son might have been able to rule, or at least survive until he came of an age to succeed his father. Philip, however, had, from the time of his accession to the throne, his nephew Amyntas available to succeed him if Alexander was unborn or not of age at the time of Philip's death; the Argead dynasty, therefore, would have likely survived. While very little is known about Amyntas' years under his guardian, he was married to Philip's daughter Cynnane, and that is pretty much the extent of our knowledge. Alexander saw him as enough of a threat that he had him killed (Just. 12. 6. 14). Philip had stripped the once large Argead royal clan down to himself, his two sons, and his nephew. Alexander completed the process by eliminating his cousin, leaving himself, his half-brother, his young son Heracles, and the posthumous son as the only remaining members of the royal clan at the time of his death. There was to be no smooth transition in power and, in the final analysis, Alexander's family, the Argeads, would not long survive the great king's death.

Unlike the later Roman empire, in which lands secured overseas by Roman armies redounded to the benefit of the Roman state, Alexander regarded his conquests as his personal possessions, his spear-won land, acquired through his personal triumphs. Whatever national Macedonian patriotism that might have existed prior to the advance into Asia had dissipated. Alexander had proclaimed he was the King of Asia; his new capital was to be Babylon. Macedonia was very distant in both his thoughts and, at the time of his death, in miles. His father Philip had created a Macedonian nation and his Asian empire, if he had lived to create it, would have centered on Macedonia.[3] For Alexander, Macedonia was a manpower resource only. His connection to his homeland grew dimmer with every new conquest and with every step he took further into the East. This personal quality of rule was one of Alexander's major legacies to his Successors. Another of Alexander's legacies to the Hellenistic Age was that his empire was won on the battlefield, and warfare was not just the backdrop of Alexander's conquests, but also that of the entire Hellenistic period. The history of the Hellenistic Age is a story of vaulting ambition, treachery, and wars almost without cessation. The result of the continued fighting among Alexander's heirs led ultimately to the Roman acquisition of the Hellenistic world. The Romans came often to help Greek allies, to free the Greeks from the oppression of other Greeks. In fact, one could say the Romans freed the Greeks right into the Roman empire.

All of Alexander's Successors initially were faced with creating their own personal kingdoms in the face of the fictional unity of the empire in the persons of the two kings, Alexander's half-brother Arrhidaeus, now Philip III, and his young son Alexander IV, both chosen in a compromise in Babylon. When the farce of the united empire and a ruling Argead dynasty was ended by the murder of Alexander's son, heir, and king, Alexander IV, Philip III having been killed previously, the true rulers now had to establish their legitimacy based on new criteria. They were no longer the ostensible governors for the ruling kings, but kings in their own right. Antigonus and his son Demetrius assumed the diadem after Demetrius' naval victory at Salamis over Ptolemy and his acquisition of the island of Cyprus; the other Successors followed suit apart from Cassander in Macedonia. Ptolemy, after his efforts helped the Rhodians survive the siege of their island by Demetrius, assumed the diadem. In short, those proclaiming themselves kings usually did so after some military success. Then began the task of creating a dynasty.

There was another problem common to these new kingdoms. Whether it be Egypt or Asia, these new kingdoms represented foreign rulers of indigenous and culturally different populations. Alexander had attempted to create a hybrid ruling class of Macedonians, Greeks, and Asians (primarily Persians). He had proclaimed that he was the King of Asia, downplaying his Macedonian heritage but also not claiming the throne of Persia. This policy of apparent "fusion" has been extolled from Antiquity to modern times as his desire to create "a brotherhood of man." Plutarch (*Mor.* 329C) proclaims that Alexander came "as a heaven-sent governor to all, and as a mediator of the whole world ... and he brought together into one body all men everywhere, uniting and mixing in one great loving cup." Alexander was hardly the philosopher king envisioned by Plutarch, but he did realize and attempted to deal with the problem of foreign minority rule over a much larger native population and attempted to find ways to lessen the problems that then arose. Additionally, Alexander wished to conquer in the West and believed he needed more troops to hold what he already possessed and fresh troops in great numbers to conquer further. Consequently, this was not the beginning of some concept of the brotherhood of all mankind, but rather an attempt to maximize his recruiting field for skilled soldiers and administrators, minimize especially in the native elites any misgiving concerning their role in his new state, and eliminate as much as possible any unrest among the recently conquered. Not only did Alexander wish to address practical concerns but, if there was any real sense of brotherhood truly intended, it was with few exceptions primarily between the Macedonian and Persian elites and in the ranks of his army. With respect to the elites, he began in Babylon to appoint governors, satraps, from the ranks of the Persians and at Susa arranged marriages between his leading *hetairoi* and noble Persian women. Additionally, here he recognized as marriages the liaisons of 10,000 of his troops and Asian women. While this might seem to be a new form of domination, since all the grooms were Macedonians and selected Greeks and the brides mostly Persian, it is more reasonable to assume that those marriages between the *hetairoi* and the aristocratic women were a way to link the two elite groups then in Asia. Alexander could have had Macedonian women sent to Asia, but he was not interested in such alliances in Macedonia. The marriages were tied to his needs in the lands of his conquest. His *hetairoi* were in Asia as were the Persian elite women.

Increasingly, Alexander added Asian units to his ever-growing army and, at Opis, even began creating Persian units trained in the tactics of and named after existing Macedonian units. He also began to enroll Asians in these very Macedonian military bodies. Of course, one way of looking at his policy is to realize that for one contemplating his own divinity, the equality he was advocating was that all people were unified in their subjection to his autocracy. While Alexander did attempt to convince the previous ruling elites that they would become part of the new power base, he also encouraged Macedonian and Greek migration to the lands of his conquest. He created colonies of these individuals in his empire, pockets of mercenaries, injured or older soldiers, and camp followers located in strategic points within his empire. It would have been interesting to see how all of these actions would have sorted out had he lived.

Alexander's Successors all had before them the example of Alexander and his policies. The question became whether they would follow his lead in creating their new kingdoms, or follow the pattern of traditional kingship in Macedonia, or Persian practices, or an amalgam of the different traditions. Whatever they chose, there was always the reality of an increasing presence of primarily Greeks, but also Macedonians, who were flocking to the new lands to serve the ever-contesting dynasts or to take advantage of the many economic opportunities—always in the context of the far more numerous indigenous populations. How would these Successors treat the different populations? Would they attempt to unify them, or would they choose to treat them as separate entities? In the case of the latter, would this separation involve a secondary status for those who had been conquered? Isocrates, when he addressed Alexander's father Philip, encouraged him to lead the Greeks in a war of revenge on the Persian Empire, "to compel the barbarians to be helots [serfs] of the Greeks" (Isoc. *Letter* 3. 5). If not at this level of oppression, would positions of authority in the government and other institutions be dominated by one ethnic group over another; would there be ethnic divisions dependent on the particular institution? If unity was the choice, the goal would be to find ways to bind together the disparate peoples and cultures to create one people. In this regard, with the very real exception of Peucestas and the partial exception of Seleucus, none of the Successors aimed to create a single nation of these diverse peoples.

Peucestas and Seleucus were noted for their acceptance of foreign traditions and peoples. Peucestas, Alexander's satrap of Persis, wore Persian dress, learned the Persian language (Arr. *Anab*. 6. 30. 2–3), and treated many Persians as his close, personal, advisors and allies (Diod. 19. 22. 2). Later, in the second great contest of Alexander's Successors, Peucestas assembled an army that included 6,000 Persian archers and slingers, 3,000 heavy infantry made up of "men of many races . . . in Macedonian array," and 400 Persian cavalrymen (Diod. 19. 14. 5). Seleucus' later success in securing much of the East was tied to his ability "to find common ground with the native populations" (Olbrycht 2013: 168). In both Babylonia and Iran his "generosity" and "benevolence" secured the support of even the common people (Diod. 19. 91. 2, 92. 5). The problems of a rapidly increasing minority of Greeks and Macedonians and a overwhelming majority of Egyptians were faced by Ptolemy after his assignment to Egypt. His solutions have been debated with many interpretations. He has been seen as treating the two different cultural groups as distinct and separate and also as attempting to bring them together. This author believes that the evidence certainly suggests the former.

This decision regarding different populations was especially important with respect to the recruitment of soldiers for the army. Here, again, Alexander, as noted, was fashioning a very different army from the one he had led into Asia. It was no longer the national force of Macedonia and Greek allied soldiers, but a polyglot army of different nationalities, including increasing numbers of true mercenaries. Even his Macedonians, not officially mercenaries, after their years of service with Alexander, had come to exhibit many of the characteristics of such soldiers (Anson 1991: 230–47). In the early Successor period these traits became amplified. Troops tended to follow leaders who were both successful on the battlefield and excellent paymasters. Often, defeated armies would desert their now beaten general and enter service with the commander of the victorious force. The other aspect of these armies of the Diadochs was that, while they may have had Macedonian cores, the majority of the troops were increasingly Greek and Asian mercenaries. When Alexander died in Babylon, his army only consisted of approximately 2,000 Macedonian cavalry and 13,000 Macedonian infantry (Curt. 10. 2. 8). In addition to these Macedonians, there were present 30,000 infantry called the *Epigoni* or Offspring, young Asians armed and trained in the techniques of the Macedonian heavy infantry (Arr. *Anab.* 7. 6. 1; Curt. 8. 5. 1; Diod. 17. 108. 1–2; Plut. *Alex.* 47. 3, 71. 1), 20,000 Persian infantry armed in their traditional fashion, forces of Cossaeans and Tapurians (Arr. *Anab.* 7. 23. 1), 30,000 mercenary infantry and 6,000 such cavalry brought from Greece prior to Alexander's voyage down the Indus (Diod. 17. 95. 4), and unspecified forces brought to Babylon shortly before the Conqueror's death from Caria and Lydia (Arr. *Anab.* 7. 23. 1). Moreover, it is unknown how many of the original force that entered India had survived the conquest of the Persian Empire. How many subsequently did not survive the journey down the Indus, the crossing of the Gedrosian desert, or had been left behind in various garrisons or colonies. According to Curtius (8. 5. 4), the army that entered India contained 120,000 men (cf. Engels 1978: 150). While these Asian and Greek forces in the aftermath of Alexander's death are most often not specified ethnically by our sources, there are indications that Asians continued to serve in the armies of the early Diadochs in large numbers. Eumenes in 320 had an army composed of "men of many races" (Diod. 18. 30. 4). In the Battle of Paraetacene in 316, Eumenes' infantry contained 6,000 mercenaries (presumably Greek) and 5,000 "men of many races" armed in the Macedonian fashion, and in his opponent Antigonus' ranks, 9,000 mercenaries, 3,000 Lycians and Pamphylians, and 8,000 "mixed troops in Macedonian equipment" (Diod. 19. 27. 6, 29. 3; cf. 18. 40. 7). The cavalry fighting in Asia during the wars of the Successors was predominantly Asian horsemen (cf. Diod. 19. 14. 5–8, 20. 3, 27. 4, 29. 2). In the early wars of the Diadochi, however, while Asian elements may have predominated numerically, it was the Macedonian veterans who served as the core of these armies (Roisman 2012). Over time this Macedonian importance would decrease significantly but be increasingly offset by Greek migrants. For those who were now dividing up Alexander's empire, the recruitment of ever-increasing numbers of soldiers was critical. How would these manpower needs be met? Armies entirely made up of mercenaries were dangerous. There was no sense of national loyalty: success and pay ruled. To recruit from the local population could be equally dangerous.

National interests might emerge, leading to revolts from these new foreign Macedonian overlords. One solution was to follow the example of Philip II who created a loyal military by giving land to formerly landless men in exchange for military service and loyalty. It was these "citizen" soldiers who had formed the bulk of the Macedonian infantry that Alexander had brought to Asia (Anson 2020: 73–92).

Ptolemy, the son of Lagus, was in many ways the most important of all of Alexander's Successors. Unlike his contemporaries, Ptolemy died in bed of natural causes at the age of eighty-four, but before doing so he created what became the longest-lasting and most durable of all the Hellenistic kingdoms. One of the major controversies that has emerged concerning Ptolemy is whether he was different from the other contenders for power. Polybius argued more than 2,100 years ago that his dominant foreign policy was one of defensive imperialism. According to Polybius (5. 34. 9), Ptolemy ensconced himself in Egypt with the goal to protect it, surrounding that land with "a fence of client states." Therefore, instead of contending for the entire empire created by Alexander, he had settled in Egypt and made it his kingdom. Many scholars have come forth to challenge this belief and, indeed, most now proclaim that Ptolemy was little different from his fellow Successors who did clearly contend over the whole of Alexander's empire. Perhaps he was more cautious than his rivals, but his goal and their goals were the same. The contention presented here is that he was different from these other heirs of Alexander's conquests, and this gave him a significant advantage over his rivals. Never having the illusion that he could be the new Alexander enabled him to avoid the many costly and ultimately failed attempts to seize the grand prize. In the final analysis then, Polybius got this right.

Alexander's death had changed the very nature of power. While Alexander lived, the court was the center, the nucleus, of power. To be away from court was to be distant from this reality. In this new world without Alexander, if one desired independence or supremacy, being the governor of one of the districts in the empire provided a base of operations for the contests yet to come. One of the major contenders for supremacy over the entire empire in the first two decades of the Hellenistic Age, Antigonus Monophthalmus, had been left behind in 333 by Alexander as governor of the region of Phrygia in what is now central Turkey, far from the court and thereby far from the seat of power, but with the death of the Conqueror his position made him a major contender in the civil wars that followed. He had a base, his own troops, and alliances with local elites and other governors like himself distant from Alexander. With Alexander's death and the new government of two kings and a regent, some chose to stay with the regent and the kings, others sought something similar to what Antigonus possessed—all for reasons of personal ambition. Leonnatus, one of the most elite of Alexander's advisors, became the governor of Hellespontine Phrygia. Since this individual at one time appeared as a candidate to be part of the regency for the new kings, this particular satrapy might appear to be quite a demotion. Hellespontine Phrygia was the area of what is today northwestern Turkey, not one of the premier satrapies. It did have one very great advantage, however: it was across the Hellespont from Macedonia. If one planned to attack Macedonia and proclaim oneself king, this could be an ideal province. As it turns out, Leonnatus planned to invade Macedonia and marry Alexander's sister and become in essence the new Alexander. The invasion took place, but not the marriage, and Leonnatus was killed in the Lamian War, that revolt of many Greek states against Macedonian domination.

Ptolemy's assignment to Egypt was not the result of some random drawing. While Perdiccas is listed by Diodorus (18. 3. 1) as personally assigning the satrapies, Diodorus does indicate that this assignment came after consultation with the leaders of whom Ptolemy was clearly one. This choice suggests his very different ambition from that of Leonnatus and so many others. Egypt was a rich land easily able to support itself and, moreover, very isolated geographically from the rest of the world. It was a natural fortress guarded by deserts, a river, and coastal barriers. Egypt was the perfect satrapy for one who might wish to ride out the storms of war. It was self-sufficient economically and guarded from outside interference. From this base, Ptolemy could venture forth judiciously to gain footholds in those lands from which an invasion of Egypt was most possible and also to undermine the power of those whose ambitions threatened Ptolemy's hold on Egypt. For those seeking to contend for the entire legacy of Alexander, Egypt would not appear to be ideally situated. The same barriers that protected Egypt from outside invasion could also hamper Egyptian efforts to conquer other lands.

As important as Ptolemy was in this new age, his personal history is today mostly lost, if much of it ever existed. While there has been much speculation that there were histories of the Successor or Diadoch Age that followed the death of our most famous Macedonian king, which concentrated on Ptolemy, the son of Lagus, the future ruler of Egypt,[4] these have not survived, not even as titles. In the surviving histories of Alexander, even though he is a close companion of the king and a participant in the expedition, except as an historian he is not mentioned until the sixth year of the campaign and then only sporadically thereafter. This is true even though his now lost history of Alexander's expedition was a major source for what is generally considered the best of the surviving histories for that campaign. Our information concerning Ptolemy's subsequent career after Alexander's death is likewise sparse. Moreover, the narrative histories that were written at the time concerning the period as a whole, not unlike those written during the life of Alexander, have survived only in fragments. The best of these—although such a determination requires a great deal of speculation—was that of Hieronymus of Cardia, a contemporary and participant, who wrote an account of the period of Alexander's Successors and their immediate descendants, the latter known as the *Epigoni*. What does survive includes the world history of Diodorus of Sicily who likely followed, though severely abbreviating, the work of Hieronymus. Diodorus' history, however, itself becomes fragmentary shortly before the Battle of Ipsus in 301 BC. Additionally, there is a severely abridged version of the *Philippic History* by the Augustan historian, Pompeius Trogus, dating likely from the early third century AD, and abridged by the otherwise unknown Marcus Junianus Justinus (Justin); a collection of military anecdotes by the second-century AD rhetorician, Polyaenus; and finally the briefest remains also from the second century of *A History of the Successors*, covering the years from 323 to 319, by Flavius Arrianus (Arrian).[5] Fortunately, in the case of materials to address the history of Ptolemy, there do survive many contemporary inscriptional and papyri sources.

As is often said about Alexander, and is also true of those who followed him and created the kingdoms of the Hellenistic Age, their history survives through a Roman filter. Plutarch wrote biographies of only one of those who followed Alexander, Eumenes of Cardia, and two from the next generation, Demetrius Poliorcetes and Pyrrhus. Nepos left only a *Life of Eumenes*, but then his biographies of kings have not survived, and his surviving biographies of military commanders purposely omitted the deeds of kings (*Reg.* 21. 1), although he does include certain Spartan kings, since "these had the title but not the power of a king" (*Reg.* 21. 2).[6] Nepos seems to express what must have been the view of many writers from the Roman period if not from the Hellenistic period as well.

> Now, among the people of Macedonia two kings far surpassed the rest in the glory of their deeds: Philip, son of Amyntas, and Alexander the Great. There were besides many kings among the friends of Alexander the Great, who assumed their power after his death, including Antigonus and his son Demetrius, Lysimachus, Seleucus, and Ptolemy. Of these Antigonus was slain in battle, fighting against Seleucus and Lysimachus. A like death overtook Lysimachus at

the hands of Seleucus; for they broke off their alliance and warred with each other. But Demetrius, after giving his daughter in marriage to Seleucus, without thereby ensuring the permanence of their friendship, was taken captive and died a natural death in the custody of his son-in-law. And not very long after that Seleucus was treacherously killed by Ptolemy, surnamed Ceraunus or 'the Thunderbolt,' to whom, when he was exiled by his father from Alexandria and was in need of help from others, Seleucus had given asylum. But Ptolemy himself, having made over his kingdom to his son while still living, by him, they say, was put to death.[7] I think that I have said enough about these kings.

Nep. *Reg.* 2 (Loeb Classical Library translation)

It is hard to measure up to a colossus. Even Ptolemy, when it came right down to it, wrote a history not of his life and accomplishments, but rather he wrote of Alexander and secondarily of his own participation in the colossus' career. The aura of Alexander hung over everyone and everything. Plutarch did not write a biography of Alexander's father Philip, who in my estimation was as important as his son. For a man who did more than any of Alexander's Successors (the *Diodochoi*) to define the Hellenistic Age, it is a shame that we do not know more about him.

2

An Early Life Imagined

So little is known of Ptolemy's early life that most of it must be imagined from what we know of aristocratic life in Macedonia in general, and even that he was a member of this aristocratic class has been challenged. What we do know is that he was a friend and an *hetairos*, a type of official companion (explained below), of Alexander's before the latter became king (Plut. *Alex.* 10. 3–5) and he became one of the official *somatophylaces*, the most elite of the official royal bodyguards, in 330 (Arr. *Anab.* 3. 27. 5).[1] From the reign of Philip II, the king was protected by four units regarded as "guards," with all being responsible for the king's safety whether on the battlefield, during the hunt, at court, or in his bedchamber (Heckel 1986: 279). These were the hypaspists, the royal infantry guards, or more particularly the 1,000-man *agema* (the most elite members of the unit) of the 3,000-man hypaspists; the royal pages, young aristocrats who guarded his bedchamber and hunted and fought with the king; the *Ilê Basilikê*, the aristocratic "royal" cavalry squadron of the "Companion Cavalry," also in general called the *hetairoi*,[2] amounting to 300 horsemen who served as the king's cavalry guard; and finally the *Somatophylaces*, the "Seven" (later in Alexander's expedition eight) aristocratic bodyguards, who were also responsible for the king's bedchamber and were often among his chief advisors.[3] These individuals often fought in close proximity to the king or served as commanders of specific units. Unfortunately, the surviving historians of Alexander the Great on occasion applied the term *somatophylaces* to members of any one of three units: the Royal Pages, the Hypaspists, or the seven-man elite bodyguard, known officially as the *Somatophylaces*.

Beyond any official capacities, Ptolemy was always very close to Alexander, with one source proclaiming that he was "much loved by Alexander" (Diod. 17. 103. 6; cf. Curt. 9. 8. 23–4). However, except for a few brief mentions and all of these prior to the launching of Alexander's great expedition, he figured hardly at all in the surviving histories prior to Alexander's advance into India. Much of this lack of information is surprising, because Ptolemy wrote a history of

Alexander's expedition in which he is reported to have accentuated his role: "[Ptolemy] was not inclined to depreciate his own glory" (Curt. 9. 5. 21). Unfortunately, this history does not survive except in paraphrases from other later surviving works (see Chapter 9).

With this lack of information on his early career, historians must rely on brief notices in very late sources and occasional fragments from contemporary ones. According to Lucian of Samosota, a second-century AD satirist, or someone else writing under Lucian's name,[4] Ptolemy was likely born in 367/366 BC (*Macr.* 12). Lucian says he was eighty-four at the time of his death and that occurred two years after the accession of his son Philadelphus to the throne. The second-century BC historian Polybius records Ptolemy's death in the year of the 124th Olympiad, or 284/283 BC (2. 41. 1, 71. 5). This dating is challenged, because many assume that Ptolemy and Alexander were true contemporaries. This is based on another assumption that Ptolemy was a page, one of the young men raised at court with the heir apparent.[5] Alexander was born in 356 BC (Plut. *Alex*. 3. 5–9; Arr. *Anab*. 7. 28. 1),[6] but there is no good reason to reject Lucian or Pseudo-Lucian's date.[7] There is no direct statement that Ptolemy was a page.[8] Waldemar Heckel (1985: 285–9) argues convincingly that Ptolemy was one of Alexander's personal advisors (*philoi*=Plut. *Alex*. 10. 1; *hetairoi*=Plut. *Alex*. 10. 5), not a boyhood friend. This is also apparently true with respect to Erigyius, son of Larichus (Heckel 1985: 286; 2021: 182).[9]

While the terms *philos* and *hetairos* are often used interchangeably,[10] there can be a formal distinction. The first can apply to personal guest-friendship or *xenia*, while the second in the case of Macedonia was institutionalized politically, socially, and religiously within the context of the state. *Xenia* was a form of hospitality which established reciprocal relationships between individuals and families.[11] Royal *hetairoi* were official companions of the king.[12] The *hetairoi* were primarily members of the powerful landed Macedonian aristocracy, although some were from elsewhere and became *hetairoi* by royal invitation. These latter owed their appointment to the king, the native-born *hetairoi* typically inherited their status as Macedonian aristocrats. The *hetairoi* were in a very real sense the government of Macedonia. They acted as the king's ambassadors, military commanders, governors, religious representatives, and personal advisors. Moreover, they represented regional authority throughout the kingdom. Apart from the king, these individuals were the basic political institution of the Macedonian state (Stagakis 1962: 53–67; 1970: 86–102). While the *hetairideia* was a formalized state institution, the relationship with the king was regarded by the *hetairoi* as personal. The ancient *hetairos* relationship between king and nobles was built on camaraderie, not on the basis of royal absolutism (Anson 2013: 24–5). Aristotle (*Nic. Eth.* 8. 1161a-25-7, 1161b33–1162a1) declares that ideally *hetairoi* are like brothers and share in all things. These aristocratic Macedonians made up the majority of the court where they feasted and drank together with the king (cf. Ael. *VH* 13. 4; Athen. 11. 119. 508D-E; [Theopompus] *BNJ* 115 F-236; [Ephippus of Olynthus] *BNJ* 126 F-120 C-D).[13] As Frances Pownall (2010: 55) explains, these festive activities were a means of strengthening the ties between commander/king and his companions. The feasts then were in their purpose not that far different from certain modern corporate team-building practices, at least those associated with happy hours and dinner parties. The *hetairoi* were formally tied to the monarch by religious and social bonds; they sacrificed to the gods, hunted, and fought alongside the king. While there are a number of difficulties with the oft-repeated statement that the Macedonian kingship was Homeric,[14] in the particular case of the *hetairoi* there are clear parallels (Stagakis 1962: 1–38, 53–77). These were after all both warrior societies, and it was not unusual for Macedonian kings to lose their lives at the hands of disgruntled Macedonian aristocrats who believed that the king in some fashion had disrespected them. Alexander's father Philip was assassinated by an aggrieved aristocrat who believed he had been humiliated and who blamed Philip for not aiding in the recovery of his honor.[15] In point of fact, aristocratic life was all about honor and glory.

That this relationship was associated with a festival of and a sacrifice to Zeus Hetaereius (Zeus the protector of companions)[16] demonstrates that the institution took on a sacral character. Nothing could be more explicit in proclaiming the social solidarity of the institution than the association of the companionship with the greatest of the Greek gods. Even though Philip II had expanded this personal *hetairos* relationship to include the Macedonian heavy infantry as the *pezehetairoi*,[17] this relationship with his new foot companions was not the same as with his elite *hetairoi*, although we are woefully short on specific information on any of these relationships.[18] The rank-and-file infantry did not typically eat, drink, hunt, etc. with their king. The commonality in the various companion relationships included the largesse of the king, land for the foot companions, and villages for the elite, often feasting with both, although not on a regular basis except for the aristocratic *hetairoi*, and fighting with the king in battle. Macedonian kings led their troops into conflict.[19]

The power of these aristocrats was compromised through the military and social reforms of Philip II. He revolutionized warfare in the ancient world through his creation of a new form of heavy infantry better suited to the circumstances of Macedonia. While the Macedonian cavalry was second to none, Macedonia did not possess any heavy infantry until the reign of Alexander's father. The Greek city-states depended on what amounted to a heavy infantry made up primarily of middle-class individuals who were wealthy enough to afford their own weaponry. They were armed with 7–8-ft stabbing spears as their chief offensive weapon and were outfitted with shields, grieves, and breast plates. They were called hoplites and were organized into units called phalanxes. Macedonian infantry before Philip was primarily what would be called light-armed skirmishers, no match for the heavily armed hoplites. Philip, faced with a mostly rural dependent population of peasants without any substantial middle class, could not afford to train and outfit a hoplite army; rather he created a new kind of heavy infantry force. Instead of the hoplite spear, he outfitted his new infantryman with a pike of at least 15 ft in length. He then arranged these in a compact phalanx. With at least three ranks of spears sticking out in front of the unit, attacking this formation was like assaulting a porcupine. This new weapon suited Philip's situation. He had become king on the death of his brother and 4,000 Macedonian soldiers in a battle against Macedonia's northwestern neighbors the Illyrians. New recruits would be encouraged by the added distance between themselves and their opponents. In hoplite warfare you were in very close quarters when in combat—so close, in fact, that it was said you could smell the breath of your opponent. Moreover, the row of pikes was virtually impenetrable and therefore there was little need for defensive armor. This was a much cheaper form of warfare than that of the hoplites. Training was also much less intense. While hoplites often found themselves in single combat away from their cohesion in the phalanx, pikemen were very vulnerable away from their phalanx, little suited to hand-to-hand combat. The difficulty of using the long pike in single combat is seen in the contest between the Olympic champion pancratist Dioxippus and the Macedonian Corragus (Diod. 17. 100. 2–101. 2; Curt. 9. 7. 16–23). Armed only with a club, Dioxippus easily overcame the fully armed Macedonian phalangite. Of course, this new infantry unit was extremely vulnerable on the flanks and rear. While experienced soldiers could quickly form a square to resist such assaults, it was a complicated procedure. This vulnerability may be why no one else before Philip in the Greek world armed their infantrymen with pikes. Philip, however, had an excellent cavalry which could protect the new infantry from attacks on its exposed flanks or rear. Indeed, Philip used his new infantry primarily to pin down the enemy infantry while his superior cavalry probed the enemy for weaknesses and was usually responsible for victory. The creation of this new infantry made the Macedonian army a force to be reckoned with; and with each victory Philip acquired land which in part he gave out to his new infantrymen, making them no longer dependent peasants but independent landowners who owed their new status not just to Philip but to the institution of monarchy itself. Philip dubbed these new soldiers his *pezhetairoi*, his infantry companions.[20]

As the heir apparent, Alexander had already assembled a group around himself, his personal advisors and companions (cf. Plut. *Alex*. 10. 5).[21] These would include friends of his youth, such as Hephaestion, the son of Amyntor (Curt. 3. 12. 16; cf. Arr. *Anab*. 2. 12. 6; Diod. 17. 37. 5), Alexander, the son of Aëropus (Arr. *Anab*. 1. 25. 1–2), and also likely Philotas, the son of Parmenion (Plut. *Alex*. 10. 5), but it would also include more senior individuals, as was likely the case with Ptolemy. While it is unknown what actual position Ptolemy may have held, it is very possible that he was a member of the Companion Cavalry, perhaps even one of the *Ilê Basilikê*. This would appear likely in that there is some evidence that in the early part of Alexander's expedition, he was closely associated with the cavalry and in close contact with Alexander. Arrian (*Anab*. 2. 11. 8), following Ptolemy's account, states that after the battle at Issus in Alexander's pursuit of Darius' retreating forces, the cavalry crossed over a ravine filled with the bodies of the Persian dead. The impression is that Ptolemy was riding in that pursuit.

With respect to these companions of the heir apparent, there is the possibility that they were appointed by his father the king, but it is far more likely that they were chosen by Alexander himself. At the Battle of Chaeronea, Philip put Alexander in command of the Companion Cavalry, assigning to him as advisors senior military officers (Diod. 16. 86. 1). However, it is clear that in these situations these were advisors for the particular moment and not the young Alexander's regular coterie. That Philip did so implies that he did not believe Alexander's *philoi* were capable of such assistance and that those he appointed were not previously part of Alexander's inner circle. Critical to this discussion is the status of Thessalus, the tragic actor, who was sent by Alexander to Pixodarus, the current ruler of Caria, concerning a possible marriage. Plutarch reports that Philip had him traced to Corinth and ordered that he be arrested. Plutarch (*Alex*. 10. 5) states that Thessalus was one of Alexander's companions, a *hetairos*. It is then unlikely that Thessalus or any of these personal companions was chosen by Philip. This particular proposal of marriage was not approved by the king, which would suggest that he was not Philip's man. Moreover, would the king have chosen an actor as one of his son's chief advisors? In the case of the heir to the throne, those individuals chosen by Alexander to be his companions held no official position within the state. These were more, then, in the general sense of *philoi* (friends) or an *amici*[22] than formal *hetairoi*. Most of our information concerning Alexander's band of *philoi* comes from Plutarch's description of this infamous Pixodarus affair and its aftermath (*Alex*. 10. 1–5).[23] In 337, the satrap/dynast of Caria Pixodarus proposed a marriage alliance with Philip, offering his daughter to be married to Arrhidaeus, Alexander's half-brother.[24] Some of Alexander's friends ("*philoi*") and his mother convinced him that despite Arrhidaeus' limitations, Philip was grooming him to be his heir.[25] Alexander then sent an emissary to Pixodarus offering himself as the prospective bridegroom. Philip became enraged at this interference in his diplomatic affairs and berated Alexander, declaring that such a marriage was beneath his heir and he exiled Harpalus, Nearchus, Erigyius, Laomedon, and Ptolemy from among the companions of the young prince (Plut. *Alex*. 10. 5; Arr. *Anab*. 3. 6. 5). After he became king, Alexander recalled all from exile and rewarded them for their loyalty (Arr. *Anab*. 3. 6. 5). All accompanied him on his expedition. Harpalus became the chief treasurer (Arr. *Anab*. 3. 6. 4); Thessalus performed at the mass marriage ceremony in Susa (Athen. 12. 538F); Nearchus was appointed by Alexander satrap of Lycia and Pamphylia (Arr. *Anab*. 3. 6. 6) and later admiral of Alexander's Indus fleet (Arr. *Anab*. 6. 2. 3; *Ind*. 18. 10); Erigyius commanded allied forces (Arr. *Anab*. 2. 8. 9; 3. 6. 6, 11. 10; Curt. 3. 9. 8; Diod. 17. 17. 4, 57. 3) and remained as an advisor to the king (Curt. 6. 8. 17; 7. 7. 21), and his brother Laomedon was placed in charge of Persian prisoners (Arr. *Anab*. 3. 6. 6) and was a trierarch in Alexander's Indus fleet (Arr. *Ind*. 18. 4). Ptolemy became one of the king's elite *somatophylaces* (Arr. *Anab*. 3. 27. 5; 6. 28. 3–4; cf. 3. 6. 6). That Alexander rewarded them for their loyalty demonstrates the confidence that Alexander had in them. This is shown especially in the case of Harpalus, who was in some way incapable of military service (Arr. *Anab*. 3. 6. 6), but Alexander found him the position of treasurer. He even forgave him when he absconded with part of the treasury in 333 and fled to Greece (Arr. *Anab*. 3. 6. 4–7). This was his first theft and flight. When subsequently he did so again Alexander was not so forgiving (Diod. 17. 108. 7). However, when the king was first informed of Harpalus' transgressions he placed those who brought him this news in chains because he believed they were falsely accusing his friend (Plut. *Alex*. 41. 8).

The strength of Alexander's attachment to these individuals owes much to that last year of Philip's reign. Alexander had become increasingly estranged from his father. This was chiefly the result of the last of Philip's polygamous marriages to a Macedonian noblewoman, Cleopatra. This particular marriage had enraged Alexander's mother, Olympias. Why is not entirely clear, but it is likely related to her concern for her son's inheritance. Philip had married seven different women in all,[26] two of whom he wed after his marriage to Olympias. Philip's last wife, however, was different from all the rest. She was a Macedonian; none of the others, including Olympias, were. This fact was brought home when, during the marriage feast, Attalus, the uncle of the new bride and one of Philip's chief generals and advisors, proclaimed that from this new marriage might come a legitimate heir to the throne (Plut. *Alex.* 9. 6–10; Athen. 13. 557D-E). While all the guests were apparently well inebriated—in this case there was likely to be a good measure of *in vino veritas*—Alexander reacted predictably with indignation, throwing a cup at the offending Attalus. What might have passed as bad manners all around quickly escalated when Philip rose from his couch with drawn sword and approached his son. This particular situation was saved when the king tripped and fell. Apparently, he was unable to rise to his feet again. Alexander and his mother then went into voluntary exile (Plut. *Alex.* 9. 11). Was Philip actually planning through this new marriage to set aside his son? Nothing other than Attalus' remark would suggest this. It would be well over a decade before any new heir would be a viable candidate for the throne. But even though both Alexander and his mother returned from exile, the subsequent Pixodarus affair shows that—at least on the part of Alexander—all was not forgiven or forgotten. Those who were loyal to Alexander throughout this difficult year would not be forgotten either when he assumed the throne.

As the date of Ptolemy's birth and the nature of his relationship with Alexander are contested, so is his birthplace. The best evidence says he was from the Lower Macedonian canton of Eordaea (Arr. *Anab.* 6. 28. 4; *Ind.* 18. 5), but the Upper Macedonian province of Orestis is also claimed (Steph. Byz. s.v. "Orestis"[27]). Both may, indeed, be true. When Philip captured Upper Macedonia, as a result of his victory over the Illyrians in 358, he rewarded those aristocratic Upper Macedonians who were his supporters with land likely in their homeland, but also provided estates in Lower Macedonia. This may have been the case with respect to Ptolemy's father. Lands were commonly given to those *hetairoi* who were not native Macedonians, but they were also given to Macedonian aristocrats. For example, Leonnatus, the son of Anteas, is listed in Nearchus' list of the trierarchs as from Pella (*Arr. Ind.* 18. 3), but he was a member of the former royal house of Lyncestis, an Upper Macedonian canton that was independent before the reign of Philip II (*Suda* s.v. Leonnatus). Aristonous, the son of Peisaeus, is also listed as from Pella (Arr. *Anab.* 6. 28. 5) and from Eordaea (Arr *Ind.* 18. 5). Both Philip and Alexander were very liberal in their dispersal of conquered lands. While the vast majority of the *hetairoi* were native Macedonians from prominent aristocratic families, some were not, but rather foreigners attracted to Macedonia by the direct invitation of the king ([Theopompus] *BNJ* 115 F-224). Of the eighty-four individuals identified as members of Alexander the Great's *hetairoi*, nine were Greeks (Stagakis 1962: 79–87). Foreign *hetairoi*, like their Macedonian counterparts, would be given large tracts of land by the king (cf. Athen. 6. 261A). Feasting and gifting were how a monarch cemented his relationship with his *hetairoi* (Samuel 1988: 1276; cf., Billows 1995: 137; Borza 1990: 215). This was certainly part of the traditional *hetairos* relationship. Macedonian kings gave their *hetairoi* vast tracts of land which included dependent villages ([Theopompus] *BNJ* 115 F-225B; Plut. *Alex*. 15. 3–6). Philip II granted all of the land north of Agora to one Apollonides of Cardia ([Dem.] 7. 39; cf. 7. 44; Dem. 8. 64). Androsthenes from Thasos (Heckel 2021: 51), Nearchus, Alexander's fleet commander from Crete, and Laomedon, a Mytilenian (Heckel 2021: 272), are listed as Macedonians from Amphipolis (Arr. *Ind*. 18. 4). These foreign *hetairoi* obviously were the recipients of royal land.

While Macedonia was traditionally controlled by this powerful aristocratic landed class, Philip, in particular, altered the very nature of Macedonia by creating cities and giving land to the landless. City growth and city creation clearly did accelerate during Philip's reign.[29] Philip is recorded as founding "strong cities at key locations" in Thrace (Diod. 16. 71. 2; Dem. 8. 44) and along his frontier with Illyria (Dem. 4. 48).[30] In Thrace, there are references to Philippopolis ([Theopomppus] *BNJ* 115 F-110; Pliny *NH* 4. 18), Drongilus, Calybe, and Mastira (Dem. 8. 44; Str. 7. 320C). Alexander the Great is also noted as a city founder. To cement his hold on occupied territories, again following the actions of his father, Alexander created a number of cities in Asia, which according to Plutarch (*Mor*. 438e) numbered seventy. Associated with these foundations was the viritane distribution of land. While royal grants to *hetairoi* included villages and the dependent populations associated with them (Plut. *Alex*. 15. 3), lands, as shown earlier, were also given to those who had formerly been peasants and dependent pastoralists. These now became independent landowners.[31] These individuals made up Philip's new revolutionary heavy infantry.[32] They were also staunch supporters of their king, since protecting the monarch now meant also protecting their lands. The king had given these, and it was the monarchy that would guarantee continued possession. Moreover, this new landed class was a powerful ally in the king's relationship with his own *hetairoi*. It was these reforms that made possible the emergence of Macedonia as a world power.[33] Ultimately, Philip created a military force of at least 3,300 cavalry and 24,000 infantry.[34] These holders of king's land became "citizen soldiers" (*stratioton politikon*) (Diod. 18. 12. 2). Additionally, these reforms carried over into the new age that began with Alexander's death. As Billows (1995, 132–7) notes, the granting of land was "a powerful inducement to future loyalty." The practice of granting land in return for military service was continued in the Hellenistic period (Billows 1995: 146–69). With respect to traditional patronage, that related to the *hetairoi*, Philip's acquisition of lands formerly outside the king's control, such as the previously independent Macedonia kingdoms in the north and west captured during his campaign against the Illyrians in 358, lands held in Macedonia by various Greek city-states, and new territories formerly outside of what had been traditionally Macedonia, made his generosity most impressive. Philip was so generous that his 800 most elite *hetairoi* enjoyed the profits from as much land as that of the 10,000 richest Greeks ([Theopompus] *BNJ* 155 F-225) and Alexander is reported to have given away most of his crown property to his *hetairoi* as well (Plut. *Alex.* 15. 5–6).

In the case of Ptolemy, given the reference to his birthplace as both Eordaea and Orestis, his father Lagus was either an aristocrat possessing ancestral lands in Eordaea, or possibly someone whose estates in Lower Macedonia were given to him by Philip as a reward for his loyalty in addition to those he continued to possess in Orestis. To fill out the possibilities, it is also conceivable that there was, perhaps, some sort of exchange of estates. Given these disagreements concerning Ptolemy's early life, it is no surprise, then, that there is also some controversy over his parentage. Again, our best sources and most modern commentators proclaim that he is the son of the otherwise unknown Lagus (Arr. *Anab.* 2. 11. 8; 3. 3. 5, 6. 5; Diod. 1. 84. 8; Joseph. *AJ* 12. 1, 11; *BJ* 6. 435; Paus. 1. 1. 1, 6, 9. 1, 11. 5, 16. 1; 6. 3. 1, 16. 3, 17. 3; 9. 16. 1; App. *Syr.* 9. 56; Polyb. 2. 41. 2; [Porphyry] *BNJ* 260 F-2). This is an uncommon name which occurs later as the name of Ptolemy's first-born son (Athen. 13. 576E).[35] Since naming a son after the paternal grandfather was common, this would add to the likelihood that Lagus was Ptolemy's father. While Lagus was likely an aristocrat, he was not an especially prominent one. Outside of the context of being repeatedly noted as Ptolemy's father, little else is known about him. Indeed, there is even a jest that was recorded by Plutarch (*Mor.* 9. 458A-B) which is based on the father's obscurity. "Ptolemy, when he was jeering at a pedant for his ignorance, asked him who was Peleus' father; and the pedant replied, 'I shall tell you if you will first tell me who was the father of Lagus.'" While the identification of the otherwise unknown Lagus as his father would appear clear, Ptolemy was also proclaimed to be the son of Philip II, the Macedonian king and father of Alexander the Great (Curt. 9. 8. 22; Paus. 1. 6. 2). Perdiccas and Leonnatus are also claimed to be Argeads based on Curtius (10. 7. 8) proclaiming them as "stirpe regis genitos," but this is generally regarded as a reference to their descent from the former kings of Upper Macedonian kingdoms (Heckel 2021: 364). According to Libanius (11. 91), Seleucus was the descendant of Temenus, the first king of Macedonia and the founder of the Argead dynasty, which would make Seleucus a very distant relation of Alexander.[36] These particular identifications with the Argead royal house all date from the period after Alexander's death. Either purposely or the result of rumors spread by would-be flatterers, if these had been true, either Philip or Alexander would have eliminated such potential rivals or in the chaos that followed Alexander's death when an adult, capable, Argead would have easily succeeded to the throne no such claim was raised (see below).

With respect to Ptolemy, it is claimed that his mother Arsinoe was Philip's mistress and when she became pregnant by the king she was married by him to Lagus (cf. Curt. 9. 8. 22; *Suda* s.v. "Lagos"; [Satyrus] *FGrH* 429 F-21). Nina Collins (1997: 436–76) accepts this account and claims that Ptolemy II made Lagus his father's official sire to conceal "the stigma of Ptolemy's alleged illegitimate birth" (474). The difficulty with this assertion is that Arrian is most likely using Ptolemy's own designation as son of Lagus. Of course, as Waldemar Heckel points out (2018: 2n.12), if Philip was indeed Ptolemy's father, this would have made the later proposed marriage of Ptolemy to Alexander's sister, Cleopatra, incestuous. This would not have disturbed the native Egyptians but would not have been well received by contemporary Macedonians or Greeks for that matter (Pl. *Leg.* 8. 838A-C). It was Ptolemy II who first broke this taboo at least on the dynastic level. Outside of Egypt, marriages between brother and sister were still frowned upon, and certainly before the example of Ptolemy II, virtually unknown. In a variant on this theme of Philip's paternity, a fragment of Aelian (*VH* 283) proclaims that Lagus attempted to kill the infant Ptolemy because he suspected he was not his child, but an eagle intervened to save the young boy. The eagle did become a symbol of the dynasty and a mainstay on Ptolemaic currency. The eagle image, however, had a long history in Macedonia, and was first used by Archelaus on coinage (Head 1879: 165). Alexander the Great introduced coinage with Heracles' portrait on the obverse side and a seated Zeus holding an eagle on the reverse (Metcalf 2012: 178–80). The eagle was the symbol of Zeus. Ptolemy after his reconquest of Cyprus in 294 began minting silver tetradrachms with his portrait wearing the aegis of Zeus and the standing eagle on the reverse (Lorber 2012: 33–44; 2018: 79–80). There is no need, then, to connect the coinage image with the story of the eagle saving the infant Ptolemy and in fact it may be the image of the eagle that gave rise to the tale of eagle salvation.

Pausanias (1. 6. 2) does state that at least in his time, second century AD, Ptolemy was acknowledged as the descendant of Philip by the Macedonians. Additionally, Arsinoe has been described recently and without any evidence as a member of the Argead family.[37] These are great stories, but none is likely to be true, and the evidence is that these tales were not put forth by the first Ptolemy to rule Egypt. Ptolemy the son of Lagus is recorded in a mid-third-century BC official inscription commemorating the deeds of Ptolemy III, as descended from Heracles (*OGIS* 54 l. 4). The inscription, however, describes Berenice, a wife of Ptolemy I and mother of Ptolemy II as descended from Dionysus (ll. 4–5). This is an attempt to enhance the divinity of the couple by direct reference to important divine ancestors. As descendants of Heracles, Philip II and Ptolemy I could be no more than very, very distant relations. A fragment of Satyrus (*BNJ* 631 F-1) has Ptolemy being a descendant of Dionysus. That throughout Arrian's *Anabasis* Ptolemy is repeatedly listed as the son of Lagus, likely reflecting Ptolemy's designation of himself in his own history of these events (see Chapter 8), as he is a major source of Arrian's history (Arr. *Anab.* 1. Pref. 1), suggests strongly that Ptolemy was perfectly happy with being the son of Lagus (Heckel 2018: 3). In the discussions in the ad hoc assembly that took place after Alexander the Great's death, the only noted individuals of Argead descent were Arrhidaeus (the eventual Philip III), Heracles, the son of Barsine, and the then as yet unborn Alexander IV (Curt. 10. 6. 1–15, 7. 2–7; Arr. *Succ.* 1a. 1; Diod. 18. 2. 2[38]; Just. 13. 4. 1–4). If there had been others, given Macedonian tradition and the desire of the army for an Argead successor, that individual would have become king. Moreover, Philip II and his son Alexander had been responsible for taking a rather populous royal clan and diminishing it down to the previously mentioned three survivors. Philip in particular had eliminated many scions of the clan. These included Argaeus, who had ruled briefly in 393/392 (Diod. 16. 2. 6; 14. 92. 4; Anson 2020: 56–8) and his three half-brothers, Archelaus, Arridaeus, and Menelaus (Just. 8. 3. 10–11).[39] Justin remarks that Philip "desperately wished to do away with them since he saw them as potential claimants to the throne" (Just. 8. 3. 10). Another Argead who had briefly contended with Philip for the throne, Pausanias, likely died early in Philip's reign.[40] Thanks to his father Philip, Alexander had only one possible Argead contender for the throne.[41] This was his cousin Amyntas Perdicca, the son of Philip II's brother and predecessor on the Macedonian throne. While no source claims that Alexander had him killed, after Philip's assassination he disappears from the historical record. There is, however, mention of a plot by this individual against Alexander's life (Curt. 6. 9. 17, 10. 24). Given that both kings feared possible Argead claimants to their throne, that any surviving viable claimants other than Arrihidaeus remained at the time of Alexander's death is very unlikely. Moreover, one wonders what all of this might mean for Ptolemy's brother Menelaus (Diod. 19. 62. 4). Was he the true legitimate son of Lagus? If all the rumors of bastardy are true for Lagus, then Menelaus must be his younger half-brother. In a surviving will in the dating introduction, Menelaus *tou Lagou* is referenced (*P.Eleph.* 2. l.2).[42] While this might refer to some other Menelaus, this is unlikely, since the reference would make him the chief priest of Alexander in this dating formula, with his name appearing right after the date in Ptolemy's reign and therefore in 284. Menelaus served his brother's interests after Alexander's death, having campaigned for him in Cyprus and later after Demetrius' victory at Salamis and the Ptolemaic evacuation of Cyprus he returned to Egypt (Diod. 19. 62. 4; 20. 47. 1–5, 7–8; Plut. *Demetr.* 15. 2; Paus. 1. 6. 6; Just. 15. 2. 7) where, as noted above, he is the eponymous priest of the cult of Alexander in Alexandria (*P.Eleph* 2. 11). One of the Egyptian nomes was also named for him (Str. 17. 801C).

Lagus' poverty is also noted in the later tradition. Ptolemy is described as having risen from the ranks of the infantry (Just 13. 4. 10), and Plutarch (*Mor.* 458A B) refers to the obscurity of his birth. This rags-to-riches tale appears to be part of a general theme with respect to many of the Successors of Alexander. Eumenes of Cardia is described as the son of a poor freight transporter whose athletic ability brought him to the attention of King Philip, who immediately took him into his entourage (Plut. *Eum* 1.1–2). Another account has him as the son of an impoverished funeral musician (Ael. *VH* 12. 43).[43] It is far more likely that Eumenes was added to Philip's court as secretary as the result of a guest-friendship with Eumenes' father, a prominent Cardian (Anson 2015: 41–2). Antigonus Monophtalmus was the supposed son of a laborer; Polyperchon, sired by a slave and a thief (Ael. *VH* 12. 43)), and Lysimachus, the son of an impoverished Thessalian ([Theopompus] *BNJ* 115 F-81=Athen. 6. 259F-260A; [Porphyry] *BNJ* 260 F-3).[44] A passage found in Appian's *Syrian Wars* (9. 56. 1) can easily be interpreted that Seleucus crossed to Asia with Alexander as a common soldier. While there was some movement within the ranks, there does not appear to have been much promotion out of class.[45] As Waldemar Heckel states, "merit alone rarely sufficed in a world of aristocratic privilege" (2018: 3).

About all that can be said from all of this information is that Arsinoe was very likely Ptolemy's mother and Lagus his father. Moreover, the evidence is clear that he came from the aristocratic class of Macedonian society, if not, perhaps, from its upper echelons (Curt. 9. 8. 22; Paus. 1. 6. 2; Heckel 2021: 418). While promotion of non-aristocratic Macedonians in the army occurred and appears to have accelerated somewhat during the later stages of Alexander's campaign, it remained uncommon. Few examples exist, with the clearest being the promotion of the Cardian Greek Eumenes to hipparch of the Companion Cavalry. Yet, even here Eumenes was not a commoner but rather an official *hetairos* (Anson 2015: 49 and n. 19). Brian Bosworth reasonably claims that the Macedonian Corrhagus, who fought the Athenian Olympic champion Dioxippus in single combat and lost, had been promoted from the ranks of the infantry to companion status.[46] That he chose to fight as an infantryman suggests he was clearly prepared to do so, which would indicate practiced skill with that panoply. The Macedonian officer class was recruited locally and initially placed in charge of local military units (Arr. *Anab.* 3. 16. 11), and it is doubtful that this changed until well into Alexander's campaign in Asia and then likely only slightly with respect to ethnicity and class. Alexander did later put units under officers who did not come from the same districts, but there is little evidence that the class barrier, at least among the Macedonians, was much altered. Eumenes was certainly hampered by his non-aristocratic Macedonian origin when dealing with those with the Macedonian aristocratic pedigree (Anson 2015: 241–61, esp. 254–61). Even though Philip II had created a Macedonian heavy infantry, its commanders were Macedonian aristocrats. Both he and Alexander, the latter at least until late in his campaign, needed the support of the traditional *hetairoi* of the Macedonian king; the officers of the army whom Alexander commanded when he crossed to Asia were still those of his father, and one and all were all from the higher echelons of Macedonian society.

The Macedonian aristocratic class was defined by birth and a sense of entitlement. Macedonia had few urban centers prior to Philip II, with most of the land divided into large estates possessed by this elite and worked by dependent pastoralists and peasants.[47] As noted earlier, Theopompus (Polyb. 8.11. 5–13=*FGrH* 115 F 225a) declares that these landed aristocrats, whom he numbers at 800, "enjoyed the profits of as much land as any ten thousand Greeks possessing the richest and the most extensive land." This has long been thought to be an exaggeration, but Macedonia was by Greek standards a large area and given that it was apparently widely under the domination of these aristocratic families, this may be a reasonable statement.

While under Philip and especially under Alexander, promotion into the ranks of the *hetairoi* from outside the traditional Macedonian aristocracy took place, among the Macedonian aristocratic elite it was resented. The later prejudice against Eumenes is a case in point. So marked was it, that on one occasion Eumenes used it to save himself from betrayal. When one of his commanders decided to betray him, another pointed out that the individual who promised a great deal for this perfidy, if he became more powerful, would take away whatever was given and then some, while Eumenes "since he was a foreigner [Cardian Greek] ... would then never dare to advance his own interests" (Diod. 18. 62. 5–7).[48]

This was one of the issues that created much dissatisfaction among the Macedonian elite. These were the king's *hetairoi*, his companions. While the term is often and correctly applied to the elite Macedonian cavalry, Philip II and Alexander the III's hypaspists and *pezhetairoi*, these are all later extensions from the initial and central association. Moreover, while it is true that the most elite of the *hetairos* designations need not be native Macedonians, most, in fact, were. These relationships were societal institutions with both political and social importance. As noted earlier, they had traditionally made up the government apart from the king. The more junior members of this class made up the Macedonian Companion Cavalry. The more senior companions were, apart from the king, the basic political institution of the Macedonian state and this had only begun to change during the reigns of Philip and Alexander with an increasing bureaucracy and an emerging middle class, the result of major military reforms that produced a Macedonian heavy infantry.[49] But the power, though lessened, of the elite *hetairoi* remained throughout the reign of the father and, though diminished, they were still a potent force under the son.[50] Their initial and continuing authority deriving from their regional control of most of Macedonia. Even though Philip II founded a number of cities and gave land to a sizable number of formerly dependent Macedonians, much of the population and land of Macedonia was under the direct control of these individuals. Alexander, prior to leading his invasion of Asia, rewarded these companions with additional farms and villages from his royal holdings (Plut Alex. 15. 3).[51] However, these aristocratic *hetairoi* derived their authority from their position in Macedonia as regional lords. With every mile marched away from Macedonia into the heart of Asia their power diminished, while that of the king increased.

In Macedonia, there was a clear class separation between the cavalry and the infantry. The cavalry was composed of those from upper-class families and a few foreign *hetairoi* ([Demochares] *BNJ* 72 F-4; Curt. 10. 7. 20). To fight on foot, except in the most extreme of circumstances or as an officer, was considered beneath these aristocrats. For killing a boar in the hunt before the king could take his opportunity, Alexander the Great punished the page Hermolaus by having the young man whipped in the presence of the other pages and additionally by having "his horse taken away" (Arr. *Anab.* 4. 13. 2). In Amyntas' (son of Andromenes) defense of his involvement in a plot against the life of Alexander, he claimed that he retained his horses when ordered to give them up, because, if he had not, he would "have had to fight on foot" (Curt. 7. 1. 34). It was in part because of the importance of the horse that these aristocrats had such large estates. Carolyn Willikes (2023: forthcoming) has noted that equine expertise took time, energy, and wealth. Moreover, a single horse was insufficient. Much like those who play polo, having a string of trained horses was essential for combat. To be an infantry officer was one thing, but a common infantry soldier was something else. Ptolemy was clearly a cavalry man and consequently did not rise from the ranks of a common soldier. As explained above, one does not just get on a horse and become an expert warrior on horseback overnight.

Despite all the fanciful tales, the nature of Macedonian society suggests strongly that both Lagus and Arsinoe were products of aristocratic families. Even Philip's bureaucratic innovations were minimal, relying as so many Macedonian monarchs had relied before on the landed aristocrats of their realm. Non-Macedonians appointed as *hetairoi* would be especially loyal, since their status was entirely tied to the king. Their lands in Macedonia were given to them by the king, not due to hereditary possession. The fluidity of the *hetairos* institution was such that many were *hetairoi* because of their power, while others had power through their selection as *hetairoi*. As Waldemar Heckel has emphasized, actual power was indirectly negotiated often on the basis of powerful personalities and shifting coalitions (Heckel 2003: 198). In the past, often powerful coalitions of nobles limited the actual power of the monarch, but Philip dramatically altered this. As seen previously, much of the kingdom was composed of large noble estates peopled by a dependent peasantry. While Philip II created a middle class in Macedonia where by and large one had not existed before, the structure of the court and the army remained dominated by those from the Macedonian aristocracy.[52] These individuals were the king's elite *hetairoi*. While Philip introduced the concept of companionship to the army with his creation of the *pezhetairoi*, this did not introduce into Macedonian society social mobility beyond the movement of many from tenant farmers and dependent agriculturalists into the ranks of a middle class. The aristocratic *hetairoi* class remained relatively static with only occasional additions from prominent foreigners. It would, therefore, be unlikely that someone outside such prominence would come into the inner circle.

Even if Ptolemy was from a minor aristocratic family, he was raised as an aristocrat and his early life would have conformed to what is generally known concerning the life of a young Macedonian aristocrat. Macedonia was a "rough and ready" society that was marked by the importance of warfare and martial activities. Ptolemy was taught from an early age to ride and prepare to be a cavalryman. An aristocratic boy became a man when he killed an enemy in combat (Aris. *Pol.* 7. 1324b) and could only recline at table, the traditional Greek practice, when he had speared a wild boar "without using a hunting net" (Athen. 1. 18A). While the majority of the population were dependent pastoralists or tenant farmers who spent their lives engaged in these activities, the aristocrats feasted, hunted, fought, and lived off the toil of others. There is evidence to suggest that in the battles from Chaeronea to the Hydaspes Ptolemy fought alongside Alexander in the Companion Cavalry.

Ptolemy was, then, from an aristocratic Macedonian family likely originally from the Upper Macedonia region of Orestis, who began his career with King Alexander not as a Macedonian page, but as one of the young prince's trusted companions (a personal *philos*) and advisors. This position of friendship and authority he held until the Conqueror's death in June 323. He was also first and foremost an experienced cavalryman as befitted his station as a Macedonian aristocrat.

3

The Man with a Plan

Alexander's sudden death opened up both challenges and opportunities for Ptolemy. By the time of the Conqueror's death on June 11, 323 (Depuydt 1997), the ancient world had been transformed. The Persian Empire that had dominated Greek politics virtually from the time of its creation was gone and in its place was an empire which stretched from Macedonia to the Indus, its conquest the result of a decade of campaigning under the leadership of one of the most mercurial personages of all history. Virtually the entire Near East had come into the Hellenic sphere of influence. The question then became how would this world emerge from the death of its creator and what would be Ptolemy's role in that creation?

Alexander's death was most likely from natural causes. In his ten-year expedition he had received numerous wounds and had likely at one point contracted malaria.[1] Add to these traumas and possible disease the heavy drinking associated with Macedonian symposia (Carney 2007: 143–4; Sawada 2010: 393; Pownall 2010: 55–65) and the Conqueror's early death from natural causes would appear inevitable. He lived hard and died young. There were, however, rumors suggesting that Alexander had been poisoned, but none of this appears in our sources in the open discussions concerning the selection of Alexander's successor. Plutarch (*Alex.* 77. 2–5) proclaims that no one had any suspicions of poisoning immediately after the Conqueror's death and even places these rumors as originating five years after the fact (Plut. *Alex.* 77. 1).

It may appear strange that such discussion did not immediately arise during the ad hoc meeting in Babylon concerning the succession. After all, Alexander's father Philip had died at the hands of an assassin and such assassination of kings by disgruntled aristocrats was not an uncommon occurrence in Macedonian history, although poison was not the usual instrument. Moreover, the son, though given what he had endured in his short life, was still in the eyes of many considered invincible and his death then unexpected. While apparently not part of the immediate discussions in Babylon concerning the succession, the rumors probably did arise not long after his death (Diod. 17. 117. 5–118.2; Curt. 10. 10. 14–19). The most complete account of a poison plot is found in the *Liber de Morte Testamentumque Alexandri Magni*, a pamphlet reflecting these rumors (see Heckel 1988). While doubtful, poisoning was not impossible as the cause of death, and a possible poison was suggested in a symposium in 2006 in Dunedin, New Zealand. Dr. Leo Schep of the National Poisons Centre at the University of Otago, after reviewing the surviving descriptions of Alexander's death, suggested that if the death was the result of poison, hellebore was the probable agent (2009: 231–4). Conspiracy appears to be a default position in the human brain. The possibility of poison was picked up in Oliver Stone's film *Alexander* (2004). Anthony Hopkins, playing the very elderly Ptolemy, comments as an aside, "we did kill him." In the movie, Ptolemy is not confessing to being an active participant in the poisoning, however, but "by silence we consented." He knew of the plot but did nothing to stop it. But, then Hopkins/Ptolemy tells the scribe to delete these musings, declaring them to be "rubbish," and so, in fact, they are likely to be. In the various versions of the poison plot surviving from Antiquity, Ptolemy is never implicated and in fact in the *Liber* he is specifically excluded, along with Eumenes, Perdiccas, Lysimachus, Asander, and Holcias (Heckel 1988: 88, 95). The various versions of Alexander dying by poison primarily implicate Antipater and his sons (Diod. 17. 118. 1–2; 19. 11. 8; Plut. *Alex*. 77. 1; Curt. 10. 10. 14–19; Arr. *Anab*. 7. 27). Certainly, Antipater faced an unknown future, having been recalled with his replacement slowly heading to Macedonia.

What is clear from all of this speculation is that Alexander's death may not have been an unwelcome event. However, if the rumors of poisoning were present soon after his death, then why are these not part of the general discussion regarding the succession? Antipater is confirmed in Europe in some fashion in all the possible scenarios discussed and his sons are never officially brought to trial, although in 317 Olympias returned to Macedonia and killed Antipater's son Nicanor and had the tomb of another son, Iollas, overturned as revenge for Alexander (Diod. 19. 11. 8). Is it because no one in authority believed the rumors, or is Plutarch correct that these rumors were not voiced in the immediate aftermath of Alexander's death, or is it the result, in the words of Anthony Hopkins, of silent complicity? Certainly, one can make a case that many had had their fill of Alexander. Justin (13. 2. 1) states that Alexander's death brought his generals joy. Who amongst these commanders was looking forward to further campaigning? It wasn't just the soldiers who were not interested in pursuing further conquests in the east at the Hyphasis, or especially thrilled with the aftermath of Alexander's turn south battling down the Indus. This campaigning was then followed by the hike across the Gedrosian desert. Additional campaigns were planned in Arabia and, perhaps, all the way to the Pillars of Heracles (Arr. *Anab.* 7. 19. 6; Diod. 18. 4. 4). Moreover, there were the judicial murders of Philotas and Parmenion, the outright murder of Cleitus, and, while not exactly the reign of terror postulated by Badian (1961: 16–18), Alexander's actions after his return from India and the desert would have caused some concern on the part of all of his associates. Both Arrian (*Anab.* 7. 4. 3) and Curtius (10. 1. 39–42) report that Alexander was more ready to listen to accusations and inflict severe punishment often for what amounted to minor infractions.[2] Harpalus was one of Alexander's oldest *hetairoi*, who also incurred Alexander's wrath, not without serious provocation. Shortly before the Battle of Issus he had fled with part of the treasury for which he was responsible. He had been forgiven by Alexander and restored to his post after this first flight (Arr. *Anab.* 3. 6. 7), but when he heard of Alexander's return from India, he fled again (Curt. 10. 2. 1–3; Diod. 17. 108. 6–7). This time Alexander was incensed and planned to head to Europe after him, but rejoiced when he heard he had been killed (Curt. 10. 2. 3–4; Diod. 17. 108. 8). What if the *Liber de Morte* is based on a truth? What if Alexander's death was a successful poison plot? What if most of those at Medius' carouse knew of it, but were not directly part of it?[3] The unlikelihood is that it would have required cooperation on the part of at least some of Alexander's immediate subordinates whose predilection was more that of competition than cooperation with one another (Heckel 1977: 10–21; Anson 2015: 54–6). As Justin (13. 2. 1) comments, "they were all competitors for the same dignity." Moreover, the chaos that ensued after the Conqueror's death would suggest that his death was not well anticipated, at least in the context of what was to come next. Tales of poison were likely no more than that, but there is always that small doubt that there may have been human intervention, other than the wounds inflicted in battle, in the Conqueror's death.

At the time of Alexander's death, he and his army were in Babylon, the capital of his new kingdom of Asia (Str. 15. 3. 9–10). This alone would have made the process of choosing a successor unique in Macedonian history, the selection of a king away from the homeland, but then neither Alexander nor many of his Macedonian forces still with him had seen Macedonia in years. To complicate matters Alexander had not provided for a successor and the once replete Argead clan, which had held the throne for over 300 years, had dwindled down to three potential heirs. When Alexander died, he left but one son, the 4–5-year-old Heracles,[4] the result of an informal liaison with Barsine, the former wife of Memnon of Rhodes, Greek mercenary commander in Persian employ until his death in 333, and the daughter of Artabazus, an advisor to Darius and Alexander's one-time satrap of Bactria. Barsine had been captured in Damascus by Parmenion and subsequently had become intimate with Alexander (Curt. 3. 13. 14; Plut. *Alex.* 21. 7; Just. 11. 10. 2) with Heracles being the result (Curt. 10. 6. 11; Diod. 20. 20. 1). Additionally, there was Alexander's half-brother Arrhidaeus, whose competence to rule was very doubtful due to some mental incapacity.[5] Finally, at the time of his death there was the possibility of a "legitimate" son, for Alexander's wife Roxane was pregnant. (Curt. 10. 6. 9; Just. 13. 2. 5; Arr. *Succ.* 1a. 8).[6] Alexander also had two additional wives, Stateira (Heckel 2006: 256), a daughter of Darius III, the Persian king and Alexander's royal opponent, and Parysatis (Heckel 2006: 192), the daughter of Artaxerxes III Ochus, the Persian monarch from 425 to 338, but neither of these produced a possible heir. Stateira was murdered shortly after Alexander's death by Roxane, and Parysatis simply drops out of the narrative; whether she was also murdered, died a natural death, or disappeared into obscurity is unknown. What is clear is that at the time of Alexander's death there was no capable Argead ready to take his place. Moreover, Alexander had complicated matters by handing his signet ring to Perdiccas, who as chiliarch was the second-in-command, and this gesture was interpreted by some as choosing him as his successor (Curt. 10. 6. 16–17).

Not having a clear successor was not an unusual circumstance in Macedonian history. Disputed successions and civil wars had often followed a king's death. There was no constitutional process to choose a new king, and any member of the Argead clan was eligible. This particular succession crisis was notable, however. There were few possible candidates available from what had once been a very extensive clan. In the past, there had been a surfeit of possible candidates for the throne, which had given rise to numerous conflicts over the succession. Now, however, as the result of both Alexander's and his father Philip's success in eliminating possible rivals, there were only the three potential candidates left. Also, while not a constitutional requirement but the result of circumstances, most often a son followed a father as king. In the example of Philip II, an adult son was given responsibilities while the father yet lived, and through the father's efforts bonds were formed with powerful individuals in the kingdom. When Philip was assassinated, Alexander had already been regent for his father in 340 (Plut. *Alex.* 9.1) and had led the cavalry at Chaeronea in 338 (Diod. 16.86.1–4), where the victory ultimately brought to Philip the hegemony of Greece.

While there were challenges to Alexander's succession, these were dealt with quickly, both as a result of the competence of the new king and because of his allies in his father's *hetairoi*. While the perpetrator of Philip's assassination,

Pausanias, was killed fleeing the scene, others were later charged with involvement in the plot. These included three aristocrats from the Upper Macedonian canton of Lyncestis, the sons of Aëropus, Arrhabaeus, Heromenes, and Alexander (Arr. *Anab.* 1. 25. 1–2). The best evidence is that the assassin Pausanias murdered the king, not because of any political agenda, but rather to avenge what he saw as a private grievance (Diod. 17. 95. 3–94. 4). The Lyncestian brothers likely also acted for personal reasons. Philip had exiled the brothers' father (Polyaen. 4. 2. 3). Not being Argeads themselves, it is possible they hoped through the assassination to bring Amyntas Perdicca, Philip's nephew and the son of Perdiccas III, Philip's brother and his predecessor as king, to power (Arr. *Succ.* 1. 22; Just. 12. 6. 14; Polyaen. 8. 60). Plutarch (*Mor.* 327C) reports that after Philip's death, "all Macedonia was festering with revolt and looking toward Amyntas and the children of Aëropus." The personal nature of the crime may explain why it succeeded in killing Philip, but failed in achieving any loftier goals, if there were any. The conspirators wished primarily to wreak revenge; all else was secondary.

In the past, on the death of a monarch a new king was the individual Argead who had the greatest support among the aristocrats, those whom the Roman sources writing in Latin, Curtius and Justin, called the *principes*, and Arrian (*Succ.* 1a. 2), writing in Greek, the *magistoi*. At some point there might be a formal coronation where the new ruler would be presented to his people, most likely just the army, for acclamation. The evidence, however, suggests that there was no formal requirement for a coronation ceremony or even for an informal meeting of the so-called Macedonian aristocratic leadership, but rather a far more amorphous process in which powerful personalities dominated. There was no assembly of Macedonians who were responsible for choosing the Macedonian monarch (Anson 2013: 25–42). In this particular succession, virtually all of the prominent *hetairoi* were in Babylon. The only exceptions, though notable ones, were Antipater, Alexander's regent in Macedonia, and Craterus, who was in western Asia Minor on his way to replace Antipater as ordered by Alexander in 324 (Arr. *Anab.* 7. 12. 4; Just. 12. 12. 9).[7]

Most of our information concerning the immediate events after Alexander's death and the ultimate choice of a successor comes from Curtius Rufus' *History of Alexander the Great of Macedonia* and Justin's *Epitome of Pompeius Trogus*. Arrian's history of the Successor period survives only in fragments, and Plutarch ends his *Life of Alexander* with reference to the possible Argead heirs. Diodorus ends his Book Seventeen with Alexander giving his ring to Perdiccas and begins Book Eighteen with the division between the cavalry and the infantry over the succession already in place. The immediate aftermath of Alexander's death is described in detail only in Curtius and Justin and the two accounts appear to be quite different.[8] In Justin (13. 2. 4–4. 4), there are in effect three meetings. First the *somatophylaces* and, perhaps, certain others meet and ultimately decide on a regency for the yet to be born Alexander IV.[9] They then swear an oath of obedience to their as yet non-existent king. Justin then has this decision given to the "*equites*," the Companion Cavalry, who accept the decision without reservation and also swear the oath. The infantry, having been ignored in this process, becomes incensed and proclaims Arrhidaeus, Alexander's half-brother, as Alexander's successor (13. 3. 1). In Curtius (10. 6. 1–7. 21), the "*corporis eius custodes*," likely again referring to the *somatophylaces*, call all the commanders and *hetairoi* (*principes amicorum ducesque copiarum*) to a meeting in the palace to discuss the future of the empire, but the meeting is invaded by common soldiers; chaos ensues with the "*principes*" wanting to await a possible birth of an heir and having a regency, and the infantry insisting on Arrhidaeus being made king. In both accounts, the result is a brief civil war resulting in a dual monarchy of Arrhidaeus, newly named King Philip III, and eventually with the birth of Alexander's son, Alexander IV.

If it comes down to choosing one over the other, Curtius' account is superior to that of Justin. The three separate meetings suggest a certain constitutional order in the selection of a new king which, as noted, did not exist. The *principes* formally choose a king through a formal vote and with an oath of obedience. That individual is then presented to the army for discussion, but more importantly, for a formal oath of obedience. The formal oath of obedience appears as a regular practice. The evidence is that the selection process was far more amorphous and chaotic than suggested here. If it wasn't for elements found in Diodorus that correspond to the description in Justin, Justin's account could be simply ignored. Certainly, his description of the conclusion of the crisis conflicts with both Curtius and Diodorus. In Justin, after the cavalry have fled the city and an attempt has been made on Perdiccas' life, that commander proceeds to the infantry, and they are so impressed by his eloquence, not to mention his courage, that they then elect him general and there follows a reconciliation of the infantry and cavalry (13. 3. 7–4. 1). In both Curtius (10. 8. 14–22) and Diodorus (18. 2. 4), negotiations are entered into and the conflict is ended. Curtius presents a more involved negotiation and a subsequent slaughter of the infantry leaders; Diodorus simply says cooler heads prevailed. It is possible that Justin has simply compressed and misinterpreted events from the threatened assassination, then Perdiccas overawes his attackers who flee, but who in Justin's account hail him as general, concluding with the general agreement between the leaders and glossing over the slaughter of the infantry leaders by simply noting that the two sides were reconciled.

In Curtius' account there is implied a preliminary meeting of the *somatophylaces* who put forth the call for a general meeting of "the chief friends and military leaders" either to discuss the succession or to hear the decision of the *somatophylaces* (Curt. 10. 6. 1). This may correspond to Justin's first meeting. It is unclear in Curtius what was to be the actual business of this more general conclave. However, the courtyards of the palace are filled with anxious soldiers awaiting news concerning their future. As a result, many of those summoned cannot get into the meeting and the soldiers themselves enter and whatever was to take place becomes now the first true assembly in Macedonian history. Given all of the unprecedented features of the selection process, its collapse into chaos makes more sense of the general situation than Justin's three separate meetings. But, Curtius' account is not without problems. He has been strongly influenced by his Roman heritage.[10] In theory, Roman emperors were created with the approval of the Senate and the oaths of the army. Curtius' description does appear to contain these same elements. However, Curtius appears also to understand certain of the nuances of the Macedonian state. Curtius is clear that this meeting (10. 7. 1) and, indeed, those conducted by Alexander himself prior to his death are *contiones*,[11] and that he knew the difference between these non-decision-making assemblages and those that do decide—which is more than can be said for Justin, who refers to the Athenian Assembly as a *contio* (Just. 4. 4. 1–2). Curtius, on the other hand, refers to the Athenian Assembly as a Concilium Plebis (Curt. 10. 2. 3). Decision-taking assemblies were called *comitiae* or *concilia* by the Romans.

The major differences in the two accounts are the three separate meetings found in Justin but only the one clearly set forth with a hint of a preliminary meeting of the royal bodyguards in Curtius, and also the different roles played by Meleager. In Curtius (10. 7. 1–7), in the general meeting Meleager, a battalion commander, takes up a spontaneous outburst supporting Arrhidaeus' candidacy, but in Justin, after the army's enthusiastic call for Arrhidaeus to become king, Meleager is sent by the *principes* to try to convince the soldiers to change their minds (13. 3. 2). Justin's account is similar to that found in Diodorus (18. 2. 2–4), who describes the events in a very summary version, but endorses Meleager's role as described in Justin. Diodorus, however, begins his description after the division between the phalanx and the leaders has already taken place. What follows is a possible reconciliation of our sources and a likely reconstruction of events.

Justin's description (13. 2. 4) of a preliminary meeting of the "*Principes*," most likely the *somatophylaces*,[12] i.e. Leonnatus, Lysimachus, Aristonous, Perdiccas, Ptolemy, Pithon, and Peucestas (Arr. *Anab*. 6. 28. 4), soon after the Conqueror's death would appear to correspond to the compressed comment in Curtius that the bodyguards called for the meeting of the chief men (10. 6. 1). The implication is that such a call would have to have been the result of a meeting. Curtius' opening account of the meeting that then resulted and broke down into chaos is misinterpreted in Justin's and Diodorus' description and likely in what appears to have been their common source as well. The proposed meeting described by Curtius was to be of the leaders, but that then disintegrated when the uninvited soldiers crashed it. In the chaos that followed with violence in the offing, the leaders and those members of the Companion Cavalry who were present withdrew from the meeting and the city of Babylon, encamping outside the city (Curt. 10. 7. 1–8. 11). Justin's separate meetings of the cavalry and the infantry then date from the aftermath of Curtius' general meeting. His account of these separate meetings also incorporates into them some of the issues raised in Curtius' general meeting. In Justin's first meeting Meleager proposes that either Heracles or Arrhidaeus be made king (Just. 13. 2. 6–8). In Curtius' account (10. 6. 10–11) it is Nearchus who suggests Heracles and an unknown soldier who first puts forth Arrhidaeus (10. 7. 1–2). This assumes four meetings: the preliminary one described by Justin and suggested by Curtius, the general meeting of Curtius' account, and the separation of the cavalry and the infantry into two groups. This also conforms to the chronology found in Diodorus (18. 2. 2–4). Justin's supposed separate meetings of the cavalry and the infantry then took place after the main meeting had broken up and after Arrhidaeus had been proposed as king by the infantry. Diodorus (18. 2. 2–3) and Justin (13. 3. 2) state that initially the *principes* had decided to settle things by force of arms, but decided instead to send Meleager one of the phalanx battalion commanders to speak to the soldiers. He, however, then joined the ranks of the infantry. Curtius speaks of none of this. In his account, Meleager is from the very beginning opposed to Perdiccas being made regent for the as yet unborn son of Alexander (Curt. 10. 6. 20–1). When the name of Arrhidaeus is mentioned in the general meeting, according to Curtius, Meleager immediately supported him (Curt. 10. 7. 1–2).

The initial meeting of the leaders, chiefly the royal bodyguards, was to create the pathway to the new age without Alexander. Subsequently, their decisions were to be approved by the remaining *hetairoi* and commanders and the plan, endorsed by the full leadership of the army, then presented to the rank-and-file as a *fait accompli*. The need for unity on the part of the leadership was essential. The Macedonian troops could not be simply ignored, but they could be overawed by the unanimous voice of their commanders. In the chaos that ensued in the general meeting, an attempt was made to assassinate Perdiccas, but those sent to kill him were instead terrified by him and fled (Curt. 10. 8. 1–3; cf. Just. 13. 3. 8–9). The leadership speaking with one voice would be even more terrifying. However, the collective will of the army also resonated power. The changing nature of these Macedonians serving in Asia was seen in their growing corporate nature. Alexander after Gaugamela had increasingly used assemblies to cajole and justify his decisions.[13] In most every case, the exception being on the Hyphasis, Alexander got his way along with the endorsement of this army—what Errington (1978: 87–90) has called testing his *auctoritas* before asserting his *potestas*. Alexander had the kind of *auctoritas* to carry the day, his lieutenants individually did not. The regular infantry soldiers refused to be ignored. They burst into Curtius' meeting and railed against their lack of participation in the initial process (Just. 13. 2. 2). Justin's statement concerning their resentment could refer to the fact that they were not invited to Curtius' meeting.

In the initial meeting, as per Justin, different opinions were openly discussed. Perdiccas proposed that they ought to await Roxane's child and if a boy, he should be made king. In this meeting Meleager opposed waiting for the uncertain birth, declaring that if they wanted a boy, there was already Alexander's son by Barsine, Heracles, now around five years of age, or, if a man, Arrhidaeus, Alexander's half-brother, be made king (Just. 13. 2. 6–8). It is very possible that here Justin or his source Pompeius Trogus has confused two meetings and what is presented as the initial gathering of the *somatophylaces* has been confused with Curtius' general meeting, which is unmentioned by Justin. The presence of Meleager, who would not ordinarily be viewed as one of the *principes*, does suggest that Justin has confused two meetings, the preliminary one of the *somatophylaces* and Curtius' general meeting. In this preliminary meeting, as depicted by Justin, it would appear that Ptolemy proposed that the new king be chosen from among their number (Just. 13. 2. 11–12).[14] Since Perdiccas was the most likely candidate among them for the throne, if this advice from the son of Lagus was followed, Perdiccas would be king. Ptolemy was not high on any list to succeed Alexander. But is this really what is being said? This comes after Meleager had mentioned Arrhidaeus as a candidate who was present and an adult. Justin had Ptolemy respond: "*Melius esse ex his legi, qui prae virtute regi suo proximi fuerint, qui provincias regant, quibus bella mandentur, quam sub persona regis indignorum imperio subiciantur.* [Better to choose from those who stood close to their late king in personal qualities, who were the governors of provinces, who were entrusted with military campaigns—rather that than be subjected to the domination of unworthy men while the king had but nominal power]"[15] (Just. 13. 2. 12). Justin's rhetoric here is not meant to show Ptolemy's endorsement of such a proposal, but rather to quash the idea of Arrhidaeus as a worthy candidate for the throne. Their final decision was to await the birth and create a regency of Leonnatus, Perdiccas, Craterus, and Antipater (Just. 13. 2. 13). Ptolemy's proposal of a ruling council (Curt. 10. 6. 15) made in the general meeting described by Curtius would have put the entire empire on a very different path.

Having made their decision, as per Justin (13. 2. 14), a meeting was called to be held in the palace of the chief *hetairoi* and the other leaders of the army (Curt. 10. 6. 1). The soldiers, who, while Alexander yet lived, had forced their way into the southern palace of Nebuchadrezzar in Babylon (Oates 1986: 150–1) to see their dying king for the last time (Plut. *Alex.* 76. 8; Arr. *Anab.* 7. 26. 1; Just. 12. 15. 1–4; Curt. 10. 5. 1), were now assembled outside the throne room in the large, 60 x 55m courtyard, awaiting news of the decision of their leaders ("desiring to know to whom Alexander's empire would be given" (Curt. 10. 6. 1)).[16] Access to the discussion going on within was supposed to be limited to those summoned by name (Curt. 10. 6. 2). However, the palace's succession of three courtyards leading to the throne room were all filled with soldiers, and, as a result, many of those summoned could not because of the crowds secure passage to the place of meeting (Curt. 10. 6. 1–2).

The soldiers' anxiety was well placed. Alexander's death just ten days after falling ill had caught them by surprise. The shock and the traditionally amorphous Macedonian selection process, when added to the unique circumstances of this succession, made a chaotic situation almost inevitable. Any difficulties with the decision of the *somatophylaces* that might have arisen in the proposed conclave of the commanders and *hetairoi* would likely have been resolved in favor of the *somatophylaces*' proposal. However, before the meeting could even begin, the army intervened. These troops were not the old Macedonian levy tied solely to the traditions of Macedonia; this was the army that had conquered the Persian Empire. It was now, as shown earlier, a force more professional than national, with a highly developed *esprit de corps*. The soldiers, desirous of information, burst into the meeting and showed no inclination to leave (Curt. 10. 6. 1–3). In 326, many of these same troops on the Hyphasis river in what is today Pakistan had failed to accede to Alexander's desire for further advance in the East (Arr. *Anab.* 5. 25. 1–29. 1; Curt. 9. 2. 1–3. 19; Diod. 17. 93.

2–95. 2; Plut. *Alex.* 62) and had even jeered him later at Opis in 324 (Arr. *Anab.* 7. 8. 1–11. 9; Curt. 10. 2. 12–4. 3; Diod. 17. 109. 1–3; Just. 12. 11. 1–12. 12; Plut. *Alex.* 71. 2–9). They would not now be intimidated by his lieutenants. All deliberations now had to be carried out before an audience possessed of a very vested interest in the outcome. All disagreements that might arise now had to be played out before this very attentive audience. Indeed, it was this very succession crisis that gave rise to the brief period of powerful army assemblies that emerged following Alexander's death (Errington 1978: 116–17; Anson 2020: 29–44). These were the result of the troops' long service in Asia, the personal nature of that service in the period of Alexander and the uncertainties that arose in this new age.

Perdiccas, Alexander's chiliarch or second-in-command,[17] is initially found in charge of the general meeting; after dramatically placing the ring given to him by Alexander on the throne, he proposed to the assemblage what had been decided earlier in the preliminary meeting, that they await the birth of Roxane's child (Curt. 10. 6. 4–5, 9; Just. 13. 2. 5).[18] This proposal received little support (cf. Curt. 10. 6. 16). Nearchus, Alexander's admiral and companion from the Conqueror's youth, quickly suggested that Heracles, Alexander's son by Barsine, be given the throne. Nearchus was married to Heracles' half-sister (Arr. *Anab.* 7. 4. 6). The troops reacted vocally and angrily to this suggestion, "clashing their spears" (Curt. 10. 6. 12).[19] They had not been pleased with what they perceived as Alexander's Persianization of the court (Arr. *Anab.* 7. 8. 1–2, 23. 1; Plut. *Alex.* 71) and his incorporation of Asian units into his ever-growing army (Carney 1996: 19–44; Anson 2013: 162–76; 2015: 249–50).[20] As Nearchus persisted, the soldiers drew close to mutiny. Ptolemy, not wishing to advance Nearchus and sensing the mood of the crowd, declared that it would be disgraceful for Macedonians and Greeks to be ruled by someone descended from those they had just conquered (Curt. 10. 6. 13–14).[21] Ptolemy now entered the fray with a proposal for a general council of leaders to rule the empire. Clearly, he had agreed to the earlier consensus of the *somatophylaces*, but this was a different audience and likely indicates what Ptolemy had wished all along. Even his initial proposal was similar to what he now put forward in that there would have been a regency of four. In this newer proposal, those who had been Alexander's chief advisors, which would include Ptolemy himself, would come together "whenever there shall be need of general consultation and that which the majority of them shall decide shall stand approved" (Curt. 10. 6. 15). This sounds for all the world like the Commission created by Lucky Luciano in 1931 to run the Mafia, though I don't believe that Lucky knew his Curtius. Moreover, during the first twenty years of this new age, most often coalitions were formed to resist those who wished to take it all. These coalitions, when victorious, then created the new reality. In this sense, maybe in the long run Ptolemy got his ruling council. The full implication of Ptolemy's proposal, whether in the first meeting described by Justin or in that later assembly described by Curtius, is that the empire would be theoretically left intact, ruled ostensibly by a council, but with the practical rule held locally. Ostensibly, the army in the field or sequestered in various garrisons would remain under the ultimate control of the council.[22] This is strikingly similar to an arrangement made by Eumenes in 316 (Anson 2014: 103; 2015: 165–7). Here to deal with a divided command, he created the "Alexander Tent," where in the presence of Alexander's throne with replicas of his diadem, scepter, and armor, in deliberations all would be theoretically on an equal standing and orders would be issued in Alexander's name (Diod. 18. 60. 5–61. 3: Plut. *Eum.* 13. 5–8; Polyaen. 4. 8. 2). Ptolemy's objections to Alexander's heirs as not pure Macedonians were not the result of actual racism on his part. Ptolemy was exiled for promoting a marriage between Alexander and a Carian princess (see Chapter 2). His objection was tied to his opposition to the accession of Arrhidaeus. His "racism" was his acceding to the mood of the assembly to get what he wanted. Moreover, none of these proposed Argead claimants would be able to rule and the practical aspects of ruling would then fall to whoever became regent. Given the previous history of Macedonia's supposed regencies,[23] he knew it would then only be a matter of time until the regent became king. It could not have only been Meleager who realized this truth (Curt. 10. 6. 20–1). So what was Ptolemy's purpose in his proposal of a council? Did he believe his political skills were sufficiently superior to those who would be his colleagues that he would gain ascendancy in such an arrangement? At the least, however, he may have seen such an arrangement of provincial governors under the ostensible authority of the dual monarchs as an alliance designed to keep the more ambitious members of Alexander's Successors in check. An attack on one would become an attack on all. Given the great ambitions of many of his colleagues, would this arrangement have kept them in check?[24]

Some agreed with Ptolemy, fewer with Perdiccas, and none apparently with Nearchus. Aristonous, one of the elite bodyguards, now called for Perdiccas to be made king in his own right, declaring that Alexander, by giving him his ring before dying, had indicated that he wanted him as his heir (Curt. 10. 6. 16–17).[25] This suggestion received broad support, but Perdiccas hesitated, and the moment was lost (Curt. 10. 6. 18–20). Given that the monarchy had been held by the Argead clan since mythical times, Perdiccas' hesitation is understandable, but what is curious is that at this moment it was not a major concern of the majority in this ad hoc meeting. Curtius (10. 6. 18), perhaps influenced by the feigned initial reluctance of Augustus and later Tiberius to accept power, states that Perdiccas coveted the prize but hoped his hesitancy would lead to an overwhelming demand that he accept the role. This worked later for Augustus and sort of for Tiberius. But for Perdiccas, when that groundswell of support was not forthcoming, he moved from the forefront and remained quiet.

It is in what follows that the two accounts, those in Justin and Curtius, become more difficult to reconcile. With the division among the leaders now laid out for all to see, Curtius declares that Meleager, the son of Neoptolemus, spoke forcefully against this last proposal regarding Perdiccas, proclaiming that Perdiccas was unworthy of such a position and further stating that Roxane's child was only a stalking horse for what would then become the *de facto* rule by Perdiccas (Curt. 10. 6. 20–1). Meleager pointed out that the sex of the child was unknown but assumed, and accused Perdiccas of being ready to introduce a male child if necessary (Curt. 10. 6. 21). Many of the rank-and-file agreed with Meleager (Curt. 10. 7. 1). All suggestions were now actively and openly debated by the troops (Curt. 10. 6. 16–18) and the meeting quickly degenerated "in sedition and discord" (Curt. 10. 7. 1). In this emerging chaos, in Curtius' account, a virtually unknown individual proposed that the crown be given to Arrhidaeus; this suggestion was soon taken up by the soldiers (Curt. 10. 7. 1–3). The proposal brought much of the disagreement among the *principes* to an end and they were joined by those members of the Companion Cavalry who were present. This may be the second meeting that Justin lists. Pithon heaped abuse upon the mere suggestion of Arrhidaeus as king (Curt. 10. 7. 4–5). There was now a kind of division of the house: those wishing to enthrone Arrhidaeus and those who were now rallying around Perdiccas (cf. Curt. 10. 7. 8). This division roughly was one between the cavalry and the infantry, perhaps indicating the two separate meetings of these groups in Justin's account.

It is here, as suggested earlier, that the attempt to reconcile our sources becomes difficult. Justin (13. 3. 1–5) has the *principes* after the infantry had opted to endorse Arrhidaeus as king send two of their number, battalion commanders Meleager and Attalus, to the infantry in an attempt to quell their enthusiasm for Arrhidaeus (Just. 13. 3. 2; Diod. 18. 2. 2–3). These, however, pursuing their own interests joined the infantry with Meleager then becoming the infantry's leader (Just. 13. 3. 2). Perhaps Curtius' account from the first mention of Arrhidaeus to the adherence of Meleager has been compressed. When Arrhidaeus is mentioned, the infantry members begin to endorse the proposal and it is at this time that Meleager, a battalion commander and therefore well known to the soldiers, is sent to stop the developing groundswell. Now why they would send someone who had attacked their proposal and maligned the integrity of Perdiccas is troublesome, unless one assumes that Curtius has gotten the chronology wrong and the tirade against Perdiccas came after Meleager had gone to the other side. Still, Meleager would appear to be an unlikely choice to be sent to the infantry. According to Justin, he had earlier proposed that Arrhidaeus would be a satisfactory choice for king. If one assumes a gap in time between the first call for Arrhidaeus to be king and Meleager's leadership, and the entrance of Arrhidaeus to the meeting where he was hailed by the soldiers as King Philip (Curt. 10. 7. 7), then it is possible that after the initial call the *principes* did send Meleager to the infantry in an attempt to dissuade them from their position. Moreover, if this Attalus is Perdiccas' brother-in-law, he would appear an equally unlikely candidate for this betrayal, especially since he is later found in Perdiccas' good graces, but it has been suggested that the marriage came later as part of a successful attempt at reconciliation (Heckel 1992: 381–4; 2021: 119). However, neither Curtius, Diodorus, nor Arrian (*Succ.* 1a. 2) associate Attalus with Meleager. Brian Bosworth (2002: 44n. 58) suggests that this is a different Attalus, not Perdiccas' brother-in-law. Justin's claim (13. 3. 7) that this same individual attempted to assassinate Perdiccas makes this a real possibility. Moreover, Attalus was a common Macedonian name.

It's a lot to assume in order to try to reconcile the two accounts and it may indeed be a bridge too far. In any case, the result was civil war, however brief. Perdiccas with 600 loyal men, including Ptolemy and the royal pages, withdrew from the meeting to the place where Alexander's body lay, but the soldiers followed, and blood was drawn. Those with Perdiccas and the majority of the officers and the Companion Cavalry ultimately left the city and camped on the plains before Babylon (Curt. 10. 7. 20). These supported awaiting the birth with the potential guardians Leonnatus and Perdiccas, and the affairs in Europe to be left to Craterus and Antipater (Curt. 10. 7. 8–9). The infantry in the city united behind their newly proclaimed king. All other proposals were forgotten and the lines between the two sides were drawn.

While the cavalry and the majority of the *principes* were camped outside, they blockaded the city (Curt. 10. 8. 11–13). In Babylon, the majority of Alexander's former army was made up of Asian troops. These would most likely have stood with the *principes*, giving this force overwhelming superiority. With supplies dwindling, Meleager under pressure from the army sent three representatives to the cavalry (Curt. 10. 8. 15).[26] The troops demanded that their leaders, chiefly

Meleager, either come to terms with the cavalry or immediately lead them against the latter (Curt. 10. 8. 12–14). A compromise was reached (Curt. 10. 8. 14–22). In the settlement, Arrhidaeus became King Philip III (Arr. *Succ.* 1a. 3), but it was also decided that, if Roxane was delivered of a male child, then that infant would also be designated as king, King Alexander IV (Just. 13. 4. 3; cf. Arr. *Succ.* 1a. 1, 8), thus creating a dual monarchy. While Appian (*Syr.* 55) states that Philip was to reign only until Alexander IV came of age, given that no other source agrees, it is likely that Appian has misinterpreted the practicality of Philip being the active king as an adult, while Alexander IV was an infant.

Meleager would become Perdiccas' lieutenant (Arr. *Succ.* 1a. 3).[27] However, in reality Perdiccas and the other *principes* had no intention of abiding by this agreement. "The Perdiccans made the compromise only to get control of the king and to eliminate Meleager" (Errington 1970: 56). As part of the agreement with the former battalion commander, a formal reconciliation was to be staged; the period of strife had lasted a week (Curt. 10. 10. 9). Treachery was planned around a ritualistic purification of the Macedonian forces (Curt. 10. 9. 8–11). Once outside the walls, surrounded by the cavalry and their supporters in the plain, and with King Philip now leading one wing of the cavalry, the king at the instigation of Perdiccas demanded the surrender of thirty[28] of the leaders of the infantry (Diod. 18. 4. 7; Curt. 10. 9. 18; Just. 13. 4. 7–8). The dumbfounded troops meekly watched as their compatriots were taken and subsequently trampled to death by the elephants. While Meleager was not in this number, he was subsequently assassinated (Diod. 18. 4. 7; Curt. 10. 9. 21; Arr. *Succ.* 1a. 4).[29]

The cavalry leaders now returned to Babylon and held the conclave planned previously to decide the fate of Alexander's empire. This time there were no common soldiers present (Curt. 10. 10. 1–4). The dual monarchy was confirmed after the birth of Alexander IV (Arr. *Succ.* 1a. 1, 8; 1b. 1; Just. 13. 4. 3). Perdiccas emerged as both guardian and regent (Arr. *Succ.* 1a. 3; Diod. 18. 23. 2). Leonnatus, who had appeared prominently in the earlier discussions, did not become co-regent. Perdiccas had benefited from the brief civil war, but not without making concessions. While there was not to be a commission to run affairs, various areas of the empire were given out to prominent *principes*. For his acquiescence to the new order, Ptolemy became satrap of Egypt. Of all the satrapies reassigned, Egypt was the plum assignment. Ptolemy had supported Perdiccas after the beginning of the chaos in the assembly in Babylon, but so had many others. In fact, few were rewarded with satrapies. Most of these provinces were simply reassigned to those already holding the positions (Arr. *Succ.* 1a. 5–7; 1b. 2–7; Diod. 18. 2. 4–3. 2; Curt. 10. 10. 1–5).

Ptolemy's former position as one of Alexander's *somatophylaces* ended with the Conqueror's death. He was now out of a job and a new office had to be found for him. However, if Perdiccas wanted him away from court, there would have been other places to send him that did not have the potential of Egypt. Perdiccas had been with Alexander in Egypt and he knew its promise.[30] Ptolemy's appointment to Egypt was not the regent's choice, it was Ptolemy's. What then would induce Perdiccas to do Ptolemy's bidding? In the first place, both Diodorus (18. 3. 1) and Curtius (10. 10. 1) make it clear that the division was the result of the deliberations of the *principes*. Indeed, Diodorus (18. 23. 2) states that early in Perdiccas' regency his position was "not firmly established." It may not have been his desire at all that Ptolemy become the satrap of such a rich and well-protected land. Perdiccas may have needed Ptolemy's backing in initially securing his new role. Given that this position was not secure, Egypt may have been given to Ptolemy in exchange for dropping any semblance of his proposal to govern the empire by committee. This proposition had shown great appeal in the initial discussions in Babylon. More of those assembled in that chaotic general meeting in Babylon had supported Ptolemy's proposal of a ruling council than Perdiccas' proposal to await the birth of the pregnant Roxane (Curt. 10. 6. 16). While the kingship had now been settled, rule by a group could still apply to the regency.

Pausanias (1. 6. 2) declares Ptolemy was responsible for the ultimate breakup of Alexander's empire and with his arrival in Egypt that unraveling had begun. What his navigation of the chaos that followed Alexander's death says about the man is that he was an expert politician. While Alexander lived, power emanated from the central government and one's closeness to the mercurial leader, but in what followed, power lay in armies and satrapies. It was almost like a return to the days before Philip and Alexander. In those days aristocratic power came from their estates and their dependent populations. This was different in that it was a much wider world. Ptolemy had attempted to create a coalition government where his political skills might work wonders, but he was quick to see and to grasp what counted in this new world: a physical base of operations and an army.

4

The Destruction of an Empire

Ptolemy, son of Lagus, the former *somatophylax*, in the aftermath of the crisis that emerged followed Alexander's death became the satrap of "Egypt and Libya and the areas of Arabia adjoining Egypt" (Arr. *Succ.* 1a. 5; Just 13. 4. 10; Diod. 18. 3. 1). Here, according to Polybius (5. 34. 9), the second-century BC historian, he ensconced himself with the goal to protect Egypt, surrounding that land with "a fence of client states."[1] Our other surviving sources would appear to support this conclusion. Diodorus repeatedly criticizes Perdiccas and Antigonus for their insatiable greed;[2] in contrast, only on one occasion does Diodorus, in a general statement that originated probably with Diodorus himself, suggest that Ptolemy likewise had ambitions equal to those of his rivals. In this particular case, Diodorus is commenting on the attempts by many of the Diadochs, including Ptolemy, to secure the hand of Alexander's sister Cleopatra in marriage, and states with respect to all her suitors that each hoped by the marriage "to gain supreme power for himself" (Diod. 20. 37. 4). A marriage to Cleopatra, like a connection to anything associated with Alexander, would enhance one's standing in the early days of the post-Alexander world. Such connections would especially appeal to the Conqueror's veterans, which would be sufficient reason to pursue such a marriage, without any desire to possess all of Alexander's former empire. However, Ptolemy is consistently portrayed favorably in the sources because of his lack of such a desire (Anson 2015: 32–4). He is also generous with his enemies. After Perdiccas' murder during the regent's attempt to overthrow Ptolemy in Egypt, with that dead commander's army suffering from a lack of supplies, Ptolemy appeared and provided what they needed (Diod. 18. 36. 6). Previously, Perdiccas' invading force had suffered desertion to Ptolemy (Diod. 18. 33. 2) and one wonders how many in this present situation would have done the same. Later in 306, during Antigonus' and Demetrius' failed campaign to capture Egypt, after Ptolemy offered bounties for deserters, the invading commander had to set up defenses to prevent his own troops from deserting (Diod. 20. 75. 1–3, 76. 7). When Demetrius was defeated in the Battle of Gaza in

312 and his personal baggage had been captured by Ptolemy's forces, Ptolemy saw that it was returned without ransom (Diod. 19. 84. 3). Ptolemy was creating an image like Alexander before him. This was, however, to be a very different one from that of the Conqueror. Alexander wanted to be seen in life and remembered as "a great warrior, invincible, unconquerable, the son of Zeus, and as a god himself on earth" (Anson 2021: 24). Alexander would have been pleased at the growth and spread of the Romance that came to be associated with him. Ptolemy was less interested in terrifying all and sundry, for he had different goals. He was not out to conquer the world; he was putting forth an aura of nobility and moderation. As a result, where coalitions were formed readily to oppose Antigonus, no coalition was formed from fear of Ptolemy's great ambitions. In short, Ptolemy, having achieved his aims in Egypt, wished to project this image of himself as a benevolent person, brave, and capable of defending himself, but so different from his rivals. As Curtius (9. 8. 23) reports, "his manner was modest and unassuming, and particularly generous and approachable, having assumed none of the aloofness of royalty." Therefore, while Perdiccas is described as "bloodthirsty" and "grasping" (Diod. 18. 33. 3; Arr. *Succ.* 1a. 20, 28; Nepos. *Eum.* 2. 3; Just. 13. 8. 2; *Suda* s.v. Perdiccas) and Antigonus is depicted as much the same (Diod. 18. 41. 5, 47. 3, 50. 1, 52. 3; 19. 44. 1, 56. 1–2; 20. 75. 3), Ptolemy is consistently described in our sources as generous and pious,[3] with Justin praising his industry, moderation, and kindness (13. 6. 18-19). Perdiccas is arrogant (13. 8. 2) and Antigonus is shown to be both bloodthirsty and greedy (Just. 14. 1. 9; 15. 1. 9). These favorable Ptolemaic comments, especially those that highlight the greed of Perdiccas and Antigonus and the generosity of Ptolemy, suggest that much of this praise is due to the belief that Ptolemy was not seeking the grand prize—the rule of Alexander's intact empire. A more concrete example of his restraint can be found in his refusal to accept the regency for the kings which was his for the asking after his defeat of Perdiccas in Egypt in 320 (Diod. 18. 36. 6). While the ancient evidence would appear clear with respect to Ptolemy's limited ambitions, Alexander Meeus has argued that Ptolemy "aimed at becoming Alexander's true Successor for the entire empire" (2014: 265). Most recent scholars agree and proclaim that Ptolemy was little different in his ambitions from the other Diadochs.[4] The Egyptian satrap was "simply more careful" in the pursuit of his "vast ambitions" (Meeus 2014: 263, 306; cf. Heckel 2016: 238n. 46).

What then was Ptolemy's actual role in this new world? Did he seek to partition the empire or to become the next Alexander, holding the empire intact under his personal authority? It is claimed that his operations in Greece later and his overtures of marriage to Cleopatra, all in 308–307, were preludes to his desire to replace Cassander in Macedonia. These operations and the overture, however, were designed to limit the power of Antigonus and Demetrius.[5] Ptolemy had campaigned against Antigonus' possessions in Cilicia in 309 and was still, at least theoretically, allied with Cassander and Lysimachus. The Egyptian satrap clearly was hoping to beat Antigonus at his own game of appearing as the friend to the Greeks and gain their support through a "Greek Freedom" program of his own. He likely wished to recreate the former League of Corinth with himself as its leader (Billows 1990: 144–5 and n. 18; Dixon 2007: 173–4 and n. 63). Ptolemy had planned on "freeing" more Greek cities, but the Peloponnesians who had agreed to assist him in these endeavors failed to contribute the forces that they had promised, and Ptolemy returned to Egypt (Diod. 20. 37. 1–2). There is no hint of any intention to seize Macedonia, and this appears to be no more than a case of attempting to undermine Antigonus' and Demetrius' power and to deflect them from activities involving Egypt. Indeed, Ptolemy's actions were likely predicated on Antigonus being absent in the East during these years attempting unsuccessfully to unseat Seleucus from Babylonia. He returned in 308.[6] Everything in Ptolemy's actions after securing Egypt were centered on its preservation. Ptolemy's rejection of his elder son, known to history as Ptolemy Ceraunus, as his successor for the younger Philadelphus, while there were also family complications resulting from his polygamous marriages, was also the result of this desire to protect his dynasty's hold on Egypt. Ceraunus was in the cast of a Demetrius. He might have gambled away Egypt in an attempt to seize the grand prize and thus he was rejected as Ptolemy's successor in favor of the younger son.

In my view, Ptolemy was not simply in favor of partition, but in the ultimate dissolution of the empire and its attendant Argead monarchy. This would explain what might first appear to be a dramatic change in his character that occurs in 320 after the defeat and death of Perdiccas. In the immediate years after Alexander's death, Ptolemy was clearly among the most reckless of all of Alexander's Successors. Ptolemy, early on, began to act independently of the central government, i.e. the regent Perdiccas, and it was Ptolemy who, as much as Perdiccas, provoked the First Diadoch War by his capture of Alexander's corpse. Subsequently, he displayed a cautious policy that almost bordered on timidity. While it is difficult to determine what Ptolemy may have intended, one avenue to get a sense of his ambition is to examine what he actually did. Ptolemy, as mentioned in the previous chapter, had in the chaotic assembly in Babylon after Alexander's death shown his desire to abandon the Argead dynasty. His proposal to establish a council of those who had been routinely convened by Alexander (Curt. 10. 6. 15) shows he believed that Alexander's empire would not survive as an extension of the traditional Macedonian monarchy.[7] Alexander had changed the very nature of that monarchy and the lack of competent Argead heirs doomed its survival. In the past, the clan had always had a number of viable candidates for the throne, but not now. Moreover, there was no true precedent for a regency. The kingship was not a constitutional office; as Beth Carney (1995: 370–1) has shown, power "was determined not by title or office but rather by position as the dominant Argead." As a result, while the new king might act as a guardian for his predecessor's child, there would not be any question concerning who was king; it was the adult Argead. This was the case with Philip II and his nephew Amyntas Perdicca. Philip became his guardian, but he was always the monarch (Anson 2009: 276–81). Until Philip had children of his own, his brother's son—his closest male relative—would be his heir, and, hence, the guardianship. A true regent would then be someone who held power for an underage Argead, but who was not an Argead himself. This was the case with Ptolemy of Alorus, who became regent for Perdiccas III and whose regency ended when the young Perdiccas killed him (Anson 2009: 281–3). This was hardly the best of precedents. What had become clear to Ptolemy after the conclusion of the events that led to the dual monarchy was that the empire would ultimately either be partitioned among the Conqueror's generals or survive intact under the authority of one of them. Ptolemy's suggestion of collective leadership had faltered in the aftermath of the riot and brief civil war. With only the two choices—partition, or a new king—and with the certainty that Ptolemy would not be that king, even if he wanted the job, partition was preferred.

Ptolemy, as noted in the previous chapter, negotiated to secure the satrapy of Egypt (Curt. 10. 10. 1; Just. 13. 4. 10; Diod. 18. 1. 3). This may not have been a hard sell. Perdiccas must have wished to eliminate from Babylon and access to the Macedonian veterans any of those who had held prominent positions under Alexander. However, both Ptolemy and Perdiccas had accompanied Alexander to Egypt[8] and there both would have been impressed by its wealth and its natural defences. Of all the major areas of Alexander's former empire, it was the best protected, surrounded by desert on two sides, shoals in the north, and desert and cataracts to the south, a virtual natural fortress (Kahn and Tammuz 2008: 37–66). Moreover, its resources were substantial. Add to these the additional resources left by Alexander and Ptolemy began his satrapal reign in a good position. There were 8,000 talents in the treasury which Ptolemy used to hire mercenaries (Diod. 18, 14. 1) to go along with the 4,000 troops and thirty triremes that Alexander had left behind (Curt. 4. 8. 4; Arr. *Anab.* 3. 5. 3–5). Ptolemy's seizure of Cyrene in 322 gave him access to additional troops and resources (cf. Diod. 18. 21. 7–9). Perdiccas did try to check Ptolemy by appointing his new satrap's lieutenant (*hyparchos*), Cleomenes (Arr. *Succ.* 1a. 5). Cleomenes' position in Egypt prior to the appointment of Ptolemy is much discussed (Yardley, Wheatley, Heckel 2011: 90; Collins 2012: 237–42; Anson 2014: 43, n.38. There is disagreement about Cleomenes' official title and authority in Egypt. Jacob Seibert (1969: 43–4, 50), following Arrian (*Succ.* 1a. 5), declares that he was appointed satrap by Alexander, but it is more likely that he simply became the *de facto* satrap of Egypt. Alexander had initially divided authority in Egypt among a number of officials, apparently leaving no one in overall authority (Arr. *Anab.* 3. 5. 2–7). Justin (13. 4. 11) declares that Cleomenes' charge was to oversee the construction of Alexandria.

Upon becoming satrap, Ptolemy proceeded almost immediately to eliminate Cleomenes (Paus. 1. 6. 3).[9] How this was done, and how openly, is unclear, but there is no reference to Perdiccas sending out a replacement. Ptolemy also "carried on a diplomatic correspondence" with Antipater, the "*Strategos* in Europe" (Arr. *Succ.* 1a. 3; Diod. 17. 118. 1–2; Just. 13. 4. 5), an individual whose power and independence was second only to that of the regent (Diod. 18. 14. 2). Perdiccas himself, in recognition of the power of Antipater, early on requested an alliance (Diod. 18. 23. 2). The nature of the resultant "understanding" is unstated, but it would appear to have been a recognition of Antipater's hegemony in Europe and that of Perdiccas in Asia. Antipater was especially solicitous of the regent, who became his son-in-law in 321 (Diod. 18. 23. 1–3; Arr. *Succ.* 21; Just. 13. 6. 6).[10] Antipater had accepted the arrangements made in Babylon and in a number of cases had deferred matters concerning European affairs to the kings, i.e. to Perdiccas. He forwarded the question of Athenian possession of Samos for adjudication to the central government (Diod. 18. 18. 6). However, even though Antipater was greatly surprised when he discovered that Perdiccas was planning on marching on Macedonia and seizing the throne, he had hedged his bets, having made alliances with others among the Successors. When Antipater did discover Perdiccas' plan to invade Macedonia, a military alliance was quickly created with the satrap of Egypt (Diod. 18. 25. 4), likely indicating the two individuals were already in communication. Diodorus does state that he would send a delegation to Egypt to discuss concerted action, "since he [Ptolemy] was utterly hostile to Perdiccas and friendly to them." This agreement between the General in Europe and the Satrap of Egypt may also have been cemented with a marriage between Antipater's daughter Eurydice and Ptolemy (Paus. 1. 6. 8);

however, the actual date of the marriage is unclear. Antipater had many daughters and used them to create familial alliances with other Successors. Craterus married Antipater's daughter Phila in 321 (Diod. 18. 18. 17), and, as noted, Perdiccas married his daughter Nicaea in the same year (Arr. *Succ.* 1a. 21, 26; Diod. 18. 23. 3).[11] It is likely that the Egyptian satrap corresponded with others as well. With the beginning of the First Diadoch War, most of the island of Cyprus revolted in favor of Ptolemy (Arr. *Succ.* 24. 14–28).

Unlike the deference to central authority shown by Antipater, Ptolemy had acted as an independent agent from the time of his arrival in Egypt. As noted, he had eliminated his assigned lieutenant Cleomenes and in the late summer or fall of 322 he had annexed the Greek city-state of Cyrene without the approval of the central government (Diod. 18. 21. 7-9; Arr. *Succ.* 16–19; [Parian Marble] *FGrH* 239 B F-10).[12] It is unclear, however, if such approval was necessary and whether Ptolemy's action would have been regarded as insubordination. It did ostensibly represent an addition to the empire. The only evidence of Perdiccas' dissatisfaction is the statement in Diodorus (18. 29. 1)—which occurs, however, after Ptolemy's seizure of Alexander's corpse—that the regent viewed with suspicion Ptolemy's increasing power. Cyrene was in fact not made an autonomous city in the empire, but was annexed to Egypt.[13] Ptolemy's intervention in what had become a Cyrenaic civil war might also be justified in the interest of imperial stability. Moreover, it is true that while Alexander lived, satraps often interfered in the internal affairs of cities supposedly autonomous (Bosworth 1988: 257), following the Persian practice of granting satraps great authority over their satrapies. It may also have been part of a traditional concern of the Egyptians, and it had been the ambition of at least one pharaoh of Egypt to seize Cyrene as a means of securing his western frontier (Hdt. 2. 161. 4; 4. 159. 4–6). While Photius' Epitome of Arrian (*Succ.* 1a. 5) states that both Egypt and Libya were awarded to Ptolemy in Babylon, Curtius (10. 10. 1; cf. Arr. *Anab.* 3. 5. 4) suggests that this reference to Libya referred solely to those peoples routinely under the sovereignty of satrap of Egypt and not to an independent Greek city.[14] The city was then an autonomous community and acted in that capacity by inviting Ptolemy's intervention (Diod. 18. 21. 6). By contrast, the decision over Samos, dealing with a situation stemming from 366 when the Athenians had expelled the inhabitants and repeopled the island with Athenians, would be considered justified under the terms of the League of Corinth. Now the dispossessed Samians wanted the Athenians expelled and the native Samians returned to their homeland. Since mainland Greece was officially under the League of Corinth, the organization created by Philip II to end warfare among the Greeks and prepare for the "Greek" invasion of the Persian Empire, this would be considered official state business. Moreover, the failed attempt in the Lamian War to overthrow Macedonian hegemony which had broken out after Alexander's death resulted in much greater control of Greek affairs by the Macedonians. Consequently, issues such as those of Samos would come routinely under the purview of the central government. Antipater sent the Samian request to the king, i.e. Perdiccas, for adjudication (Diod. 18. 18. 6, 9). Antipater saw the need to get the approval of the central government for such actions; Ptolemy either did not see the need or chose purposefully to act independently and possibly even to annoy the central government (cf. Diod. 18. 29. 1).

What led to the request for Ptolemy to interfere in Cyrene arose from events that began, while Alexander yet lived, with Harpalus' second flight. Harpalus, as noted previously, was one of Alexander's long-standing "friends" (Arr. *Anab.* 3. 6. 5; Plut. *Alex.* 10. 4), who because he was unfit for military service was made Alexander's royal treasurer (Arr. *Anab.* 3. 6. 6). He had fled shortly before the Battle of Issus, taking with him part of the treasury, but had returned and was forgiven by Alexander and reinstated in his job. In 324, he fled again. He had used funds from the treasury to live a life of extreme luxury and debauchery (Diod. 17. 108. 4; Plut. *Mor.* 648C-D; Athen. 13. 594F-595C), but when he learned that Alexander had returned from the East, he was afraid of the king's possible reaction and fled to Athens with 5,000 talents from the Babylonian treasury and 6,000 mercenaries (Curt. 10. 2. 1; Diod. 17. 108. 6; 18. 19. 1), some of whom aided in the later unsuccessful revolt from Macedonian authority, the so-called Lamian War (Diod. 18. 9. 1). Harpalus ultimately was slain in Crete by his supposed friend Thibron (Diod. 17. 108. 8; 18. 19. 2; Curt. 10. 2. 3), who after the assassination took command of the mercenaries who had followed Alexander's former treasurer to Crete (Arr. *Succ.* 1a. 16; Diod. 17. 108. 6; 18. 19. 2). After the murder, associating himself with certain exiles from the North African city, Thibron defeated the Cyrenaeans in battle, seized control of the harbor and began to besiege the city (Diod. 18. 19. 2-3; Arr. *Succ.* 1a. 16). As a result, the Cyrenaeans agreed to give him 500 talents and become his ally. Thibron now planned a campaign to subdue much of Libya, but these intentions began to go awry when he had a falling-out with one of his commanders, who convinced the Cyrenaeans to renounce their treaty. As the fighting dragged on, the wealthy Cyrenaeans, having been driven from the city by "the commons," appealed to Ptolemy, who sent a fleet and an army (Diod 18. 20-21. 7). The "democratic commanders" in the city joined forces with Thibron. In the ensuing battle, Ptolemy's general Ophellas won a complete victory, capturing Thibron, and delivering control over the entire region to Ptolemy (Diod. 18. 21. 8–9). Near the end of the campaign, Ptolemy himself appeared and the annexation was complete (Arr. *Succ.* 1a. 19).

The clearest act of insubordination committed by Ptolemy, however, occurred in the winter of 321/320, when the Egyptian satrap seized Alexander's body which was supposed to be on its way to Perdiccas in Asia Minor (Arr. *Succ.* 24. 1–4; 25; 1. 25; Diod. 18. 28. 2–3; Str. 17. 1. 8). Not only was this in violation of the will of the regent, but Ptolemy used violence against a force sent by the regent to forestall the satrap's action (Arr. *Succ.* 1a. 25, 24. 1). Now, there is considerable debate concerning the decision reached in Babylon concerning Alexander's burial site. Diodorus (18. 3. 5; cf. 18. 28. 3) states that it was decided in the conclave of the *principes* in Babylon following the reconciliation of the cavalry and infantry that the body was to be transported to Siwah for burial.[15] Here Diodorus is, perhaps, reflecting Alexander's personal wish (Curt. 10. 5. 4; Arr. *Anab.* 7. 26. 3; Diod. 17. 117. 3; Just. 12. 15. 7; 13. 4. 6), one of those last plans of the dead king rejected by the army in Babylon (Diod. 18. 4. 1–6) or, perhaps, reflecting a detail from his source for Alexander's campaign, or something he may have heard on his own visit to Egypt (Diod. 1. 44. 1; cf. 1.10. 6–7, 22. 2, 61. 4). The body was most likely meant to go to Aegae from the beginning (Paus. 1. 6. 3), the traditional site for the burial of Macedonian kings (Just. 7. 2. 2–5, 11. 2. 1; Diod. 17. 2. 1; Borza 1990: 167, 259).[16] However, Perdiccas may have made the decision to reroute the body from its original destination in Egypt as part of his plan to invade Macedonia and declare himself king. In the winter of 321/320, Perdiccas had made the decision to seize the throne for himself.[17] The importance of the dead conqueror's body was that all things associated with Alexander were sources of authority with the Macedonian veterans. In 318, Eumenes and his forces formally worshipped the dead king (Diod. 18. 60. 5–61. 3; Plut. *Eum.* 13. 5–8; Polyaen. 4. 8. 2). Alexander's body as a talisman continued long past that of the immediate period after his death. In 30 BC, Octavian traveled to Alexandria and visited Alexander's tomb (Suet. *Aug.* 18. 1; Cass. Dio 51. 16. 5).[18] Francisco Bosch-Puche has stated that by not only visiting but touching the body, Octavian was symbolically assuming the inheritance of Egypt and universal dominion (2014: 103–4). The propaganda value of returning Alexander's body to his homeland for Perdiccas then is obvious, although the assumption that possession of the body conferred legitimacy of rule is to give the corpse too much power.[19] For Perdiccas, it was one part of a far more extensive use of the memory of the dead king. He would divorce Nicaea, Antipater's daughter, and marry Cleopatra, Alexander's sister, while being welcomed back in Macedonia by Alexander's mother Olympias (Diod. 18. 25. 3; Arr. *Succ.* 1a. 21; Just. 13. 6. 4).[20] Finally, he would oversee the burial, a traditional duty of the dead ruler's successor (cf. Just. 11. 2. 1).

This plan began to unravel when Arrhidaeus, a Macedonian commander, and not the king,[21] in the winter of 321/320[22] violated his instructions, and, perhaps in collusion with Archon, the satrap of Babylonia,[23] diverted the funeral cortege to Egypt (Arr. *Succ.* 1a. 25), where the body was interred temporarily in Memphis with elaborate rites (Paus. 1. 6. 3). Arrhidaeus' reason for disobeying the regent is unknown. He may have wanted to fulfil Alexander's personal desire to be buried at Siwah, or he may have suspected Perdiccas' grand intentions to seize power, which in the *ad hoc* meeting that occurred in Babylon following Alexander's death, Meleager had stated to the assembled that seizing the throne was Perdiccas' intention. However, Meleager's accusation came during the initial disturbance and the ultimate decision by the leaders in Babylon was to confer the regency on Perdiccas. Of course, these suspicions did become a reality. Perdiccas in the summer of 321 did determine to proclaim himself king.

Diodorus' chronology, however, places the seizure of the Conqueror's corpse before any real knowledge of Perdiccas' ambitious plans became known (Anson 2013: 56). The funeral carriage had begun its journey west about the same time that events were unfolding which would lead to the regent's plan to become king (Anson 1986: 212–13). It was the murder of Alexander's half-sister, Cynnane, in the summer of 321 that would be the catalyst for Perdiccas' active and immediate designs on the throne. In that summer, Cynnane, the daughter of Philip II and Audata, and the widow of Amyntas Perdicca, Philip II's nephew and Alexander's cousin, arrived in Asia demanding that her own daughter Adea be married to King Philip (Arr. *Succ.* 1a. 22; Polyaen. 8. 60; cf. Diod. 19. 52. 5). Cynnane had raised a troop of her own and had forced her way out of Macedonia despite Antipater's attempt to block her departure (Polyaen. 8. 60). Perdiccas sent his brother Alcetas north to intercept her. When her determination proved unshakeable, Cynnane was murdered by Alcetas probably on Perdiccas' orders (Diod. 19. 52. 5; Arr. *Succ.* 1a. 22–3; Polyaen. 8. 60). The army reacted violently, forcing Perdiccas to agree to the marriage. Adea now changed her name to Eurydice and became the wife of King Philip III (Arr. *Succ.* 1a. 23; Polyaen. 8. 60; Diod. 19. 52. 5). It was this incident that precipitated a change in the policy of the regent. Prior to the appearance and murder of Cynnane, Perdiccas had married Antipater's daughter Nicaea, in preference to a proposal from Cleopatra, indicating that he was at least at that moment not interested in seizing power in his own name. He had assumed that this was unnecessary at this juncture. The royal army had proven loyal in a couple of campaigns and the regent's authority to this point had not been seriously challenged. The episode with Cynnane now convinced Perdiccas that his control of the army and hence the empire was not as firm as he had assumed. He now decided that in order to cement his authority he would have to become king in his own right, and preparations were made for an invasion of Macedonia. As noted earlier, the plan was to marry Cleopatra and in the company of his new wife, Alexander's brother and son, and welcomed by Alexander's mother Olympias, and with the Conqueror's body, return to his homeland, where he would formally bury Alexander in Aegae and declare himself king (Anson 2013: 55–6). After all, Macedonian regencies had been extremely rare and rarer still those that long survived (Anson 2009: 276–86).

Arrhidaeus, therefore, likely started his journey unaware of these events unfolding in western Asia. His journey began in the late summer of 321 (Anson 1986: 212–13), with his rendezvous with Ptolemy in northern Syria in the winter. It was in this same winter that knowledge of Perdiccas' plan to invade Macedonia and seize the throne became known. The news was revealed by Antigonus, the Phrygian satrap (Diod. 18. 25. 3–5; Arr. *Succ.* 1a. 24; [Parian Marble] *FGrH* 239 B F-10, 11), and it came as a shock to Antipater who with his now colleague Craterus[24] was then in the midst of a winter campaign in Aetolia (Diod. 18. 25. 1–3). Diodorus (18. 23. 3) indicates that Antigonus was well informed of the intrigues involving Cleopatra and Perdiccas. Menander, an Antigonid ally[25] and satrap of Lydia, was ideally situated to know of the activities involving the Conqueror's sister, since she was then resident in Sardis (Arr. *Succ.* 1a. 26). Menander may have become disenchanted with the regent, who apparently made the satrap subservient to the authority of Alexander's sister (Arr. *Succ.* 25. 2). Upon his arrival in Macedonia, Antigonus warned Antipater of Perdiccas' designs (Diod. 18. 25. 3; Arr. *Succ.* 1a. 24). He stated that Perdiccas would soon divorce Nicaea and marry Cleopatra as a preliminary to invading Macedonia and proclaiming himself king. Whatever proof Antigonus supplied, it was convincing. The source may well have been someone in Cleopatra's immediate circle who passed that evidence to Menander, who in turn passed it on to Antigonus (Anson 2013: 57–8). Antipater and Craterus immediately made peace with the Aetolians and began to prepare for an invasion of Asia (Diod. 18. 25. 3–5). Given that Arrhidaeus violated the commands of the regent before any news of Perdiccas' impending attempt to undo the decisions made in Babylon, this collusion with Ptolemy must have been in place, perhaps, from as early as the arrangements made shortly after Alexander's death. Our sources make it very clear that Arrhidaeus did not suddenly in Syria decide to take the body to

Ptolemy. The Egyptian satrap was not summoned to Syria after the funeral cortege arrived there, but rather he rendezvoused with Arrhidaeus in Syria (Diod. 18. 28. 3; cf. Arr. *Succ.* 1a. 25; Paus. 1. 6. 3; Str. 17. 1. 8). Even a cavalry force traveling from Memphis to Damascus, a journey of about 500 miles, would have taken some time to make that journey and Damascus is in southern Syria.[26] Moreover, Ptolemy apparently marched from Egypt with a significant number of troops, for Arrian (*Succ.* 1a. 25; 24. 1; cf. Diod. 18. 28. 3) records that he was harassed by a Perdiccan force sent to stop him all the way back to Egypt, but the agents of the regent were unable to prevent the satrap's return. While the reasons for Arrhidaeus' actions can only be guessed, it is clear that Ptolemy knew exactly what he was doing; he was precipitating a war. But, why? If he believed that that empire was doomed to partition, why not wait? The answer is likely that Ptolemy began to have his doubts. The Greek rebellions, east and west, had been crushed,[27] the regent had successfully campaigned in Asia Minor and had installed one of his loyal lieutenants, Eumenes the Cardian, there; at the same time Antigonus, who had long dominated the region, was under fire and preparing to flee, Craterus had willingly accepted his subordinate role in Macedonia, Leonnatus was dead, Antipater was old. Ptolemy had been acting as if the central government did not exist in anticipation of its imminent collapse, but it now looked as if it might survive a bit longer. While this was likely only a delay of the inevitable, that delay along with Perdiccas' growing power made Ptolemy anxious for his position. What if Ptolemy was the last man standing of the old guard? Before Perdiccas grew any stronger, now was the time to act. It was a dangerous decision and not in the least a cautious one.

The murder of Cleomenes and the seizure of Cyrene would have been pretext enough to justify such a declaration from Perdiccas, but the seizure of Alexander's corpse in direct opposition not only to the wishes of the regent but also the use of force against those operating under the regent's authority (Arr. *Succ.* 1a. 25; 24. 1–4) made war inevitable. Ptolemy could not have known when he caballed with Arrhidaeus of the impending war between Perdiccas and Antipater. He might have anticipated that Perdiccas would make an attempt to become king in his own right and prepared for such an eventuality back in Babylon with Arrhidaeus. Ptolemy clearly had suspicions of Perdiccas' ultimate ambitions. He had the measure of his fellow Diadoch from their long association on Alexander's expedition, and was watching with alarm the regent's growing power. Still, it must have been a pleasant surprise when word came along with the request for an alliance with Alexander's old Macedonian regent (Diod. 18. 25. 4). While, as noted, there had been some earlier understanding between Ptolemy and

Antipater (Diod. 18. 14. 2; cf. Paus. 1. 6. 8), it is very clear that a military alliance aimed against the regent had not existed before this latter request, which originated with Antipater. In any case, Ptolemy must have known that he would face Perdiccas alone. Even if an offensive and defensive alliance was in place with the Macedonian general, Antipater was in no position to intervene in time to prevent an invasion of Egypt. He was involved in a war in Aetolia at the time of Antigonus' arrival with the news and, until early in 320, forces ostensibly loyal to Perdiccas controlled the royal fleet, and hence the Hellespontine crossing. Cleitus, the fleet commander, did, however, desert the Perdiccan cause in the spring of 320 (Anson 2015: 106–11). Ptolemy, therefore, exhibited a great degree of confidence in his ability to deal with Perdiccas without the assistance of allies. Even given the natural defenses of Egypt, Ptolemy was taking a great risk in facing the regent who commanded the bulk of Alexander the Great's former army.

It is clear from his actions that Ptolemy wished at the least to destroy Perdiccas' power from the very start of the regency. As to any other ambitions, it is equally clear from later events that the Egyptian satrap did not wish to become the new Perdiccas himself. After the defeat and assassination of the then regent, when the regency was apparently his for the asking, he demurred (Diod. 18. 36. 7), proclaiming his loyalty to the kings and his support for Pithon, the satrap of Media Major (Arr. *Succ.* 1a. 5; Diod. 18. 3. 1; Just. 13. 4. 13; Curt. 10. 20. 4), and Arrhidaeus, the transporter of Alexander's corpse, as the new regents (Arr. *Succ.* 1a. 30; Diod. 18. 36. 7). While Joseph Roisman (2014, 471; 2012, 106–7; cf. Worthington 2016, 98) is correct that the regency was never actually officially offered to Ptolemy, it is unlikely that its mention in this context is simply a piece of Ptolemaic propaganda. Diodorus' narrative is clear and fits the situation. After the assassination of Perdiccas, "Ptolemy came, greeted the Macedonians, and spoke in defence of his own attitude; and as their supplies had run short, he provided at his own expense grain in abundance for the armies and filled the camp with the other needful things. *Although he gained great applause and was in position to assume the guardianship of the kings through the favor of the rank and file, he did not grasp at this*" (italics are mine). Perdiccas was dead; the royal army was in Egypt and Ptolemy was being very generous. Even without Diodorus' comment, it would appear obvious that Ptolemy was in a position to secure the regency had he wanted it. Clearly, he did not.

Perdiccas plainly appeared to Ptolemy as the greatest danger to his position. The other Diadochs would have appeared far less dangerous to Ptolemy in 321. Perhaps the most ambitious of them all, Leonnatus was dead, having died responding to a call from Antipater in the Lamian War and in anticipation of seizing the throne in his own name (Plut. *Eum.* 3. 7–8; Diod. 18. 15. 1), and Craterus, another very prominent lieutenant of the dead Alexander, had shown a muted ambition, moving to Macedonia and deferring to Antipater.[28] Antipater himself appeared content in Macedonia. Lysimachus was fully occupied in Thrace (Lund 1992: 19–50). The later, clearly ambitious and talented Antigonus and Seleucus had not as yet shown forth either their ambition or their skill. Ptolemy encouraged the awarding of the regency after Perdiccas' death to the lackluster pair Arrhidaeus and Pithon. By encouraging this arrangement, Ptolemy would realize a regency weakened both by its duality and its unimposing leaders. Even later at Triparadeisus where the regency passed to Antipater, Ptolemy must have realized that the old Macedonian was not interested in reclaiming Alexander's former empire. Later that winter Antipater in possession of the kings passed back to Macedonia never in the brief time left to him to return to Asia (Anson 2013: 73).

Ptolemy's policy was that if there had to be a central government, it should be as weak as possible. In the case of Antipater, who clearly was not weak, the focus of the new regent was clearly Macedonia and Greece. He couldn't wait to get out of Asia. He assigned to Antigonus the royal army, having exchanged 8,000 fresh Macedonian troops for the same number of Alexander's more independent veterans, and the war in Asia against Eumenes and the other remaining Perdiccans (Arr. *Succ.* 1a. 38; Diod. 18. 39. 7–40.1; Just. 14. 1. 1). Richard Billows believes that Antipater wished to designate Antigonus as his successor (1990: 69–71). Antigonus had proven to be loyal and capable, and at Triparadeisus, a life saver (Arr. *Succ.* 1a. 33). The army with its new regents had proceeded north to rendezvous with Antipater. At Triparadeisus in northern Syria what had been general insubordination in the ranks of the royal army was now close to mutiny. Under pressure, Pithon and Arrhidaeus abdicated in favor of Antipater, who was not present but near. When Antipater finally arrived, the troops were demanding their arrears in pay. Antipater addressed the army, attempting to quell their anger. In the resulting rioting, Antipater was almost killed, but saved by the recently arrived Antigonus (Arr. *Succ.* 1a. 31–3, 39; Diod. 18. 39. 1–4; Polyaen. 4. 6. 4). Antipater then, taking the kings with him, departed for Macedonia as quickly as he could, leaving before the end of winter (Bosworth 1992: 59), and he did not involve himself further in the affairs of Asia. After a protracted illness, he died in the late summer of 319 (Diod. 18. 48. 4; 47. 4; Plut. *Phoc.* 31. 1; *Eum.* 12. 1),[29] at the age of seventy-seven years (*Suda* s.v. "Antipatros"). The new regent was not Antipater's eldest son Cassander, nor any of his six sons (Heckel 2006:

35), but Craterus' old second-in-command, Polyperchon, who had accompanied that commander to Cilicia and then to Macedonia (Diod. 18. 48. 4; Plut. *Phoc.* 31. 1; cf. Plut. *Eum.* 12. 1). He had remained in charge of the country when Antipater and Craterus had crossed to Asia to attack Perdiccas (Just. 13. 6. 9) and was held in high regard by the Macedonians (Diod. 18. 48. 4). Cassander was made chiliarch, or Polyperchon's official second-in-command (Diod. 18. 48. 4–5). Antipater's death and this slighting of his eldest son would see the beginning of the second war over Alexander's inheritance. Craterus had likely been Antipater's preferred Successor, but he had died fighting in Asia Minor against Perdiccas' lieutenant Eumenes (Arr. *Succ.* 1a. 27; Diod. 18. 30. 5; Plut *Eum.* 7. 3; Nepos *Eum.* 4.1).

During the fall Cassander privately gathered support (Diod. 18. 49. 2). Given that Polyperchon had strong backing in Macedonia, Cassander was forced to seek allies elsewhere. He therefore sought alliances with "other commanders and cities," who had been allied with, or "friends" of, his father (Diod. 18. 49. 3). His supporters in Macedonia he sent secretly to the Hellespont in preparation for his own flight from Macedonia (Diod. 18. 54. 2). Outside of Greece, he sent envoys to Ptolemy to renew their friendship and to secure an alliance (Diod. 18. 49. 3; 54. 3). Cassander asked that Ptolemy send a fleet to his aid (Diod. 18. 49. 3). While there is no evidence that Ptolemy complied, some arrangement was reached (Diod. 18. 54. 3). To understand Ptolemy's actions, it is necessary to return to his suggestion at the original meeting in Babylon that a ruling council be created as opposed to choosing a single successor for the Conqueror. Polyperchon now represented centralized imperial authority; Cassander, at least judging from his later actions, did not. Antipater's son wished to establish himself as the legitimate ruler of Macedonia (Landucci Gattinoni 2003: 124–36; 2010: 113–21) and whatever other parcels might come his way. His ambitions, like those of the other Diadochs, with the exception of Ptolemy, was personal. The rivalry among the Successors was not that of the heads of national states, but rather conquerors holding spear-won lands as their own personal possessions. What was most important in the eyes of the Egyptian satrap was that turmoil in Europe would free Ptolemy from any fear of interference from that quarter.

It is with this same desire to destroy the unity of Alexander's empire that the seizure of Alexander's body must be seen. It would provoke the regent to war and would also enhance Ptolemy's standing in the coming conflict. Perdiccas would now be determined to remove Ptolemy from power and put one of his "friends" in his place and recover the body of the dead king (Arr. *Succ.* 24. 1). For the moment the Macedonians, who now had likely forgotten any grievances they had had against Alexander, now delighted in their status as his veterans, and wished to be associated with all things Alexander. As seen, both Perdiccas and Ptolemy had realized the propaganda value of securing the body of the dead king.

In these early actions, Ptolemy is anything but cautious. He was obviously confident both in his own ability and the defensive strength of his Egyptian satrapy. Ptolemy meant to provoke a confrontation with the regent, a confrontation he was prepared to win on his own, and which, indeed, he did with little assistance from any of the other heirs to Alexander's legacy. Brian Bosworth (2000: 228) suggests that Ptolemy and his dynasty did come to center their rule in Egypt, not as deliberate policy, but simply as the result of circumstances. However, Ptolemy's actions later do indicate a more circumspect ambition, which after the lack of caution early on, make this later strategy appear to be most probably a deliberate choice. Other than Egypt, Ptolemy did show an interest in the eastern seaboard of the Mediterranean, Cyprus, the Aegean Islands, coastal Asia Minor and occasionally parts of the Greek mainland. Of these areas outside Egypt, his primary interest was in the acquisition of Phoenicia, Coelê Syria, and Cyprus. All three areas had historically been of special interest to the Egyptians during those periods of Egyptian independence. Necho II is reported to have led an army to the Euphrates in 609 (2 *Kings* 23: 29–35; 2 *Chron.* 35: 20–22, 36: 4; *Jer.* 46: 2), and is generally regarded to have controlled the eastern seaboard of the Mediterranean, even establishing a league of maritime states (Boast 2006: 38). His fleet also explains those acquisitions along the coast of Asia and elsewhere as naval bases (Hauben 1974: 40). These operations provided Egypt with buffers and a strong fleet protected Egypt from any outside interference. These were Ptolemy's goals. For these he was ready to run great risks to obtain and retain. A strong naval force was necessary to achieve this goal. It has even been claimed that Ptolemy was simply following traditional Egyptian foreign policy. Gunther Hölbl (2001: 28) puts Ptolemy I's policy succinctly "as defensive imperialism." Diodorus (18. 43. 1) states that Ptolemy saw Phoenicia and Coelê Syria as critical bases for any contemplated invasion of Egypt. It has also been suggested that part of Ptolemaic policy was to maintain strong ties with areas of the Greek world to foster immigration to Egypt (Mueller 2006: 180). Perhaps the best explanation of Ptolemy's policy is provided by Roger Bagnall (1976B: 2): "Ptolemy I had no sooner acquired Egypt in the division in Babylon in June, 323, than he began looking outside Egypt; in the ensuing decades he worked cautiously but energetically to create an empire that would complement Egypt." His actions in Cilicia, Caria, and in the Aegean were by and large attempts to win allies in his ongoing struggle with Antigonus. With the death of Antigonus at Ipsus in 301, Ptolemy had taken control of Coelê Syria and Syria remained relatively dormant until 294. With Antigonus' son Demetrius intriguing and eventually gaining control of Macedonia, Ptolemy moved to retake the last of those key areas that he had previously lost to Antigonus. He recaptured Cyprus in 294 (Plut. *Demetr.* 35. 3-4, 38. 1). He further seized Tyre and Sidon and took possession of coastal areas in Caria, Lycia, Pamphylia, and Cilicia from those loyal to Demetrius (Wörrle 1977: 59–60; Meadows 2006: 460–1).[30]

Ptolemy was also not the first ruler of Egypt to see the importance of controlling Cyrene as a means to secure the western approaches to Egypt. Apries II made an unsuccessful attack on the Greek colony around 570 to stop the Greek city's expansion into territory controlled by Egyptian allies (Diod. 1. 68. 2).[31] Ptolemy then in these areas outside of Egypt was simply following earlier Egyptian interests. Phoenicia and Coelê Syria were seen by Ptolemy as critical bases for any contemplated invasion of Egypt (Diod. 18. 43. 1). Along with the possession of Phoenicia went a dominant navy. Such a force would prevent or at least seriously hinder any invasion of Egypt, given that a fleet was usually essential for a successful invasion. As in Antigonus' and Demetrius' invasion of 306 where their fleet was to convey supplies to the invading army and to secure entrance into the Nile, but failed in its mission, Cyprus was a shield to protect Phoenicia and Syria (Balandier 2007: 153). Getzel Cohen (1995: 35) emphasizes that the island controlled the shipping lanes, was a major source of timber, and a center for ship building, in addition to being conveniently located for an attack on Egypt. Successful invasions of Egypt were usually the result of land and sea coordination by the invaders (Anson 2016: 88). At the beginning of the conflict between Ptolemy and Perdiccas, known as the First Diadoch War, the Cypriots declared for Ptolemy (Arr. *Succ.* 24. 6), likely indicating that Ptolemy's emissaries had been active on the island previously. The island remained mostly under Ptolemaic control until Demetrius' great sea victory over the Ptolemaic fleet at Salamis in 306, when it fell under Antigonid domination (Diod. 20. 46. 5–47. 4, 7–53. 1; Plut. *Demetr.* 15–17. 1; Just. 15. 2. 6–9; Polyaen. 4. 7. 7; Paus. 1. 6. 6; App. *Syr.* 54). It was regained by Ptolemy in 287 (Plut *Demetr.* 35. 7) and retained until the end of his life.

With respect to Phoenicia and Coelê Syria, in the spring of 318, the Egyptian satrap captured these regions from their "lawful" satrap, Laomedon (Diod. 18. 43, 73. 2; [Parian Marble] *FGrH* 239 B F-12), and thereafter consistently sought to retain their possession. Despite a brief interlude when Eumenes occupied

Phoenicia in 318 (Diod. 18. 73. 2),[32] Ptolemy occupied the region until 314, when these areas were taken by Antigonus (Diod. 19. 58. 1–4). Here, except for a short period after the Battle of Gaza (Diod. 19. 83. 1–3; Plut. *Demetr.* 5. 1–3; Just. 15. 1. 7), the region remained in Antigonid hands until 301. In that year occurred the Battle of Ipsus and the defeat and death of Antigonus (Plut. *Demetr.* 28–30. 1; *Pyrrh.* 4. 4; Diod. 21. 2, 4b; App. *Syr.* 55; Just. 15. 2. 16–17, 4. 21–2; Polyb. 5. 67. 8). Even though Ptolemy had not participated in the battle, he demanded and did receive Phoenicia and Coelê Syria (Diod. 21. 1. 5). The Egyptian dynast claimed that in the negotiations that had created the alliance to oppose Antigonus, he had been promised these areas (Polyb. 5. 67. 8–10). Seleucus acquiesced "on account of their former friendship" (Diod. 21. 1. 5). Ptolemy, now fearing Seleucus' ambition, formed marriage alliances with both Cassander and Lysimachus in 299 (Wheatley and Dunn 2020: 286, 293). At this time Demetrius, Antigonus' son, still occupied the two of the major Phoenician cities, Sidon and Tyre (cf. Plut. *Demetr.* 22.9), but these were again under Ptolemy's control by 295/4 (Hölbl 2001: 23).

The last area where Ptolemy did show a sustained interest was the Aegean. Here, as in the case of Cyprus, he finally gained the upper hand after the collapse of Demetrius' rule in Macedonia and the withdrawal of many of that commander's former allies. Ptolemy then took over the Nesiotic League (Hammond and Walbank 1988: 228 n. 2, 232; Anson 2013: 181–2) which had been established by Antigonus in 313 ostensibly to guarantee the islands' independence (Billows 1990: 118; Anson 2013: 139). This policy was then continued by Ptolemy less in the breach as during the Antigonid administration, however, and more in the observance. A decree issued by the League, perhaps in 280, praises Ptolemy for "having liberated the cities, restored their laws, established to all their ancestral constitutions" (*Syll.*3 390. ll. 11–16). Ptolemy's legacy with these Aegean states was, therefore, not then as ruler and subjects but as *Soter*, Savior, and saved. The various states on the Greek mainland became as the islanders in the League, allies not dependencies.[33]

> Be it resolved by the common body of the delegates, since King Ptolemy [I] Soter has been responsible for many great blessings to the islanders and the other Greeks, having liberated the cities, restored their laws, reestablished to all their ancestral constitution and remitted their taxes ...
> *Syll.*³ 390. ll. 11–16 (translation Austin 1981: 359)

The nature of Ptolemy's activities outside of Egypt can be seen most clearly in his reaction to Demetrius' attack on the island of Rhodes in 305. While the island had been allied with Antigonus it had failed to join in the attack on Cyprus or the abortive invasion of Egypt the previous year. The Rhodians had proclaimed that they were at peace with all parties (Diod. 20. 81. 2, 4). They did, however, incline towards Ptolemy because of close trade connections with Egypt (Diod. 20. 81. 4). Antigonus was not content with their response to his request for an active alliance, and sent Demetrius with a well-equipped force, including numerous siege engines, to bring the Rhodians to heel. The other Diadochs supported the Rhodians with supplies and reinforcements (Diod. 20. 96. 3, 100. 2). In particular, Ptolemy contributed substantially to the Rhodian defense (Diod. 20. 88. 9, 94. 3–5, 96. 1–3, 98. 1, 100. 2). The siege ultimately failed. Other than convincing Ptolemy, and perhaps the other Diadochs, that it was time to become kings—the last of the kings, Alexander IV, was murdered by Cassander in 310 (Heckel 2021: 27)—the results of the siege were modest. Antigonus and Demetrius had already proclaimed themselves kings after Demetrius' great victory in the Battle of Salamis in 306, the battle that forced the evacuation of Cyprus by all Ptolemaic forces. Ptolemy was given the title of "*Soter*," Savior, by the grateful Rhodians, a name that would become a commonly applied epithet to the Egyptian ruler from then on. Moreover, with the acquiescence of the Oracle of Zeus at Siwah, Ptolemy henceforth would be worshipped as a god by the Rhodians (Diod. 20. 100. 3–4).[34] Ptolemy's primary goal as shown in his actions with respect to the Rhodians was to prevent wherever possible the increase in power of any of the other Diadochs. This was done less through acquisition of territory but rather through supporting the independence of those states resisting the aggression of his rivals. Ptolemy's primary concern was to undermine his rivals' grander ambitions. With respect to Asia Minor he did attempt to establish garrisons in certain coastal cities in Cilicia, Caria (cf. Diod. 20. 37. 2), and Lycia (Diod. 20. 27. 1–2; Wörrle 1977: 43–66). Ptolemy's occupation was always in opposition to their being held by someone else (Diod. 20. 19. 3, 27. 1) and most often tied in some fashion to his stated desire to "free the Greeks." Moreover, these areas were never claimed by him in any of the peace settlements (Diod. 20. 19. 3–4). As with respect to Asia Minor, so also with the Greek mainland, while Ptolemy made forays into Greece, he acquired no territory that he retained for any substantial period, nor did he ever demand these as part of any settlement. In 308, he acquired Sicyon and Corinth and garrisoned both (Diod. 20. 37. 2). This acquisition was unusual. Most often he operated as he did in the case of the Athenians, sending help and supporting the local government against the more acquisitive Diadochs (*SEG* 28. 60). With the death of Alexander, the son of Polyperchon, in 313, that individual's widow,

Cratesipolis, took control of her husband's army and established her rule over these two cities, possessions of her former husband (Diod. 19. 67. 1–2; cf. Diod. 20. 37. 1). The widow surrendered these to Ptolemy (Diod. 20. 37. 1; Polyaen. 8. 58), perhaps in hopes that he would add her to his many wives (Mahaffy 1895: 48; Carney 2000: 229). He did not. During this expedition to the Greek mainland, Ptolemy also acquired briefly the city of Megara (D. L. 2. 115; Hauben 2014: 254). Ptolemy had called on the Greek cities to join him in what would have amounted to a war of liberation, creating in Greece an association, perhaps, not unlike the League of Islanders or the original League of Corinth.[35] Their independence would ensure that Cassander would be kept in Europe. When the Greeks did not rush to his banner, he patched things up with Cassander, then in control of Macedonia, and, perhaps hearing of Antigonus' return from Babylon, returned home to Egypt (Diod. 20. 37. 2). Sicyon remained in Ptolemaic hands until "liberated" by Demetrius in 303 (Diod. 20 102. 2). Prior to the fall of Sicyon, Corinth was found in the control of Prepelaus, a commander in the employ of Cassander (Diod. 20. 103. 1). Brian Bosworth saw this episode in an entirely different light. He associated Ptolemy's interest in Greece with the demise of the Argead family and the attempt of Cleopatra to seek a marriage with the Egyptian dynast, and all as a prelude to Ptolemy's seeking the throne of Macedonia (Bosworth 2000: 238–9).[36] Ian Worthington (2016: 151) adds that Ptolemy's attempt to "bring back the League of Corinth ... shows that he wanted to be king of Macedonia." While this scenario is possible, it is not probable. Diodorus (20. 37. 1–2) makes no mention of such an ambition and along with the *Suda* (s.v. "Demetrios Antigonou") states that the purpose of this agreement was to liberate Greek states in order to protect their freedom. Certainly, this reflects Ptolemaic propaganda, but there never is any serious attempt by Ptolemy to involve himself in Macedonian affairs. Ptolemy's actions here appear more in line with an attempt to limit Cassander's growing power. Garrisons were likely included in Sicyon and Corinth and, perhaps, Megara, not to control the local population but rather to protect the cities. Cassander was, after all, the ruler of Macedonia, with a considerable presence in Greece and a much wider ambition. In the spring of 314, Cassander had demanded that Antigonus surrender Cappadocia and Lydia to him (Diod. 19. 57. 1–2), and in the winter of 313 he sent an army into Caria (Diod. 19. 68. 2).

Ptolemy's interest in Asia Minor and the Greek mainland was fleeting at best. As noted, these were never part of his demands in any settlement of hostilities with his fellow Diadochs. His interest in southern, coastal, Asia Minor may simply have been tied to maintaining Egypt's trade routes in the Aegean and providing harbors for the Ptolemaic fleet (Hauben 2014: 245). Ptolemy also never expressed any interest in possessing his homeland of Macedonia or in lands east of Thapsacus. After Antigonus' return to the West in 314, at the conclusion of the Second Diadoch War, Ptolemy demanded Syria from his erstwhile ally (Diod. 19. 57. 1; App. *Syr.* 53) but made no claims on Asia Minor or Greece. It was his ally in this particular war, Cassander, who made demands for parts of Asia Minor. The Third Diadoch War ended with a general understanding that the parties would retain what they held at the start of the war (Anson 2013: 148–9). With the conclusion of the Fourth Diadoch War, once again Ptolemy only demanded as compensation Phoenicia and Coelê Syria (Polyb. 5. 67. 8–10).

The question then becomes whether this was absence of any real evidence of desire for these distant areas or control in its entirety of Alexander's former empire due to circumstances and caution, or to a limited purpose in the first place. The evidence suggests that Ptolemy was simply different in his aspirations from so many of the other Diadochs. Support for his desire to hold the empire intact as Alexander's heir is non-existent. When the opportunity arose, he left Babylon to become the satrap of Egypt. He turned down the regency when it could have been his. All still might be assigned as part of his caution, as Alexander Meeus claims, but from the very beginning Ptolemy's efforts were not in the interests of unity, nor early on very cautious either. His proposal of a ruling council would only have encouraged the empire's breakup. In his foreign policy in many ways Ptolemy followed what had been the typical foreign policy of independent Egypt, which was to control the eastern coast of the Mediterranean, from which most of the invasions of Egypt originated, and Cyprus, from which attacks could be easily launched. Ptolemy clearly knew the strengths of Egypt. He did not choose to meet Perdiccas in open battle and certainly had no intention of meeting him outside the confines of Egypt. Indeed, on several occasions he demonstrated a clear reluctance to take on any of the major contenders for power personally outside of his natural fortress. Seleucus had to encourage him to engage the young Demetrius at Gaza in 312 (Diod. 19. 80. 3), and when he heard that Antigonus had returned to the area, Ptolemy quickly fled back to Egypt (Diod. 19. 93. 6). Prior to the Battle of Ipsus, on the rumor that Antigonus was approaching, Ptolemy, who had promised to support his allies Lysimachus and Seleucus, turned back to Egypt and failed to appear as his allies had expected and as he had promised (Diod. 20. 113. 2).[37] His addition to what had been the general defensive strategy for Egypt was his desire to neutralize the Aegean, most often fostering autonomy amongst the island and mainland states.

All of Ptolemy's actions outside of Egypt can be tied to a determination to make Egypt safe and his control of this rich country secure. Ptolemy worked to win over the people under his authority (Diod. 18. 14. 1; Just. 13. 6. 18–19), especially establishing close ties with the various Egyptian priesthoods, and as part of this strategy he had accepted all the traditional trappings of pharaoh (Müller 2009: 172–5). As Catharine Lorber (2018: 60–83) relates, even his monetary policy centered on Egypt. The other Diadochs, unlike Ptolemy, did not much concern themselves with the needs and interests of their subject peoples. In the final analysis, the claim that, at least with respect to the first Ptolemy, Ptolemaic foreign policy and military activities were to create "a fence of client states" to protect Egypt is on the mark. The only addition would be his desire to forestall any and every attempt to unify the empire. His actions reflected a desire to prevent his many Diadoch competitors from dangerously expanding their horizons. The Egyptian satrap and later king's goal from the time of the death of the great Conqueror had been to dismember the empire and secure his possession of what he must have considered its jewel, Egypt.

One element of his lack of interest in securing all of Alexander's empire is found in his monetary policy. While his currency at various times in its iconography played to his connection to Alexander and later placing his own countenance on Egypt's coins might suggest an attempt to sell himself to the new Hellenistic world, Ptolemy made the currency such that it could only be used in Egypt. He created a closed monetary zone where foreign currencies had to be exchanged at the border.[38] While this could have been a side result of an attempt to increase the money supply in Egypt, when that problem was eliminated, he did not abandon the reforms.

Once his goals concerning Egypt were achieved, the adventurous actions of Ptolemy in the First Diadoch War gave way to Ptolemy's more cautious ones of subsequent years. His goal was attained, his primary ambition achieved. His concentration on Egypt was one of his greatest strengths. While others kept acquiring new territories, these lacked the cohesion and purpose that came with the close association with a particular place and people. At the conclusion of his life, Egypt was secure and the greatest threats to Egyptian independence, Perdiccas and Antigonus, were dead, and the united empire of Alexander an increasingly distant memory.

5

The General

Ptolemy was a competent, but not a brilliant, military commander. He showed his bravery and his ability to carry out orders, but the evidence suggests that in the military scheme of things he was no Alexander nor for that matter an Antigonus, a Demetrius, a Perdiccas, a Seleucus, or a Eumenes. Polyaenus (4. 19; cf. Frontin. 4. 7. 20) only offers one stratagem associated with Ptolemy:

> When Perdiccas had marched down to the river opposite Memphis, with the intention to cross it, Ptolemy tied his baggage to a number of goats, swine, and oxen, and left the herdsmen with some of his horses to drive them. The baggage thus dragged along the ground by those animals raised a prodigious dust; and exhibited in appearance the march of a numerous army. With the rest of his cavalry Ptolemy pursued the enemy, and came up with them as they were crossing the river, part having already passed it; who, from the dust, suspecting a numerous army in their rear, some fled, others perished in the river, and a great number were taken prisoners.
>
> translation: Krentz and Wheeler 1994[1]

For comparison, Antigonus (Polyaen. 4. 6) has twenty stratagems, Demetrius (4. 12) twelve, Seleucus (4. 9) six, and even Perdiccas (4. 10), who left the stage relatively early, has two. Ptolemy did not shine on the battlefield but had other more important skills. While Heracleitus declared that "war was both the king and father of all," a truer statement might be that politics is king and father of all. Ptolemy's career as a military commander with Alexander got off to a slow start in part because, as is so often stated, Alexander's initial commanders were those appointed by his father Philip. Ptolemy would not have been part of Philip's army, since, as a result of the Pixodarus affair, he was in exile at the time Philip was putting the finishing touches to his expeditionary force.[2] He became a military commander apparently only after the battles on the Granicus, at Issus and Gaugamela. In short, after the major contests were over, Alexander could afford to transform the command structure of his army into something more to his liking peopled with his loyal supporters. Cleitus, in the arguments that led to the incident with Alexander and his death, accuses the king of "scorning the soldiers of Philip" (Curt. 8. 1. 46).[3] Increasingly, Alexander came to believe that in matters of strategy and tactics, he was sufficient unto himself. In his mind, and given his successes he was probably correct, he had the brilliance sufficient to win every battle and overcome every obstacle. What he needed were competent and loyal, not necessarily brilliant, officers. Ptolemy would come to fit that bill. In the aftermath of Alexander's death, competency was seldom good enough and yet Ptolemy not only survived but created a kingdom and a dynasty that outlasted every other Successor kingdom and dynasty. While Ptolemy was successful in defeating two invasions of Egypt and defeating Demetrius at Gaza, he most often was reluctant to engage the other Diadochs except in Egypt. After the victory at Gaza, at the approach of Antigonus, he fled back to Egypt; at Salamis he was defeated by Demetrius in the sea battle and had to abandon Cyprus; at the Battle of Ipsus he was a no show. In the case of his three great successes, two were in part owed to Egypt itself and the third likely owed something to Seleucus.[4] His joining with Seleucus was perhaps only due to his fear of Antigonus and his desire to create another broad coalition to oppose this new nemesis (cf. Diod. 19. 56. 3–4, 57. 1; Paus. 1. 6. 4). As Antigonus had brought the news of Perdiccas' ambitious intentions to Antipater and Craterus in 321, so Seleucus brought the news of those of Antigonus to Ptolemy (Diod. 19. 56. 1–3). With the exception of the two invasions of Egypt where he was on his own, in every other campaign he was part of a coalition and while others gained the glory, in the treaty negotiation he retained his hold on those territories he had sought from the very beginning: Egypt, Cyprus, and Coelê Syria. As Curtius (9. 8. 23), points out, he was better known for his skills in the arts of peace than in those of war. To put it another way, he was a consummate diplomat and politician and knew how to win the hearts and minds of others.

In this new world two things were seemingly essential for a king and kingdom to be successful: money and soldiers. Certainly, in the early Hellenistic period the two were closely intertwined. Without money, in this age where soldiers were mostly mercenaries and would often desert a defeated commander to join with the victorious one, a commander could lose everything. The obvious example of the fickleness of these troops is found in the career of Eumenes of Cardia, whose army not only deserted him but surrendered him to his opponent.[5]

The good commander was both a good paymaster and a successful general. Even during Alexander's lifetime many of his Macedonians had shown certain mercenary characteristics. Often in the latter stages of his campaign in Asia he had to resort to promises of riches and booty and more personal appeals to keep his troops' loyalty (Curt. 9. 2. 27; Arr. *Anab.* 5. 26. 8; Diod. 17. 94. 1–3; cf. 104. 5–7). Earlier Alexander had encouraged his troops in national terms: territories were not secure and further campaigns were necessary (Curt. 3. 3; Plut. *Alex.* 47. 1–4; Just. 12. 3. 4). In the era of the Successors, it became customary to enroll defeated troops into your own army. Antigonus created a massive force through this process of assimilation. In his first battle against Eumenes, Antigonus had 10,000 foot soldiers with an additional 3,500 in reserve, 2,000 cavalrymen, and 30 elephants (Diod. 18. 40. 7), with many of the defeated enrolling in the victor's ranks (Diod. 18. 41. 4). Eumenes' army contained 20,000 infantry and 5,000 cavalry (Diod. 18. 40. 7–8). Later, Antigonus' army had grown to 40,000 infantry and 7,000 cavalry (Diod. 18. 45. 1). This growth represented his addition of the survivors of Eumenes' force from the previous battle and also—now that Antigonus, as royal general in Asia, had access to the royal treasuries—the addition of mercenaries both Greek and Asian. After his subsequent defeat of Alcetas and the other surviving Perdiccan commanders, his army stood at 60,000 foot soldiers, 10,000 cavalrymen, and 70 elephants (Diod. 18. 50. 1–3). Ptolemy, while not known for his great victories over his opponents outside of Egypt, did have the other half of what held an army's loyalty. He was an excellent paymaster both monetarily and by granting land and position in Egypt. Much of this tied to the cleruchy system, land for military service (Bagnall 1984: 7–20). This system which was used throughout the Hellenistic states eliminated one serious problem. During the early days of this period, armies resided with their families and worldly possessions in the camp. This made the transfer of allegiance to another paymaster relatively easy. This also made the camp a worthy target for any enemy force. Eumenes of Cardia lost his army and his life when, during the course of the Battle of Gabene, Antigonus acquired the Cardian's camp. The battle had ended in a draw with Antigonus' forces suffering more, but those who had lost their families and possessions to Antigonus readily surrendered (Plut. *Eum.* 17. 2–4; Diod. 18. 43. 8–9; Polyaen. 4. 6. 13; Just. 14. 4. 1). Also, Ptolemy was in possession of the richest area in the Mediterranean world, and he took advantage of it. These revenues in conjunction with those from Cyprus, Cyrene, and Coelê Syria have been estimated at between 3,000 and 7,000 talents a year (Fischer-Bovet 2014: 67–70).

While Ptolemy may not have been a military genius, he was a brave soldier, having been wounded twice in India (Arr. *Anab.* 4. 23. 3; Diod. 17. 103. 3–6; Curt. 9. 8. 14–20, 23). Arrian (*Anab.* 2. 11. 8), likely here following Ptolemy's own account, states that after the Battle of Issus and in the pursuit of Darius' retreating forces, the cavalry crossed over a ravine filled with the bodies of the Persian dead. This would then appear to suggest that Ptolemy was part of this pursuit and also that in the great battles he accompanied the Companion Cavalry under the command of Alexander. This was likely also the situation at Chaeronea and in Alexander's subsequent campaigns in the north after Philip's death (cf. Arr. *Anab.* 1. 2. 7).[6] As one of Alexander's *philoi* and as an aristocrat, this would have been Ptolemy's role as a battle-hardened veteran there to protect his younger companion. In short, while he may not have commanded units personally in the great battles of Alexander's campaign, Granicus, Issus, Gaugamela, he did participate in these, accompanying Alexander personally. Given Alexander's propensity to dive into the action, Ptolemy likely saw a good bit of combat. There survive two accounts of Ptolemy's *aristeia*: his single combat with an Indian prince in 327 (Arr. *Anab.* 4. 24. 3–5) and his personal stand against the forces of Perdiccas at the Fort of Camels during Perdiccas' invasion of Egypt (Diod. 18. 34. 2).

In what appears to be Ptolemy's first command at the Persian Gates (Arr. *Anab.* 3. 18. 9),[7] he showed competence, but not initiative or particular brilliance. After first being stymied by a Persian force blocking this narrow pass into Persia proper, Alexander discovered a way to arrive behind the Persian force. Ptolemy was part of an operation to prevent the escape of as many Persians as possible, which apparently he and others did successfully. This may have been responsible for his criticism of Perdiccas at the siege of Thebes, that he did not await Alexander's orders. Perdiccas showed initiative. After the Battle of Gaugamela, Alexander moved rapidly both in pursuit of the defeated Persian king but also to occupy the Persian heartland before any further serious resistance could be assembled. Moreover, he wished to take possession of the vast sums in the various Persian treasuries and in particular that which existed in the Persian capital of Persepolis (Fuller 1960: 228–34). To get to the capital there were two routes, one longer but through easily traversed country and another through a narrow pass known as the Persian Gates.[8] Alexander sent Parmenion along the longer route, while he with the bulk of his forces moved to the gates. To bypass the gates would give the initiative to the Persians and leave a sizable hostile force in his rear. This was also, it must be remembered, Alexander. One did not avoid a challenge. Initially, Alexander attempted to attack the gates directly in a frontal assault, but the Persians—according to Arrian (*Anab.* 3. 18. 2) a force of 40,000 infantry and 700 cavalry, or in Curtius' account (5. 3. 17) 25,000 foot soldiers (no mention of cavalry)[9]—had built a wall across the narrows and had stationed archers in the heights above the pass. Alexander and his forces were repulsed with heavy losses. Subsequently, Alexander quickly discovered a way around the Persian defense and adjusted his strategy accordingly. He not only wanted to get through the pass, but he wanted to eliminate as many Persians as possible to forestall their escape back to Persepolis where, perhaps with the treasure or as much of it as they could carry, they could extend the war in the Persian heartland. To prevent such an eventuality, Alexander wished to block every possible escape route, which he did most effectively. Curtius (5. 4. 33) claims that Ariobarzanes, the Persian commander, forty horsemen, and 5,000 infantry escaped, while Arrian (*Anab.* 3. 18. 9) states that only the commander and a small number of horsemen got away. In either case, the effectiveness of Ariobarzanes' force had been substantially reduced and now having cleared the pass, Alexander's race to Persepolis was all but won. Ptolemy led one of the smaller forces whose job it was to block any escape routes and he along with the others apparently did his job competently.[10] In the course of the battle, as Alexander and his forces descended on the rear of the Persian force and Craterus, with a force that had been left behind as Alexander moved behind the Persian position, moved to a frontal attack on the wall, it was Ptolemy's task to attack the wall from behind, take possession of it and block this avenue of Persian retreat (Arr. *Anab.* 3. 18. 8–9). Ptolemy's role was, therefore, important, but only part of a much larger operation. He did, however, what he did most often during the lifetime of Alexander: he obeyed his commander and accomplished his task. Alexander reached Persepolis in January/February, the Persian Gates perhaps delaying the journey a week.[11]

Arrian next mentions Ptolemy as other than an historical source as the individual who accepted the surrender of Bessus in 329 (Arr. *Anab.* 3. 29. 7=*BNJ* 138 F-14). Bessus, the newly self-proclaimed Artaxerxes V, King of Kings, had fled the great Persian defeat at Gaugamela with the Persian king Darius, but subsequently had killed his king and assumed that role himself (Arr. *Anab.* 3. 21. 4–22. 1, 25. 3–8, 3. 30. 1–5; 4. 7. 3; Curt. 5. 8. 4–13. 25; 6. 3. 9–14, 4. 8, 6. 13; 7. 5. 19–26, 38–43, 6. 14, 10. 10; Diod. 17. 73. 2–4, 78. 1–2, 83. 3, 7–9; Just. 12. 5. 10). Spitamenes and Dataphernes, two supposed allies of Bessus, sent messengers to Alexander offering to surrender their new king to him. These declared that Bessus had already been placed under arrest and, if a "small force" was sent, he would be handed over. According to Arrian (*Anab.* 3. 29. 7) and only Arrian, the job of retrieving Bessus was given to Ptolemy. Instead of a small force, Ptolemy was sent out in command of three units of the Companion Cavalry, all the mounted javelin men, an infantry battalion, one-third of the hypaspists, all the Agrianes, and half the archers. This was a very considerable force. Its size would indicate that Alexander was not certain that this was not a trap, and, indeed, upon Ptolemy's arrival, according to Arrian, the two would-be conspirators were still debating whether to surrender Bessus (Arr. *Anab*. 3. 30. 1). Ptolemy was ordered to proceed by forced marches to rendezvous with Bessus' former associates as soon as possible. According to Ptolemy he did so, completing the journey in four days which should have taken ten (Arr. *Anab*. 3. 29. 7). Ptolemy's prompt arrival and his considerable forces made the decision to surrender Bessus much clearer. At the Macedonians' approach, however, Spitamenes and Dataphernes fled, "being ashamed to hand him over personally" (Arr. *Anab*. 3. 30. 2). Once in possession of Bessus, Ptolemy sent a message to Alexander asking how he wished the newly captured "king of kings" to be treated. Alexander ordered the regicide stripped naked, bound, placed in a wooden collar, and left by the side of the road that the army would be proceeding along (Arr. *Anab*. 3. 30. 3). Ptolemy did as requested. Both Curtius (7. 5. 36–40) and Diodorus (17. 83. 7–9) describe the capture very differently and without reference to Ptolemy. Curtius (7. 5. 36) has Spitamenes personally delivering Bessus to Alexander, "bound, stripped, and with a chain around his neck," and Diodorus just says he was surrendered by Bessus' generals (Diod. 17. 83. 8). Aristobulus (Arr. *Anab*. 3. 30. 5=*BNJ* 139 F-24) also offers a slightly different version from Ptolemy's where the followers of Spitamenes and Dataphernes accompany Ptolemy and deliver Bessus to Alexander. As Bosworth declares, Aristobulus' account diminishes Ptolemy's role somewhat. The only true discrepancy between Arrian's two major sources is that Aristobulus appears to be saying that Ptolemy led these individuals to Alexander who then turned Bessus over to the king. Arrian in his preface declares that wherever Ptolemy and Aristobulus agree in their accounts of Alexander's expedition he accepted their testimony, and I believe he followed this practice. Both wrote histories of Alexander's expedition, and both were present on the campaign.

This operation suggests that Alexander trusted Ptolemy to carry out what amounted to more of a diplomatic mission than a military one, but that is not to say that it could not have turned into a military one if this surrender turned out to be a trick. Moreover, whatever doubt the conspirators may have had concerning their decision to hand over their leader ended with the quick arrival of Ptolemy. If Arrian is to be believed concerning the size of the force sent with Ptolemy, then it suggests that Alexander expected treachery and sought to protect his friend by sending him with such a large force. It also needs to be noted that giving Ptolemy this command showed the king's confidence in Ptolemy's military ability and might even point to there having been other commands besides that at the Persian Gates before this operation that have not been reported in our sources. Arrian does, indeed, point to one other additional independent command prior to the invasion of India. In 328, according to Arrian (*Anab*. 4. 16. 2–3), when Alexander divided his forces into five parts for the invasion of Sogdiana, one of these was commanded by Ptolemy. No other source supports this claim and Curtius speaks of only three columns (8. 1. 1), none of which is led by Ptolemy.

The other sources only begin to report Ptolemy's military career in India.[12] Curtius (8. 13. 18–19, 23, 27, 14. 15) first notes Ptolemy in a military capacity in the battle on the Hydaspes in 326 against the Indian prince Porus and is the only source that mentions Ptolemy as directly commanding troops in this campaign. There is no such reference in Arrian (*Anab*. 5. 13. 1), who only notes that Ptolemy joined Alexander, Lysimachus, Perdiccas, and Seleucus on a thirty-oared vessel which crossed the Hydaspes. Porus and his forces were on the other side of the monsoon-swollen river, the modern Jhelum, awaiting in force any attempt by Alexander to cross.[13] According to Curtius (8. 13. 18–19), Alexander deployed Ptolemy with a cavalry force to move away from the point where Alexander planned to cross and make it appear that he was preparing to cross further away. Arrian (*Anab*. 5. 9. 2) relates that Alexander broke up his army into many different groups and had them move about the river in order to confuse and disperse Porus' forces. According to Curtius, Ptolemy did this for a number of days and succeeded in getting most of Porus' force to move from Alexander's planned crossing site and the crossing was made successfully. What seems here to be a singling out of Ptolemy's activities by Curtius of what appears from Arrian to have involved many others is similar in this respect to Arrian's discussion of Ptolemy's role at the Persian Gates. These discrepancies suggest that these inclusions or exclusions may simply be the result of their respective authors' choice of emphasis, and not, for example, in the case of Arrian's reference to Ptolemy's actions at the Persian Gates, reflective of Ptolemy's highlighting or exaggerating his activities. Once the crossing was accomplished Curtius has Ptolemy joining Alexander along with Perdiccas and Hephaestion in an attack on Porus' left flank. Curtius provides no further information on Ptolemy's participation.

The next reference to Ptolemy in a command position comes in the winter of 328/327 but is not associated with combat. During the siege of the fortress of Sisimithres, also known as the Rock of Chorienses, in order to attack the city a ravine that surrounded it had to be filled. Alexander oversaw this operation during the day with half the army and at night the other half was divided into three watches under the commands respectively of Perdiccas, Leonnatus, and Ptolemy (Arr. *Anab.* 4. 21. 4). All four commanders were then in charge of filling the ravine. Later in India, during the campaign in the Swat valley, Ptolemy along with Alexander and Leonnatus was wounded fighting the Aspasians (Arr. *Anab.* 4. 23. 3). Curtius only notes the wounding of Alexander (Curt. 8. 10. 6) but does provide, at least in the case of Alexander, that it occurred during a siege of an Aspasian city. No details are provided. At least in the case of Ptolemy, the wound apparently was not serious (Heckel 2021: 430), since soon after comes the only account of Ptolemy's *aristeia* during Alexander's lifetime: his single combat with an Indian prince (Arr. *Anab.* 4. 24. 3–5). Alexander's forces approached another of the Aspasian cities, having already taken a great many (cf. Curt. 8. 10. 21), but in this case the inhabitants set their community on fire and fled into the neighboring mountains. Ptolemy, in charge of one of the parties pursuing the fleeing Aspasians, came upon "the actual leader of the Indians" and Ptolemy with a much inferior force pursued the fleeing group and catching up with them, dispatched their leader in single combat. Bosworth (1995: 161) has accurately described Arrian's depiction of this event as Homeric in its presentation. (See a full translation in Chapter 8.)

Ptolemy continues to enjoy commands during the journey down the Indus. Many of these involved the numerous sieges that occurred. The last of these was the Rock of Aornus to which much of the population in the area had fled on Alexander's approach. This city was thought to be impregnable, so much so that the legend was that even Heracles could not capture it (Arr. *Anab.* 4. 28. 1; Diod. 17. 85. 1; Curt. 8. 11. 2). On a more practical note, its capture would secure Alexander's supply lines. Alexander learned from locals the best place from which to assault the rock. According to Arrian (*Anab.* 4. 29. 1–2), Ptolemy was dispatched with the Agrianians, other light-armed troops, and some hypaspists to occupy this location. He secured the position with a stockade and successfully resisted a determined attempt by the inhabitants to retake it (Arr. *Anab.* 4. 29. 3). The following morning Alexander and the rest of the army joined Ptolemy and attempted to advance and secure the rock. The direct assault failed and Alexander then had the soldiers fill in the gap between the Macedonians' position on the nearby hill and the enemy's position. With the mound complete, the Indians offered to surrender and began to evacuate. After they had evacuated the outer defenses, Alexander and a force of 700 attacked the retreating forces (Arr. *Anab.* 4. 29. 4–30. 4).[14] Curtius (8. 11. 5), however, omits all reference to Ptolemy and lists the leader of the force not as Ptolemy, as in Arrian, but a certain Myllinas, a "royal scribe."[15] Since there is some evidence that this individual did exist beyond this passage (*IG* XII 9 197 l.2), this reference cannot be rejected out of hand, but it is likely that Curtius' statement that he was in overall command is incorrect. Bosworth (1995: 186; cf. Ma 2013: 12) suggests that this individual was simply in charge of the light-armed troops, who were the first to occupy the position under Ptolemy's overall command. Curtius only references the light-armed troops, but Arrian makes reference to hypaspists as well as Agrianians and light-armed troops. This was not a diplomatic mission or an inconsequential military one, but key to the successful capture of Aornus. Is it likely that Alexander would put someone without clear military experience in charge? Ptolemy had participated in a great many sieges by this time and would be a suitable choice for this particular operation (Curt. 8. 10. 21).

Ptolemy is listed as one of the many who were wounded at Harmatelia, "the last city of the Brahmans."[16] This was in the area known as the Sindh occupying roughly the last third of the Indus valley down to the Indian Ocean. Alexander's journey to the sea had been a bloodbath and here was no exception. Resistance to Alexander was met with indiscriminate slaughter and enslavement (Bosworth 1996: 94–7). During an attack on the city, Ptolemy among others was struck with an arrow tipped in poison (Diod. 17. 103. 3–6; Curt. 9. 8. 14–20; cf. Str. 15. 723C). Later, he shares a command with Leonnatus campaigning with light-armed troops against the Oreitai in Gedrosia (Curt. 9. 10. 6–7; Diod. 17. 104. 5–6). Ptolemy was "to plunder the area by the sea" (Diod. 17. 104. 6) and Leonnatus that of the interior. Both achieved what their commander intended. The land was pillaged, thousands were killed, and the others so impressed that they submitted to Alexander's authority (Diod. 17. 104. 6–7). Ptolemy's final campaign prior to Alexander's death was against the Cossaeans (Arr. *Anab.* 7. 15. 1–3), a tribal people inhabiting the Zagros mountain region in what is today western Iran and long noted for their raiding (Str. 11. 13. 6, 16. 1. 17--18; Arr. *Anab.* 7. 15. 2). No specifics are given of the campaign beyond that it ended the brigandage. As Heckel (2021: 431) points out, Ptolemy's prominence may be due to the absence of more senior commanders, Perdiccas and Craterus having been sent on other tasks, and the earlier death of Hephaestion. In any case, Alexander had clearly achieved a level of confidence in Ptolemy's ability and his military standing, now joined with his personal ties to his king, to make him one of Alexander's chief confidants. Ptolemy's military credentials show him to be brave, disciplined, obedient, and competent.

Alexander's death brought about a whole new world. Ptolemy became a satrap away from court but possessed of one of, if not the, richest provinces among Alexander's conquests, and easily the most defensible one. In theory,

Alexander's empire and Argead rule had survived the death of the Conqueror, but in reality, as seen in Chapters 3 and 4, it was but a pale reflection of either and neither would long survive Alexander's death. Alexander's empire had been just that, Alexander's empire. Alexander was the glue that held it together and without him it was difficult to see it surviving intact. This empire was not an extension of Macedonia, Alexander had planned his new capital to be Babylon and he described himself as the Lord of Asia (Hammond 1986: 73–85; Fredricksmeyer 2000: 136–66). This was a personal empire. As Alexander had moved beyond his homeland physically, he also moved away from seeing himself as the head of a clan or the ruler of an extended Macedonia. He had become a true autocrat, but with his death the only precedents for what should happen next came from the traditions of his homeland. Unfortunately, these traditions now hardly applied. What had once been a very populous clan had been culled considerably, first by his father Philip and subsequently by Alexander himself. Nor was Alexander much concerned with preserving Argead rule. This lack of interest in perpetuating Argead domination is found in his waiting to marry, with the ultimate result being the dual monarchy of an infant son and half-brother, two of the last surviving Argead males. Of course, he did not plan on dying so young, but he had resisted earlier calls to marry and produce a child (Diod. 17. 16. 2). If Macedonia had been a constitutional monarchy, Argead rule might have survived, but then it was not, nor had it ever been.[17] Meleager had voiced in the meeting in Babylon what any astute observer would have known. Whoever became regent for the kings would be the *de facto* king and ultimately the official ruler of Alexander's legacy. Moreover, Alexander's state was a hodgepodge administratively, an amalgam of satraps, garrison commanders, city leaders, treasury officials, and allied kings, who all ostensibly owed their obedience directly to the central government, which when Alexander yet lived was Alexander (Anson 2013: 121–52). Satraps often did not have authority over garrison commanders or treasurers.[18] These individuals would be answerable to the king and not the local satrap (Anson 2010: 141–5). Many cities were autonomous, owing allegiance only to the king. It would have taken another Alexander to hold this together and the new regent for Alexander's heirs, Perdiccas, was not a new Alexander—but then, as time would tell, neither was anyone else.

As seen in the previous chapter, Ptolemy began early in his administration of Egypt to act independently of the kings or, in reality, their regent. He had seen to the murder of Cleomenes, ostensibly Ptolemy's lieutenant appointed by Perdiccas, and had annexed the city of Cyrene without clearing it with the central government. Now Ptolemy was not the only satrap who had ignored the new central government. Antigonus, the satrap of Greater Phrygia, had been ordered by Perdiccas to assist Eumenes in the acquisition of Cappadocia, but had not done so (Anson 2015: 80–8). As a result, Antigonus was summoned in the late spring of 321 to answer charges of insubordination before King Philip (Diod. 18. 23. 4). Antigonus had operated with great independence in Asia Minor since Alexander had appointed him satrap in 333 (Arr. *Anab*. 1. 29. 3). At the time of Alexander's death, the Phrygian satrap controlled roughly two-thirds of Macedonian held Asia Minor (Billows 1990: 46) with alliances with many of the independent native rulers in the area (Anson 1988: 471–7). Antigonus' refusal to aid Eumenes led to Perdiccas and the royal army leaving Babylon and proceeding to Asia Minor where Eumenes was installed through the efforts of the royal army in his satrapy. Perdiccas, as part of his general campaign in Asia Minor, in the spring moved to secure Pisidia where two cities continued to resist Macedonian authority, those of the Larandians and of the Isaurians (Diod. 18. 22. 1). These people had murdered the Cilician satrap Balacrus sometime late in Alexander's reign (Diod. 18. 22. 1; cf. Arr. *Anab*. 2. 12. 2). There were, indeed, many regions in Asia Minor that had resisted Macedonian conquest or had simply been bypassed by Alexander. The existence of independent rulers and recalcitrant satraps threatened the hold of the central government on these regions of Alexander's legacy. Antigonus' failure to aid Eumenes was a further concern, which Perdiccas also moved to rectify. In 321, he ordered Antigonus to appear before the king to answer charges of insubordination.[19] Antigonus gave every indication that he would appear, but in the end he fled to Macedonia in the winter of 321/320 (Diod 18. 25. 3–5; Arr. *Succ*. 1a. 24).[20]

While Perdiccas' authority was facing challenges in Asia and in Egypt, in Macedonia his relationship with Antipater showed no cause for concern. While the original agreement in Babylon and Craterus' failing to challenge for the authority in Macedonia, and the defeat of the Greeks' attempt to overthrow Macedonian hegemony in the Lamian War had left Antipater securely in charge of Macedonia and Greece, that individual had been most correct in his dealings with Perdiccas and the central government. He had forwarded the question of Athenian possession of Samos for adjudication to the kings (Diod. 18. 18. 6), even though he was the "General in Europe."[21] Perdiccas' actions with respect to Antipater were not so transparent. The regent had been in communication with the Aetolians, one of the last of the Greeks still fighting against the Macedonians (Diod. 18. 38. 1), and he had received communications from the Athenian politician Demades inviting him to cross to Europe (Diod. 18. 48. 2). None of this had been revealed to Antipater. But what would lead to conflict between the forces in Macedonia and the regent, what would come to be termed the First Diadoch War, was the decision made in the summer of 321 by Perdiccas to invade Macedonia in the following spring and declare himself king in his own right (Diod. 18. 23. 3, 25. 3, 6). The plan was that Perdiccas would marry Cleopatra, Alexander's sister, who had arrived in Asia offering herself in marriage to the regent (Arr. *Succ.* 1a. 21; Diod. 18. 23. 2; Just. 13. 6. 4) and with the kings bring back Alexander's body to Aegae for royal burial (Diod. 18. 25. 3). He was in communication with both Cleopatra and her mother Olympias, who may have been responsible for the initial marriage proposal (Carney 2006: 66; Anson 2015: 96). Unfortunate for the plan, it was discovered by Antigonus, who fled with the news to Antipater. Worse yet, Ptolemy intercepted the body of the dead king and brought it to Egypt. Perdiccas was now facing a possible war on two fronts. Ptolemy's seizure of Alexander's body was a direct and physical attack on the regency of Perdiccas and done for the express purpose of eliciting a response. Perdiccas' plans now changed. Facing a war on two fronts, it was decided to attack Egypt first. He would leave a force in Asia Minor and with it coordinate with the royal fleet in the Aegean, both of which might at least inhibit the crossing and delay the progress of the Macedonians. The plan was predicated on distance. Even if Antipater and Craterus succeeded in crossing to Asia in the spring of 320, which they did, and Perdiccas headed to Egypt in the same season, the royal army, it was thought, would defeat Ptolemy in time to turn north and catch the Europeans between the force advancing from Egypt and the forces that had been left behind in Asia Minor.[22] That was the scenario if the defense at the Hellespont failed. The plan's weakness was that Perdiccas would be dividing his forces. He would not have his entire fleet or his full complement of troops for this invasion because forces had been diverted to meet the threat coming from Europe. The real weakness, however, was that Ptolemy had to be defeated in short order.

In 320, the then regent for the Macedonian empire invaded Egypt with what amounted to the army of Alexander the Great. While the total number of forces involved is not specified in our sources, it is clear that this was both a substantial force and a very experienced one. Egypt was a natural fortress protected on all sides by formidable natural barriers (Kahn and Tammuz 2008: 39, 41–3). To the west is the great expanse of the Sahara Desert; to the east the Sinai Peninsula with its heat, lack of potable water, and quicksand; to the north the Mediterranean sea and the shoals and marshes[23] that guard the coast, even including that before Alexandria. While the Nile river emptied into the Mediterranean through seven separate branches, only two, the Pelusiac and the Canopic, could admit ships larger than fishing boats and even these were guarded by marshes, reefs, sandbars, etc. (Diod. 1. 31). Moreover, the Nile itself protected Egypt especially when in flood stage, which occurred from July to October.[24] The delta was further traversed by additional branches of the great river plus numerous canals, which especially protected Egypt from invasions from the east (Hdt. 2. 108. 2; Diod. 1. 33. 5–8, 34. 2, 57. 2–3; Str. 17. 1. 4). Those cities, such as the ancient capital at Memphis, were predominantly on the western side of the Nile, but even cities such as Pelusium could be effectively protected by the river through the use of canals. The entire area could be flooded. To these natural defenses, the Egyptians added manmade impediments. During Artaxerxes III's failed invasion in 373 (Diod. 15. 42. 2–3), the Egyptians fortified all the Nile channels on the Mediterranean with towers and bridges and inundated all the land approaches to these fortresses. Similar measures were in place during that king's subsequent invasion of 343 (Diod. 16. 46. 7–8). The Nile was also routinely patrolled by river boats equipped for combat (Diod. 16. 47. 6). While these measures are not commented on with respect to all the invasions, it is probable that they were commonly employed, as they likely were in 320. Of course, in the case of Alexander the Great, the Persian defenders simply surrendered (Arr. *Anab.* 3. 1. 1–2).[25] Given unity, commitment, and competence, if the Egyptians chose to react to the invasion defensively, using the natural defenses of the country, the result was most often defeat for the invaders and their evacuation of Egypt.

In an analysis of those expeditions that proved successful, a number of elements were present and apparently essential for the positive result. The first is the time of the year the invasion took place. The Nile flood and the heat of these summer months, and the Etesian winds of August, virtually precluded invasions at this time of year and forced the attacking force to retreat. The need for an accompanying fleet further limited the time period for a successful invasion. The sailing season in the Mediterranean traditionally closed from November to March (Casson 1995: 270–2). While sailing in the winter was done, it was dangerous because of the winter storms. When tied to the Nile flood season, this meant that a successful invasion of Egypt had to take place either in the spring before the start of the flood or in the late fall or early winter after the waters had receded, but not during the time of the winter storms. There was, therefore, no perfect time to invade Egypt, only better times. Coming in the spring after the winter storms but before the flood afforded the invader only a limited timeframe in which to accomplish the conquest before the rising water of the Nile. Arrival in the fall gave the invader more time, but the winter storms curtailed this time period as well. The resources needed and the time requirement typically meant that the invader had to be free of other concerns. Egypt was able to revolt and remain free for considerable periods to a great degree because the Assyrians and the Persians had other commitments that kept them from a full-scale invasion.

During the Age of the Successors there were two major invasions of Egypt, the first, Perdicaas' invasion, in 320 and the second in 306. Both failed. In the first, the invasion was launched in the spring with the invading army arriving in Egypt likely in late May. Its success depended on victory being achieved quickly. This was necessitated both by the coming Nile flood and also an approaching relief force on its way from Macedonia. With the time constraints, the only real hope of victory was for the then satrap of Egypt, Ptolemy to meet the invaders in open battle, which the wily commander had no intention of doing. While Ptolemy presumably had possession of the 4,000 troops and thirty triremes left by Alexander in Egypt (Curt. 4. 8. 4; Arr. *Anab*. 3. 5. 3–5) and had found 8,000 talents in the Egyptian treasury with which to hire additional soldiers (Diod. 18. 14. 1), Perdiccas, however, possessed the bulk of Alexander's former army. Even with the subtraction of the forces left behind in Asia Minor to resist the expected invasion coming from Macedonia (Diod. 18. 29. 1–3; Just. 13. 6. 14–15; Nep. *Eum*. 3. 2; Plut. *Eum*. 5. 2), the army set to invade Egypt was large and highly experienced. When Alexander died, his army contained approximately 2,000 Macedonian cavalry and 13,000 Macedonian infantry (Curt. 10.2.8), but also 30,000 infantry called the *Epigoni* or Offspring, young Asians armed and trained in the techniques of the Macedonian heavy infantry (Arr. *Anab*. 7. 6. 1; Curt. 8. 5. 1; Diod. 17. 108. 1–2; Plut. *Alex*. 47. 3, 71. 1), 20,000 Persian infantry armed in their traditional fashion, unspecified numbers of Cossaeans and Tapurians (Arr. *Anab*. 7. 23. 1), 30,000 mercenary infantry and 6,000 hired cavalry (Diod. 17. 95. 4), and unspecified forces brought to Babylon shortly before the Conqueror's death from Caria and Lydia (Arr. *Anab*. 7. 23. 1). To these forces were added those left in Cilicia by the departing Craterus, including the 3,000 elite infantry guards, the argyraspids, formerly the hypaspists. How many of all these troops were still present in the royal army approximately three years after Alexander's death can only be guessed. Consequently, while the exact size of Perdiccas' invading army is unknown, it would still have been far larger than any army that Ptolemy could present in opposition. Moreover, those Macedonians with Perdiccas were veterans of both Alexander's wars and those of Perdiccas himself.

Ptolemy, therefore, took up a defensive position on the western bank of the Nile, having first garrisoned the delta fortresses, in particular Pelusium (Diod. 18. 33. 1, 3), and assembled a mobile force to respond to any attempted crossing of the Nile (cf. Diod. 18. 34. 1). Without a direct confrontation in open battle, this was an invasion virtually doomed to failure from its inception. From the very beginning the troops showed little enthusiasm for the campaign against the Egyptian satrap. Upon entering Egypt, the regent, in an attempt to convince them of the need for this invasion, assembled them and recited the charges against Ptolemy (Arr. *Succ.* 1a. 28). The army was not impressed. These grumblings were due in part to the disinclination to fight another Macedonian commander and some at least of their former comrades-in-arms (Roisman 2014: 456–7, 460). Even though the "many" did not accept Perdiccas' rationale for the war, Perdiccas continued the campaign anyway (Arr. *Succ.* 1a. 28). After all he was regent and King Philip had officially authorized the war.

The campaign itself from the beginning did not go well. Failing to take Pelusium which had been garrisoned by Ptolemy, Perdiccas hurried south to another potential crossing near a fortified position called the Fort of Camels (Diod. 18. 33. 6). At Pelusium, according to Diodorus (18. 33. 1–2), Perdiccas had attempted to clear a canal, but the Nile flooded the operation and the attack was abandoned (Diod. 18. 33. 1–2). It is likely what took place is that on Ptolemy's orders, that area of the delta was flooded and Perdiccas attempted to empty the flooded land by opening a seldom used canal, and that endeavor failed. Diodorus' account of the campaign appears to indicate that Perdiccas had not brought any true besieging equipment with him. The only gear noted in that author's account are scaling ladders (Diod. 18. 33. 6, 34. 1, 4).

At the Fort of Camels, while in the process of crossing, Ptolemy and his forces appeared and occupied the fort. It is surprising that there is no mention of patrol boats, but that may be an oversight on the part of our sources, or it may be encompassed in the mobile forces under Ptolemy's command. The "siege" was abandoned and the Perdiccan troops returned to their camp (Diod. 18. 34. 5). It was here at the Fort of Camels that Ptolemy displayed his own personal bravery defending in person (Diod. 18. 34. 2). Having failed in these two actions, during the following evening, the regent moved his forces south to Memphis. At this location there was an island large enough to hold a whole army. Perdiccas began to transfer his forces to the island. In the process, the river bed was disturbed especially by the actions of horses and elephants, with the result that water which had initially come up to the armpits of those crossing first was over the heads of those who followed (Diod. 18. 35. 4). Panic set in and the crossing was halted, with many drowning in the river or being captured, or even being eaten by beasts (presumably crocodiles) (Diod. 18. 36. 3). Polyaenus (4. 19. 1) and Frontinus (*Str.* 4. 7. 20) suggest that the crossing was thwarted by Ptolemy using herds of animals to raise a cloud of dust, which was interpreted by Perdiccas' men as an approaching large army. Diodorus' account is to be preferred as likely coming from Hieronymus and therefore more likely to be accurate. This was a veteran army that would be unlikely to panic at the approach of a cloud of dust. Aelian (*VH* 12. 64) records that Perdiccas was tricked by a fake Alexander corpse into stopping his invasion. These last are all fanciful tales, but little else.

The mood in the Perdiccan camp was hostile. In addition to the disasters incurred, supplies were running short (Diod. 18. 36. 6). That night in a conspiracy of his commanders Perdiccas was assassinated (Diod. 18. 36. 4). Perdiccas failed in the main because he had to be in a hurry. The one thing that was necessary for a successful assault on Egypt, despite the problems associated with the river flood and the storms of winter, was still time, but with Antipater approaching from the north, time was something Perdiccas did not have. He needed to defeat Ptolemy quickly so he could turn and meet Antipater before that commander made it to Egypt. It was on account of this need to dispatch the Egyptian satrap in a timely fashion that led to the many abortive attempts to cross the river. Moreover, while Perdiccas brought a war fleet to Egypt, there is no reference to his use of it, except perhaps, as noted, at Pelusium. In any assault on Memphis, the key to ultimate success was a fleet. Perdiccas' death occurred likely in early July (Anson 2014: 59, 81n. 38).

The information for the invasion in 306 is fuller. Here, as before, the failure was due to the defensive strategy of Ptolemy, poor planning on the part of the invaders, and the time constraints placed on the expedition by outside circumstances. According to our sources, the Diadoch Antigonus decided to cap what had been a most successful campaign year with a full assault on Egypt (Diod. 20. 73–6; Paus. 1. 6. 6). The planning was rushed, and the various environmental factors given little consideration (cf. Diod. 20. 76. 5). However, the forces brought to bear were impressive. Antigonus' land army consisted of 80,000 infantry, 8,000 cavalry, and 83 elephants. As in 320, Ptolemy garrisoned all key points (Diod. 20. 75. 1). Antigonus' son Demetrius was to parallel the army's movements with a fleet of 150 warships and 100 transports. The expedition reached Gaza eight days before the setting of the Pleiades in early November (Diod. 20. 73. 2–3), making the time of the arrival probably in late October. The setting of the Pleiades was the customary end of the sailing season in the eastern Mediterranean and the start of the winter storms. Demetrius' pilots advised against the invasion based on the lateness of the season, but Antigonus pushed ahead. While the fleet was still passing along Sinai, a storm came up, resulting in the dispersal of the fleet, with some ships running aground on the shoals, others destroyed at sea (Diod. 20. 74. 3–5; Plut. *Demetr.* 19. 4). As with Perdiccas' expedition, there was also significant dissatisfaction in the ranks, causing Antigonus to go to extreme measures to curb desertions to the enemy (Diod. 20. 75. 2–3). Archers, slingers, and catapults were stationed along the river to stop those seeking to desert, and those captured while making the attempt were tortured (Diod. 20. 75. 3). Ptolemy promised a large payment to all who did desert (Diod. 20. 75. 1). The situation was not helped by the appearance in the camp of those sailors who had survived the storm (Diod. 20. 75. 4–5). It was the failure of the fleet to force an entrance into the Nile (Diod. 20. 75. 4–5, 76. 4), Ptolemy's strong defensive position on the western bank of the river (cf. Diod. 20. 73. 1, 4, 76. 1, 3), and a growing lack of supplies (Diod. 20. 76. 4–5) that forced Antigonus to give up the operation and return to Syria. Clearly, the fleet was key to an understanding of Antigonus' underlying strategy. The ships were to sail up the Nile, enabling both a crossing and to aid in the siege of Memphis. With the failure of the fleet even to gain an entrance to the Nile, the expedition had to be abandoned. This failure, since the depth of the river was sufficient for the ships to travel south, was the direct result of Ptolemy's countermeasures. The Pelusiac channel was blocked, and river boats equipped with ordnance plied the river (Diod. 20. 76. 3–4). Moreover, while not in the same precarious position faced by Perdiccas, the danger of being trapped between two armies, Antigonus did have significant enemies who threatened his possessions elsewhere. His window for success, therefore, was likewise limited. With all points of access blocked, Antigonus and his army returned to Syria (Diod. 20. 73–6. 6; cf, Plut. *Demetr.* 19. 4). Ptolemy had once again thwarted what would have appeared to be overwhelming forces through his shrewd use of Egypt's natural and enhanced defenses.

Aside from these two successful defenses of Egypt, Ptolemy did not much directly participate in the warfare of his time. In the case of his acquisition of Cyrene, Ophellas was his general, with Ptolemy only showing up after most of the fighting had concluded with the revolt in its final stages (Arr. *Succ.* 1a. 19). His only other appearances of any consequence were in the Battle of Gaza, where with Seleucus he defeated Demetrius, and the sea Battle of Salamis that took place in Cyprus in 306, where he lost to that commander. Prior to the invasion of Egypt by Perdiccas, Ptolemy had achieved alliances with the Cyprian kings of Salamis, Soli, Paphos, and Amathus (Arr. *Succ.* 24. 15–19). At the conclusion of this war with Perdiccas (First Diadoch War), Ptolemy was secure in Egypt, but also in possession of Coelê Syria (Beqaa Valley) and Phoenicia and had alliances with four of the kings of Cyprus. Coelê Syria had been acquired by his general Nicanor in the winter of 320/319 (Diod. 18. 43; Paus. 1. 6. 4). Nicanor captured

Laomedon, the satrap of Syria, secured the cities of Phoenicia with garrisons, and returned to Egypt. In the case of Laomedon, who had with Ptolemy been exiled as a result of the Pixodarus affair, Ptolemy had first tried to buy the satrapy from him, but Laomedon had refused (App. *Syr.* 9. 52).

In the summer of 319, Antipater, the regent after Perdiccas and the brief regency of Pithon and Attalus, died. His death set in motion events that led to the Second Diadoch War, which began in 318. This war was between two coalitions. The first consisted primarily of Eumenes in Asia and Polyperchon, Antipater's successor as regent for the kings who with their new guardian were all in Macedonia. They faced Cassander, Antipater's son, Ptolemy, Antigonus, who at this time controlled most of Asia Minor, and Seleucus, the satrap of Babylonia. In the fall/winter of 318, Eumenes occupied Phoenicia (Diod. 18. 63. 6), but this brief interruption of Ptolemaic possession ended when Eumenes abandoned the region in the summer of 317 (Diod. 18. 73. 2). That commander had in the late fall or winter of 318 occupied the area without opposition. Ptolemy did not attempt to confront him. But as the result of actions elsewhere, Eumenes abandoned the region, never to return in the fall of 317. Ptolemy then reoccupied most of the area with the exception of "northern Syria" (the area from the Amanus mountains to the Eleutheris river[26]) (cf. Diod. 19. 57. 1) and held it until the start of the Third Diadoch War in 314, when Antigonus invaded Phoenicia (Diod. 19. 58. 2–6).

Antigonus had fulfilled his commission given him at Triparadeisus to defeat the last supporters of Perdiccas remaining from the First Diadoch War and after the death of Antipater in 319, in the resulting Second Diadoch War he had defeated Eumenes finally and that commander's ally Polyperchon was replaced in Macedonia by Cassander. Antigonus emerged from these two conflicts controlling most of Asia and with the desire to become the new Alexander and ruler in its entirety of his empire. In Persia, he was proclaimed king by the Persians, with Diodorus (19. 48. 1) adding "as if he was being acknowledged as Lord of Asia." This was the title claimed by Alexander himself. With the conclusion of the Second Diadoch War, Antigonus' former allies demanded that they share in the spoils of these campaigns. Cassander demanded Lycia and Cappadocia in Asia Minor; Lysimachus, Hellespontine Phrygia; Ptolemy, all of Syria, and Seleucus, Babylonia. Antigonus had also gained control of the empire's treasuries and his former colleagues demanded a share of the spoils as well (Diod. 19. 57. 1); these amounted to more than 40,000 talents and his annual revenue added 11,000 more (Diod. 19. 46. 6, 48. 7–8, 56. 5). With respect to the demands made to Antigonus, those of Ptolemy and Lysimachus were specious at best. Neither, as far as can be told from our sources, had any serious role in the recent war (the Second Diadoch War).

To challenge Antigonus on the battlefield would be a formidable task. Antigonus' army was substantial. Against Eumenes at Gabene his forces consisted of 28,000 heavy infantry, 10,600 cavalry, 65 elephants, and roughly 15,000 light infantry (Diod. 19. 27. 1, 29. 2–6; cf. Anson 2015: 124n. 37). Given that there were garrisons scattered about Asia and with many of Eumenes' defeated forces at Gabene enlisting with Antigonus, his army dwarfed those of the other Successors.[27] Antigonus' response to the demands from his former allies was war (Diod. 19. 57. 2). This war, known as the Third Diadoch War, saw a new coalition of virtually everyone against Antigonus. In the eastern Mediterranean, at the start of this war, Ptolemy controlled Cyprus through alliances with the kings there (Arr. *Succ.* 1a. 10. 6; cf. Diod. 19. 59. 1, 62. 5), and many of the Aegean islands were also tied to him as well (cf. Diod. 19. 62. 9). Part of Antigonus' response to this coalition was to seek to undermine Egypt's control of the sea. While Antigonus had the most formidable land army, he was woefully inferior on the sea. His fleet, which had defeated Cleitus in the Hellespont, had during his absence in the East been acquired by Ptolemy and Cassander (Diod. 19. 58. 1–2, 5). To offset this naval deficiency, he sent an agent to Cyprus and marched himself into Phoenicia where he planned to raise a naval force to compete primarily with Ptolemy's dominance on the sea (Diod 19. 57. 4, 58. 1–6). Here, all of the Phoenician cities, except Tyre, came over to him. It alone had a Ptolemaic garrison (cf. Diod. 19. 61. 5). Phoenicia was the center of the Ptolemaic navy with Cyprus as a second. Ptolemy, when he took over the region from Laomedon, had also acquired the Phoenician fleets. He had evacuated these to Egypt during Eumenes' brief occupation of this area and with Antigonus approaching, now did the same. Antigonus would use the Phoenician shipyards now in his possession to build his navy from scratch. In Cyprus, Antigonus' agent had some success. The kings of Cition, Lapithus, Marion, and Ceryneia, had concluded a treaty with Antigonus; however, the majority of the kings of Cyprus, including Nicocreon, the king of the most powerful city, Salamis, remained loyal to Ptolemy (Diod. 19. 59. 1). Given the evacuation of the Phoenician fleet to Egypt, even with Antigonus in possession of Phoenicia and making inroads in Cyprus, Ptolemy's fleet still ruled the seas and would for the next few years.

In the spring of 314, Antigonus called together the kings of the chief Phoenician cities, now his allies, still with the exception of Tyre, and his commanders in Syria to begin the construction of his new fleet. This fleet would be essential for the implementation of a full blockade on the city of Tyre, and also to counter his enemies' naval forces in the Aegean. Shipyards were established at Tripolis, Byblus, and Sidon, with two additional ones in Cilicia and Rhodes (Diod. 19. 58. 2–5). Diodorus (19. 58. 3) reports that 8,000 men alone were employed to cut down the trees and trim the timber, with 1,000 draught animals to haul the lumber from the forests of Lebanon to the building sites. Antigonus promised his allies that "in that very summer" he would take to sea with 500 warships (Diod. 19. 58. 5). While the fleet was being constructed, Antigonus began the siege of Tyre. After having left a force behind to continue operations against the holdout Phoenician city, Antigonus moved further south and captured the cities of Joppa and Gaza, both of which he garrisoned. He then returned to the on-going siege of Tyre (Diod. 19. 59. 2). An attempt by Seleucus, leading a Ptolemaic fleet of 100 warships, to seize the Ionian coastal city of Erythrae failed (Diod. 19. 60. 2–4; 62. 4). That commander had on his way to the Ionian city attempted to intimidate the forces besieging Tyre by sailing past knowing that Antigonus was powerless to interfere, thus clearly demonstrating to all of Antigonus' allies Ptolemy's domination of the sea (Diod. 19. 58. 5–6).

Seleucus' presence in Egypt was the result of Antigonus' actions in the eastern provinces. Even though Seleucus had been an Antigonid ally against Eumenes, Antigonus had forced him from his satrapy of Babylonia in 315. Antigonus was in the process of removing those satraps who were popular with their populations or who had held prominent positions with Alexander, or both popular and prominent. Peucestas was replaced in Persia (Diod. 19. 48. 5) and Pithon was murdered (Diod. 19. 46. 4). Seleucus with but fifty friends had fled to Egypt where he was welcomed by Ptolemy (Diod. 19. 55. 2–56. 1). He then entered that satrap's service.

After his failure to acquire Erythrae, Seleucus proceeded to Cyprus to join the Ptolemaic forces there (Diod. 19. 62. 4). Receiving no help from outside, in the summer of 313, Tyre was forced by starvation to capitulate. The siege had lasted a year and three months (Diod. 19. 61. 5). The Ptolemaic soldiers present in the city were given a safe conduct to depart with their possessions. The response of Ptolemy to Antigonus' activities in this area would be described as passive. He sent no reinforcements to Tyre. The troops freed were those who had been placed there before the siege began. Similarly, he did not intervene to protect Gaza. He did, however, respond to an Antigonid proclamation made at Tyre.

To counteract Cassander's opposition, Antigonus had made an alliance with Polyperchon who was designated the General of the Peloponnesus; the new alliance was ratified by the former regent's son, Alexander, who had been sent to Tyre to endorse the alliance formally (Diod. 19. 60. 1). After his retreat from

Macedonia, Polyperchon had established a power base in the Peloponnesus, holding amongst other communities the important cities of Patrae, Sicyon, and Corinth (Diod. 19. 54. 3–4, 66. 3, 67. 1). After Alexander's arrival and after making the alliance official, Antigonus summoned a "general assembly" of the soldiers and "the people dwelling there." Before this *ad hoc* group he accused Cassander of the murder of Olympias and excoriated his ill-treatment of King Alexander IV and Roxane. In 316, Cassander had successfully invaded Macedonia, seizing control of the country, and besieging Olympias who had taken refuge in the city of Pydna. Olympias herself had returned to Macedonia at the invitation of Polyperchon in the previous year. The then regent for the kings had hoped that her presence would shore up his support among the Macedonians, but her actions upon arrival proved to be far less than helpful. She saw to the deaths of King Philip III and his wife Eurydice along with many other prominent Macedonians. When Pydna surrendered in 315, Alexander's mother was put on trial by Cassander and eventually murdered. Subsequently, Cassander had the remaining king, Alexander, and his mother Roxane imprisoned.[28] In addition to his charges respecting Olympias and Alexander IV, Antigonus also declared that Cassander had taken Thessalonice, Alexander the Great's half-sister, in marriage by force, and that he was undermining Macedonia by rebuilding Thebes, destroyed by Alexander, and resurrecting Olynthus, which Philip II had destroyed by his creation of Cassandreia and peopling it with many displaced Olynthians (Diod. 19. 61. 1–2). When the assembled, as Antigonus had intended, reacted with rage, he introduced a decree that Cassander should be considered an enemy unless he destroyed the two cities, returned Alexander IV and Roxane to the Macedonians, and acknowledged Antigonus as the rightful regent. The decree continued that all Greek cities were to be free and autonomous and without foreign garrisons (Diod. 19. 61. 3). He then put these proposals, commonly known as the "Tyre Proclamation," to a "vote of the soldiers," who approved them overwhelmingly. The meeting operated much like a good modern-day political rally, designed as much to energize his base as his actual proposals were to undermine the authority of his rival in Macedonia. Antigonus now sent out messengers carrying copies of the decree far and wide, in the hope—as Polyperchon before him had attempted to do with respect to his nemesis Cassander, but ultimately unsuccessfully—to use the promise of freedom and autonomy to gain the active participation of the Greeks in the war on Antigonus' behalf. Polyperchon had earlier in 319/318 issued in the name of King Philip III a decree calling for a restoration of "the peace and the constitutions that our father Philip [II] established . . . preparing peace and such governments as you enjoyed under Philip and Alexander" (Diod. 18. 56. 2–3). As Diodorus (18. 55.4–56. 8, 64. 3) relates, even though not specifically noted in the decree itself, this decree meant the restoration of democratic governments and a return of those specifically exiled by Antipater in the Spartan and Lamian Wars.[29] This arrangement was based on that inaugurated by Alexander the Great's father, Philip II, who put forth the decree establishing the famous League of Corinth in 337, in which the cities then were to retain their traditional governments, i.e. those in existence "when they took the oath concerning the peace" ([Dem.] 17. 10; *IG* II². 329, lines 12–14). While Polyperchon's and Antigonus' proclamations mirrored many of the features of Philip's League of Corinth, these were not simple recreations of that former alliance (Poddighe 2002: 187; contra Dixon 2007: 151–78). For one thing, the decrees have very different purposes. Where Philip's original league was geared towards uniting the Greek world for the invasion of Persia, both Polyperchon and Antigonus wished to use these new alliances as ways to undermine those governments created after the Lamian War by Antipater (Diod. 18. 18. 3–9) and now favoring his son Cassander. Moreover, the decrees do not mention "freedom" or "autonomy" specifically, even though these concepts are found in the subsequent correspondence with the Greek cities (Diod. 18. 64. 3–5; 66. 2; 69. 3–4; Plut. *Phoc.* 34. 4).

With Antigonus' proclamation, many island cities now decided to break free from their association with the Athenians. Lemnos (cf. Diod. 19. 68. 3), Delos, and Imbros likely took advantage of the proclamation to declare their independence (O'Sullivan 1997: 112). These were encouraged by the appearance of an Antigonid fleet provided by the Rhodians (cf. Diod. 19. 61. 5, 62. 7, 64. 5). Rhodes, an independent city since the death of Alexander (Diod. 18. 8. 1), was allied with Antigonus and very supportive of his Proclamation of Greek Freedom (cf. Diod. 19. 77. 3; van Dessel and Hauben 1977: 326–7; Berthold 1984: 61). The proclamation was, of course, primarily aimed at Cassander to keep him occupied in Greece. Ptolemy, though not lifting a hand to save Tyre or Gaza, did publish a similar decree of his own, indicating that he too was in favor of Greek freedom and autonomy (Diod. 19. 62. 1). Given his objectives, Greek freedom and autonomy fit in well with his own interests.

In the winter of 314/313, Ptolemy, stirred from his seeming lethargy, secured an alliance with Asander in Caria (Diod. 19. 62. 2). Asander was apprehensive concerning Antigonus' intentions, and in the summer of 313, Ptolemy also sent his brother Menelaus with an army of 10,000 men and a fleet of 100 warships to Cyprus (Diod. 19. 62. 2–4).[30] After consultation, the Ptolemaic commanders present on the island decided to divide their forces. Polycleitus, the fleet commander sent with Menelaus, was to proceed to the Peloponnesus with fifty ships to aid in the campaign against the coalition of Antigonus' general Aristodemus and Polyperchon. However, when Polycleitus arrived at Cenchreae, the eastern port of Corinth, he discovered that Polyperchon's son Alexander had changed allegiance. He then sailed to Cilicia and there finding that Antigonus' commander Theodotus was sailing from Lycia to Caria, accompanied by a land army marching under Perilaus, he arranged a successful ambush on both land and sea. The Antigonid army and fleet were captured. Theodotus was wounded and later succumbed to his injuries; Perilaus was captured. The victorious Polycleitus then sailed back to Cyprus and then on to Egypt. Perilaus and certain others were subsequently released by Ptolemy when requested to do so by Antigonus. Ptolemy then met with Antigonus at a point east of the Nile delta to discuss peace, but nothing came of the encounter, for Antigonus was not willing to agree to Ptolemy's demands (Diod. 19. 64. 4–8). The terms discussed are not specified, but after Polycleitus' victory, it is doubtful that Ptolemy's demands were much altered, if at all, from the original ones which brought on the war, i.e. Ptolemaic possession of Phoenicia and Syria.

"In this same summer" of 312 (Diod. 19. 79. 1), the people of Cyrene revolted from Ptolemy, freeing their city and putting the garrisoned citadel under siege. The Egyptian satrap sent an army under Agis, an otherwise unknown commander, who retrieved the situation, recapturing the city (Diod. 19. 79. 1–2).[31] With the revolt crushed, Ptolemy himself now took an army to Cyprus and attacked the kings still in alliance with Antigonus (Diod. 19. 79. 3–80. 2). Once these were subdued and the cities on the island his (Diod. 20. 21. 1), he left Nicocreon, the king of Salamis, in charge of the army and sailed across to northern Syria. There he sacked two cities and sailed on to Cilicia where he captured the community of Malus, selling the inhabitants into slavery and plundering the surrounding countryside, before returning to Cyprus and subsequently to Egypt (Diod. 19. 79. 4–7, 80. 3). This represented one of the few Ptolemaic excursions out of Egypt, but another was in the offing.

Back in Egypt in the fall of 312, at the urging of Seleucus, Ptolemy decided to confront the 22-year-old Demetrius (Plut. *Demetr.* 5. 2) and began marching his army north (Diod. 19. 80. 3). While the young man had participated in his father's operations against Eumenes (Diod. 19. 29. 4, 40. 1), this was his first command (Plut. *Demetr.* 5. 1–2). Demetrius summoned his troops from their winter quarters and prepared to confront the satrap of Egypt and his ally Seleucus. The advisors that Antigonus had left with the young commander advised him not to take the field. Demetrius, however, was anxious to show his ability. Ptolemy marched across Sinai with an army of 18,000 infantry, including mercenaries and a "great number" of Egyptians, some armed (Diod. 19. 80. 4),[32] most support personnel, 4,000 cavalry, but no elephants. Demetrius prepared to meet his opponents to the south of the city of Gaza. He and his associated commanders led a force of 11,000 heavy infantry, consisting of 8,000 mercenaries, 1,000 Lycians and Pamphylians, and 2,000 Macedonian phalangites; 4,400 cavalry, 2,150 light-armed infantry, and 43 elephants (Diod. 19. 82).[33] In the battle, Demetrius commanded the left wing with 2,900 heavy and light cavalry, 1,500 light infantry, and 30 elephants; his right contained 1,500 mostly light cavalry. The infantry phalanx of some 11,000 was deployed in the center, with 13 elephants in front, interspersed with 650 light-armed troops. Demetrius ordered his right wing to refuse battle until the issue had been decided on the left. Initially, Ptolemy and Seleucus had placed the majority of their cavalry on their left, but learning of Demetrius' deployment, they transferred these, along with 3,000 heavy cavalry, to their right wing. To deal with Demetrius' elephants, they placed a screen of archers, javelin men, and men equipped with caltrops—spikes connected to chains—to be thrown in front of the elephants. The allies' center consisted of their infantry phalanx, with the left wing protected by only 1,000, probably light, cavalry. Demetrius' right wing was then far superior to that of his enemy's left, but, as per the allies' plan, their left never fully engaged during the battle (Diod. 19. 83. 1–3).

The battle opened with the two strong cavalry wings attacking one another. While the cavalry battle on this flank was progressing, those in charge of Demetrius' elephants advanced to the attack. The elephants were stopped by the light-armed infantry. The ultimate result was that Ptolemy's and Seleucus' forces captured all of the surviving elephants. The defeat of the elephants caused a general panic among Demetrius' cavalry, which began to flee the battle in large numbers. The battle ended in a rout. Of Demetrius' forces, 500,[34] mostly cavalrymen, were dead, and 8,000, primarily infantry, captured. This battle was the only major confrontation between the forces of the principal antagonists during this entire war (Diod. 19. 83. 4–85; Plut. *Demetr.* 5. 2–4; Just. 15. 1. 6–9). All three, Seleucus, Ptolemy, and Demetrius, directly participated in the combat as cavalrymen (Diod. 19. 83. 4–5).

After the conflict Demetrius retreated with the remnants of his forces to Tripolis in Phoenicia, and then to Cilicia, summoning troops from garrisons throughout the area to augment his now very depleted army. Ptolemy acquired Gaza that very night after the battle (Diod. 19. 84. 7–8) and subsequently was able to occupy Phoenicia, including the ports of Sidon and Tyre (Diod. 19. 85.

5–86. 1–2³⁵). This victory increased significantly Ptolemy's military power. He gained at Demetrius' expense a number of elephants³⁶ and 8,000 prisoners, most of whom joined Ptolemy's forces and were made cleruchs and settled in Egypt (Diod. 19. 84. 4–5, 85. 4; Plut. *Demetr.* 5. 2; Just. 15. 1. 6–9). Having collected what forces he could, Demetrius had moved from Cilicia back to Upper Syria. Ptolemy, still encamped in Phoenicia, sent his general Cilles with an army to dislodge his beaten opponent. Demetrius learned of the enemy's approach and also that the force was carelessly encamped and proceeding rapidly by forced marches with light-armed troops, caught the enemy by surprise in the early morning hours. He captured the army without a battle and made Cilles his prisoner. The latter along with his staff was subsequently repatriated to Ptolemy (Diod. 19. 93. 1–3; Plut. *Demetr.* 6. 27), possibly in recompense for the Egyptian satrap's similar generosity after the Battle of Gaza with respect to officers captured from Demetrius' force (Diod. 19. 85. 3). After this success, which Demetrius believed retrieved his previous defeat (Diod. 19. 93. 2),³⁷ he wrote to his father urging him to come immediately. Antigonus was in winter quarters in Celaenae when the request reached him. He quickly left his base and within a few days joined his son in Syria. When Ptolemy learned of Antigonus' arrival, he rapidly retreated back to his safe haven of Egypt. However, before leaving the coast of the eastern Mediterranean he razed a number of the cities he had captured, including Gaza, which stood on the threshold of Egypt. Antigonus regained possession of that important coast without striking a blow (Diod. 19. 93. 1–94. 1).

After the victory at Gaza, Seleucus requested that his Egyptian benefactor give him forces for the reconquest of Babylonia (Diod. 19. 86. 5). Ptolemy outfitted him with a small force of 800 infantry and 200 cavalry.³⁸ It is peculiar that Seleucus was not sent with a larger force. Opening a new front in the east that would likely draw Antigonus away would certainly appear to be in Ptolemy's interest. Despite the small numbers and the apprehension of his supporters, Seleucus was convinced of his eventual success. He had been popular in Babylonia before his flight, and he assumed he would be so again on his return (Diod. 19. 90). Also, Antigonus had been very high-handed in his replacement of officials in the east without much concern for the ill feelings such action might cause among the populace. In fact, he had eliminated Peucestas because of his popularity with the Persians.

During this winter (311/310), three of the antagonists, Antigonus, Cassander, and Lysimachus, reached a settlement ending the Third Diadoch War, basically recognizing the boundaries that existed between them at the start of the conflict.

This agreement had been made perhaps as early as the late summer. Ptolemy only joined in the winter. A letter from Antigonus to the city of Scepsis (Bagnall and Derow [*OGIS* 5] 1981: 11–12) makes it clear that an agreement had first been made with the Europeans (*OGIS* 5 ll. 25, 35), and only subsequently with Ptolemy (*OGIS* 5 ll. 30, 35). The earlier peace created a serious dilemma for the ruler of Egypt. With both Cassander and Lysimachus out of the war, Ptolemy would have stood alone against Antigonus in the west (Billows (1990: 113–14). Seleucus and Polyperchon were now the odd men out (Mehl 1986: 120–4; Billows 1990: 132). Moreover, while the status quo was recognized for Lysimachus and Cassander, Antigonus was to remain in control of those areas taken from Ptolemy.

So, Ptolemy was in effect the only loser. He retained Egypt and Libya, but he had lost all his possessions on the eastern seaboard of the Mediterranean and had abandoned his ally Seleucus. Additionally, there was discovered that Nicocles, the King of Paphos in Cyprus, was plotting to betray the city to Antigonus (Diod. 20. 21. 1). Ptolemy sent agents to Menelaus, who was now acting in his brother's interest here as king, and Nicocles was forced to commit suicide (Diod. 20. 21. 2–3). To these setbacks was added the overall increase in Antigonus' power; not only at Ptolemy's expense, but he was now generally recognized as the "leader" of, or the "first" in, all Asia (Diod. 19. 105. 1). After the peace, Antigonus had gone east to bolster his control there, and, in particular, to oust Seleucus who had, indeed, reestablished his position in Babylon. In the absence of the powerful dynast, Ptolemy attempted to gain some advantage. While Antigonus was strengthened on the one hand by his extensive family, his sons and his nephews, in the case of the latter, these were not always a blessing. His nephews were competent commanders, but not always loyal to their uncle. In particular, Polemaeus had revolted from his relation and was garrisoning Greek communities in violation of one of the terms of the general treaty that ended the last war and which acknowledged Greek freedom and autonomy.[39] Ptolemy, ignoring that Polemaeus was no longer an agent of Antigonus, charged Antigonus with breaking the treaty, and using this claim as an excuse, sent an army north, which captured cities in western Cilicia that had been allied with Antigonus (Diod. 20. 19. 4). These successes were fleeting, for Antigonus' sons recovered the lost territory. Antigonus' youngest son Philip countered Polemaeus in the Hellespontic region and Demetrius drove Ptolemy's forces out of Cilicia (Diod. 20. 19. 5; Plut. *Demetr.* 7. 3). The year 309 saw the death of the last Argead. His half-brother Alexander IV and his mother Roxane had been murdered on Cassander's orders in 310 (Diod. 19. 105. 2). The now seventeen-year-old

Heracles was murdered by Polyperchon in another of that commander's displays of dazzling incompetence and here also blatant stupidity (Diod. 20. 28. 2). He had been using the young man successfully as his way to regain his power in Macedonia against Cassander, when Cassander "amazingly" convinced him that it would be a good idea to kill this last male Argead (Carney 2014: 14).

In the spring of 309, Ptolemy left Egypt himself for Lycia, where he captured the cities of Phaselis and Xanthus, then sailing on to Caria he captured the city of Caunus. He further sent to those cities controlled by Cassander and Lysimachus asking for their cooperation. His purpose was to prepare for Antigonus' return (cf. Diod. 20. 19. 4; Seibert 1969: 176–83). These operations secured for Ptolemy important ports in Asia Minor and gave him additional access to rowers and revenue. As part of his attempt to counter Antigonus' resources, Ptolemy sailed to the island of Cos where he summoned Polemaeus to a meeting. Antigonus' rebellious nephew left Chalcis to meet the ruler of Egypt. This potential alliance, however, collapsed when Polemaeus attempted to subvert Ptolemy's commanders with gifts, and was forced to drink hemlock (Diod. 20. 27. 4). Ptolemy proceeded to win over the troops previously loyal to their now dead commander and these were distributed throughout his ranks (Diod. 20. 27). Ptolemy spent the winter of 309/308 in Caria (cf. Diod. 20. 37. 1).

The following spring saw Ptolemy again active in the Aegean, sailing from Myndus in Caria, through the islands, where he separated Andros and likely many others from their alliance with Antigonus, and with his large fleet proceeded to the Greek mainland. Here, he acquired Sicyon and Corinth from Cratesipolis, the widow of the now deceased Alexander, the son of Polyperchon (Diod. 20. 37. 1; Polyaen. 8. 58). The Egyptian satrap clearly was hoping to beat Antigonus at his own game and gain the support of the Greeks through a "Greek Freedom" program of his own. He likely wished to recreate the former League of Corinth with himself as its leader (Billows 1990: 144–5 and n. 18; Dixon 2007: 173–4 and n. 63). Ptolemy had planned on "freeing" more Greek cities, but the Peloponnesians who had agreed to assist him in these endeavors failed to contribute the forces that they had promised, and Ptolemy returned to Egypt (Diod. 20. 37. 1–2). While Ptolemy had proclaimed that Greek cities should be free and autonomous, he garrisoned both Sicyon and Corinth prior to his withdrawal from Greece (Diod. 20. 37. 2; Plut. *Demetr.* 15. 1; *Suda* s. v. *Demetrius*), which only confirmed Greek doubts concerning his commitment to Greek freedom. It is likely that the garrisons were placed to defend the cities from the other Diadochs, not to maintain control of them, but the image of placing garrisons at the same time one is proclaiming freedom and autonomy is not a good one. In any case, freedom and autonomy were never more than slogans to gain some advantage by one party or another. The later Romans were to use the concept of Greek freedom greatly to their advantage. For Ptolemy this was a way to keep Greece disunited. With the failure of the program to gain any traction, he returned to Egypt. His return was hastened by Antigonus' return from his failed attempt to unseat Seleucus (Wheatley 2002: 45–6).

After his inability to remove Seleucus, Antigonus returned sometime in the summer of 308. His arrival in the west was soon followed by the death of Alexander's sister, Cleopatra. She had been sought in marriage by many of the Diadochs: Leonnatus (Plut. *Eum.* 3. 9–10), Perdiccas (Diod. 18. 23. 1), and more recently by Lysimachus, Ptolemy, and perhaps even Antigonus (Diod. 20. 37. 4). Her death was occasioned by the recent proposal of marriage from Ptolemy (Diod. 20. 37. 3). Antigonus killed her to prevent any additional enhancement of the Egyptian satrap's charisma due to some further connection to Alexander.

Due to Polemaeus' betrayal and his own absence in the east, much of Greece was now allied to and/or garrisoned by Cassander and Ptolemy. Demetrius was sent in the spring of 306 (Paus. 1. 6. 6; [Parian Marble] *FGrH* 239 B F-21) with a force of 15,000 infantry, 400 cavalry, and 163 warships to Cyprus. Ptolemy's general on the island, his brother Menelaus, contested the invasion with 12,000 infantry and 800 cavalry. The battle was of short duration with Demetrius winning a complete victory, killing 1,000 and capturing 3,000 of the enemy. Menelaus, however, with the remainder of his force retreated inside the port city of Salamis. Demetrius promptly put the city under siege. While the siege was in progress, Ptolemy arrived with a relief force of 140 warships and 200 transports. Menelaus in the safety of his harbor commanded 60 additional warships, bringing the Ptolemaic fleet total to 200. Demetrius' armada totaled 180. In the sea battle that ensued, both commanders placed the larger and more powerful ships on their left, preparing to hold back their right as much as possible. The successful fleet would then be the one that succeeded in destroying the enemy's right and rolling up the center before the opposing fleet could do the same. Ptolemy set his fleet facing the harbor, forcing Demetrius' ships to put their sterns towards Salamis. When the two fleets engaged, Menelaus was to sail out and attack the rear of the enemy line. To counter this move, Demetrius stationed ten of his best ships facing the harbor entrance. In the course of the battle these ten were able to delay Menelaus' relief force long enough for Demetrius' fleet to achieve its objective first, routing Ptolemy and his forces. One hundred transport ships carrying 8,000 men were captured along with 40 warships. Eighty Ptolemaic warships were sunk. The result of the sea battle was the surrender of the entire island to Demetrius. The victorious commander, having taken all of the cities and their garrisons, enrolled the captured into his army. The number of those thus incorporated was 16,000 infantry and 600 cavalry. The victory came in June of 306;[40] Ptolemy now deserted Cyprus and Demetrius occupied the entire island (Diod. 20. 53. 1).

With this victory, Antigonus had himself and his son proclaimed kings (Diod. 20. 53. 2; Plut. *Demetr.* 17. 2–18. 1; cf. [Heidelberg Epitome] *FGrH* 155 F-1.7), and in this action they were followed later by Ptolemy in the first half of 304,[41] and shortly thereafter by Seleucus (Diod. 20. 53. 4; Parker and Dubbenstein 1942: 18; Gruen 1985: 258–9), Lysimachus, and Cassander (Diod. 20. 53; Plut. *Demetr.* 17–18; [Heidelberg Epitome] *FGrH* 155 F-1. 7; Wheatley 2013: 17–29). Cassander, while addressed as king by others, continued in the traditional fashion of the Argeads of being addressed by his subjects by his name without title (Plut. *Demetr.* 18; App. *Syr.* 54).[42] The delay in proclaiming what must have seemed inevitable to most did come only after Cassander's murder of Alexander IV and his mother Roxane.

After the success in Cyprus, the Antigonids, father and son, prepared to invade Egypt. As noted previously, this invasion, like that of Perdiccas before it, failed. Ptolemy's strong defensive position on the western bank of the river (cf. Diod. 20. 73. 1, 4, 76. 1, 3), the storms that crippled the invading fleet, and a growing lack of supplies (Diod. 20. 76. 4–5) led to Antigonus returning to Syria (Diod. 20. 73–6. 6; cf, Plut. *Demetr.* 19. 4). In 305, the nature of Ptolemy's activities outside of Egypt can be seen most clearly in his reaction to Demetrius' attack on the island of Rhodes. While the island had been allied with Antigonus, it had failed to join in the attack on Cyprus or in the abortive invasion of Egypt the previous year. The Rhodians had proclaimed that they were at peace with all parties (Diod. 20. 81. 2, 4). They did, however, incline towards Ptolemy because of close trade connections with Egypt (Diod. 20. 81. 4). Antigonus was not content with their response to his request for an active alliance and sent Demetrius with a well-equipped force, including numerous siege engines, to bring the Rhodians to heel. The other Diadochs supported the Rhodians with supplies and reinforcements (Diod. 20. 96. 3, 100. 2). In particular, Ptolemy contributed substantially to the Rhodian defense (Diod. 20. 88. 9, 94. 3–5, 96. 1–3, 98. 1, 100. 2). The siege ultimately failed. Other than convincing Ptolemy, and perhaps the other Diadochs, that it was time to become kings, the results of the siege were modest. Ptolemy was given the title of "*Soter*," Savior, by the grateful Rhodians, a name that would become a commonly applied epithet to the Egyptian ruler from then on. Ptolemy had once again thwarted an invasion of Egypt by what would have appeared to be overwhelming forces through his shrewd use of Egypt's natural and enhanced defenses, and his support of the Rhodians had certainly aided in their surviving Demetrius' siege. Ptolemy's last hurrah, although a muted one, occured in 302 when once again a coalition was formed to thwart Antigonus' ambitions. This one contained Seleucus, Lysimachus, Cassander, and Ptolemy (Diod. 20. 106. 3–5; Plut. *Demetr.* 28. 2; Just. 15. 2. 17, 4. 1). The Fourth Diadoch War would soon begin; however, it hardly came after a peaceful interlude.

It was decided by the allies that Cassander would remain in Greece, while Lysimachus, taking with him part of the Macedonian's forces under the command of Cassander's general Perpelaus, would cross to Asia. Here he would be joined by Seleucus and Ptolemy. During this same winter, on his way to join his allies, Ptolemy moved to take advantage of the absence of Antigonus to recapture Phoenicia, but, arriving at Sidon, he was told that the great battle had already been fought and that Antigonus, the victor, was advancing into Syria. Ptolemy immediately retreated back to Egypt (Diod. 20. 113. 1–2). While Ptolemy would not be a factor in the coming battle, Antigonus was defeated and killed while Demetrius escaped. True to form, no sooner was this war over than disagreements broke out among the allies. The triumphant Seleucus journeyed south to Phoenicia only to find that Ptolemy had occupied the region with garrisons. Ptolemy claimed that these lands had been made subject to himself and were not part of Antigonus' holdings when he met his death. Additionally, he stated that he had been an ally in the recent war and deserved some reward. Seleucus responded that to the victors belonged the spoils, and that the victors in the actual battle were himself and Lysimachus, and that Ptolemy was not present (Diod. 21. 1. 5). But the Egyptian dynast claimed that in the negotiations that had created the alliance to oppose Antigonus, he had been promised Phoenicia (Polyb. 5. 67). Seleucus finally stepped back, stating that on account of their former friendship he would not push the issue (Diod. 21. 1. 5). The quarrel was in truth over who would have the option of obtaining two of the major Phoenician cities, for Sidon and Tyre remained under Demetrius' control (cf. Plut. *Demetr.* 22. 9). Fearing Seleucus' future activities, Ptolemy now arranged marriage alliances with both Cassander and Lysimachus. Although Antigonus was dead and his vast empire was now being divided up, his son Demetrius was still very much alive and a force still to be reckoned with. While his land forces had been seriously diminished (Plut. *Demetr.* 30. 2), his fleet, the largest in the Aegean, was still intact. Cyprus (cf. Plut. *Demetr.* 25. 6), the Phoenician cities of Tyre and Sidon (Plut. *Demetr.* 32. 10), and his League of Islanders remained steadfast.[43] In

300, with Demetrius at large in the Aegean and Seleucus a special concern, Ptolemy, Lysimachus, and Cassander formed a new alliance. Ptolemy here used his daughters to cement these relationships. Lysimachus divorced his wife and married the young daughter, Arsinoe, of his new partner in Egypt. His eldest son, Agathocles married Ptolemy's daughter, Lysandra (Plut. *Demetr.* 31. 3–5; Just 15. 4. 24). Demetrius returned to Cilicia and took possession of that region, sending his wife Phila to her brother Cassander to try and smooth things over. Seleucus, aware of the apparent dangers that this new alliance represented, made a rapprochement with Demetrius. He then arranged an alliance between Ptolemy and Demetrius, with Demetrius marrying another of Ptolemy's daughters, Ptolemais (Plut. *Demetr.* 31. 3–32. 7). Ptolemy was clearly hedging his bets. Why Seleucus would be arranging an alliance between these two individuals is unclear. This is especially the case since he was soon to make rather pointed requests of Demetrius regarding lands under the latter's control, lands that were contested between himself and Ptolemy. Perhaps these alliances were pointed towards Lysimachus, who had emerged more or less from the shadows as a major player now in Diadoch affairs.

Another player in the politics of the post-Alexander the Great wars now appeared: Pyrrhus. Pyrrhus was scion of the Epirote royal house, the son of Aeacides, who would become king of Epirus in 307 at the age of thirteen but lost the throne in 302 and regained it in 297. His early history coincides with a turbulent time in Epirus.[44] His father was overthrown in 316 with the young Pyrrhus barely escaping with his life (Diod. 19. 11. 1–2, 36. 4–5; Paus. 1. 11. 3–4; Just. 14. 5. 9). He was taken in by the Illyrian king, Glaucias, with whom he lived for the next twelve years (Plut. *Pyrrh.* 3. 1–6; Just. 17. 3. 17–20). In 307, Glaucias invaded Epirus and put Pyrrhus on the throne (Just. 17. 3). He was all of eleven years of age. When he was seventeen, while visiting Glaucias in Illyria, his supporters were driven out of Epirus and a new king placed on the throne. Pyrrhus fled south and joined his brother-in-law, Demetrius, the son of Antigonus. Demetrius had married Pyrrhus' sister Deidamia and was then campaigning against Cassander in southern Greece. In 302, when Demetrius joined his father and engaged in the Battle of Ipsus the next year, he had been accompanied by Pyrrhus. After the defeat at Ipsus, Pyrrhus had remained with Demetrius and in 300 the young man was sent to Egypt as a hostage for Demetrius' good behavior. As a hostage in Egypt, Pyrrhus impressed his host and his host's young wife Berenice (Plut. *Demetr.* 4. 6–7). She was the cousin of Ptolemy's third wife, Eurydice, the daughter of Antipater, and had served as a lady-in-waiting for her cousin before catching the eye of Ptolemy (Carney 2000:

173–4). While in Egypt, Pyrrhus married Berenice's daughter, Antigone, by a previous husband (Plut. *Demetr.* 4. 7). Both Ptolemy and Demetrius were polygamists. Ptolemy married four times.[45] He had married Artacama in the famous marriages that took place in Susa in 324 (Arr. *Anab.* 7. 4. 6), but this wife disappears from the record after the notice of the marriage. Probably in 321, he had married one of Antipater's many daughters, Eurydice, and later, he married Berenice (Paus. 1. 6. 8).

With respect to Pyrrhus, the excellent relations he had established with his host in Egypt brought him back to Epirus.[46] Ptolemy, in 297, sent the young man and his new wife home with treasure and an army to enable him to regain his throne (Plut. *Pyrrh.* 5. 1; Paus. 1. 11. 5). Likely Ptolemy hoped that by reinstating Pyrrhus he would foment new conflicts in that part of the world. Pyrrhus, instead of engaging the then king Neoptolemus in battle, formed an alliance with him and they reigned jointly. Plutarch suggests that Pyrrhus made this bargain because he was afraid that Neoptolemus would appeal either to Macedonia or to Lysimachus for assistance. If this was the case for the former seeking to avoid conflict, it was even a stronger incentive for the latter. Pyrrhus had come with forces sent by Ptolemy and he was the ally also of Demetrius. As one would suspect, the dual monarchy did not last long, which likely was not a surprise to Ptolemy. Outside of Sparta there was something that did not love a dual monarchy unless it was formed of a father and a son. The two individuals plotted each other's demise. Pyrrhus struck first, inviting the former to dinner and there murdering him in 297 (Plut. *Pyrrh.* 5).

The alliances supposedly cemented by these marriages and arranged by Seleucus broke down almost as soon as they were formed. Seleucus requested that Demetrius sell to him the newly conquered Cilicia, and when the latter refused, demanded the surrender of Tyre and Sidon instead (Plut. *Demetr.* 32. 10). Demetrius, in 298, secured his possessions in Asia with garrisons and sailed to Attica to overthrow Lachares' tyranny (Plut. *Demetr.* 33. 1). The latter was the former agent of Cassander. A relief force sent from Ptolemy failed to break the stranglehold Demetrius had on the city. With this failure, Lachares fled, escaping to Thebes, and Demetrius "freed" the city for a second time in April of 294 (Plut. *Demetr.* 33. 1–34. 1; Polyaen. 3. 7. 1–3, 4. 7. 5; *IG* II² 646 ll 1–5). The year 294 would see Demetrius cap his remarkable recovery from the disaster at Ipsus with his becoming King of Macedonia. Cassander had died in the winter of 298/297 ([Euseb. *Chron.*] *FGrH* 260 F-3.4; *P.Oxy.* 2082=257a F-3).[47] While Demetrius had assembled quite a collection of possessions in the Greek peninsula, he had lost his possessions in Asia Minor and Cyprus to Lysimachus and Ptolemy respectively (Plut. *Demetr.* 35. 3; 38. 1).

Demetrius' emergence as king of Macedonia is just another stage in this individual's mercurial career. In Macedonia, after the death of Cassander, his son Philip (IV) had succeeded to the throne, only to die four months later of the same malady that had afflicted his father (*P.Oxy.* 2082=*BNJ* 257a F-3; [Euseb. *Chron.*] *BNJ* 260 F-3.5; Plut. *Demetr.* 36. 1). The result was a struggle for the throne between his two younger brothers, Alexander and Antipater. The boys' mother, Thessalonice, insisted that the two brothers share the rule. The kingdom was partitioned, with Alexander receiving the western part and Antipater the eastern.[48] The mother's preference was for the younger Alexander over the sixteen-year-old Antipater. This particular dual monarchy lasted only two-and-a-half years (*BNJ* 260 F-4.5). The crisis was precipitated by Antipater's murder of his mother. The young Alexander, then, properly fearing for not only his share of the kingdom, but also for his life, sent letters both to Demetrius and to Pyrrhus, who was once again king of Epirus (Plut. *Demetr.* 36. 1–2; *Pyrrh.* 6. 3; Paus. 9. 7. 3; Diod. 21. 7; Just. 16. 1. 5). Given the distances involved and Demetrius' engagement in the Peloponnesus (Plut. *Pyrrh.* 6. 2), which even though he ended it, still delayed him, Pyrrhus, coming from Epirus, was the first to respond and more than settled things in Alexander's favor. Demetrius now arrived. Alexander welcomed his now unneeded and unwanted rescuer. While the two pretended to be amiable, they were in fact plotting against one another. Demetrius succeeded in murdering his host and proclaimed himself king of Macedonia (Plut. *Demetr.* 36; *Pyrrh.* 7. 1; Just. 16. 1. 8–18; [Euseb. *Chron.*] *BNJ* 260 F-3.6). As he prepared to address the Macedonian troops in the hope of securing their backing, they proclaimed him king. In Macedonia, Demetrius was well received (Plut. *Demetr.* 37; *Pyrrh.* 7. 2; Just. 16. 1. 17–18). Antipater fled to Thrace and Demetrius occupied the entire kingdom. Demetrius became king of Macedonia in the fall of 294.[49] He was to rule for roughly six years ([Euseb. *Chron.*] *FGrH* 260 F-3.6). By becoming king, Demetrius had reached the high-water mark in his independent career. In addition to Macedonia, he also gained control of Thessaly, in part through his foundation of Demetrias in 294/293, at the head of the Gulf of Pagasae (Str. 9. 5. 15; Cohen 1995: 111–12).

As with so many of Alexander the Great's Successors, and in this case with the son of one of them, there was no sense of contentment in what one possessed, but always the goal of adding more. The new struggles began in the fall of 288 ([Euseb. *Chron.*] *BNJ* 260 F 3.5, 6; Wheatley 1997: 21–2). With Ptolemy sailing to Greece to undermine Demetrius' hold there, both Pyrrhus and Lysimachus simultaneously invaded Macedonia. The new government in Athens sent Crates the philosopher to negotiate with the former king of Macedonia. He advised Demetrius to return to Asia, and the ever-changeable commander decided to follow his advice (Plut. *Demetr.* 46. 1–3). Here he was captured by Seleucus and died in captivity in 283. Ptolemy, the adroit politician, had now gained all he could reasonably expect from the alliance against Demetrius. He was in complete control of Cyprus, and by virtual default was now the new patron of the Nesiotic League (Hammond and Walbank 1988: 228n. 2; 232). His taking over the league was seen as a liberation and he was later honored during the reign of his son Philadelphus as a "Soter" in a decree issued by the league (*Syll.*³ 390). To complete what he had long desired, he also seized control of Tyre[50] and Sidon and for good measure Lycia as well (Merker 1974: 125–6; Wörrle 1977: 56). At the time of his death in 282, Ptolemy had now achieved his ultimate goal. Egypt was secure and the "fence" in place.

Lysimachus and Seleucus remained, but no real threat to Ptolemy during the remainder of his life. Lysimachus, like his predecessors at the apex of their power, was due to suffer an eclipse. Here, the coming disaster was one of his own making, a by-product of his polygamy. Lysimachus' eldest son, Agathocles was the grandson of that Antipater who had been regent of Macedonia during Alexander the Great's expedition to Asia. As part of the ever-changing alliances often cemented, however briefly, by marriage, Lysimachus had married, in addition to his son Agathocles' mother, Nicaea, Ptolemy's daughter Arsinoe, and by her had three sons.[51] With his mind poisoned against his eldest son by his new wife, he had Agathocles executed for treason (Just. 17. 1. 4). Those who had supported the young man were massacred. This led to an exodus of family members and supporters. These included Lysandra, Agathocles' wife, and her brother Ptolemy Ceraunus, who had fled to Lysimachus about the time his father Ptolemy Soter had set him aside for his younger half-brother, also named Ptolemy, who became co-ruler in 285. It was this son Ptolemy, so-called Philadelphus, who did succeed to the throne on the death of his father in 282 ([Euseb. *Chron.*] *FGrH* 260 F-2.3; Hazzard 1987: 140, 146–7, 149–50, 154). The forces of the two aged dynasts, 77-year-old Seleucus and 74-year-old Lysimachus (Just. 17. 1. 10), met at Corupedium early in 281. In a battle about which virtually nothing is known, Lysimachus met his death (Just. 17. 2. 1; App. *Syr.* 62). This death was followed later the same year by that of Seleucus, murdered by Ptolemy Ceraunus.[52] Seleucus was the last of those generals who had served the great Alexander. An age had ended.

Of the Diadochs clearly the most successful, Ptolemy in his lifetime had created the most enduring of all the Hellenistic kingdoms. This was done by design. Ptolemy did everything in his power to see that his legacy would be a kingdom and a dynasty. From his very audacious and risky baiting of the regent Perdiccas to his far more cautious later life, it was all meant to secure his hold on Egypt and to protect Egypt by what Polybius accurately saw as his fence. He joined coalitions and fought wars to prevent the emergence of a winner in the Alexander sweepstakes. When the regency was his for the asking, he did not grasp it. His military skills were ideal for his ambitions. He was what would be called in boxing a great counterpuncher. He lacked not just the ambition, but also the ability to conquer the world. After the Perdiccan invasion, he never risked it all; the closest he came was at Gaza. However, here he was accompanied by Seleucus and he was facing to this point the untested Demetrius. When he heard that Antigonus was approaching, he retreated back to Egypt. He was likely present in all of Alexander's great victories as a valiant cavalryman, but not in command of major offensive units until after the defeat and collapse of the Persian Empire. On the Hydaspes, he commanded a diversionary force and having accomplished his goal, as he likely had done on the Granicus, at Issus, and at Gaugamela, joined Alexander and fought bravely. He was not present at Ipsus. As an admiral, he and his brother lost the Battle of Salamis. If, as so many proclaim, he desired to be Alexander's successor and master of that commander's entire world, he was not willing to run great risks to achieve this goal. At the very least, he lacked the necessary "fire in the belly." He would run risks, but only those to achieve his more limited objectives. When he sailed to Greece and acquired Corinth and Sicyon and attempted to build a coalition, he never made even the slightest feint towards Macedonia. When it became clear that his desire to undermine his rival might only be achieved by his moving into Europe in a big way, then he went home. The Greeks were not willing to carry the load. He did not have the mercurial military career that so many of his rivals achieved, but he, not them, died in bed of natural causes (Just. 16. 2. 7; cf. Lucian *Macrob.* 12),[53] leaving behind a kingdom and a dynasty that lasted until 30 BC.

6

The Lord of Egypt

"The Hellenistic kingdoms were founded by upstarts, acquired and subsequently underpinned by military strength." This statement by Jane Rowlandson (2007: 29) is certainly true. Underlining every one of these Hellenistic states was the importance of "military prowess," and a drive to establish legitimacy among those who backed up this military prowess. As R. M. Errington[1] would say, the ultimate importance of *potestas* never left these kingdoms. However, there was a measure of *auctoritas* that eventually emerged, which brought a semblance of order to those states that arose from Alexander's empire in their day-to-day functioning. These Hellenistic territorial states were monarchical in their organization and Ptolemaic Egypt was no exception. This is not too surprising since the major political traditions in existence at this time and in this place, Macedonian, Persian, and Egyptian, were all based on the authority of hereditary monarchies. After the chaos that ensued on Alexander's death occasioned by the collapse of the Argead monarchy in most respects except in theory, and by 304 with there being no more true Argeads, those of Alexander's still surviving Successors began the process of establishing their own dynasties. In a reciprocal relationship, dynasty was critical to establishing legitimacy to rule and legitimacy to rule was critical in creating a dynasty. Ptolemy inaugurated the practice of designating his successor and establishing a joint rule with his designee ([Porphyry of Tyre] *BNJ* 260 F-2; Just. 16. 2. 7–8).[2] A problem that existed both in the traditional Argead dynasty and also in the Ptolemaic one, among others, was that often legitimacy was complicated because of the practice of polygamy (Carney 1992: 169–89; 2000: 23–7). In many respects Ptolemy was lucky that this designation of one of his sons proved successful. There was every possibility that it could have erupted into civil war. Ptolemy fathered as many as seven sons with at least three different women. With Thaïs, his concubine/wife?, he had two sons (Plut. *Alex.* 38. 2; Athen. 13. 576E). With Eurydice, the daughter of Antipater, Alexander's regent in Macedonia and also for his heirs from 320 until his death in 319, he had two sons (Paus. 1. 6. 8, 7. 1, 9.7; Plut. *Demetr.* 46. 3), and with Eurydice's cousin Berenice, a son and his heir Ptolemy II Philadelphus, and, perhaps, one additional son (Theoc. *Id.* 17; Paus. 1. 6. 8).³ After the appointment of Ptolemy II as co-ruler, Meleager and Ptolemy Ceraunos,⁴ sons who were bypassed in the succession, fled Egypt and eventually both served for a short time as kings of Macedonia (App. *Syr.* 10. 62; Nep. 21. 3. 4; Diod. 22. 4; [Porphyry] *BNJ* 260 F-3. 10). Two other sons, Argaeus and another unnamed son, were put to death by Ptolemy II, the ironically called Philadelphus (Paus. 1. 7. 1).⁵ While polygamy often led to succession crises, it did have the advantage of producing girls who were useful in establishing alliances. Where Alexander the Great's father Philip married seven times with, perhaps, only the last not being to cement an alliance,⁶ Ptolemy only married once as part of an alliance.⁷ As noted earlier, he married Eurydice, a daughter of Antipater. However, his own daughters cemented a number of alliances. Ptolemy married his daughter by Thaïs, Eirene, to Eunostus, the king of Cyprian Soli ([Cleitarchus] *FGrH* 137 F-11=Athen. 13. 576E), Lysandra, daughter of Eurydice (Paus. 1. 10. 3), was married to Alexander V, Cassander's son and briefly king of Macedonia, and subsequently she married Agathocles, the eldest son of Lysimachus (Paus. 1. 16. 2), and Arsinoe, daughter of Berenice, married Lysimachus (Just. 17. 1. 4–6).⁸ While his marriage alliance with Antipater proved most useful, the other marriage alliances proved much less helpful.

The marriage and alliance with Antipater became most useful during the unsuccessful invasion of Egypt by Perdiccas (see Chapter 4). Perdiccas, the regent for Alexander's heirs, the Conqueror's half-brother and infant son, had determined to become king in his own right. His plan was to marry Cleopatra, the dead Alexander's sister, march to Macedonia with the royal army, with the two supposed kings, bring Alexander's body home for burial, and seize the kingship in his own name. His plans were disrupted when Ptolemy seized Alexander's body, taking it to Egypt, and Perdiccas' plot was prematurely revealed to Antipater and Craterus, who were in command of the forces in Macedonia.⁹ With the likelihood of invasion from Europe, Perdiccas had to divide his forces before proceeding to Egypt. Perdiccas with the bulk of the royal army and most of the officer corps proceeded to Egypt, while part of the army and most of the fleet would be left behind to resist Antipater and Craterus, who were preparing to invade Asia. The Cardian Greek Eumenes was given the overall command for the defense of Asia Minor (Diod. 18. 29. 1–3; Just. 13. 6. 14–15; Nepos *Eum.* 3. 2; Plut. *Eum.* 5. 2). In Asia Minor, the first line of defense was the Hellespont (Diod. 18. 25. 6, 29. 1–3). While most of the transport ships sailed for Egypt, the main battle fleet sailed from Cilicia to the Hellespont.¹⁰ It is unknown if the presence of the main fleet, which remained in the Hellespont to thwart any invasion from Europe into Asia, would have made a difference by its presence in Egypt. It might have prevented its commander, Cleitus, from subsequently deserting to Antipater.[11] The presence of the extra forces left in Asia Minor might have made a difference, as might the presence of experienced officers like Perdiccas' brother Alcetas and Perdiccas' close ally Eumenes, but Perdiccas still had what appeared to be an overwhelming force. His inability to force a crossing to the left bank of the Nile doomed his invasion. He was assassinated by his own officers (Diod. 18. 36. 4–5; Paus. 1. 6. 3; cf. Arr. Succ. 1a. 28; Str. 17. 1. 8). What hindered this undertaking most of all was that Perdiccas faced two enemies and feared being trapped between them.

The rule of Hellenistic kings in general was basic autocracy, in the sense that the king theoretically could work his will but was limited practically by a heavy reliance on the army and, in a foreign land, on local control and traditional practices. Samuel (1993: 192) is basically correct that in terms of ruling ideology Hellenistic kings were constrained "by qualities of character rather than position."[12] There was no sovereign assembly, no shared rule with a council—in short, there was no constitutional agency with independent authority with which to contend[13]—but there were constraints that arose from social and economic forces that had to be accommodated. These constraints, however, were not immoveable objects, but to ignore them could lead to unrest. Ptolemy, like Alexander, changed what he believed to be necessary and those things that did not undermine his authority he let stand. Ptolemy's acquisition of Egypt presented him with a very defensible base, but also for himself and his descendants the complication of gaining legitimacy in two different traditions, the Graeco-Macedonian and the Egyptian. This was not unique to Egypt as all the Successors with the exception of the Macedonian dynasts faced similar problems, and in the case of Ptolemy he was helped considerably by the very nature of Egypt. The same deserts that defended Egypt from the outside world also created a specific territory that was Egypt—a relatively narrow band of land roughly 600 miles in length with the river Nile acting as a highway through the middle. The Nile was and is navigable both north and south. The current flowed north, but prevailing winds were northerly and northwesterly (Khalil 2012: 72). A ship with favorable wind could travel south at twenty-five miles a day (Khalil 2012: 72; Bagnall 1993: 19). This compactness had since the Old Kingdom period encouraged political unity and a centralized bureaucracy. Both were encouraged by the necessity created by the Nile flood. The predictability of the flooding made possible a system whereby during the major flood stage, July into

October, the waters were permitted to inundate the land. The water would remain for forty to sixty days before being drained by canals. Once the fields had dried out, they were sown.[14] This operation needed coordination and cooperation, both of which encouraged the growth of political unity. These conditions made possible far greater centralization of the Egyptian government and economy than was possible elsewhere. However, this was still a pre-industrial society and such centralization had serious limitations. Traditionally, the administration was based on priest-scribes and taxes were levied and collected through the temples. Ptolemy, at the local level, retained the traditional administrative nomes of Egypt with their native officials in overall charge of agricultural production, finance, and record keeping. These individuals were answerable to the *Dioscetes*, the chief financial minister of the ruler. While policy could be made at the highest level, its enforcement was in the hands of local authorities. Indeed, Ptolemy left the basic organizational system in Egypt intact. Nomes, the traditional districts, and villages remained the basic organizational system in Egypt. Royal peasants still tilled the royal estates. Taxes paid in kind were in most cases the truth of the proclaimed Pharaonic ownership of the land of Egypt. A large part of arable land was controlled by the temples (Hobl 2001: 25). Under Ptolemy the son of Lagus, taxes were still mostly paid to the local temple. Beginning with his heir Ptolemy Philadelphus, taxes were paid to tax farmers contracted by the government.[15] Even with tax farming, the routine Egyptian nome organization remained as seen in a contract from 203/202: "Those who obtain the contracts shall present to the [nome's] finance officer and royal secretary sureties ... Those obtaining contracts may subcontract, apprising the financial officer and royal secretary ..." (Lewis 1986: 19–20). Over time the Ptolemaic tax system was so expanded that it has been claimed its impact on the population was such that it was responsible for the late third century's revolts in the south and a general decline in the overall financial health of Egypt. Eric Turner (1984: 134–59) declares that the rule was so oppressive that over time Egypt was bankrupted by this system. One important change that was introduced by the first Ptolemy was the acceleration of the use of coined money which began to replace the traditional trade in kind (von Reden 2007: 300–91; Colburn 2007: 105–9; Lorber 2018: 60–83).

What is debated is the nature of Ptolemy rule with respect to his two different populations, the native Egyptians and the Greeks, Macedonians and others who emigrated to Egypt in large numbers. Were they treated separately, fused, or a little of each? It has been called "strict segregation" (Lewis: 1986: 4; Samuel 1988: 9) and depicted as the king being double-faced, "the one face directed toward his

Macedonian and Greek subjects and the other ... toward the Egyptians" (Koenen 1994: 26–7). Some have seen unification of the two cultures taking place through religion (Wellendorf 2008: 35). This argument entails the identification of the Greek and Egyptians gods, and the emergence of a new religious cult, that of Serapis (see Chapter 7). This was a process that certainly was as old as Herodotus. The Cult of Serapis is seen as an amalgamation of the Egyptian gods Osiris and Apis, and Hades and Dionysus of the Greeks, which became a new cult having adherents in both ethnic groups (Plut. *Mor.* 362B). The evidence, however, that the union of the two cultures was a goal of first Ptolemy or of his descendants is mostly nonexistent (Turner 1972: 167; Lewis 1986: 154–5). The rulers were predominantly imbued with Greek and Macedonian culture. The language at court was Greek. Indeed, that Cleopatra VII was the first Ptolemy to speak Egyptian is telling (Plut. *Ant.* 27. 3–4). Ptolemy the son of Lagus crafted what would be a monarchy where both Greek and Egyptian traditions would be accommodated. However, the court, the capital, even the army until the Battle of Raphia in 217, was almost exclusively Greek and Macedonian. "As far as politics and the higher administration in the broad sense are concerned, the Ptolemies never sought real cooperation with the native Egyptian aristocracy" (Mooren 1981: 299–300). Ptolemy moved the capital of Egypt from Memphis to Alexandria sometime before 311.[16] Moreover, Alexandria became not just the capital of Ptolemaic Egypt but the major center for Greek and Macedonian culture throughout the Hellenistic world, while Memphis remained a parochial center of Egyptian life. Alexandria had all the attributes of a Greek *polis:* the agora, gymnasium, theater, etc. (Str. 17. 10). Alexandria became the center of the Ptolemaic kingdom in a way that no other city in either the Antigonid or Seleucid kingdoms ever did. Strootman (2012: 39–40) correctly describes these other Successor regimes as peripatetic.

Within Egypt, the central government of the Ptolemies and the native Egyptian religious authorities remained in a state of wary coexistence. In the case of Thebes, the capital of Upper Egypt, wariness by the end of the third century became outright hostility and revolt.[17] Such hostility was not derived solely from the activities of the new dynasty. There was always some tension between Lower and Upper Egypt, Memphis and Thebes, and the respective dominant gods of the two cities, Ptah and Amun (Crawford 1980: 8). Ptolemy, however, always presented himself as a patron of these temples. Whatever Alexander the Great had intended by his marriages at Susa,[18] or the banquet at Opis,[19] whether a true "brotherhood of all mankind" (Tarn 1950: 137–48), or—as is much more likely—that Alexander was in need of the administrative and troop resources of the Persians and that this unity was nothing more than in all peoples' obedience to Alexander (Anson 2013: 156–63), this was not a policy much followed after the Conqueror's death. In any case, with respect to Ptolemy, Alexander was speaking of Persians, or more broadly Asians, he was not speaking of Egyptians.

With respect to his Greek constituents, Ptolemy certainly played on his closeness to Alexander in his claims of legitimacy. He had seized Alexander's body which he initially interred in Memphis (Paus. 1. 6. 3), but subsequently moved to Alexandria (Diod, 18. 28. 3). He minted coins with Alexander's portrait (Lorber 2018: 67–77). However, while these ties were important, they were not so important as to have crippled Ptolemy's greatest opponent Antigonus Monophthalmus' rise to prominence. While this Successor's personal connection to Alexander ended in 333 when he was left behind as the satrap of Phrygia (Arr. *Anab.* 1. 29. 3), yet from 315 until 301 he was clearly the most powerful of all the so-called Successors.

Following the Macedonian tradition, these Successors of Alexander relied on a coterie of personal advisors. Certain of the Macedonian institutions inaugurated by Philip II remained, such as the pages and the *somatophylaces*.[20] With respect to the pages, these were the sons of aristocratic Macedonians whose duties were to guard the king while he slept or dined (Curt. 5. 1. 43; 8. 6. 2, 5–6), mount the king on his horse "in the Persian style," attend him on the hunt (Arr. *Anab.* 4. 13. 1; Curt. 5. 1. 42; 8. 6. 4), unobtrusively bring concubines to the king (Curt. 8. 6. 3), and serve with him in combat (Curt. 8. 6. 4). The institution came to serve as a sort of school for future military commanders (Curt. 5. 1. 42; 8. 6. 6). They were also educated with the king's sons (Curt. 8. 6. 4). The king's sons and the other pages received an education under the supervision of a court dignitary in later times usually called the *tropheus* (Polyb. 31. 20. 3; Plut. Ant. 5. 31; *OGIS* 148, 256; 1 *Macc.* 11. 1; Jos. *AJ* 12. 127; Diod. 33. 4. 1). Indeed, Philip's pages were educated along with Alexander at one point by Aristotle (Plut. *Alex.* 7. 3–4). The initial purpose was twofold: to hold the sons as guarantors of their fathers' good behavior, and to forge the loyalty of the next generation of aristocrats to the Macedonian king and his heir. This institution was continued in Ptolemy's court in Alexandria and throughout the time of the Ptolemaic kings (cf. Curt. 8. 6. 6).

The seven *somatophylaces* were the most elite of the guard units protecting the king.[21] The title carries over into the Hellenistic Age where it is supplemented by the additional title of *archisomatophylaces* after 197 (Rowlandson 2007: 34). With Philip and Alexander this was seen as a most privileged position in the Macedonian court. The *somatophylaces* fought alongside the king and, like the pages, also guarded his bedchamber (Arr. *Anab*. 1. 6. 5; 6. 28. 4). After Alexander's death, while the institution was not continued with Philip III or Alexander IV immediately, later after the death of Perdiccas in Egypt and at the settlement at Triparadeisus in 320, the new regent Antipater appointed Autodicus, the brother of one of Alexander's former *somatophylaces* Lysimachus (Heckel 2021: 121), Amyntas, the brother of another of Alexander's former *somatophylax* Peucestas (Heckel 2021: 45–6), Alexander, the son of Polyperchon the later regent (Heckel 2021: 30–1), and Ptolemy, the son of another former *somatophylax* who died at Halicarnasus (Heckel 2021: 428), as Philip III's *somatophylaces* (Arr. *Succ*. 1a. 38). Antipater also apparently did the same for Alexander IV (*IG* 2² 561; cf. Diod. 19. 52. 4).[22] While the title appears in Hellenistic times (Diod. 30. 10. 2, 11. 1; Polyb. 15. 27. 6, 32. 6; Mooren 1975: nos. 0279–0280), in the late third century BC Ptolemaic dynasty, they were the highest-ranking officers in the Ptolemaic army (Fischer-Bovet 2014: 150). There were also in this later period other vestiges of Argead Macedonia. There was a royal cavalry and a foot guard (Fischer-Bovet 2014: 148–53). With the army, as with so much else of the Hellenistic institutional world, the Macedonian legacy of Philip and Alexander dominates.[23]

This is also seen in the Hellenistic institution of *philia* or friendship. This is much like the concept of *hetaireia*, companionship, of Argead Macedonia. While both are alike in the sense that those who are part of these institutions are in many respects the functionaries and courtiers of the king, differences, however, do abound. In the case of Argead Macedonia, the *hetairoi* often possessed power especially at the local level that transcended their standing with the king. There was also an understood camaraderie that diminished the separation between king and these elite individuals. The king was seen as a first among equals. Even during the reign of Philip II with his introduction of pages and *somatophylaces*, there was still the sense that the king was not the boss, but the leader. Alexander did much to put an end to this concept. In the most simple fashion, most of the *hetairoi* were landed Macedonain aristocrats who controlled entire villages of dependents. In short, much of their power came from their local authority. They were responsible in times of war for recruiting from their regions the troops necessary to fill the army and usually leading those contingents that they raised. As Alexander moved ever further into Asia and ever more distant from Macedonia, this source of power diminished. The king was becoming preeminent. The Argead sense of companionship was emphasized by the king and his companions feasting together. Beginning with Alexander, those who had been *hetairoi* were increasingly becoming the king's *philoi*, his friends. Those in the

Hellenistic Age with the title of *philoi*, like the *hetairoi*, served the king as courtiers, agents, military commanders, diplomats, as well as policy advisors.[24] The title *hetairos* disappears entirely in Ptolemaic designations. This disappearance represents the chief difference in the Successor period between the two titles. An *hetairos* could be created by the monarch, but they also existed traditionally by hereditary right, while *philoi* were created by the monarch. Their power existed through the king's authority and, at least in theory, not from their own. The following anecdote exemplifies the difference.

> When a young man, the son of a brave father, but not himself having any reputation for being a good soldier, suggested the propriety of his receiving his father's emoluments, Antigonos said: "My boy, I give money and presents for the excellence of a man, not for the excellence of his father."
>
> Plut. *Mor.* 183D

During the reign of Alexander, our sources often use the two terms interchangeably primarily because their sources were writing during the transitional period and because the two terms with respect to function often were identical. While a king's *philoi* in many respects at the various Hellenistic royal courts were similar in function to the former *hetairoi*, they also served in the capacity of those who in the earlier period were more commonly called *xenoi* and *proxenoi*. This was a practice that began in the Greek Archaic Age (800–479). The aristocratic elites of the various communities established relations based on the institution of *xenia*, guest-friendship. *Proxenia* was a more formal and state-oriented form of this ancient practice. *Xenia* was a system of hospitality establishing reciprocal, often hereditary, relationships between individuals and families in which significant services would be provided as a matter of courtesy.[25] These services could be as little as personal generosity or the providing of political or military support (Mitchell 2002: 13). These individuals remained in their home communities serving in the capacity designated by the terms as *xenoi* and *proxenoi*. There were no permanent foreign embassies in the various states (Perlmann 1958: 187). At a formal level, states established connections with foreign governments through local individuals given the honor of representing a foreign state's interests in a relationship between the two states. This was called *proxenia*.[26] Here a state would contract a relationship with a *proxenos*, a person representing the interests of the contracting state in their own community (Antiph. frg. 67). These were then relationships on the state level. Those who served as *proxenoi* were usually prominent individuals who took active roles in the political life of their own cities. In this traditional relationship the *proxenos* was not a foreign agent working for the foreign party at the expense of his own state. Loyalty to one's own state was paramount. In the words of Plato (*Leg.* 1. 642b):

> Stranger of Athens, you are not, perhaps, aware that our family is, in fact, a "*proxenus*" of your state. It is probably true of all children that, when once they have been told that they are "*proxeni*" of a certain state, they conceive an affection for that state even from infancy, and each of them regards it as a second motherland, next after his own country.
>
> Loeb Classical Library translation

The duty of this individual was to look out for the interests of the contracting party but ideally never to compromise loyalty to the home state. In the case of city-states, it was assemblies that usually established these relationships formally, but in Macedonia the king determined who would be *proxenoi* for the Macedonian state and, therefore, act in fact in the king's interests in the Greek world. Philip had many *xenoi/proxenoi*, those looking after his relations with those outside of Macedonia (Anson 2020: 93–100). With the gift-giving aspect of the reciprocal relationship there was always a problem with respect to actual loyalties. As with the former *hetairoi*, the king was expected to reward his "friends."[27] Demosthenes (Dem. 18. 41, 295; 19. 145, 167, 265, 306) commonly referred to those who could be regarded as Philip's *xenoi* or *proxenoi* (the problem here is, of course, that for all practical diplomatic purposes Philip was the Macedonian state) as traitors, the paid agents of the Macedonian king.[28] An example of *proxenoi* from the time of Ptolemy son of Lagus concerns two Kaunians, Amyntas the son of Euthon and Sosigenes the son of Zopyros, who served as Ptolemaic representatives in Limyra, Lycia:

> In the 36th year of the reign of King Ptolemy, in the month of Dystros, it was resolved by the *polis* of Limyra and those who dwell around it as follows. Since the Kaunians Amyntas son of Euthon and Sosigenes son of Zopyros, having been appointed by King Ptolemy as *oikonomoi*[29] of the land, have been fair, honourable and just towards the *polis* of Limyra, towards those who dwell around it and towards the rest of the Lycians, with good fortune, it is resolved to praise the Kaunians Amyntas son of Euthon and Sosigenes son of Zopyros for their virtue and good will towards them, and that they should be regarded as Benefactors and *Proxenoi* of the *polis* of Limyra, and to give them citizenship, the right to possess land and immunity from all of the taxes levied by the city, and the right of entry and exit in war and peace, unmolested and without formality, and they shall be allowed to participate in the sacred life of the city just as the citizens of Limyra do.
>
> *SEG* 27. 929 (Translation: http://www.attalus.org/docs/seg/s27_929.html)

Similar to the Argead *hetairoi*, *philoi* could be military commanders, such as Cilles, a general defeated by Demetrius soon after the Battle of Gaza (Heckel 2021: 242), Callicrates, the Ptolemaic commander in Cyprus (Heckel 2021: 233), and, indeed, Seleucus, the future ruler of most of Asia, who commanded Ptolemaic fleets in the 310s (Diod. 21. 1. 5). They could also serve at the royal court representing their *polis* and in allied communities representing the king in their home cities (Strootman 2011: 149). A classic example of the former is Callias of the Athenian deme Sphettus. During the Athenian revolt of 287 against the suzerainty of Demetrius Poliorcetes, "Kallias learned the impending danger to the state, and choosing a thousand of the mercenary troops stationed with him on Andros, paying their wages and providing rations of grain, he came at once to the city to help the people, acting in accordance with the good will of King Ptolemaios towards the people" (*SEG* 28. 60. ll. 18–23).[30]

Callias was one of Ptolemy's agents commanding a mercenary force on the island of Andros (*SEG* 28. 60. ll. 20–1), and he returned to Egypt after the completion of this operation. The Macedonian *philos* Pelops served as the commander of the Ptolemaic garrison on Samos and later received Samian citizenship (Rowlandson 2007: 35), making him in effect both the Ptolemaic *proxenus* on Samos and the Samian *proxenos* in the Ptolemaic court. Whereas in Argead Macedonian even commoners, let alone aristocrats, had the "right of petition" to have their grievances heard by the king (Adams 1986: 43–52), in the Ptolemaic court no such right existed.[31] These examples indicate the change from the concept of companions wherein the king is the first among equals to those who are creatures of the court, serving at the king's pleasure.

The king's relationship was one of domination over his "friends." While power dynamics within the coterie of friends influenced and could on occasion even compel a king's actions, their power ultimately came from their standing with the king. This ritualized friendship following the pattern long set by the tradition of *xenia* was accompanied by the king granting landed estates to his "friends" (Herman 1987: 108). These individuals were typically Greeks and Macedonians (Strootman 2014: 126–31). Only one Egyptian is described as a *philos* of the first Ptolemy and that individual was Manetho, the Egyptian priest and author of *Aegyptiaca*, a history of Pharaonic Egypt written in Greek (Habicht 1958: 5–6; Dillery 1999: 109n.54).

Another difference with the Argead model was the nature of the army. Philip II had founded a heavy infantry virtually out of thin air through a combination of military and economic reforms which created on a large scale a middle class that owned its own resources[32] and was skilled in the new innovations in Macedonian warfare.³³ While Ptolemy was well versed in the nature and tactics of the Macedonian military, he was not the ruler of Macedonia and had but very limited access to the recruiting fields used by Philip and Alexander. He basically had three choices in his creation of an army in this age of almost continuous warfare: he could enlist native Egyptians as his major military force—in the past, the Egyptians had been able to maintain their independence against the greatest of western Asian empires;³⁴ he could create an army primarily from those Macedonians and Greek mercenaries in Asia and already in Egypt; or he could use some combination. Ptolemy and the majority of his dynasty created their armies from non-Egyptian sources. Being in Egypt, this dynasty had an advantage. Naphtali Lewis (1986: 8) has called Egypt "the Eldorado on the Nile." The wealth of Egypt was long known and would attract anyone seeking better times.

Alexander had left 4,000 troops in Egypt (Curt. 4. 8. 4). With the 8,000 talents also left there by Alexander, Ptolemy recruited troops feverishly (Diod. 18. 28, 5).³⁵ He had acquired soldiers in his acquisition of Cyrene (Fischer-Bovet 2014: 67–70) and from numerous desertions from Perdiccas' invasion force in 320 (Diod. 18. 33. 2, 36. 1–2). These then became the nucleus of Ptolemy's army and also Ptolemy's first cleruchs (Bagnall 1984: 16–18). Keeping large forces continually under arms was both expensive and dangerous. As an alternative, following the example of Philip and Alexander, Ptolemy established them on lands scattered throughout Egypt.³⁶ Later, during his reign there was a general (*strategos*) placed in charge of those cleruchs in a particular nome. Unlike the agricultural and financial officials of the nome, the general was answerable to the king, not the chief financial official of Egypt, the *dioicetes*. For Bagnall, the military cleruch population of Egypt was created primarily during the reigns of the first Ptolemy and subsequently made up of their descendants. They then became an hereditary class. Most later emigrants came for economic and political opportunities (1984: 18–20). This conclusion has recently been challenged and it appears that immigration from Macedonia and the Greek mainland continued, as did the creation of additional military cleruchs, at least until the end of the third century (Stefanou 2013: 108–31). This would appear clear from the poet Theocritus' fourteenth idyll (ll. 58–68) written likely sometime in the 270s BC:

> If you really mean to emigrate, Ptolemy [II] is the freeman's paymaster, the best there is ... bestower of much upon many, no denier of favors, as befits a king ... Well, if you are ready to clasp the military cloak on you right shoulder, if you have the courage to plant your legs firmly to withstand the attack of a bold warrior, get you quickly to Egypt.
>
> translation: Lewis 1986: 11

Cleruch land, like all land in Egypt, technically belonged to the king. The cleruch could not sell or mortgage, neither technically could the land be inherited. In practice, however, these lands were inherited, but so was the military obligation. Moreover, these individuals were not all of European descent. In 318, Ptolemy in acquiring Coelê Syria, primarily the Beqaa Valley, reportedly captured and brought back to Egypt 100,000 captives "from the land of the Judeans," from whom 30,000 were settled in the country as garrison troops ([Ps-] Aristeas 4, 12–13, 36). Now, this particular source is generally regarded as neither appropriately attributed to the otherwise unknown Aristeas nor is its information to be trusted (Bagnall 2002: 349–52). Certainly, the discussion regarding the Library in Alexandria and the context of the translation of Biblical texts are at odds with generally accepted facts and part of a serious attempt to distort the truth, but does this make the information concerning Ptolemy son of Lagus totally unreliable as well? Likely most would answer in the affirmative. However, the particular reference to Ptolemy may be based in some fashion in reality. Josephus (*Ap.* 186–205) speaks of "a few ten thousands" Jews being removed after Alexander's death to Egypt and Phoenicia. While the enslavement of 100,000 people declared by [Pseudo] Aristeas and their transport to Egypt directly relates to the author's subsequent claim that Ptolemy Philadelphus then freed these individuals, there was early on and continued to be a large Judean presence in Alexandria (*CPJud* 1. passim). Josephus (*Ap.* 2. 33–44) also speaks of a large population of "Judeans" resident in Alexandria in the time of this same Ptolemy. [Pseudo] Aristeas (4. 36) further states that Ptolemy attached many of these individuals to his respective army units. It is declared they joined many others who had settled in Egypt previously. According to Josephus' *Against Apion* (2. 33) a settlement of Jews had been established near Alexandria by Alexander himself.[37] Certainly, in [Pseudo] Aristeas either the numbers are exaggerated, since just the logistics of moving 100,000 cooperative people would be difficult and those facing slavery would present seemingly insurmountable problems, or the status of the individuals as slaves is false, or likely the truth includes a bit of both.[38] Josephus (*Ap.* 2. 44) does appear to confirm that Ptolemy the son of Lagus had placed large numbers of Jews as garrison troops in Cyrene and in the cities of Libya. Many of these might be listed as mercenaries in the description of Ptolemy's forces at the battle before Gaza. Ptolemy is reported to have had 18,000 infantry, Macedonians, mercenaries and Egyptians (Diod. 19. 80. 4). Cleruchs, both military and otherwise, made up a privileged class in Ptolemy's Egypt with their own language, culture, and social structure.

While Ptolemy followed in the footsteps of Philip and Alexander in many ways, in one he clearly diverged. Both Philip and Alexander were the founders of a great many cities, with both of them using urban foundations as ways of securing their hold on the lands where the cities were founded.[39] Unlike his fellow Successor Seleucus, Ptolemy did not found many cities on the Greek model. Indeed, only one in Egypt is noted, Ptolemais Hermiou, which after its creation became the capital of Upper Egypt, replacing Thebes, much as Alexandria replaced Memphis in the north. In addition to being the administrative center for Upper Egypt, it was for administrative structures and settlement for Greek immigrants placed in this region. There were then in Egypt other cities that were on the design of the Greek *polis*: Heracles-Thonis, Naucratis, and Canopus. These communities also enjoyed a special status within the Ptolemaic kingdom. With respect to the three most important Greek cities of the Ptolemaic dynasty, Naucratis was of long standing, having been founded in the sixth century, while Alexandria and Ptolemais Hermiou had their own legal status as *poleis* with their own assemblies and councils (Höblb 2001: 26–7; O'Neil 2006: 25). Most of those who immigrated to Egypt, however, found themselves living in Egyptian villages with only the nome capitals providing some of the benefits associated with *polis* living (Grabowski 2013: 58). Of course, the nature of the Greek *polis* changed with Philip and Alexander from the freewheeling independence that had characterized, at least philosophically, the Classical Age, to something more akin to what the Greek cities of western Asia had been experiencing for centuries. These had long been and continued in the Hellenistic Age to have their independence circumscribed by the overriding authority of kings. Yet, much autonomy outside of foreign affairs remained and the Hellenistic kings styled themselves as the benefactors and protectors of these communities. James O'Neil (2000) concludes that Hellenistic kings interfered in the affairs of Greek cities mostly to mediate. Indeed, these empires were in many ways, as described by Rolf Strootman (2011: 144), "hegemonic empires." In the cities, there was a reciprocal arrangement whereby the community supplied the king with revenue and the king provided the city with protection. The central governments collected revenue in the form of tribute or taxes while exercising minimal centralized administrative control. In fact, most foundations not only exercised a degree of autonomy but their governments were at least moderate democracies. This was certainly the case with the Seleucid Empire, but much less so with respect to Ptolemaic Egypt with only a few *polis*-style cities and a long-standing tradition of centralized administration with respect to agriculture. Egypt relied not on cities, but nomes and temples. By the standards of the time,

Egypt would be seen as exercising considerable supervisory authority in the collection of tribute and tax.

Hellenistic cities followed a pattern created in Macedonia by Philip II. In 357, when Philip captured Amphipolis, the city maintained many of its institutions (cf. *GHI* 49) and its assembly was able to pass decrees (cf. *GHI* 49. ll, 1–15).[40] Inscriptional evidence shows that the practice continued throughout the cities in Macedonia. An inscription from the last quarter of the fourth century from the Macedonian religious center of Dion lists magistrates, selected committees, and the "voting and publishing of decrees, erecting statues, and [the] responsible for the organization of festivals and games" (Hatzopoulos 1996A: 129; 1996B: 73–4). While coming from the time of Alexander the Great, an inscription accepted as a letter from Alexander to the Chians may show how such arrangements were made by Philip, by Alexander, and by the Conqueror's successors. In this surviving inscription, a Chian by the name of Alcimachus is praised to the people of Chios and—more importantly for the current discussion—he is called Alexander's "*philos*" (*GHI* 84 B. l. 13; Piejko 1985: 242 l. 13):

> Inasmuch as this (man) Alcimachus protested that he had departed led by force, and he became my friend and was well disposed toward your folk, for he made continuous efforts to restore the exiles and was instrumental in the freeing of your city from the oligarchy which had previously been set up among you, and since both in words and in deeds he acted in your interests, I believe it would be fair in return for all he has done on behalf of the people, whether by himself or on all those occasions when he cooperated with me in matters concerning you, to rescind the things voted against his father, to restore to him as the first among those who are returning what the city took away, and to treat him and his friends with (all) honor and trust, as a man who has always been devoted to the city. Such action on your part would please me, and if you should require anything of me I would be even more disposed to succor you.
>
> translation, Piejko 1985: 243

There was usually, however, someone in the city, sometimes an official called an *epistates*, who acted as a go-between for the city and the king (Sherwin-White and Kuhrt 1993: 165–6).[41] These officials likely date from the time of Philip II (Hatzopoulos 1996A: 388–9; Hammond and Walbank 1988: 476) and are based on a long-standing practice of *xenia* and *proxenia*, as described earlier. It was the tradition of *proxenia* that evolved into the position of *epistates*.[42] In the Hellenistic Age, the *epistates* was not just an official, but, as was the case with Philip II, also the *philoxenos*, the foreign friend of the king.

The basic autonomy of the city may, indeed, have been part of the reason for the lack of further *polis* creation in Egypt. The land was already highly organized politically and economically under the authority of whoever oversaw the land in its entirety, whether that be a satrap, a king, or a pharaoh (Grabowski 2013: 58). While the two *poleis* of Alexandria and Ptolemais Hermiou were necessary for the general administration of Egypt, the local authorities of temples and villages carried on the day-to-day activities. The Ptolemies did encourage the settlement of Greeks and others in Egypt, but typically "outside the framework of urban settlement" (Mueller 2006: 3; Grabowski 2013: 58). This followed a pattern practiced by Philip II. While he did found and refound cities, he also gave out land to individuals for military service without the creation of an urban center. When Methone was captured and razed to the ground and later Olynthus and the other thirty-two Greek cities in Chalcidice captured by Philip were leveled and their citizens sold as slaves, their land was distributed viritane to Macedonian settlers (Diod. 16. 34. 5; Dem. 4. 35; Dem. 9. 26; Justin 7 .6. 14–16). Much of the earliest settlement of foreign elements in Egypt was done in this fashion. This was especially the case in the area known as the Fayum, the Arsinoite Nome, where a major reclamation project was begun by the first Ptolemy and, while the population here as elsewhere was predominantly Egyptian, much of the reclaimed land was given to those who were enrolled in the army.

As noted, the Ptolemies established only one *polis* in Egypt which was a real city as understood by the Greeks; this was Ptolemais Hermiou, founded by the dynasty's creator. As noted, apart from Ptolemais Hermiou, there existed only two *poleis* of significance: Alexandria and Naucratis. Most of the settlement of Egypt, whether foreign or native, was organized in villages all along the Nile, and only the main towns of the districts, the nomes, while not formally *poleis*, had many of the amenities similar to what would be found in the cities of the Greek world, but just not with the local autonomy associated with Greek *poleis*. Much of the settlement distributed throughout the Nile river valley associated the newcomers with existing Egyptian communities. The settlements that come to the fore, however, are those whose purpose was to solve one of the urgent problems which the Ptolemies, similarly to the Seleucids, had to face: the creation of their own soldier recruitment bases.

This was the case with respect to Ptolemy's foundations. The basic local governments of Alexandria (Fraser 1972: I. 93–115) and Ptolemais Hermiou (Bowman and Rathbone 1992: 108–9) were broadly democratic with councils and assemblies. Cyrene, while not part of Egypt itself, was part of the Ptolemaic possessions down to Ptolemy Apion, whose father, the Egyptian pharaoh Ptolemy

VIII, had gifted the city to him, and at the former's death by will it became a Roman possession in 96 BC (Tac. *Ann.* 14. 18; cf. *SEG* 9.7). It was initially given a constitution by Ptolemy son of Lagus. This was not part of Egypt proper and it was an existing Greek city which had recently undergone a civil war, but it may display some aspects of Ptolemaic rule with respect to "Greek" cities.

> Shall be citizens [men born from [a Cyrenaean father] and a Cyrenaean mother, and [those born from] the Libyan women between Catabarthmos and Authamalax (the boundaries of the state of Cyrenaica) and those born from [settlers] from the cities beyond Thinis (unknown), whom the Cyrenaeans set as colonists [and those] Ptolemy designates, and those admitted by the body of citizens, in conformity with the following laws. The body of citizens shall consist of the Ten Thousand. The members shall be the exiles who fled to Egypt, [whom] Ptolemy shall designate, and any whose property together with that of his wife is estimated at twenty Alexander minas (roughly a third of a talent) ... (there follows some qualifications on this calculation) and not below the age of thirty ... The Council shall consist of 500 men appointed by lot and not below the age of fifty; they shall serve as councillors for two years and in the third year they shall eliminate by lot half of their number, then they shall let two years elapse. If the number is insufficient, they shall select by lot the others from those over forty years of age. There shall be 101 Elders appointed by Ptolemy. In case of an Elder who dies or resigns, the Ten Thousand shall appoint another man to make up the 101 from those not below the age of fifty ... (there follows some additional restrictions) Ptolemy shall be general for life. Besides him five generals shall be appointed from those who have not yet held the office of general and are not below the age of fifty; if a war breaks out, (there follows regulations on the appointments giving this responsibility to the Ten Thousand) ...
>
> *SEG* 9. 1; translation: Austin 1981: 443–5[43]

Here the citizen body is defined largely by property and age, but at least here the city's independence seems clear and Ptolemy's ability to interfere circumscribed. Moreover, it would appear that Ptolemy while restricting the size of the citizen body was actually broadening it from what had existed before (cf. Diod. 18. 21. 6–7). Unmentioned is the presence of the garrison placed in the city (cf. Diod. 19. 79. 1).

Alan Lloyd (2002: 117–34) has made a strong case that with respect to the vast majority of Egypt and Egyptians, not much changed outside of the court in Alexandria and that Egypt remained much as it had been for millennia. "Members of the [Egyptian] elite may not have had such ready access to the highest civil and military functions in Alexandria itself, and many would have been able to find ample consolation playing the local pasha in ancient provincial cities where their families had been lording it for generations" (Lloyd 2002: 131). Beginning with the first Ptolemy, these individuals came under the authority of "generals" of Greek and Macedonian origin. These generals were initially created as a way to organize those military cleruchs living in the nomes.

One of the advantages Ptolemy found in Egypt was that by Egyptian tradition the king, the pharaoh, had responsibilities to the land, to the water, and to his people (Thompson 2012: 136–7). He was to maintain Ma'at, the cosmic order. "In this role, the king acts as a mediator to transmit the cosmic to the human world" (Howe 2018: 158–9). He was in theory for all intents and purposes "the fountainhead of all authority" (Frankfort 1948: 31). With respect to his responsibilities to the people, benevolence was a required characteristic of the ruler. In practice, the Hellenistic king's relationship with the governed, however, changed depending on the group he was in fact governing. Hellenistic satraps, kings, etc. dealt with native populations and Greeks and Macedonians were seen typically as separate categories. Greeks and Macedonians were the dominant social group and exercised control over the administration and the army. They were settled throughout Egypt and dominated the nome capitals. The Egyptians, who made up the bulk of the population, might find their way into the lower rungs of the civil service, but were principally peasant cultivators. This relationship in the case of Egypt was, according to Michael Rostovtzeff (1941: 1. 271),[44] one of exploitation, with the Ptolemies owning the land and compelling the people to work it. Others proclaim that the king may have been the "director," but there was no centralized planning, "local elites and a growing bureaucracy" oversaw the system (Manning 2010: 44). This is to say that the basic pattern of irrigation, growing, planting, harvesting, and storing of crops was at it had been for much of the duration of Egyptian history. Central planning in a pre-industrial society often has little to do with what takes place at the local level. During the regime in Egypt of Cleomenes, Ptolemy's predecessor, the nomarchs were in charge of the collection and sale of grain and the payment of taxes (Arist. *Oen.* 2. 1352A). One problem in attempting to understand the policies of the first Ptolemy is that so little information remains that many conclusions are based on later bits of information. Undoubtedly Ptolemy the son of Lagus was a far different individual as man and ruler than many of his successors over time. In any case, this was not a laissez-faire economy. The satrap, king, pharaoh could interfere at any time, but such interferences in basic patterns of life were seldom.

However, Ptolemy did change the fiscal system, established new settlements, and moved existing populations. All in all this was not that much different from the pattern found in Macedonia during the reign of Philip II or Alexander the Great. It was the nature of autocracy in a pre-industrial world. While the ruler had the final word on domestic and foreign policy, this would still have to be carried out through established institutions. While there is evidence of dissatisfaction in the Egyptian population with Ptolemaic control of Egypt, it did not manifest itself in any serious fashion until the latter half of the third century when there were revolts. One of the questions that then arises is why, if there was this general dissatisfaction, the revolts do not occur much earlier? After all, the Egyptians rose successfully and unsuccessfully again and again against foreign rule during periods when Assyrians and Persians were ostensibly in control. One partial answer is that the Ptolemies were not ruling Egypt from far away through surrogates; they were ever present except for the occasional foray elsewhere, but their homeland was Egypt. The other Successors were continually attempting to increase their holdings of territory; their kingdoms were agglomerations of lands. Egypt, thanks to the river Nile, was a self-contained, fairly homogenized society "ripe for centralized political control."[45] Ptolemy, like Alexander before him, was regarded favorably due in large part to the Egyptian perception of their years under Persian rule (Hdt. 3. 29. 1–3, 37. 1–3, 64. 3; *Suda* s.v. "Apis"; Diod. 10. 14. 2–3; 16. 51. 2; Ael. VH 4. 8. 6). Curtius (4. 7. 5) relates that Alexander respected Egyptian traditions and Arrian (*Anab.* 3. 1. 4) reports that he sacrificed to Egyptians gods. Whether accurate or not, the perception of Persian rule was negative in the extreme. Alexander himself did not have to fight his way into Egypt, he was welcomed as a liberator (Arr. *Anab.* 3. 1. 2; Curt. 4. 7. 2; Diod. 17. 49. 2). Ptolemy also to a certain degree was aided in his acceptance by the Egyptians because of complaints against his Greek predecessor in Egypt, Cleomenes (Arr. *Anab.* 7. 23. 6, 8).[46] Aristotle (*Oen.* 2. 1352A 16-B 25) lists a number of Cleomenes' extortion plans. He recounts that during a famine, Cleomenes first prohibited the export of grain, then permitted it but demanded much higher duties. When a companion was killed by a crocodile, Cleomenes threatened to retaliate against the species; those priests who worshipped the creature collected all the gold they could find and bought him off. Moreover, the Ptolemies owed much of their success within Egypt to Alexander the Great's foresight. In his empire, he not only placed garrisons in key locations, but he created cities to be inhabited by Greeks and Macedonians. His city creation in Egypt would become Egypt's capital, a major port in the eastern Mediterranean, and a Greek and Macedonian stronghold virtually immune to those physical features of Egypt that made Egypt's previous revolts not only possible but so often successful. Alexandria was on the western side of the Nile with its port giving easy access to the important cities on that bank of the Nile, while at the same time defending Egypt from attacks from Libya.[47] While the actual development of Alexandria in Egypt was the work of Ptolemy and his descendants, it was Alexander who saw the site's potential and began the process of its creation (Arr. *Anab.* 3. 1. 5; Str. 17. 1. 6–7). Ptolemy, again following the example of Alexander, was also attuned to the traditional elites of Egypt and maintained their status under his regime. With both Alexander and Ptolemy, the powerful priesthoods were given special deference.

Traditionally Egypt was an autocracy ruled by a living god, the pharaoh, the incarnation of the god Horus, and the champion of cosmic order and the preventor of chaos. Consequently, with respect to the native Egyptians and their ruler, this meant the Macedonian needed to assume the powers if not the position of pharaoh. There is in general a reluctance in current scholarship to accept that foreigners could ever become true pharaohs and enjoy the kind of obedience and reverence traditionally associated with that office (Burstein 1991: 139–45; Collins 2009: 179–86). The argument often centers on the very elaborate coronation ceremony and that Alexander was not in Egypt long enough to have accomplished all of its intricacies. It appears clear, however, that traditionally accession to the throne was immediate but that the full ritual process of coronation could take up to a year. The first year itself was in large part a ceremonial means of establishing full legitimacy (Barta 1980: 49–51). There was a division between being accepted by the gods as the ruler of Egypt and the cosmic confirmation by the gods. Alexander apparently did do part of the official ceremony. He did travel to Memphis, not once but twice, and spent six months in Egypt, much of it there in Memphis. In Memphis, he sacrificed to Apis (Arr. *Anab.* 3. 1. 4, 4. 5–5. 1) and may have done a couple of other parts of the official ceremony as well. He may have walked around the walls of Memphis and attended the feast of the appearance of the king, but Alexander likely did not remain in Egypt long enough to accomplish all that was seemingly required. Alexander then received an abbreviated version of the official coronation rites (Bosworth 1988: 70–1; Burstein 1991; Stewart 1993: 124),[48] yet he is pictorially associated with all the powers and titles of a pharaoh (Bosch-Puche 2013: 131–54). Moreover, he received the five names (Horus, Nebty, Golden Horus, Throne, Personal) associated with being the pharaoh (Bosch-Puche 2013: 132–54; see Chapter 7) and announced at the coronation of the new pharaoh (von Beckerath 1999: 232–3).. Bernadette Menu (1998: 262) has argued that the priests persuaded Alexander to have himself formally crowned for his power to be made legitimate. The theoretical role of the pharaoh as the key to cosmic order made it essential to the priests that there be a pharaoh, for their existence was tied to the ruler's theological importance. They wanted Alexander to be pharaoh as much as Alexander wanted their support. In terms of ritual formality, Alexander is depicted in ritual scenes in the temples in traditional Egyptian pharaonic regalia performing the rituals guaranteeing the continuing existence of Egypt. Such depictions are found throughout Egyptian history, whether the "pharaoh" was native-born or foreign. Visual evidence such as this would be comforting for most Egyptians. To a degree, as long as there was a ruler who did not act contrary to what was expected, the vast majority of the Egyptian population, who were agricultural workers with a serf-like status, would be content. The ruler was essential for the cosmic order and as long as that individual did nothing to upset that order, the ruler was acceptable and indeed required. If the rhythm of the Nile flood and the sun rising in the sky continued, etc., the cosmic order was in place and the pharoah was doing his job. With respect to the priests, they were the ones responsible for the imagery. It was simply in the interest of both parties, the Macedonians and these elite Egyptians, to forge such an alliance.[49] This was clear to Alexander and to Ptolemy as well. Stanley Burstein, while rejecting the idea of a formal coronation for Alexander the Great, acknowledges that Alexander was accepted as pharaoh by the Egyptian priesthood (1991: 140–1). Even with respect to the Ptolemies there are only two Ptolemaic coronations that are clearly documented. Ptolemy V's coronation is noted on the Rosetta Stone (*OGIS* 90, ll. 46–7) and Diodorus (33. 13) records Ptolemy VIII being crowned according to "the traditional manner."

While it is debated about Alexander the Great's status in Egypt, Ptolemy presents a far more complicated situation. For almost two decades he was officially the satrap of Egypt; only in 304 did he proclaim himself king.[50] As Giles Gorre (2018: 129) has commented, "for almost twenty years, nobody in Egypt knew exactly how to address the new leader of the country." Moreover, while our literary sources speak of a dual monarchy of Philip III and Alexander IV, contemporary Egyptian and Babylonian documents appear to acknowledge only one king at a time, with Alexander IV appearing as such only after the death of Philip III.[51] For example, the Dra Abu el-Naga Papyrus (29-86-508) dates 314 as the third year of the reign of Alexander IV.[52] This complication can be seen in the so-called Satrap Stele, dated November 311. Ptolemy is called "the great prince,"[53] "the great ruler of Egypt," and "satrap."[54] The king recognized here, however, is Alexander IV, who is called "beloved of the gods," "ruler of the entire land," "King of Upper and Lower Egypt," "Son of Ra." Indeed, he is associated with all the royal nomenclature of a pharaoh (Ockinga 2018: 167). It is very clear that, while receiving these titles, Alexander IV was never officially enthroned in Egypt. In fact, in this document, he is said to be living in Asia. These titles given the king then imply a full ritual coronation, but in this case are simply acknowledging the same fiction regarding the governance of Alexander's legacy that the Diadochs themselves paid lip service to. In official documents, Alexander the Great, like his son, was given the full title of the Egyptian king which consisted of five names, the Horus, Nebty/Two Ladies,[55] Golden Horus, King of Upper and Lower Egypt (throne name), and Son of Ra (personal) names. These ritual names come to be associated also with Ptolemy after his proclaiming himself king (von Beckerath 1999: 234–5). Ptolemy's pharaonic names translate as "Great of strength and brave king" (Horus name), "Who has seized with power, the ruler Sile"[56] (Nebty name), "Chosen by Ra and beloved of Amun" (throne name), and "Ptolemy, Son of Ra" (personal). So what is the importance of completing all of the seeming coronation requirements? Not only did Philip III receive pictographic recognition of his rule replete with the pharaonic titles, but Alexander IV, three years old during his brief stay in Egypt during Perdiccas' unsuccessful invasion, after the death of Philip III, also receives these same recognitions as pharaoh (von Beckerath 1999: 232–3). It points to a great positive for Ptolemy in his securing control of Egypt. Egypt was used to being ruled by god-kings. The priests in particular were seeking a way to accommodate the new reality. It is not so much that Ptolemy was seeking to be pharaoh as the role was thrust upon him.

By 311 and the publication of the Satrap Stele, the dual monarchy was now just Alexander's son. Philip III was killed in 317. What is clear, however, is that the wielder of power in Egypt is Ptolemy. It is Ptolemy who brought the "sacred images of the gods which were found in Asia, together with all the ritual implements and all the sacred scrolls ... so he restored them to their proper places" and it was "Ptolemy who defeated the Syrians." Even though Ptolemy is not the king, he possesses many of the attributes of such an individual (Schäfer 2011: 193; Ockinga 2018: 168–83, 191). He is a

> youthful man, strong in his two arms, effective in plans, with mighty armies, stout hearted, firm footed, who attacks the powerful without turning back, who strikes the face of his opponents when they fight, with precise hand, who grasps to himself the bow without shooting astray, who fights with his sword in the midst of battle, with none who can stand in his vicinity, a champion whose arms are not repulsed, with no reversal of what issues from his mouth, who has no equal in the Two Lands or the foreign countries.
>
> Satrap Stele (Ritner 2003: 393)

While not the *de jure* king, who the document proclaims is living in Asia, Ptolemy was the *de facto* one (Ockinga 2018: 194). It is he who protects and restores. After his adoption of the royal title in 304,[57] he is "Great of strength and a brave king" and "Chosen by Ra and beloved of Amun" (von Beckerath 1999: 234–5).

Ptolemy maintained good relations with the priests of Egypt (Müller 2009: 172–5, 204; Thompson 2012: 100, 106–8). While this has been seen as a general truism, Gilles Gorre (2018: 128–54) has challenged this view, stating that the close relationship began with Ptolemy II and not with his father. Gorre emphasizes the role of the priests themselves in attempting to maintain their establishments and their elite status in the absence of any real involvement by the new power brokers, the Macedonians. Against his argument, then, whether Ptolemy I or Ptolemy II, the priests and the ruler have the same need of one another, and the Satrap Stele along with the pharaonic depictions and other inscriptions and papyri would appear to demonstrate the close connection between the first Ptolemy and the priests. Given this basic need one for the other, for an intelligent new ruler and a foreigner this would be an ideal situation, benign neglect forcing the priests to go out of their way to please the man in charge. However, while sparse, the evidence shows that Ptolemy the son of Lagus did engage in a meaningful way with Egyptian authorities on various occasions. There is the episode noted in the Satrap Stele of his restoring the religious objects to the temple and additionally giving back to the priest of the native gods Pe and Dep the lands that had been confiscated by the Persians. These lands included "all its towns, all its villages, all its inhabitants, all its acreage, all its water, all its cattle, all its flocks, all its herds and everything that derives from it and which has been part of it previously." It was traditional belief that the well-being of Egypt was tied to the well-being of the temples (Crawford 1980: 7–9, 15). Ptolemy is also recorded signing a decree forbidding the alienation of sacred property (*SB* 16. 12519; Rigsby 1988: 273–4). When the sacred Apis bull, the incarnation of the premier god of Memphis died of old age, its funeral was underwritten by Ptolemy (Diod. 1. 84. 8). This would be in obvious contrast to the Egyptian belief concerning the Persian king Cambyses' murder of an Apis bull (Hdt. 3. 29. 1–3; Plut. *Mor.* 368F) and the many reported outrages of Artaxerxes Ochus (Diod. 16. 51. 2; Ael. *VH* 4. 8. 6; Plut. *Mor.* 355C, 363C).[58]

Ptolemy in a very real sense stood astride two peoples and two civilizations. Even in the case of law there were two sets, one for native Egyptians and one for the others (van der Spek 2009: 103). In most instances he became king to the Greeks and Macedonians and in whatever fashion pharaoh to the Egyptians.

Pierre Briant has remarked with respect to Alexander the Great that "[he] was able to create the conditions for a balance between his own ambition and the [indigenous] nobility's desire not to perish in the turmoil" (Briant 2002: 870). In general, Alexander was adept at accommodating the previous elites by maintaining their economic and political status (Briant 2002: 842–4, 1046–60). This could just as easily have been said about Ptolemy in Egypt. He had secured Egypt from external threat and his actions further saved her from internal ones as well.[59]

7

Ptolemy and Religion

For Ptolemy the son of Lagus, religion was a tool to be used to increase his personal and his family's authority. Here as elsewhere he used religion differently depending on the population he was hoping to influence. While eventually he became a god in Egypt, with the Macedonians and Greeks he never proclaimed his divinity. For Ptolemy, especially early on, such a general claim might have incensed his Macedonian and Greek veterans given Alexander the Great's experience with respect to such a status.[1] His divinity was only proclaimed to the Egyptian Hellenic community by his son and successor, Ptolemy II Philadelphus, after the father's death. While the first Ptolemy did not seek in any fashion to be seen as divine in the context of Hellenic Egypt, it was outside of Egypt on one occasion at least thrust upon him. The Rhodians had been most grateful for his assistance in resisting the son of Antigonus, Demetrius' famous siege (Paus. 1. 8. 6; Diod. 20. 100. 3). They awarded him the title of Soter, Savior, which he did accept and indeed incorporated it into his standard nomenclature. The Rhodians had also sent a delegation to Siwah which approved their request to worship Ptolemy as a god. These honors were commonly awarded to those powerful Diadochs who brought assistance to cities in their times of need. Ptolemy accepted the honors, but other than the title of Soter, he did not transform his relationship with the Egyptian Hellenic community. In native Egyptian ceremony and occasionally elsewhere among the Greek communities, especially in the Aegean islands, he might receive the honors due a god, but not among the non-native inhabitants of Egypt.

With respect to this rush among many Greek communities to honor their benefactors as living divinities, the most outrageous of these "honors" were those awarded by the Athenians to Demetrius and Antigonus in 307 (Plut. *Demetr.* 10. 3–4). The son had "liberated" the Athenians from the control of Cassander. The father and son were hailed as "Savior-gods," along with a dedicated priesthood and altar. Additionally, the spot where Demetrius landed in Athens was consecrated and an altar was erected, officially "the Altar of

Demetrius Alighter." Other extravagant honors included gold statues of both Antigonus and Demetrius in a chariot placed near the statues of the supposed earlier liberators of Athens, Harmodius and Aristogeiton,[2] gold crowns, having two new tribes in their names added to the ten Cleisthenic tribes, annual games in the "Saviors'" honor, having their names along with those of the gods woven into the ceremonial garment fashioned before the Panathenaic festival and draped on the statue of the goddess Athena (Diod. 20. 46. 2; Plut. *Demetr.* 10. 3–7). When Demetrius visited the city subsequently, as lodging he was provided the rear chamber of the great Temple of Athena, the Parthenon. Demetrius now often referred to the goddess Athena as his sister. Moreover, he shared the Parthenon with at least four professional ladies: Lamia, often called "the love of his life" (Wheatley and Dunn 2020: 163–8), Chrysis, Demo, and Anticyra (Plut. *Demetr.* 23. 3–24. 1, 25. 9; Demochares *BNJ* 75 F-1). Two of Demetrius' mistresses, the aforementioned Lamia and a new lady, Leaina, were granted religious sanctuaries by the Athenians, and certain of his companions, altars and libations (Athen. 6. 253A).

Ptolemy's position in Egypt was complicated. While Egypt would appear to give its possessor an advantage in that the ruler was in some capacity believed to be divine, Ptolemy for almost two decades was the agent, the satrap, of the accepted pharaoh, at first Philip III, Alexander's half-brother, and subsequently Alexander IV, Alexander's son. It was only after the end of the Argead dynasty and Ptolemy's proclamation of himself as king that he then became for the Egyptians pharaoh in his own right, eventually receiving four of the official pharaonic names associated with the office. These were routinely announced at the coronation of the new pharaoh (von Beckerath 1999: 232–3). Like Alexander before him, Ptolemy was seen to worship the Egyptian gods and to bestow his patronage upon their temples. He paid special attention to Apis, the sacred bull god, as had Alexander the Great (Arr. *Anab.* 3. 1. 3–4), and later his son and heir, Ptolemy Philadelphus provided one hundred talents of myrrh for the burial of one of the sacred bulls (*PSI* 4. 328). The sacred bull was worshipped and was a central part of the pharaonic coronation rites. "Some explain the origin of the honor accorded this bull in this way, saying that at the death of Osiris [died but resurrected god of the dead] his soul passed into this animal, and therefore up to this day has always passed into its successors at the times of the manifestation of Osiris" (Diod. 1. 85. 4; cf. Plut. *Mor.* 359B, 362D),[3] the animate image of Osiris (Plut. *Mor.* 43. 368B). Apis was also seen as the embodiment of Ptah (Pfeiffer 2008: 389), the god of creation. In addition to participating in the worship of Egyptian deities and in particular with respect to Apis, Alexander also wished to make certain that Egyptian religious institutions and practices were protected after his departure in the so-called Saqqara Papyrus,[4] issued by order of a certain Peucestas, most likely one of Alexander the Great's appointed generals, Peucestas the son of Macartatus, who was left in charge of the army in Egypt after Alexander's departure (Arr. *Anab*. 3. 5. 5; Heckel 2021: 372). The papyrus states: "By order of the C[ommander]-in-C[hief], Peucestas. Out of bounds to troops. Ritual area."[5] It is very likely that the shrine being here protected was the burial chamber of the Apis bulls (Turner 1974: 241; Wojciechowska 2016: 85). Ptolemy continued those policies begun by Alexander. When the bull died, Ptolemy lent those in charge fifty talents of silver to aid in the financing of what was a very elaborate and expensive burial ceremony (Diod. 1. 84. 8).

In the Egyptian context Ptolemy followed their religious practices, although he left most of the day-to-day operations of Egyptian religious institutions in the hands of the priests. This would explain one of the controversies involving the maintenance and building of temples. What was the nature of Ptolemaic involvement? Did Ptolemy play an active role or was most of the planning and financing in the hands of the priests? The evidence would suggest that in this regard Ptolemy was helpful, but in most respects remained outside active participation except in those ceremonies and activities expected of the ruler (Caneva 2018: 90). The Satrap Stele provides insights into the Ptolemaic policy. While taking control of Coelê Syria and Phoenicia, he obtained sacred statues, ritual instruments, and sacred scrolls which he returned to the appropriate priests (ll. 16–17). He also returned to the possession of the priests of Pe and Dep lands that had been taken from them by the Persians (ll. 62–70). Nowhere in this document is Ptolemy telling the priests what they are to do with his benefactions. It is to be noted that the fifty talents that were given to help pay for the burial of the Apis bull were not a donation but a loan. In other words, Ptolemy's policy was a form of benign participation. He performed his ritual duties as pharaoh as seen again in the Stele, where it is noted that he was celebrating a holiday connected with the gods of Upper and Lower Egypt. He performed his functionary activities, gave the occasional donation, especially when he could be seen as righting a wrong inflicted by the previous Persian administration,[6] but in the main stayed out of direct interference in temple affairs. The best evidence of Ptolemy's lack of interest in playing an active role in the traditional religious institutions of Egypt is his abandonment of Memphis for the more cosmopolitan and Hellenized city of Alexandria. As long as the revenues continued to flow, the local affairs of Egypt could be conducted by the long-standing traditions of Egypt (Trigger 2003: 208).

Ptolemy's position with the Greeks was more complicated. He certainly had the example of Alexander before him if he had wished to embark on that course. Alexander had used his new position in Egypt as the son of Amun to establish himself in the Greek and Macedonian setting as the son of Zeus. His entire purpose in traveling to the Oracle at Siwah was to accomplish this goal (Anson 2003: 117–30; 2013: 97–109). Later, he was to claim that he was not just the descendant of the king of the gods, but a god in his own right (Bosworth 1988B: 288–9; Anson 2013: 114–20). Of course, even before the proclamation made by the priest at Siwah he was already seen as descended from Zeus, for his Argead ancestry made him the descendant of Heracles who was himself a son of Zeus. Alexander in Egypt simply wished the connection to Zeus be closer, much closer. Ptolemy could have followed the course certainly after the end of the Argead dynasty and his becoming the king/pharaoh of Egypt and declared his divinity. That he did not, and in fact his divinity was proclaimed only after his death, suggests that his memory of the issues that similar actions by Alexander raised between that commander and his army influenced his decision. Moreover, unlike Ptolemy, Alexander did not have competition for the services of his Macedonian veterans. He was the only show in town. Certainly, it can be argued that times have changed. After all, Alexander got push-back from the Athenians. In the year prior to Alexander's death, the Athenian orator Demades had proposed enrolling Alexander as one of the "Twelve Gods." For his efforts, he was heavily fined (Athen. 6. 251B; Ael. *VH* 5. 12). When this response is compared with the Athenian actions with respect to Demetrius, it appears clear that times had changed significantly. As Peter Green (1990: 402) observes, "Sacrifices, sacred enclosures, tombs, statues, prostration (*proskynesis*), hymns, altars, and other such divine appanages are all, as Aristotle [*Rhet.* 1361a34–6] specifically states, simply marks of honor, the gesture itself, not its recipient (whether god or man), is the important thing, that is, mortals were simply sharing 'some of the gods' divine prerogatives.'" The practicality of these in seen in a hymn written to honor Demetrius:

> The greatest of the gods and those dearest to our city are here, for the occasion brought both Demeter and Demetrios to this place. She comes to celebrate the holy mysteries of the Maiden (i.e., Persephone), and he is joyful in his presence here, as is proper for a god, and is handsome and laughing. His appearance is something majestic, with his friends all around him, and he himself in their midst, and his friends are like the stars, while he is like the sun. Hail son of most powerful Poseidon and Aphrodite! The other gods are either far away or they do not have ears or they do not exist or they do not pay any attention to us at all, but

we see that you are present, not made of wood or stone, but here in reality. And so we pray to you.

BNJ 76 F-13; translation Frances Pownall

The power of individuals like Demetrius, Antigonus, Ptolemy, etc. to alter outcomes made them practical gods. However, these proclamations of divinity are not put forth by the Diadochs themselves, but rather initiated by the various cities. They would also be worshipped as founders in those cities that they created. None of the Successors officially deified themselves. Ptolemy, as with the Rhodians and the Egyptians, let others proclaim his divinity. He did not establish his own cult; that was done by his son after the father's death.

Ptolemy, amongst his many favorable qualities highlighted in our sources, is consistently described as pious. He honored Alexander with a sacred precinct and games and sacrifices (Diod. 18. 28. 3-4). He gave proper rites to dead enemy soldiers (Diod. 18. 36. 1). His victory over Perdiccas is ascribed by Diodorus, perhaps reflecting his source, as due to the gods (18. 28. 6). This was part of Ptolemy's projected persona. To proclaim himself to his Macedonian veterans, to his Greek mercenaries, a living god would have been too dangerous even if he was so inclined. Indeed, this was not something lost on the Successors. Being proclaimed by some grateful city as a living deity was one thing; to attempt to impose such belief and—even more importantly—practice on these forces was not something any of Alexander's immediate successors dared to do. Certainly, it presented Ptolemy with an added wrinkle to his dichotomy of rule. To the Egyptians he was viewed as divine,[7] but to the others in his realm, a human king. As Dorothy Thompson (2012: 117) has implied, the Egyptians were ready for a full-blown cult of Ptolemy the son of Lagus, but reluctance on the part of the ruler kept that from being fulfilled until after his death. With Ptolemy II Philadelphus, the cult of a living ruler was inaugurated.

It may have been a desire to address this dichotomy in his rule that led to the Cult of Serapis.[8] Could there be some unifying religious force for the non-Egyptians that through patronage and association could be seen as endorsing his and his descendants' rule? Sarapis (in Latin, Serapis) was a Greek form of a combination of the Egyptian Osiris and Apis. As Stambaugh (1972: 60–7) has shown, the origin of the name is not certain even in our ancient sources, however it appears to have been a version of the Egyptian Cult of Apis, hence the name. Over time, while the Memphian cult remained basically as it had been since time immemorial, the Hellenic version diverged with increasing emphasis on the Osiris part of the Egyptian cult and a virtual demise of the Apis animal worship aspects. Sarapis/Serapis is unknown in the Classical period and is found at the earliest in the fourth century BC. The prominence of the Cult of Serapis begins in earnest in the following century and takes off from there, becoming one of the dominant religious cults of the Hellenistic Age and enduring into the late Roman Empire. The importance for the Egyptians of the cult's antecedents, the worship of Osiris and Apis, was immediately grasped by both Alexander the Great and Ptolemy. It was the latter who likely witnessing the growing popularity of the Hellenic version among the Greek population in Memphis of this cult and to some degree served as its promoter and patron, especially after the change in capital from Memphis to Alexandria—what Dorothy Thompson (2012: 197) has called "that Greek masterpiece of adaptation of an old Egyptian cult." The distinction, however, was maintained. While the Cult of Serapis developed from the Memphian cult of Osiris-Apis, they remained distinct. The Hellenized Cult of Serapis did not replace the Memphian observance among the Egyptian population (Thompson 2012: 190–206, 273–5).

It is generally believed that it was the first Ptolemy, the son of Lagus, who initiated this cult,[9] but there are many who question the extent of his role (for example, Caneva 2018: 101). The oldest documentation for the god Serapis is a fragment from the writings of Menander (*Encheiridion* fr. 139), who died in 292/291 BC. However, Plutarch (*Mor.* 361E) cites concerning Serapis the fourth-century BC philosopher/astronomer Heraclides of Pontus, and Demetrius of Phalerum, who founded the Library in Alexandria during the time of Ptolemy son of Lagus, was supposedly cured of blindness by Serapis and wrote hymns of thanksgiving to Serapis in response (Artemidorus *Onirocritica* II, 39.). This evidence then makes it clear that Serapis existed during the time of the son of Lagus as ruler. The logic, then, is that it could not have originated with a subsequent Ptolemy. The son of Lagus' successors may have strengthened it, altered it, but did not create it. This does, however, open the door to an earlier creation than simply during Ptolemy's time in Egypt. Part of the argument for the first Ptolemy as the creator of the cult is a common belief that this was a conscious creation to blend the two peoples, Greeks and Egyptians.[10] This claim is only partially accurate. Ptolemy was looking for something to unite the people of his capital in Alexandria. It appears clear that it was never his intent to unite the Hellenic and the native Egyptian populations in this worship (Caneva 2018: 97–8). For one thing, Serapis was centered in Alexandria and the ritual cult of Apis remained in Memphis. Indeed, many likely believed with the later Plutarch (*Mor.* 379E) that:

[in] doing [religious] service to the animals themselves and in treating them as gods, [the Egyptians] have not only filled their sacred offices with ridicule and derision, but this is the least of the evils connected with their silly practices. There is engendered a dangerous belief, which plunges the weak and innocent into sheer superstition, and in the case of the more cynical and bolder, goes off into atheistic and brutish reasoning.

There are numbers of complications with respect to this general belief that Ptolemy was the cult's originator, however. In the so-called *Ephemerides*, the supposed royal diaries of Alexander the Great, it is stated that during the Conqueror's last illness he was taken to the Temple of Serapis in Babylon ([Ephemerides] *BNJ* 117 F-3a=Arr. *Anab* 7. 26. 2; cf. Plut. *Alex.* 76. 9).[11] Nor is this the only such reference to Serapis in the Alexander tradition. As Alexander approached Babylon,

> he once took off his clothes for exercise and was playing ball, and when it was time to dress again, the young men who were playing with him beheld a man seated on the king's throne, in silence, wearing the royal diadem and robes. When the man was asked who he was, he was speechless for a long time; but at last he came to his senses and said that his name was Dionysius, and that he was a native of Messenia; in consequence of some charge brought against him, he said, he had been brought here from the sea-board, and for a long time had been in chains; but just now the god Serapis had come to him and loosed his chains and brought him to this spot, bidding him put on the robe and diadem and sit on the throne and hold his peace.
> Plut. *Alex.* 73. 7–9, Loeb Classical Library translation

Now Lionel Pearson (1955: 438–9) has argued that the mentioning of a cult of Serapis in Babylon in 323 is anachronistic and therefore in the case of the *Ephemerides* is indicative of a late date for the composition of these supposed diaries. This argument is based, however, on the firm belief that the cult did not exist before Ptolemy. Certainly, in the Roman period that appears to have been the common belief. Tacitus (*Hist.* 4. 83–4) and Plutarch (Plut. *Mor.* 361F–362B) claim that the Egyptian priests themselves during the second century AD identify Ptolemy, "the first of the Macedonians to place the power of Egypt on a firm foundation," as the creator of the worship of Serapis in Alexandria.[12] Tacitus does, however, also note that other priests give the honor to Ptolemy III. Both Tacitus and Plutarch, however, in their descriptions of Ptolemy's role in the creation of the cult in the new capital city, disconnect the creation from the Temple of Apis in Memphis.[13] Ptolemy's role as originator of the cult is also called into question by both Nicholas Hammond and Brian Bosworth. Hammond (1988: 144) questions the wisdom of using very limited inscriptional evidence to determine the date of the establishment of this cult outside of Egypt. Bosworth (1988A: 167–70) puts forth the more compelling argument that the cult made reference to in the quotation from the *Ephemerides* was not perhaps the same as that instituted by Ptolemy, but rather a forerunner based on the worship of Osiris-Apis. Evidence exists of Greek interest in this particular cult as early as the fifth century BC (Thompson 2012: 181). It is very possible that the cult was spread to Alexandria by those who had practiced it in Memphis prior to moving to Alexandria and such migrants may have been responsible for its spread elsewhere.

The ritual associated with the cult of Apis, the bull-god, however, was very much tied to Memphis. Animal deities were common in Egypt, with the living animal being the embodiment of a god (Ael. *NA* 11. 10). In the case of Apis, this was no simple male cow:

> This Apis, or Epaphus,[14] is a calf born of a cow that can never conceive again. By what the Egyptians say, the cow is made pregnant by a light from heaven, and thereafter gives birth to Apis. The marks of this calf called Apis are these: he is black, and has on his forehead a three-cornered white spot, and the likeness of an eagle on his back; the hairs of the tail are double, and there is a knot under the tongue.
>
> Hdt. 3. 28, Loeb Classical Library translation

When the Apis bull dies the entire country, in addition to mourning, goes on the hunt to find the new Apis. After the discovery, "the priests who have the care of it first take the young bull to Nilopolis, where it is kept forty days, and then, putting it on a state barge fitted out with a gilded cabin, conduct it as a god to the sanctuary of Hephaestus [Ptah] at Memphis" (Diod. 1. 85. 2). Here, Apis resides except for holy processions in which the "god" is celebrated with dances and feasts (Ael. *NA* 10. 10). Having lived a most pampered life, when the bull dies of old age, it is given very elaborate funeral rites. The Egyptians would mourn his passing for seventy days with crowds in their thousands in attendance. The bull would be mummified and placed in the Serapeum at Saqqara (Thompson 2012: 184–7; Asheri 2007: 428).[15] The inner coffin containing the bull would include sacred symbols of Osiris and a message of resurrection. In death Apis had become Osiris. The death of the bull would inaugurate a frantic search all over Egypt to find the new Apis bull. Great rewards were offered to whoever found it. On one occasion Darius III, the ruler of the Persian Empire, in an attempt to win

Egyptian support, offered 100 talents for the discovery of the appropriate bull (Polyaen. 7. 11. 7).

For the Greeks present in Memphis these rituals were translated with respect to the mysteries associated with Dionysus (Diod. 1. 96. 7–8; Plut. *Mor.* 364E-F, 365D; Thompson 2012: 188; Stambaugh 1972: 53–9; Bommas 2005: 31). Dionysus was associated with numerous sacred animals, especially the bull, but more importantly he was associated with resurrection and reincarnation. In truth, what arose in Alexandria was very different from the Cult of Apis. As noted, associated with the cult of the bull was the god Osiris. Osiris was the god of the dead and also of resurrection. His prominence among the native Egyptians went far beyond the Cult of Apis. While Osiris was very important in the Egyptian pantheon of gods, the Cult of Serapis made little headway among the native Egyptians (Höbl 2001: 100). The cult of Serapis likely had its origins in the Greek population in Memphis as the cult of Osorapis (Höbl 2001: 100). The cult related both to Osiris and to Apis had attracted a number of non-Egyptian followers in Memphis (Thompson 2012: 24–6, 177).[16]

This would not have been unusual for a Greek population. There was a tendency best exemplified in Herodotus of seeing equivalencies between Greek gods and those of foreign peoples. The Oracle at Siwah visited by Alexander is a prime example of this religious syncretism. The oracle was an offshoot of the worship of Amun-Ra in Thebes, for which at some subsequent time, perhaps in the sixth century BC, a branch of the Theban cult had been established in the Libyan desert (Classen 1959: 349–55; Parke 1987: 194–5). While in origin an Egyptian foundation, it came to be seen very early by the Greeks as an oracle of Zeus (Parke 1987: 203–37; Brunt 1976: 474–5). By the middle of the fifth century, Zeus/Amun of Siwah had already appeared in an ode of Pindar's (*Pyth.* 4. 29; Paus. 9. 16.1), and Amun and Zeus were equated in a long discourse by Herodotus (1. 46; 2. 32, 52–6). Clearly, by the fifth century the oracle in the Libyan desert was ranked by Greeks with those at Dodona and Delphi (Parke 1967: 109–17). It was because of this syncretism that Alexander journeyed to Siwah. While the Oracle of Zeus/Amun was one of the premier oracles in the Mediterranean world, questions regarding his father's murderers and his subsequent success could have been easily asked at Delphi or Dodona, and with respect to the latter in a sense were. Of the questions that our sources state that Alexander asked, only one would have caused him to journey to Siwah—the one regarding his birth. The other item of interest here is that he was not seeking any validation from his newly acquired Egyptian population. He was for all attempts and purposes recognized as pharaoh by the priests and people of Egypt, as his five royal titles affirm.[17] Even if it is true that the pharaoh was only divine while performing the duties of a pharaoh and human at other times (Malek 1997: 227), it is doubtful that the average Egyptian or a newly arrived Macedonian would recognize this nuanced position. Alexander was proclaimed "the Guardian of Egypt" (Horus name),[18] "The Son, great of might, who takes possession of mountains, lands, and deserts" (Nebty), "The Bull who protects Egypt, the ruler of the sea and of what the sun encircles" (Golden Horus), "Chosen by Ra and beloved of Amun" (throne), and "Alexander" (personal). In inscriptions in the temples of Luxor and Karnak, Alexander was hailed as "Son of Amun" and "Son of Ra." It has been argued that associating foreign rulers with divine parentage was used to legitimize the rule of a foreign king (Bosch-Puche 2014: 96). It was this emphasis on sonship that led Alexander to Siwah. The dual nature of the oracle meant that if Alexander was acknowledged as Son of Amun, which given his position in Egypt was acknowledged both in Thebes and Memphis, then he was also son of Zeus, since Zeus and Amun were two different ethnic names for the same god with respect to Siwah. His special status as the son of a god would not then just be acknowledged in Egypt, but throughout the Greek world as well.[19] Apparently it was not the spirit of the omen that counted in these situations, but the letter of the omen. Alexander, prior to the battle on the Granicus, was reminded that the Macedonian king during the month of Daesius was not to take an army into the field and he was preparing to do just that. Alexander proclaimed that the current month was a second Artemisius (Plut. *Alex.* 16. 2). Since he won the battle, his calendrical manipulation was in the eyes of the gods permissible.

Ptolemy and the other Successors were concerned with how the Macedonian veterans would respond to any of them claiming similar parentage or divinity itself. With respect to Alexander, after his death all was forgiven. His troops forgot any misgivings they had had concerning his religious claims or even his rapprochement to the Persians. Ptolemy wished to take advantage of the respect and new reverence for the Conqueror. As shown, he stole Alexander's body and paid him religious rites. He may even have had the thought that the worship of Alexander could be the linchpin he was looking for to unite the people at least of Alexandria. Ptolemy did establish the worship of the Conqueror in Alexandria and may have done so preliminarily in Memphis. There were in fact two cults of Alexander in Alexandria. The first was the founder's cult. Alexander was the official founder of the city and was worshipped as such. The tombs of city-founders were traditionally accorded honors due a god, their cult and their influence were associated with their actual tomb. A good example from the fifth century BC occurs in the case of the Spartan Brasidas and the city of Amphipolis. After the Spartan commander's death in the battle before Amphipolis, he was honored with a public funeral, annual contests and sacrifices, and the creation of a *temenos*, that is, a sacred enclosure (Thuc. 5. 11. 1). Brasidas had fought and died in a battle ensuring Amphipolis' independence from the Athenians, who had initially colonized the city, and he came to be regarded as the new founder of the city and also as the city's Soter (Savior). Greek colonies were typically sent out with an official "founder" who, as in the case of Brasidas, were honored as heroes after their deaths. The Greek concept of hero was that they occupied an intersection between mortal and immortal, man and god.[20] For their achievements on earth, they would be given this special status after death.

The second cult of Alexander was begun with Ptolemy's seizure of Alexander's corpse (Diod. 18. 28. 2). At first, Alexander's body was brought to Memphis (Paus. 1. 6. 3) where it was treated with sacrificial honors and later transferred to Alexandria, where he was entombed in a magnificent temple honoring him with sacrifices and games (Diod. 18. 28. 4). Ptolemy's treatment of Alexander brought him the respect and support of the soldiers who had served with the Conqueror (Diod. 18. 28. 5). In a similar fashion, Eumenes of Cardia created a cult of Alexander in his army (Diod. 18. 60. 5–61. 3; Plut. *Eum.* 13. 5–8; Polyaen. 4. 8. 2). Facing increasing insubordination from his ostensibly subordinate commanders, Eumenes declared that in a dream he had seen Alexander in full regalia presiding over his regular council and giving orders. He then proposed that all the commanders meet in a tent in the presence of Alexander's throne and regalia.[21] Each morning they would meet, prostrate themselves, and offer incense before the throne. Orders would then be decided by the group and issued in Alexander's name. While it is obvious this was an attempt to eliminate the problems in Eumenes' command, Diodorus (18. 61. 3) speaks of the growing reverence for the king which filled them with confidence.

While the creation of the Alexander cult benefitted Ptolemy through his connection to Alexander and his patronage of the respective cults, ultimately it was his involvement in the cult of Serapis that solidified his dynasty with the Greek and Macedonian population of Egypt. Theoretically, in Egyptian belief, the pharaoh was the chief priest of every Egyptian deity, but the practical and visual aspect of this was the ruler's patronage. Royal patronage established a bond of religious sympathy between the ruler and the devotees (Trigger, Kemp, O'Connor, and Lloyd 1983: 294–5). This cult, as noted, began in Memphis and had proved to be attractive among the more Hellenized population and it was this that brought Ptolemy's attention to its possibilities. Then, what is very likely is that Ptolemy was responsible for promoting the cult of Serapis, but not creating it.

In the cult established in Alexandria there were no sacred bulls and the emphasis very quickly turned to the Osiris connection (Pfeiffer 2008: 391–2). Now elements of both Egyptian and Greek features were present, which might suggest the hand of Ptolemy or Manetho, but in reality this would appear to be more in line with the gradual evolution of the cult from its Egyptian origins. What would appear most likely is that with the construction of Alexandria and with the migration of many Greeks and Macedonians from Memphis to the new capital, they brought with them the partially Hellenized version of the Memphian cult. This, then, in the presence of increasing emigration from both inside and outside of Egypt, led to the evolution of the cult. Ptolemy's role then was to patronize what for him must have been a welcome unifying force in the new city of such a diverse population. This would also explain the rapid expansion and wide diversity of the roles played by Serapis. He became in many ways a universal god. In the later Roman sources Serapis is identified with a great number of Greek/Roman gods. Tacitus (*Hist.* 4. 84. 5) proclaims,

> Many regard the god himself as identical with Aesclepius, because he cures the sick; some as Osiris, the oldest god among these peoples;[22] still more identify him with Zeus/Jupiter as the supreme lord of all things; the majority, however, arguing from the attributes of the god that are seen on his statue or from their own conjectures, hold him to be Father Dis/Hades.
>
> Loeb Classical Library translation

Plutarch (*Mor.* 362B; cf. *Mor.* 356B, 364D) declares that many insist

> the body is called Hades, since the soul is, as it were, deranged and inebriate when it is in the body, [but they] are too frivolous in their use of allegory. It is better to identify Osiris with Dionysus and Serapis with Osiris, who received this appellation at the time when he changed his nature. For this reason, Serapis is a god of all peoples in common, even as Osiris is; and this they who have participated in the holy rites well known.
>
> translation from the Loeb Classical Library edition

The Egyptian god Osiris was an intriguing and attractive deity—a god who had been resurrected and oversaw the resurrection of the dead. "He was the ruler and king of the dead" (Plut. *Mor.* 381E).[23] Apis was merely an earthly manifestation of resurrection from death to become Osiris. The so-called Egyptian Book of the Dead, whose real title is *Coming Forth by Day*, not only promises that for correct behavior and ritual purity the reward is life after death, but also "splendor in heaven and might upon earth and triumph in the land of the dead" (Wallis Budge 1967 [1895]: 15. 10 [255]). In death one could become one with the gods. "I am one of the gods," proclaims the dead scribe Ani in his funerary papyrus scroll likely composed sometime between 1500 and 1400 BC (1. 6 [271]). While, given the possible blessings that await in the afterlife, it is easy to see why the worship in some fashion of Osiris would be popular, what Ptolemy gained is not so obvious. While the importance of Apis in the coronation ceremony (Hölbl 2001: 81, 88–9) made this particular cult very important in an Egyptian setting, that importance for a non-Egyptian audience is unclear. As a patron of the cult, he would derive the support of those associated with its worship. If, as proposed, this worship of a Hellenic form of the Egyptian cult had arisen and gained popularity within the Alexandrian Hellenic community as a popular movement, then Ptolemy would be tying himself to this increasingly popular cult. It would also suggest that, as with his involvement in Egyptian religion, he supported what was accepted without any great interference. Additionally, there is a connection between the ruler and Osiris that derives from Egyptian tradition. According to Herodotus (2. 144. 2):

> Before these men, they said, the rulers of Egypt were gods, but none had been contemporary with the human priests. Of these gods one or another had in succession been supreme; the last of them to rule the country was Osiris' son Horus, whom the Greeks call Apollo; he deposed Typhon, and was the last divine king of Egypt. Osiris is, in the Greek language, Dionysus.
> translation from the Loeb Classical Library edition

Also, in the Pyramid Texts (Utterance 213. 134) in one associated with Unas,[24] a pharaoh of the Fifth dynasty in the twenty-fourth century BC, "O Unas, you have not gone dead. You have gone alive to sit on the throne of Osiris. Your scepter is in your hand, and you may give orders to the living . . ." Osiris is often associated with kingship (Plut. *Mor.* 355E, 356D). By the time of Ptolemy III and possibly during the reign of Ptolemy II, the Cult of Serapis was merged with a cult of the ruling dynasty (Pfeiffer 2008: 400–3).[25] The association of the pharaoh with the cosmic order was part of Egyptian belief. For Egyptians, pharaoh is the penultimate representative of the gods on earth. Even without the theological aspect and more likely with respect to the non-Egyptian population, he was the ultimate practical source of patronage and protection. Even without proclaiming himself a god, in his ability to confer benefits or inflict suffering in a polytheistic society he was little different from a god. While Ptolemy was careful not to revive or highlight those issues which had put Alexander at odds with his troops, he did astride the Hellenistic Egyptian world, whether Egyptian or Hellenic, like a god.

Moreover, Serapis/Osiris was closely associated with Isis, the goddess and wife of Osiris, who brought him back from death. Ptolemy II and his wife Arsinoe in their iconography identified themselves and the holy couple of Osiris/Serapis[26] and Isis (Pfeiffer 2008: 387). This association marking Serapis as Osiris is found in early inscriptions from the Alexandrian temple. The first is dated to the first Ptolemy and the second to Ptolemy II.

> Delok[les had it (i.e. the statue) m]ade. Aristodemos, son of Dio[. .]os, Athenian, had it (dedicated) to Serapis and to Isis.[27]

> On behalf of King Ptolemy, son of Ptolemy and Berenike, the saviours, Archagathos, son of Agathokles, the overseer of the (nome Libya and his wife Stratonike, (have dedicated) the temenos [precinct] to Serapis and Isis.[28]

This association is also clear in the ritual found with respect to Apis in Memphis where Isis is viewed as his mother (Thompson 2012: 27–8). Alexander the Great, when laying out his plan for Alexandria, located both Greek and Egyptian temples; a temple honoring Isis is specifically mentioned. The association of Serapis and Isis becomes very clear in later Roman sources (Paus. 2. 4. 6, 34. 10; 3. 22. 13; 7. 26. 7; Vitr. 1. 7. 1; Tac. *Hist.* 4. 84; Plut. *Mor.* 361E). The attractive power of these deities is easily seen. Osiris was the ruler of the dead and through his good graces to those who were worthy all would be given. This was a most important aspect of Egyptian religion and when translated into Greek form, would be most attractive to Hellenic audiences as well. Ptolemy the son of Lagus noticed the attraction and used it to his advantage. His capital was becoming the most cosmopolitan city in the Mediterranean basin. It was as a result the most diverse in customs and religion. Serapis remained, however, a Greek deity, never widely worshipped by the native Egyptians (Pfeiffer 2008: 392), nor does this appear to have been part of Ptolemy's purpose in promoting the cult. With a population coming from over 200 different locations in the Greek world alone (Lewis 1986: 10), the argument is that something was needed to unite them. Unity tied exclusively to a political philosophy, as has been more than demonstrated recently, is not always enough to ensure unity and concord; other factors such as religion can be sources of accord or just as easily its reverse. The Cult of Serapis, while based mostly on Osiris, also took on the attributes of other gods as well. Osiris comes to be seen as responsible for the fertility of the soil (Plut. *Mor.* 363D-

E). He is proclaimed as both the Nile and the Sea (Plut. Mor. 364A).[29] Serapis became in many ways a melting pot of divine attributes. Through his patronage of the new cult, Ptolemy could enhance the loyalty of his non-Egyptian populace and at the same time unite them in this new, initially Alexandrian religion. While Ptolemy likely saw the advantages for himself and his dynasty, it is doubtful that he saw the full ramifications of what he was fostering. As the cult caught on, it spread widely throughout the Mediterranean basin. While it has been claimed that it was Ptolemy's purpose to use the cult to spread his influence throughout the Mediterranean world (for example, Youtie 1948: 9–29), Apollonius' letter (*IG* 11. 4. 1299) relating to the Temple of Serapis on the island of Delos speaks of the early difficulties of getting the cult established and attributes its success to the intervention of Serapis. There is no indication of help or initiation from the Egyptian government. Moreover, it appears from the evidence that the priesthood was inherited in families (Moyer 2011: 163–4); not in any way was the selection affected by the state. It is also clear that each temple outside of Egypt saw to its own financing. Even while such patronage was practiced in Egypt, it was not a major activity. As Ptolemy did not expend his energy attempting to gain for himself the glory of an Alexander, he also was not in the realm of religion attempting in any way to convert the world, or for that matter even seriously to evangelize the cult of Serapis in Egypt. The evidence of the Apollonius letter suggests that while he patronized the cult in Alexandria, outside of Egypt the spread was due to individual efforts, not part of some state activity. In one case, a request is made to a different Apollonius than the letter writer and, indeed, the chief financial officer of Egypt, for financial assistance to build a temple of Serapis in Memphis, but it is clear that the impetus for the temple was from a private individual and it is unknown if the requested patronage was forthcoming.[30]

> To Apollonius, greetings, from Zoilus, Aspendian, of the … and recommended to you by the king's friends. While petitioning the god Sarapis for your health and success with King Ptolemy, it had been happening to me that Sarapis often ordered me in dreams to sail over to you and present you with this order of his, that there must be built for him … and a precinct in the Greek quarter by the harbor, and for a priest to officiate and to sacrifice on the altar in your behalf. When I asked … that he release me from this task, he cast me into illness so great that I was in danger of my life. So I prayed to the god that he cure me, so that I might submit to the duty and do what he had ordered. When at once I became well, someone from Cnidus came who set about building a Sarapeum in that place and imported stones; but later the god warned him not to build it, and he left. When I came to Alexandria and hesitated to meet with you about these

things but instead about the business you had granted to me, once again I relapsed for four months, so I was unable to come to you promptly. So, Apollonius, it would be well for you to act in accord with the god's orders, so that Sarapis be gracious to you and make you far greater with the king and more conspicuous in bodily health. Do not be alarmed by the outlay, that will be a great expense to you, to the contrary it will be by way of substantial profit to you; for I will join in overseeing all these things. Farewell.

P.Cair. Zen. 1 59034; translation: Rigsby 2001: 117–18[31]

The ultimate consequences of the Cult of Serapis were found in the corresponding Cult of Isis, which came to be even more so than the Cult of Serapis a major religious force in the Mediterranean world. Isis was transformed into a goddess very much at home in the Hellenistic and Roman cultural milieus. The worship of Isis was not new to the Greek world. Herodotus (4. 186. 2) reports that "the women of Cyrene consider it wrong to eat cows' flesh, because of Isis of Egypt; and they even honor her with fasts and festivals." This adoption of an Egyptian goddess and cult likely resulted from the intermarriage of Greek settlers and the inhabitants of Libya (Corcella 2007: 710).[32] There was even a temple of Isis in Athens prior to 333/332. In an Athenian Council decree (*GHI* 92 [464]; Tod 2. 189 [250]), Citian merchants from Cyprus requested that they be given the right to build a temple to Cyprian Aphrodite, which was granted. At the end of the decree, it states: "Grant to the merchants of Citium the right to acquire land on which to found a sanctuary of Aphrodite, just as the Egyptians have founded the sanctuary of Isis" (ll. 42–5). Also, apparently during the fourth century the worship of Isis was found in Eretria as well (*IG* 12. Supp. 562; cf. *GHI* 2003: 465). The full transformation of what had originated as a bastardized version of the cults of Osiris and Apis can be seen in the second-century AD writer, philosopher, and rhetorician, Lucius Apuleius' *Metamorphosis*. In a most critical passage, Isis addresses the long-suffering Lucius, who has been transformed magically into an ass. Here can be seen the full impact, perhaps, of Ptolemy's support, however limited, for the new cult of Serapis—a most unintended consequence, no doubt.

> I, mother of all Nature[33] and mistress of the elements, first-born of the ages and greatest of powers divine, queen of the dead, and queen of the immortals, all gods and goddesses in a single form; who with a gesture commands heaven's glittering summit, the wholesome ocean breezes, the underworld's mournful silence; whose sole divinity is worshipped in differing forms, with varying rites, under many names, by all the world. There, at Pessinus, the Phrygians, first-born

of men, call me Cybele, Mother of the Gods; in Attica, a people sprung from their own soil name me Cecropian Minerva [Athena][34]; in sea-girt Cyprus I am Paphian Venus [Aphrodite]; Dictynna-Diana to the Cretan archers; Stygian Proserpine to the three-tongued Sicilians; at Eleusis, ancient Ceres; Juno to some, to others Bellona, Hecate, Rhamnusia [Nemesis]; while the races of both Ethiopias, first to be lit at dawn by the risen Sun's divine rays, and the Egyptians too, deep in arcane lore, worship me with my own rites, and call me by my true name, royal Isis. I am here in pity for your misfortunes, I am here as friend and helper. Weep no more, end your lamentations. Banish sorrow. With my aid, your day of salvation is at hand. So listen carefully to my commands … And have faith in my power to oversee the execution of my orders, for at this very moment when I am here with you I am with my priest too telling him, in dream, what he must do. When I wish, the heaving crowd will part before you, and amidst the joyous rites and wild festivity no one will shrink from your unseemly shape, nor treat your sudden change of form as sinister and level charges at you out of spite. Remember one thing clearly though, and keep it locked deep within your heart: the life that is left to you, to the final sigh of your last breath, is pledged to me. It is right that all your days be devoted to she whose grace returns you to the world of men. Under my wing, you will live in happiness and honour, and when your span of life is complete and you descend to the shades, even there, in the sphere beneath the earth, you will see me, who am now before you, gleaming amidst the darkness of Acheron, queen of the Stygian depths; and dwelling yourself in the Elysian fields, you will endlessly adore me and I will favour you. Know too that if by sedulous obedience, dutiful service, and perfect chastity you are worthy of my divine grace, I and I alone can extend your life beyond the limits set by fate.

translation: A. S. Kline https://www.poetryintranslation.com/PITBR/Latin/TheGoldenAssXI.php#anchor_Toc353982291

8

The Royal Historian

Ptolemy sometime during his lifetime wrote a history of Alexander's expedition,[1] which, unfortunately, has not survived and all that remains are what are generally called "fragments," statements quoted or paraphrased purportedly from the original text.[2] Even the title of the history is unknown. The major source for twenty-nine of these forty generally recognized fragments is the history of Alexander's expedition, the *Anabasis of Alexander*, written by Lucius Flavius Arrianus, Arrian for short, an historian of the second century AD.[3] His account is generally considered to be the best surviving narrative of Alexander the Great's expedition and consequently his proclaimed reliance on Ptolemy's history would enhance the reputation of the latter's account and, as it happens, vice versa. Clearly from the number of references to Ptolemy's history and the nature of many of these ascriptions, it appears that Arrian (cf. *Anab*. 1. 2. 7, 8. 1; 6. 2. 4) relied heavily on Ptolemy, especially when describing military operations (Hammond 1993A: 191–204; Howe 2018A "Ptolemy" *BNJ* F-3 com.).[4] Given that this appears to be so, the best if not virtually the only way to evaluate Ptolemy's history, its biases and general nature, would be through an analysis of Arrian's history. In his preface, Arrian does proclaim:

> Wherever Ptolemy, the son of Lagus, and Aristobulus have both given the same accounts of Alexander, the son of Philip, it is my practice to record what they say as completely true ... in my view Ptolemy and Aristobulus are more trustworthy in their narratives since Aristobulus took part in king Alexander's expedition, and Ptolemy not only did the same, but as he himself was a king, mendacity would have been more dishonorable for him than for anyone else ... both wrote when Alexander was dead, and neither was under any constraint or hope of gain to make him set down anything but actually happened.
> Arrian, *Anabasis* Book 1, Preface (Loeb Classical Library translation)

Arrian, however, is not a cipher, he is an author who is capable of using many sources which he is able to edit to achieve his aims (Bosworth 1980: 17; 1988: 14;

Stadter 1980: 66–76), with an ultimate stated goal to relate, in his words, "what actually happened." Indeed, as Arrian (*Anab.* 1. Pref. 3) notes, he has included information from other sources (the *legomena*), but only where he has found these to be "worth mention and not entirely untrustworthy." To damn these others with faint praise! Arrian (*Anab.* 1. 12. 2–4) proclaims his desire "to make Alexander's deeds known to men," and he here is also setting forth his worthiness to produce the definitive work on Alexander, "a master of warfare" (Arr. *Anab.* 1. 12. 5). This entire section makes it very clear that Alexander is to be Arrian's focus, which is emphasized again in his concluding comments regarding him "a man beyond all other men" (*Anab.* 7. 30. 2). These comments also make it clear that Arrian was a fan. What Arrian has written is virtually an encomium on the Conqueror (Bosworth 1980: 30). Arrian's stated reliance on Ptolemy and Aristobulus and his very sympathetic attitude towards Alexander suggests that Ptolemy's account was also favorable, thought to be trustworthy, and concentrated on the Conqueror, not on the author. While Arrian may rely heavily on Ptolemy's history, Arrian's purpose was not to extol the virtues and achievements of that history's author. After all, if Ptolemy's history was an account of Ptolemy's activities in Alexander's expedition, it is doubtful, given Arrian's stated purpose in writing this account, that Ptolemy would have been a preferred history, even given his presence on the expedition and his later kingship.

It becomes clear that Arrian is attempting to correct the more mistaken accounts then in circulation. In his comment on Alexander's wound received in India at the hands of the Mallians, Arrian states: "A great many other stories have been written by the historians about this disaster, and legend has handed them on as the first falsifiers told them, and still keeps them alive to this day; and will indeed never cease handing on these falsehoods to others in turn unless it be checked by this my history" (Arr. *Anab.* 6. 11. 2).[5] The favorable nature of Arrian's account not only suggests that Ptolemy's history was favorable as well, but that this also may have had something to do with the latter's selection as a major source, even though this is nowhere expressed by Arrian. Ptolemy, indeed, has been criticized for leaving out of his history episodes that might have damaged Alexander's image. Of course, such arguments are based on these omissions originating with Ptolemy and not Arrian. There are even claims where the episode is reported in Arrian, but the assumption is made that Ptolemy had omitted it. A case in point deals with the supposed omission from Ptolemy's account of the death of Cleitus (Seibert 1969: 18–19; Worthington 2016: 48–9). This is assumed because Arrian does not reference Ptolemy's work for anything involving this incident. Ptolemy is noted by Arrian as one who tried to defuse the argument by separating the two individuals. This reference in Arrian is attributed to Aristobulus (4. 8. 9). Curtius (8. 1. 45) says both Perdiccas and Ptolemy attempted to separate the two individuals. Aristobulus is quoted by Arrian (Anab. 4. 8. 9) as proclaiming that "the entire fault lay with Cleitus." Ian Worthington argues that Ptolemy eliminated the incident because he might have seen this as a failure on his part, since as a bodyguard, a *somatophylax*, he should have been able to prevent the incident (Worthington 2016: 49). While Ptolemy's history is not specifically mentioned, Arrian comments that with respect to Cleitus' murder many *legomena*, different tales, abound (Arr. *Anab.* 4. 9. 3), which suggests that this is likely true for the entire episode (Roisman 1984: 377–8). This is further supported when Arrian notes that Aristobulus ignored the origins of the drinking bout, which Arrian reports. This should not imply however that Ptolemy did the same. In fact, if he had, would not Arrian have noted that as well? The death of Cleitus at Alexander's hands is highly sanitized in Arrian's account,[6] and this may reflect what he found in Ptolemy. In fact, his death is described by Arrian as a tragedy that "caused Alexander much suffering" (*Anab*. 4. 8. 1), and Cleitus is "strongly blamed for his insolence towards the king" (Arr. *Anab*. 4. 9. 1), an insolence that was dearly punished. According to Curtius (8. 2. 12), in an *ad hoc* meeting of the army it was decreed that Cleitus had been justly put to death, and if Alexander had not given him his proper funeral rites, the army was ready to deny him proper burial.

One part of Arrian's preface has generated much discussion with respect to his claim that kings are less likely to lie than other people. Such a statement does appear at first glance to demonstrate naivety on the part of the author, but in general most accept Arrian's account and his reasoning for selecting his primary sources, and in the main, his history is seen as reasonably accurate.[7] After all, this claim about the veracity of kings is a subsidiary reason for his use of Ptolemy. In the first place, he is not saying that kings are always truthful, but rather that they should be. Lying is simply "more dishonorable for [a king] than for anyone else." As Brian Bosworth (1980: 43) has suggested, this was a "commonplace," a trope, a cliché, in Hellenistic and Roman literature. Plutarch (*Alex*. 59. 6–8) proclaims that Alexander stained his military career by his actions in his siege of Massaga. Alexander made a truce with the mercenary fighters in the city that they were free to leave, but when they did, they were massacred by the Macedonians. What is apparently being criticized, since Alexander's massacres are not otherwise condemned, is that here Alexander violated his word. Timothy Howe (2018B: 155–77) has suggested that at least part of this emphasis on truth telling was the result of Ptolemy's personal propaganda, which in turn was based on traditional Egyptian belief in a ruler's responsibility to maintain Ma'at, the personification of "Truth, Justice and Order" (2018: 156).

While it is likely that Ptolemy was Arrian's primary source ("Ptolemy of Lagus whom I chiefly follow" [Arr. *Anab.* 6. 2. 4]),[8] for Arrian this supposed royal quality of honesty appears of secondary importance, since Aristobulus was not a king and yet was seen by Arrian as a very acceptable source because of his actual participation in the campaign. Ptolemy's account would be superior only because of his direct participation in the military aspects of what was primarily a military campaign. Moreover, it would appear Ptolemy's history was anything but a bestseller. If it was not for Arrian, one would hardly know that he had written a history. This would suggest that this work, dare I say it, was a dry, loaded with detail, history. There are but two testimonia and one of these is, indeed, Arrian's preface,[9] and thirty-six fragments, only ten of which are not from Arrian, six of these dating from the Byzantine period. Of these ten, none could be described as "tall" or "fabulous" tales; all are either related to military activities or geography. Fragment 28a (Plut. *Alex.* 46. 1–2) has Ptolemy denying that Alexander ever met with the Amazon women—not conclusive evidence of a fact-based account, but telling nonetheless.

There are other reasons for Arrian's selection of his sources that are of primary importance. First is that these two individuals have by and large given similar accounts. Secondly, they both were with Alexander on his expedition. Lastly, they wrote after the Conqueror's death and consequently, Arrian believed, would not be compelled by Alexander to alter their accounts.[10] This may be an allusion to Callisthenes' incomplete history, which was written under the strict gaze of the Macedonian king. Of course, there may have been very personal reasons to stray from a truthful telling of events. Unfortunately, as seen, most of what we know of Ptolemy's work comes from the later work of Arrian.

Given the scarcity of information concerning Ptolemy's history, even the proposed date of its composition becomes important. Modern commentators for the most part believe that Ptolemy wrote his account late in life and consequently, being already established in Egypt, had no political reason to falsify it and wrote "simply for the sake of writing history" (Roisman 1984: 385), simply to eliminate the fog of the Alexander Romance and to set the record straight. Certainly, his later denial that he had anything to do with saving Alexander's life in the siege of the Mallian city where the king was seriously wounded would suggest this (Arr. *Anab.* 6. 11. 8; cf 6. 10. 1–2).[11] The argument for late composition typically is tied to the idea that he was too busy earlier to take the time to write his history. As Joseph Roisman has properly observed, this particular argument, if taken by itself, is "seriously flawed" (1984: 373). However, there are certain other considerations that would appear to support a late composition. It was this first Ptolemy who began the institutions that would ultimately make Alexandria the cultural center of the Greek world: the Museum and Library of Alexandria.[12] These efforts, along with his patronage of the Cults of Serapis and Alexander, were, in part, designed to encourage Greek migration to this new addition to the Greek world. His history may have been at least in part his way of demonstrating that he was not just a patron of the arts but an active participant in this cultural renaissance. This last consideration would suggest a later production of his history. The Library and Museum were begun in earnest after the arrival of Demetrius of Phalerum in Alexandria in 297 BC (Diod. 20. 45. 4; D. L 5. 78).[13]

Even if Ptolemy had no political reason to embellish his role or extol the virtues of his former commander, a history written near the end of his life still could be his personal attempt to secure his immortality as the friend, companion, confidant, fellow-soldier, and true successor—at least in a broad sense—of the now more than legendary Alexander; in short, his attempt to partake of that legend with, perhaps, the occasional slap at those he had long resented. This would most likely then be in the form not of falsification but of omission. Timothy Howe (2021: 54) sees Ptolemy as presenting himself *in imitatio Alexandri,* who became, especially during the Indian campaign, "Alexander's military right hand and true heir" (Howe 2008: 216). In point of fact, at the time of Alexander's death, his second-in-command was Perdiccas (Diod. 18. 3. 4; Plut. *Eum.* 1. 2), but no such reference is found in Arrian's *Anabasis*. Curtius (9. 5. 21) does relate, "[Ptolemy] was not inclined to depreciate his own glory." As noted earlier, Arrian (*Anab.* 1. 12. 2–4; cf. 7. 30. 2) proclaimed that it is his purpose "to make Alexander's deeds known to men," and that Arrian is hardly a cipher for his sources. Therefore, it is then, of course, possible that many of those passages that so impressed Curtius as reflecting the deeds of Ptolemy were excised by Arrian. As noted above, I do believe that Ptolemy did write his history late in life, but there is no hard evidence to suggest when he wrote his history.

Arguments that it was written earlier proclaim the history a work of propaganda designed to enhance Ptolemy's standing with Alexander and denigrate that of others, especially the reputations of his rivals in the struggles that dominated the early Hellenistic Age. For this to be the case, then Ptolemy's history was written earlier, and perhaps much earlier.[14] Again, with the proviso that the general nature of his history can be determined from Arrian's history, the evidence appears to show that his history was for the most part a factual account of one of the most important military expeditions of all time by one of the most mercurial figures in history—an attempt to set the record straight. Does this mean that there is no exaggeration of Ptolemy's personal exploits, or the occasional dig at some enemy? No, but it does mean that this history is unlikely to have any strong political motive.

Certainly, the importance of Arrian in any reconstruction or evaluation of Ptolemy's history is critical, and the best way to do such an evaluation is to examine both those passages attributed to Ptolemy and those depicting his activities in general and compare these descriptions with those of Alexander's other companions and commanders. One thing that is quickly noted in such a survey is how infrequently Ptolemy's name comes up. In Arrian's history, prior to Alexander's attempted entrance through the Persian Gates, Ptolemy's name does not appear other than as a source. He is mentioned some fifty times in Arrian's *Anabasis*, with less than half of these not related to his history, but rather to his activities. However, for comparison, his later Diadoch rival Perdiccas has twenty-five such references in Arrian, but with a number of these being in reference to his battalion. It is, therefore, important to note that Ptolemy's first appearance other than as an historian comes in his description of the Persian retreat from Issus in which Arrian quotes him as saying that the cavalry crossed over gullies filled with Persian corpses, implying that he was with Alexander in the pursuit of the retreating Persian king as a member of the Companion Cavalry (Arr. *Anab*. 2. 11. 8=[Ptolemy] *BNJ* 138 F-6). As Waldemar Heckel (2018: 1) states, "Ptolemy was a man who emerged from the shadows." In the campaign against the Triballians during Alexander's first full year as king, Ptolemy's activities are not mentioned in passages attributed to him, but those of others are (Arr. *Anab*. 1.2–34=[Ptolemy] *BNJ* 138 F-1, cf. F-2), the same with respect to the assault on Thebes (Arr. *Anab*. 1. 8. 1–8=[Ptolemy] *BNJ* 138 F-3),[15] the siege of Halicarnassus (Arr. *Anab*. 1. 20. 2–23. 7).[16] He is absent from the accounts of the battles on the Granicus (Arr. *Anab*. 13–16. 4; Diod. 17. 19–21. 6), at Issus (Arr. *Anab*. 2. 6–11. 10; Diod. 17. 33–35. 1; Curt. 3. 9–11. 19; Just. 11. 8. 1–9. 11), and Gaugamela (Arr. *Anab*. 3. 8. 2–15. 6; Diod. 17. 57–61. 3; Curt. 4. 12. 5–16. 33; Just. 11. 13–14. 7). However, in the latter half of Alexander's campaigns, he appears as one of the major commanders along with Hephaestion, Leonnatus, Craterus, and Perdiccas (Arr. *Anab*. 4. 16. 2, 21. 4, 24. 10, 25. 2–3, 29. 1–6; 5. 23. 7; 6. 5. 3–7; 7. 15. 1–3; Curt. 6. 8. 17; 8. 1. 45, 48, 10. 2, 14, 15, 21; Diod. 17. 104. 5–6). Much of this change from early in the campaign to the prelude to the invasion of India has to do with the loss of many of those who commanded earlier. Parmenion,[17] Philotas,[18] Nicanor,[19] Amyntas, the son of Arrhabaeus,[20]

Socrates,[21] Amyntas,[22] son of Andromenes, and Philip,[23] son of Amyntas, Calas,[24] Philip,[25] son of Menelaus, commanders who participated in the battle on the Granicus were no longer present, making the promotion of others necessary. Neither Leonnatus nor Hephaestion have significant roles prior to India. In Arrian (*Anab.* 4. 22. 7), Hephaestion appears in other than a possible cavalry command for the first time somewhere near the Cophen river in 327/326 (Bosworth 1995: 149–50), and Leonnatus slightly later (Arr. *Anab.* 4. 21. 4). He, like Ptolemy, was present in the battle on the Hydaspes accompanying Alexander and the cavalry (Curt. 8. 14. 15).[26]

Ptolemy's first actual command comes in Alexander's attack on the defenders of the Persian Gates in 330, where an unspecified Ptolemy, but likely the son of Lagus (Bosworth 1980: 328; Howe 2015: 167–90; Heckel 1980: 169n. 7, cf. 2018: 3), was stationed with a force as part of an operation to prevent a successful Persian retreat, a task which was accomplished with great loss on the part of the Persians (Arr. *Anab.* 3. 18. 9). The reference to Ptolemy, a popular Macedonian name, appears without patronymic, which is most unusual given the routine reference to the historian and companion of Alexander as son of Lagus (twenty-two times) and if omitted, then an identifying reference to him as an historian (Arr. *Anab.* 1. 2. 7; 5. 15. 1, 20. 2; 6. 10. 1) or in association with Aristobulus (cf. Arr. *Anab.* 2. 12. 6; 3. 26. 1; 4. 3. 5; 4, 14. 1; 5. 7. 1, 20. 2; 6. 11. 5; 7. 13. 3, 26. 3), or clearly identifiable in the context (cf. Arr. *Anab.* 1. Pref. 1. 1, 2; 3. 6. 6, 18. 9, 30. 2; 4. 24. 4, 29. 2, 3, 4, 5, 6; 5. 13. 1, 24. 1, 2, 3; 6. 5. 7; 7. 4. 6). The lack of a patronymic at 3. 18. 9 led Jacob Seibert (1969: 6–10) to doubt that the reference is to the son of Lagus. There are, indeed, other Ptolemys in Arrian's history. The Ptolemy mentioned in Arrian's *Anabasis* (1. 22. 4, 7) without patronymic is not the son of Lagus (Bosworth 1980: 148; Heckel 2021: 417), nor is the Ptolemy without patronymic noted in 1. 23. 6 and 2. 5. 7 (Bosworth 1980: 196; Heckel 2006: 235), nor the battalion commander at Issus, also listed as Ptolemy but without patronymic (Arr. *Anab.* 2. 8. 4),[27] nor is a patronymic provided for the Ptolemy, the commander of the Thracians (Arr. *Anab.* 4. 7. 2).[28] The absence of epithets in fact in the early stages of the expedition is especially unusual because, as seen above, there are these other individuals named Ptolemy, not just the son of Lagus, who are involved in military operations. Later, Ptolemy the son of Lagus is noted, and yet the identification is most often clear without the need of the epithet. It is certainly possible that the omission of the epithet identifying the father was the result of carelessness on the part of Arrian; such omissions are common when the individual is not the son of Lagus. The prominence of the epithet for the son of Lagus suggests that in Ptolemy's history he may have associated his name and patronymic with every reference to himself. He wrote his history in the third person.[29] After all, he was writing a history of Alexander's deeds. Writing in the third person would highlight Alexander and also keep his name ever before the readers. Since there would always be confusion with the very popular name Ptolemy, the son of Lagus likely wished to make certain that his deeds were not attributed to others of the same name. As noted earlier, Curtius (9. 5. 21) proclaims that Ptolemy the son of Lagus wished to make certain his actions were clearly proclaimed. While the lack of the patronymic for Ptolemy the son of Lagus is unusual, it is not for the other players in the Alexander saga. More than forty of these appear without patronymic and more than twenty have it appear only after the individual is first mentioned. For example, Arrian's *Anabasis* includes eight apparently different Macedonians named Amyntas.[30] Of these, only four have patronymics. There are also nine individuals named Philotas in Arrian, of which only two have patronymics. The problem with all these suppositions making the son of Lagus the Ptolemy of Arrian *Anabasis* 3. 18. 9 is that they cannot rise above the status of a very likely assumption.

However, if not the son of Lagus, then who might be this particular Ptolemy? Of those other Ptolemies mentioned earlier in Arrian, one dies at Halicarnassus (Arr. *Anab*. 1. 22. 7) and another, the son of Seleucus, dies at Issus (Arr. *Anab*. 2. 12. 2), thus ruling both of them out of the running. Seibert (1969: 8–10) believes Arrian *Anabasis* 3. 18. 9 may refer to Ptolemy the son of Philip (Arr. *Anab*. 1. 14. 6). This particular Ptolemy appears in and disappears from the record with the battle on the Granicus.[31] Seibert and Berve both suggested that Ptolemy the son of Philip may be identical with the Ptolemy listed as the commander of the Thracians (Berve 1973: 336; Seibert 1969: 9). It is also possible that this is a Ptolemy different from these others. As noted earlier, Arrian's *Anabasis* includes eight apparently different Macedonians named Amyntas, of which only four have patronymics, and seven Philips without patronymics or some other clear identifiers (Heckel 2006: 208–15). Much of the argument for the identification of the Ptolemy at the Persian Gates as the son of Lagus is rather backhanded. No source other than Arrian mentions a Ptolemy in this battle nor describes the action at the Persian Gates itself in the same way.[32] The argument appears to be that the incident described in 3. 18. 9 either did not happen or was inconsequential,[33] and only its connection to Ptolemy the son of Lagus would make it worthy of Arrian's notice.[34] Both Tarn (1950: 319–26) and Badian (1959: 144–57) attribute the passage to Ptolemy's desire for self-promotion. Howe (2015: 188–9) goes further, claiming that Ptolemy may have had a very subsidiary role but chose rather to present himself as responsible for a significant part of the victory at the Persian Gates.³⁵ However, Ptolemy's claimed role here is strikingly similar to that carried out by Craterus with respect to the Uxians (Arr. *Anab*. 3. 17. 5; cf. 3. 17. 4), and also one conducted by Ptolemy in India against the Mallians (Arr. *Anab*. 6. 5. 6–7). Alexander liked his victories to be complete, annihilating as many of the enemy as possible. Whether in his pursuits of defeated opponents or in his securing paths of escape, as with the Uxians, the Persians at the Gates, and the Mallians in India, he wished to inflict maximum casualties on his enemies.³⁶ In the case of the Uxians, Craterus was sent ahead of Alexander's main force to seize the heights to block any Uxian escape (Arr. *Anab*. 3. 17. 4). In the operation at the Persian Gates, Craterus with Meleager was left in charge of the camp at the entrance to the pass (Arr. *Anab*. 3. 18. 4; Curt. 5. 4. 14). Alexander, having been rebuffed in a direct frontal assault on the entrance which had been reinforced by a wall, left to turn the pass by a different route. Craterus was to await Alexander's signal and then attack the Persian wall (*Anab*. 3. 18. 5; Curt. 5. 4. 16, 29).³⁷ As Alexander moved to this new position to the rear and above the Persian camp, he detached Philotas, Coenus, and Amyntas to bridge the Araxes river which crossed the area between the pass and Persepolis (Curt. 5. 4. 20). Their location would also prevent the Persians using this route to retreat to the capital.³⁸ Alexander descended from the heights and began his attack on the Persian camp and at the same time Craterus, responding to the signal, moved to the wall. This would have taken some time, since the camp was three miles distant (Curt. 5. 3. 23; Polyaen. 4. 3. 27).³⁹ The chaos in the Persian camp must have been substantial. Moreover, whether 25,000 or 40,000, the Persian camp would have been elongated in the relatively narrow space. Some would have turned to resist Alexander; according to Arrian, most attempted to flee (Arr. *Anab*. 3. 18. 8). In the chaos, Ptolemy, as ordered, moved to secure the wall. The Persians still defending the wall now found themselves under attack from both sides (Arr. *Anab*. 4. 18. 9). These Persians were then caught between the forces led by Alexander and Philotas and those under the command of Ptolemy and Craterus. Curtius (5. 4. 33) claims that Ariobarzanes, the Persian commander, forty horsemen, and 5,000 infantry escaped, while Arrian (*Anab*. 3. 18. 9) states that only the commander and a small number of horsemen got away. Ptolemy's role is, therefore, important, but not critical to the success of the operation. Ptolemy was to block escape from the wall until Craterus was in place on the other side. Why is he not mentioned in our other sources? The simple answer may be that his role was not seen by these other sources as significant enough to warrant a separate reference. That his role in Arrian is given primacy over that of Philotas and the forces with that commander is likely the result of Arrian's source (Ptolemy) emphasizing his part in the battle. Not a great argument, but what else would give the role of Ptolemy in this battle significance enough to merit it being subsequently mentioned by a later source than that one's primary source may for the first time be appearing in a command role of some significance? Indeed, this campaign may have been more significant than it is often given credit for. General Fuller points out that the pass was not the only way into Persis and Parmenion was on his way to Persepolis by the longer route which avoided the pass (Arr. *Anab*. 3. 18. 1; Curt. 5. 3. 16). Alexander was most interested in preventing the Persian garrison in Persepolis or Ariobarzanes moving to Persepolis from seizing the treasure that the city contained and using it to extend the Persian resistance (Fuller 1960: 228–34). If Alexander continued on the longer route, the Persian commander could easily arrive in the Persian capital well before Alexander. A Persian commander with 40,000 men[40] and all that bullion could be a most formidable foe. Moreover, if Alexander remained stymied at the gates, Parmenion's force would be placed in danger of attack with Alexander unable to intercede. Taking the shorter route through the pass was a gamble. Ariobarzanes would be forestalled from moving to Persepolis (Fuller 1960: 228), but the lack of success in breaking through the Persian defense could have led at the very least to an extended war, if not actual disaster. Alexander left a sizable force behind in the camp about three-and-a-half miles from the gates and had them pretend to be the entire complement to create the impression that the entire army was still there (Curt. 5. 4. 14). By so doing, Alexander convinced Ariobarzanes that Alexander's advance into Persian had been stymied. For Alexander, however, the key to a fully successful operation was the elimination of Ariobarzanes' force. Ptolemy was part of that campaign of elimination. Accepting Arrian's figure for the number of Persians who survived, this was a very effective operation. Even if Curtius' numbers are correct, 5,000 survivors out of an original force of 25,000 would still indicate a significant victory.

If the episode at the Persian Gates is not our introduction to the son of Lagus as a fixture on Alexander's expedition, then that honor falls to that commander's involvement in the pursuit and capture of Bessus in 329 (Arr. *Anab*. 3. 29. 7=[Ptolemy] *BNJ* 138 F-14). There are two sections of Arrian where Ptolemy is given considerable ink. The capture of Bessus is the first. Here, Ptolemy demonstrates his competency, but the capture is not dramatically described. The only semi-remarkable thing noted is that Ptolemy and his forces completed in four days what should have taken ten (Arr. *Anab*. 3. 29. 7). Of course, since the other sources omit any mention of a role for Ptolemy in this operation, the question may be raised whether his involvement happened at all? However, it needs to be noted that these other accounts also differ one from the other. Both Curtius (7. 5.36–40) and Diodorus (17. 83. 7–9) describe the capture very differently and without reference to Ptolemy. Both of these accounts have Bessus' companions surrendering him directly to Alexander, though highlighting different Bactrian individuals in the surrender. Aristobulus also offers a variation on Ptolemy's account, having Spitamenes and Dataphernes accompanying Ptolemy and handing over Bessus to Alexander personally (Arr. *Anab.* 3. 30. 5=[Aristobulus] *BNJ* 139 F-24). That Aristobulus includes a role for Ptolemy is sufficient justification for concluding that he was involved.

Could Arrian's account, likely based on Ptolemy, be what has been termed "invented tradition"?[41] While in this operation Ptolemy's derring-do is not apparent and it appears in many ways a mission more diplomatic than military, his competency and Alexander's trust are on display and the capture of Bessus is certainly an important event, even if Ptolemy's role is only that of an escort. Indeed, the armed force with Ptolemy, including three hipparchies of the Companion Cavalry, all the mounted javelin men, an infantry battalion, a chiliarchy of the hypaspists, all the Agrianes, and half the archers (Arr. *Anab.* 3. 29. 7) would appear to be overkill, since Bessus' associates Spitamenes and Dataphernes had asked that Alexander send a small force to them and they would surrender their commander (Arr. *Anab.* 3. 29. 6). On the one hand, the large force suggests a lack of trust in Bessus' soon to be former allies, and on the other a sense that prior to this operation Ptolemy had proven his worth to Alexander as a military commander.[42] It would therefore suggest that there may have been other commands before and after that have not been reported in our sources prior to this operation. Our sources pick up Ptolemy's military career in India. Curtius (8. 13. 18, 14. 15) first mentions Ptolemy as leading a force on the Hydaspes against Porus, and Justin (12. 10. 3) when he is poisoned by the arrow in the Oreitan campaign.[43] As mentioned earlier, Arrian's history concerned Alexander, and even though using Ptolemy's history—which may or may not have included much information concerning the author's activities, but likely did so—it was to be and, in fact, was centered on Alexander. It is certainly then possible that while Ptolemy's history may have been an encomium to both Alexander and secondarily to himself, much of that related to his exploits was, as they say with respect to a different genre, left on the cutting room floor.

However, given Arrian's stated purpose to present a true account of Alexander's expedition concentrating on Alexander, would he have chosen a history, however trustworthy in his eyes, that did not do the same? Curtius, while mildly criticizing Ptolemy for extoling his role in the expedition (9. 5. 21), later describes him as "a valiant warrior," "modest and affable," "generous," dear to his king and his fellow Macedonians (Curt. 9. 8. 23–4). He is also proclaimed by Curtius to be a son of the previous king, Philip (Curt. 9. 8. 22). In fact, it could be argued that Curtius' account offers more praise of Ptolemy than does Arrian's history. Moreover, Arrian's constant reference to "son of Lagus" suggests the rumor that Ptolemy was a son of Philip was certainly not part of Ptolemy's history (see Chapter 2).

While the passage related to Ptolemy's involvement in the capture of Bessus is a fairly straightforward description of the operation, in India, during the Aspasian campaign, there occurs an account of Ptolemy's single combat with an Indian prince (Arr. *Anab.* 4. 24. 3–5), which Bosworth (1995: 161) has accurately described as Homeric in its presentation (see below).

> The actual leader of the Indians of this district Ptolemy son of Lagus saw close to a hill, and some of his guards with him, though he [Ptolemy] himself had a much inferior force with him, yet he continued to pursue him on horseback, but when the hill proved difficult for his horse to ascend he left it there, handing it to one of the guards to lead; but he himself, on foot as he was, followed the Indian, who then seeing Ptolemy drawing near, turned round with his guards; and the Indian with his long spear struck at close quarters through Ptolemy's breastplate, the breastplate checking the blow; but Ptolemy pierced right through the Indian's thigh, drove him to the ground, and despoiled him.
>
> translation from the Loeb Classical Library edition[44]

This particular act of bravery is echoed later in 320 during Perdiccas' invasion of Egypt. On this occasion, Ptolemy stood in the forefront of one such confrontation engaging the enemy directly (Diod. 18. 34. 2):

> Ptolemy, however, who had the best soldiers near himself and wishing to encourage the other commanders and friends to face the dangers, taking his long spear and posting himself on the top of the outwork, put out the eyes of the leading elephant, since he occupied a higher position, and wounded its Indian mahout. Then, with utter contempt of the danger, striking and disabling those who were coming up the ladders, he sent them rolling down, in their armor, into the river.... The battle for the wall lasted a long time, as the troops of Perdiccas, attacking in relays, bent every effort to take the stronghold by storm, while many heroic conflicts were occasioned by the personal prowess of Ptolemy and by his exhortations to his friends to display both their loyalty and their courage.
>
> translation from the Loeb Classical Library edition

Only two such examples of Ptolemy's *aristeia* are found in our sources, and they do come from two different sources, likely Ptolemy himself in the first and Hieronymus of Cardia in the second,⁴⁵ and refer to two different timeframes. It would appear that there must have been other examples of Ptolemy's bravery in combat. He was wounded twice (Arr. *Anab.* 4. 23. 3; Diod. 17. 103. 3–6; Curt. 9. 8. 14–20). That more examples have not survived could indicate that Ptolemy may have been more circumspect concerning his activities in his history than Curtius (9. 5. 21) implies, or simply that Arrian was not that interested in Ptolemy's exploits

In general, Arrian's material on the opening campaign in India up to the spring of 326 appears fuller and without discernible "*logomena*" (Bosworth 1995: 141),⁴⁶ suggesting far greater reliance on Ptolemy and Aristobulus. This is an assumption based on Arrian's preface concerning his use of Ptolemy and Aristobulus, for nowhere in this section is either Ptolemy's or Aristobulus' account directly cited and not again until 5. 7.1. It is also in India that Ptolemy makes his presence as one of Alexander's premier commanders. It is clear that in the Indian campaign Ptolemy takes on an increasingly important role and this is reflected in Arrian. In the campaign against the Aspasians, Alexander divided his army into three parts. One of these, which included a third of the hypaspists, two infantry battalions, two chiliarchies of archers, the Agrianians, and half the cavalry, was assigned to Ptolemy (Arr. *Anab.* 4. 24. 10; Curt. 8. 10. 21).⁴⁷ Subsequently, he is again found leading troops into battle (*Anab.* 4. 25. 2–4). It needs to be noted that Leonnatus is also mentioned here for his success. This particular passage may reflect the nature of Ptolemy's practice. While his part in the campaign is given more detail, praise is awarded to others as well. Alexander's actions, of course, are rarely given short shrift. If, again, Arrian is reflective of Ptolemy's work, the latter's history was about Alexander, not himself. Previously, in Alexander's invasion of Sogdiana, Ptolemy commanded a fifth of the force (Arr. *Anab.* 4. 16. 2). While Curtius (8. 1. 1) speaks of only three divisions, headed by Hephaestion, Coenus, and Alexander himself, most accept the evidence of Arrian. If this is an attempt by Ptolemy to fabricate his own importance, it might appear curious that in the same breath he does so for Perdiccas as well. The two added commanders in Arrian's account are Ptolemy and Perdiccas.

It becomes clear that in Sogdiana, if not earlier, Ptolemy had become one of the chief commanders. In the siege of the Rock of Chorienes, while Alexander conducted the siege in person, at night the work was divided between Perdiccas, Leonnatus, and Ptolemy (Arr. *Anab.* 4. 21. 4). With respect to the Rock of

Aornus, Ptolemy played an important and dangerous role (Arr. *Anab.* 4. 29. 1-6).[48] Ultimately, however, the attempt to take the rock by direct assault failed (Arr. *Anab.* 4. 29. 6)[49] and it was captured by other means in which Ptolemy is not mentioned (Arr. *Anab.* 29. 7–30. 4). In India he was regularly in charge of mixed forces (Arr. *Anab.* 5. 23. 7-24. 3; 6. 5. 6; 7. 15. 3).[50]

As mentioned, it has been claimed that Ptolemy used his history to denigrate his rivals among the Diadochi, in particular Perdiccas and Antigonus,[51] but his rivals are not much maligned in Arrian's account. Antigonus, his most enduring opponent, was left behind in Phrygia in 333 (Arr. *Anab.* 1. 29. 3) and not mentioned again in Arrian until a brief reference to his death at Ipsus in 301 (*Anab.* 7. 18. 5). Their actions are in certain cases ignored, but then, as seen, it is likely that so are some of Ptolemy's. Arrian's history highlights Alexander's deeds but omits many of those of his underlings. It has been claimed, however, that this is not solely the result of Arrian's selections of material, but rather reflective of his source Ptolemy's attempts to accentuate his actions and eliminate or minimize those of his rivals (Errington 1969: 233). Perdiccas is reported by Ptolemy as not awaiting Alexander's signal for battle during the siege of Thebes, but precipitously engaging (Arr. *Anab.* 1. 8. 1). Other sources report that Perdiccas was following Alexander's orders (Diod. 17. 12. 3–4).[52] At Halicarnassus, Diodorus (17. 25. 5) describes a situation similar to the one found in Arrian with respect to Thebes. Diodorus reports that Perdiccas' soldiers became drunk and made a "wild" attack on the wall of the citadel. In the case of Thebes, the attack by Perdiccas' forces led to the quick fall of the city (Arr. *Anab.* 1. 8. 2–8). There is little doubt that however long Alexander might have waited for a surrender, the Thebans were not about to do so. Those who precipitated the attack on the Macedonians in the Cadmea knew they would be executed and so encouraged resistance (Arr. *Anab.* 1. 7. 11). Moreover, there are no noted repercussions for Perdiccas' claimed disobedience. Of course, this might be because of the outcome. In any case, Perdiccas remained in charge of his battalion (Arr. *Anab.* 1. 14. 2). One of the chiliarches or taxeis of the infantry was throughout the campaign in Asia named for Perdiccas (eg. Arr. *Anab.* 1. 14. 2, 20. 5). Moreover, during the attack on Thebes, Perdiccas, while fighting in the first ranks, was wounded and had to be carried from the field (Arr. *Anab.* 1. 8. 3). Errington (1969: 237), however, claims that the supposed insubordination of Perdiccas was part of an attempt by Ptolemy or Arrian to free Alexander from the repercussions of destroying one of the great Greek cities. However, Alexander was facing serious problems from other of his erstwhile Greek allies and the destruction of Thebes brought all of that agitation to an end. This was a clear example of the doctrine of Shock and Awe.[53] While he did turn the final decision with respect to Thebes over to those allies who had joined him in the siege, most of these were long-standing enemies of the Thebans. The Macedonian king therefore knew what he was doing in giving the decision regarding Thebes to those who had been that city's enemies for years (Diod. 17. 8. 1, 5–6; Just. 11. 2. 7–9; Arr. *Anab.* 1. 7. 4, 10. 1–2). At most, this might have given Alexander a fig leaf of deniability, but no one was fooled. While it is likely that Alexander was angry at the Thebans' actions, this decision was reached through cold reason. When the Thebans refused to make peace with him, Alexander saw the destruction of the city as the way to forestall future revolts. The Athenians had promised assistance to the Thebans (Diod. 17. 8. 5; Arr. *Anab.* 1. 7. 4; Dein. 1. 18), as had the Arcadians (Diod. 17. 8. 5–6; Arr. *Anab.* 1. 10. 1), the Eleans (Diod. 17. 8. 5; Arr. *Anab.* 1. 10. 1), and the Aetolians (Arr. *Anab.* 1. 10. 2). These now all made their peace with Alexander.

In the attack on the chief Mallian city in India where Alexander was severely wounded, it is claimed that Arrian intimates that Perdiccas was at least partially responsible for Alexander's serious wound. Arrian (*Anab.* 6. 9. 1–10. 4) reports that for the assault on the city the army was divided between Alexander and Perdiccas. Apparently, most of Perdiccas' troops, since the outer wall had been abandoned, believed there was no wall to scale and therefore they did not bring any scaling ladders. When they discovered that the citadel's walls were indeed occupied, many went back to get them and others began to undermine the wall.[54] Alexander became frustrated at what he took to be dawdling and, seizing a ladder, climbed the wall and jumped down inside, where he was seriously wounded (Arr. *Anab.* 6. 9. 3–10. 2).[55] In this section, Arrian does not state that it was on the order of Perdiccas that the ladders were not initially brought, and he only references Ptolemy with respect to Alexander's wound and states that while many sources listed Ptolemy as well as Peucestas covering the wounded Alexander with their shields, Ptolemy himself says he was not there with Alexander when he was wounded (Arr. *Anab.* 6. 11. 8). The passage in Arrian then does not directly criticize Perdiccas, nor even the troops who assumed the city had been taken and hence no need for ladders. If anything is by implication put forth as responsible for Alexander's very serious wound, it was the impatience of the commander himself (Arr. *Anab.* 6. 8. 3).[56] While it is likely the material comes from Ptolemy, it is not directly attributed to him. If this is meant to be a denigration of Perdiccas, and if here Arrian is reflective of his source, it is a very nuanced criticism indeed. Again, as with respect to the possible incident at Thebes, no recrimination from Alexander is recorded and in this latter case Perdiccas remained in Alexander's confidence as one of the elite bodyguards

(Arr. *Anab.* 5. 13. 1; 6. 28. 4), was one of those who along with Alexander was married to a Persian princess in Susa (Arr. *Anab.* 7. 4. 6), and at the time of Alexander's death was the Conqueror's second-in-command (Diod. 18. 3. 4; Plut. *Eum.* 1. 2).

The case for the conscious omission of Antigonus' exploits is even less convincing. Now it is true that this commander is referenced exactly once in the *Anabasis*. Other than the notice of his posting in Phrygia (Arr. *Anab.* 1. 29. 3), he is absent from Arrian's narrative of Alexander's expedition. In the first place, both Ptolemy and Arrian were writing about Alexander, whom after his posting in Phrygia Antigonus never saw again. He did have one major accomplishment prior to Alexander's death. In the aftermath of the Battle of Issus, many escaping from the battle fled north and attempted to recapture Lydia, but Antigonus in four battles defeated them (Curt. 4. 1. 34-35). Arrian (2. 13. 2) refers to 8,000 fleeing the battle, but in his account these head to Tripolis and escape to Cyprus and Egypt. Antigonus' heroics are nowhere found in Arrian and the assumption is that they were omitted from the account of Ptolemy as well. However, they do not appear in either Diodorus or Justin. Moreover, Antipater's defeat of Agis is mostly missing from Arrian's account as well, with but a brief mention that Alexander sent to Macedonia money to Antipater for "the Lacedaemonian War" (Arr. *Anab.* 3. 16. 10). These events did not directly involve Alexander. Once Alexander has moved inland, most of what he has left behind is omitted from Arrian's narrative. This may have been true of Ptolemy's as well. While this is not definite, it is noteworthy that Arrian's history ceased with the death of the Conqueror (Arr. *Anab.* 7. 26. 3).

There are also other occasions where particular individuals are mentioned in other sources but omitted from Arrian's account. For example, Diodorus (17. 61. 3) and Curtius (3. 16. 32) report that Coenus, Hephaestion, Menidas, and Perdiccas were wounded at Gaugamela, but Arrian only reports Coenus, Menidas, and Hephaestion, omitting any reference to Perdiccas suffering an injury (Arr. *Anab.* 3. 15. 2). Hermann Strasburger (1934: 50–4) believed these omissions were simply to amplify Alexander's role, but Errington (1969: 233–4, 240–1) see them as emanating from Ptolemy's purpose to present all of Alexander's officers as relatively equal under the supremacy of Alexander. Certainly, as noted earlier, this concentration on Alexander was part of Arrian's stated purpose and likely Ptolemy's as well (Arr. *Anab.* 1. 12. 2–4; 7. 30. 2). On the death of Hephaestion, Perdiccas was promoted to second-in-command to Alexander (Diod. 18. 3. 4; Plut. *Eum.* 1. 2). While it is true that this information is not found in Arrian's *Anabasis*, it also is absent from Book Seventeen of Diodorus and Plutarch's *Life of Alexander*. Diodorus (17. 110. 8) does declare that Perdiccas was put in charge of conducting Hephaestion's body to Babylon. Nor does Arrian mention that on his death Alexander handed his ring to Perdiccas (Diod. 17. 117. 3; Curt. 10. 5. 4; Just. 12. 15. 12–13). Curtius (10. 6–9) also clearly presents Perdiccas as in charge in the aftermath of Alexander's death. While these omissions might be telling, as noted above, Arrian reports that both Ptolemy and Aristobulus end their works with the death of Alexander (*Anab.* 7. 26. 3). Only the lack of a reference to the new authority given to Perdiccas after Hephaestion's death is then notable. Why it does not appear in the sources relating the events of Alexander's life is unclear. What is clear is that, while there are omissions, there are also occasions where, for example, Perdiccas is mentioned by Arrian and omitted by the other historians. Arrian (*Anab.* 4. 30. 9)[57] reports that Hephaestion and Perdiccas accomplished the bridging of the Indus, while Curtius (8. 12. 4) only mentions Hephaestion. Plutarch (*Alex.* 41. 5) mentions that Perdiccas, while hunting, accidentally wounded Craterus; no mention of the incident in Arrian—maybe then missing from Ptolemy's account as well? The best argument is the one presented by Joseph Roisman (1984: 381), that Ptolemy's work was not an attempt to undermine Perdiccas or any of the other Diadochs. In the case of Perdiccas, the period of their open hostility is remarkably short and without much of an afterlife. This would then have had to have been a history hastily written and copied and distributed to achieve any real political value. It is even more problematic when considering the population one would most want to influence: the mostly illiterate veterans.[58]

Ptolemy, also on the basis of Arrian, is thought to have neglected the activities of others as well. Aristonous, it has been argued, was ignored by Ptolemy (Tarn 2003: 109; Errington 1969: 235–6). His later connection to Perdiccas is seen as the reason for his exclusion from the narrative.[59] He is mentioned only once in Arrian's *Anabasis* (6. 28. 4)[60] simply listed as one of the *somatophylaces*. However, he is not much noted in any of the Alexander historians. Neither Diodorus, nor Justin, nor Plutarch's *Life of Alexander* mention him at all in their accounts of Alexander's life. Curtius (9. 5. 15–16, 18) only mentions him as one of those, in addition to Peucestas, Timaeus, Leonnatus, and Aristobulus, who protected Alexander when he was seriously wounded in the attack on the Mallian city. Curtius further reports that Aristonous himself was severely wounded in this incident and Timaeus was killed. Diodorus (17. 99. 4) only lists Peucestas as saving Alexander's life; Arrian (*Anab.* 6. 10. 1–2) says the saviors were Peucestas, Abreas, and Leonnatus. This omission of Aristonous from Arrian's list of those who helped save Alexander, then, is not significant. Given that Ptolemy and

Aristobulus appear in agreement and Curtius has no support from the other sources, it is likely that Aristonous' inclusion was part of what Howe has called "invented memory" on the part of one of the many no longer surviving accounts of Alexander's expedition.

Leonnatus is another individual believed to have his accomplishments omitted by Ptolemy. In the so-called Conspiracy of the Pages, Curtius (8. 6. 22) reports that it was Leonnatus and Ptolemy who revealed the conspiracy to Alexander. Arrian (*Anab.* 4. 13. 7) only mentions Ptolemy. Plutarch (*Alex.* 55. 3–4) simply says the plot was revealed, mentioning neither. Leonnatus is, however, mentioned a number of times in Arrian's account. Alexander sent him to Darius' mother, wife, and children to assuage their concerns that Darius was dead (*Anab.* 2. 12. 5); it is noted that he was one of the elite *somatophylaces* (*Anab.* 3. 5. 5; 4. 24. 10; 6. 22. 3, 28. 4), he along with Perdiccas and Ptolemy held a command during the siege of the Rock of Choriones (*Anab.* 4. 21. 4), was wounded along with Ptolemy in an attack on an Aspasian city (*Anab.* 4. 23. 3), commanded one-third of the force against the Guraeans and was successful in fulfilling his part of the operation (Arr. *Anab.* 4. 24. 10, 25. 3). Leonnatus was one of the individuals who defended Alexander inside the Mallian city (Arr. *Anab.* 6. 9. 3–10. 1. 11. 1–2), he acted in a number of military capacities during the voyage down the Indus (Arr. *Anab.* 6. 18. 3, 20. 3, 22. 3), and Alexander awarded him along with Peucestas a golden crown for his actions saving the king's life (Arr. *Anab.* 7. 5. 5).[61] These many favorable references imply that the earlier omission had no ulterior purpose.

The argument here is less that Ptolemy directly attacked his rivals, but rather did so mostly through the omission of their accomplishments; "the general levelling of the officers' prestige under Alexander and the concealment of Perdiccas' closeness to Alexander in the last months of the king's life ... might even have been the crucial factors in retaining the long-term loyalty of Ptolemy's Macedonian supporters" (Errington 1969: 233–7, 241–2). This assessment depends on an earlier date for the composition of Ptolemy's history, sometime soon after 320, and also on these so-called omissions being attributed to Ptolemy and not to Arrian himself. Moreover, it further depends on both a literate and a very sophisticated population to draw the conclusions Errington assumes from what can only be described as some very nuanced criticism, if that is what it is.

So, what can be known with some degree of certainty? Ptolemy did write a history of his famous commander. His account, if Arrian is any indication, was primarily military and mostly devoid of the fanciful aspects that became the Alexander Romance. He did, however, have Alexander led to Siwah by talking snakes (Arr. *Anab.* 3. 3. 5).[62] While most writers embraced the account of

Alexander meeting with the Queen of the Amazons (Plut. *Alex.* 46. 1), it was missing from both Ptolemy's and Aristobulus' histories (Arr. *Anab.* 7. 13. 3; Plut. *Alex.* 46. 2). Beyond these few conclusions, it is difficult to say. Was it a work of propaganda designed to enhance Ptolemy's standing in the wild world of the Diodochi? I have a difficult time seeing the value in such propaganda. The subtlety of damning by omission would be lost on rank-and-file soldiers, or even on their commanders who would be very familiar with the truth. As Joseph Roisman (1984: 375) remarks, "the author must have been a master of subtle propaganda, of a propaganda indeed so subtle that its usefulness may be doubted." Moreover, when Antigonus had a letter sent into Eumenes of Cardia's camp to persuade his soldiers to desert him, it had to be read to the assembled army (Diod. 18. 63. 1–2). This was not the most literate of ages. Additionally, the increasingly mercenary character of the armies serving in Asia and Egypt lessened over time the importance of Alexander. These soldiers were more concerned with pay and successful leadership (Anson 1991: 230–47). Antigonus, who had the least connection to Alexander, became until his death in 301 the most dangerous and successful of the Diadochs. In the case of Antigonus or Cassander, neither attempted to create some fictional tie to the dead Conqueror himself, but rather to gain some such connection through marriage respectively to Cleopatra, Alexander's full sister or to Thessalonice, his half-sister. Cleopatra had favorably responded to a proposal of marriage from Ptolemy, but to prevent the marriage Antigonus had her killed (Diod. 20. 37. 3–6).

The ineffectiveness of propaganda is seen in the example of Eumenes of Cardia. Eumenes was not a native Macedonian and yet competed in the struggle after Alexander's death. When Neoptolemus, a former commander of the hypaspists/argyraspids and a Macedonian aristocrat, attempted after Alexander's death to subvert Eumenes' Macedonian forces by proclaiming that Eumenes was but a secretary to Alexander, he was laughed to derision, for the soldiers remembered that Alexander had bestowed many honors on the Cardian Greek and had even thought Eumenes "worthy of a relationship through marriage" (Plut. *Eum.* 1. 6). This last was in reference to the marriages arranged in Susa by Alexander between his senior officers and Persian princesses (Arr. *Anab.* 7. 4. 4–7). Perdiccas and Ptolemy are both mentioned specifically as part of this same ceremony in Arrian's account. Many attempts were made to subvert Eumenes' troops after the death of Perdiccas, but until the very last all had failed. While Eumenes and other former supporters of Perdiccas were condemned by the royal army in Egypt, Eumenes' condemnation, in particular, was the result of his defeat of the popular Craterus in battle and the death of that commander in that struggle

(Diod. 18. 37. 1–2; Plut. *Eum*. 8. 3). Those Macedonians serving with Eumenes were not impressed by the actions of their fellow soldiers in Egypt and even created a thousand-man bodyguard for Eumenes (Plut *Eum*. 8. 6). When Ptolemy attempted to undermine Eumenes' authority, he didn't write a pamphlet, he sent individuals to attempt to undermine the Cardian directly (Diod. 18. 62. 1). Ptolemy's agents reminded those serving Eumenes that he had been condemned by the army in Egypt after the assassination of Perdiccas. Nothing apparently was said concerning Eumenes' earlier involvement with Alexander. Diodorus (Diod. 18. 62. 1) reports that "no one" paid attention because "the kings and Polyperchon, their then guardian, and also Olympias, the mother of Alexander, had written to them that they should serve Eumenes in every way." Antigonus sent similar individuals and a letter which was read to Eumenes' troops (Diod. 18. 62. 3–7). These offered material rewards for the Cardian's betrayal, money, and satrapies. When these incentives proved fruitless, Antigonus threatened open war. In the one plot that succeeded against Eumenes, it was not due to any slurs on his character or distortions of his actions, but rather a trade by elements in Eumenes' army to recover their property and families that had been taken by the enemy by surrendering Eumenes (Anson 2015: 202–3, 257–9).[63]

Other examples of subtle propaganda have been claimed to be seen in other aspects of Ptolemy's history. With respect to Alexander's journey to Siwah, much is made of Ptolemy's description of snakes, instead of ravens, guiding his expedition when it became lost, and his claim that Alexander did not return from Siwah the way he had gone, but rather across the desert to Memphis. In the case of the snakes, this is contrary to Aristobulus' and other writers' insistence that it was ravens who led him when lost. It is argued that snakes became associated with the Ptolemaic dynastic myth and this was a way of joining the legend of Alexander and the legitimacy of the Ptolemies (Howe 2013: 63–4; Pownall 2021: 34; cf. Ogden 2009: 161–2). What makes attribution of a purpose to Ptolemy's giving another creature of the desert credit is that these spoke.[64] This makes the entire incident a clear example of the intervention of the divine (Arr. *Anab*. 3. 3. 5=[Ptolemy] *BNJ* 138 F-8). This emphasis on divine assistance was likely Ptolemy's main purpose in providing this more sensational tale. That the symbols of this divine aid should be snakes might indeed be part of Ptolemy's attempt to connect the two dynasties, but if so, it has been done very subtly. The second point of dispute, the excursion across the desert directly to Memphis from Siwah, is presented by Arrian in the simple phrase, "Ptolemy, son of Lagus, by a different way, direct to Memphis" (Arr. *Anab*. 3. 4. 5). There is no elaboration. Howe argues that Ptolemy wished to separate the founding of Alexandria from the consultation with the oracle. "A god-like, prescient Alexander should not need advice on how to plan his most famous city" (2014: 78). Not even from his father Zeus/Amun? I am more inclined to agree with Bosworth (1980: 274) that this different route and direct trip from Siwah to Memphis was the result of Arrian's confusion. Arrian's very next sentence is that Alexander received delegations in Memphis (Arr. *Anab*. 3. 4. 5).

The role of propaganda was essentially waged orally. Perdiccas was assassinated by his officers after his failure in the Egyptian campaign, not as the result of any pamphlet that diminished in their eyes his previous status with Alexander (Anson 2014: 68–9). Philip did not advertise his war of revenge against the Persians by writing a history of their interference in Greek affairs over the years, nor did he inaugurate some great revival of Herodotus. If Ptolemy's history was a piece meant to enhance his association with Alexander as a way to diminish the power and authority of his enemies in real time, then when did he write it? If he wished to undermine Perdiccas' power in the early days, then such subtlety in addition to what I noted earlier about the lack of reading skills on the part of the troops would hardly undermine what all veterans of Alexander's campaign knew. As with the earlier discussion with respect to Eumenes, they knew who Perdiccas was and his position under Alexander, as is shown in the failed attempt to assassinate him back in Babylon. If written later to undermine the standing of Antigonus, the problems remain with this assumption as well. While this would have been a far easier task, for Antigonus was left behind in Asia Minor in 333, there are no reported attempts to undermine his authority by referring to his absence from the majority of Alexander's campaign. It is never, at least as far as our sources would indicate, brought up.

Timothy Howe (2021: 54–64; cf. Bosworth 1980: 376) believes that Ptolemy's history was all part of an attempt by Ptolemy to present himself as some sort of mirror image of Alexander. "Both Arrian and Ptolemy take pains to underscore the fact Alexander has chosen Ptolemy to act as his proxy and that Alexander approves of Ptolemy's actions and trusts him more than any other commander in his army. The conclusion we are expected to draw is that Ptolemy was a second Alexander" (Howe 2021: 63–4). This is a very interesting take on the purpose of Ptolemy's history. But instead of a mirror image, if this was the history's purpose, the result is more like a pale reflection. From the little that can be gleaned from Arrian's use of Ptolemy's history, the primary focus was Alexander. Ptolemy was to be seen standing in his shadow as a loyal and brave lieutenant.

Ptolemy's history was not an attempt, however nuanced, to secure political power, but rather an endeavor to be closely associated with the growing legend of his former commander. After all, he did not write a history of his own considerable achievements, but rather those of Alexander, attempting wherever possible to connect himself with that commander. While this might suggest an early date for the composition of his history, in the immediacy of Alexander's death such connections to the Conqueror might be powerful inducements to support, but what little that can be gleamed of his original composition from Arrian suggests to me more the recollections of an older individual remembering the time—and the glorious time at that—of his youth. As a younger man, such a history might give some very slight advantage, but as shown by Roisman, too subtle to be of much use; it was actual physical connections to Alexander, such as possessing his body, marrying his sister, and so on, that could bring political advantages rather than writing histories to impress what was primarily an illiterate public of army veterans and mercenaries. Everyone who had fought with Alexander inherited part of the Conqueror's charisma. The example of Alexander's hypaspists, the later argyraspids, shows how many clung to their attachment to the Conqueror.[65] Ptolemy's history then was not for the present—it was for posterity.

Ptolemy had created what would grow in Alexandria into the great cultural institutions of the Hellenistic Age, the Museum and the Library. His history was to be part of his contribution to this cultural and historical foundation. Moreover, if written late in life, which I believe is certain, with virtually everyone who could contradict him dead and if Arrian's account fairly reflects in whatever truncated version Ptolemy's story, his history was remarkably free of self-aggrandizement. His glory came from his association with another. His actions then would be subtly enhanced and those of his opponents equally subtly diminished. This might not even have been done consciously. If written late in life, what need to do more? His major opponents were dead and in direct conflict with each he had won, defeating the respective invasions of Egypt by Perdiccas in 320 and Antigonus in 306.[66] To diminish their reputations too much would diminish his own as the one who defeated both. Moreover, the truth concerning his earlier career with Alexander was in and of itself sufficient to secure his legacy with respect to that legendary time. He had accompanied the great Alexander on his expedition, was his close companion, and came to be one of the Conqueror's chief advisors and commanders. What need to go much beyond the facts? Having been proclaimed a living god and a king would ensure his present and immediate memory, but being remembered through the ages as part of the greatest epic adventure of almost any time would immortalize him in the same way the heroes of the *Iliad* transcended time.

9

Ptolemy: A Conclusion

Ptolemy set the pattern for his descendants in treating Egypt as if in many ways it was two different nations, which in many respects it was to the end of the Ptolemaic era. Alexander was not the philosopher king attempting to unify the world's people, as proclaimed by W. W. Tarn, but a brilliant enough individual to realize that empires in the East could not survive as the rule by a minority of Greek speakers over a vast sea of native peoples in such a perilous world. The Successors, as Ian Worthington (2016: 197) states, "heavily taxed and marginalized their native subjects." The Romans demonstrated what freer citizenship meant: fewer revolts and much bigger battalions for the endemic wars. Ptolemy became the pharaoh of the Egyptians and the king of the Greeks and others. While local authority remained primarily in the hands of native Egyptians, from the regional nomes to the central government in Alexandria Greek and Macedonians were in charge. Whatever Alexander's purpose in attempting to bring the conquered into his government and army, that was not the policy followed by Ptolemy. His relationship with his subjects was as the traditional pharaoh for the Egyptians and a Hellenic king for the others. While this was an opportunity missed, it would have been a difficult task to join as one people two such diverse cultures. Some have claimed that he did make such an attempt with his support and, perhaps, even his introduction of the Cult of Serapis. However, the evidence is that Serapis was never meant to, nor did it succeed in transforming the traditional worship of Apis among the native Egyptians into a universal cult. What Ptolemy did accomplish was a stable regime. Alexandria became the cultural, educational, and creative center of the Hellenistic world. Ptolemy's cultural creations and foreign policy did change the focus of Egypt from a relatively isolated North African state turned ever inwards into one at least with respect to its non-Egyptian population whose focus was on the Mediterranean. Through Alexandria in particular, Ptolemy opened up Egypt to the world. It became the conduit through which much of what had so intrigued Herodotus about Egypt now began to flow into the mainstream of Hellenic culture. Aspects of Egyptian theology were very attractive to Greek audiences and the Cult of Serapis was one result of this fascination. However, the cult that emerged, while incorporating many of the theological aspects of its Egyptian origins, was Greek in its ritual practices and those theological aspects became associated with Greek myths. Ptolemy promoted the cult in Alexandria, but did not create it, nor did he use it as a means to dominate the Mediterranean. Ptolemy's descendants fully associated the new cult with Ptolemaic rule. Ptolemy wished to make Alexandria the cultural capital of the Greek world and his descendants achieved his vision. Alexandria was not just the Ptolemaic capital, it was the center of their Hellenic kingship. Alexander may have seen the potential of the site of the future Alexandria militarily and economically, but it was Ptolemy who realized the city's full potential.

Ptolemy created the longest-surviving Hellenistic state and unlike his fellow Successors left this world, in a play on a supposed motto from the American West, "he died with his sandals off." His achievements with respect to Greek culture were truly significant. He began the Library and the Museum. His other achievements are less obvious and more nuanced. His dynasty lasted for almost three centuries, being the last to succumb to the great power that arose in the West and went down only after a strong final resistance. While true that long before it was absorbed into the Roman Empire it had been a Roman protectorate, it took defeat in the Battle of Actium in 31 BC to end Egypt's independence. It was the deft diplomacy of its last Ptolemaic ruler, Cleopatra VII, bolstered by her Roman paramours Julius Caesar and Marcus Antonius, that gave Egypt a chance of avoiding incorporation into the Empire. With her death, Egypt became a province in that Empire.

That the Hellenistic world failed to survive the advance of Rome was due to a Hellenic inability to unite into one people politically. The history of the Greek world was one of cultural unity but political division. Alexander's empire added such immense potential for a new political reality which was never realized. Instead of one great empire stretching from the Adriatic to the Indus, there arose independent kingdoms, free city-states, an expanded Greek world culturally, but with the enduring inability to unite often even when self-interest demanded it. While this was not the fault of Ptolemy alone, he did work from the very beginning to bring about the division of Alexander's empire. Ptolemy also, like his fellow Successors, failed to unite into one people those whom he ruled. Using the Roman Republic as an example of successful empire building, the Romans unified first central Italy and eventually all of Italy into the Republic through a combination of alliances, grants of citizenship, and colonization. As

Hannibal discovered, the Romans had by the standards of the time in the late third century BC a huge citizen base. Consequently, despite Hannibal's brilliance, Rome was able to suffer massive defeats and yet fight on to victory. As Napoleon supposedly explained and likely plagiarized, "God always favors the big battalions." Of course, this did not work out so well for the Persians against Alexander, but in general, most things being equal, the ability to replace losses with fresh soldiers was an advantage that the Roman Republic exploited. What might have resulted from the accomplishments of Philip and Alexander did not happen, nor did it result from the efforts of any of the later Hellenistic dynasties. A united Greek world clearly would have stood a good chance of resisting Rome. It was one of the great accomplishments of this age, however, that the Hellenistic world greatly influenced the Roman world.

The Hellenistic kingdoms themselves, by their creation of what amounted to two different societies operating under one central government and thereby not utilizing fully their population resources, further exacerbated the problem. Here, Ptolemy Soter was guilty of setting a course for future Egyptian history as a country of two different nations. Egypt had in truth two capitals, the overall controlling one in Alexandria, the culturally Greek capital, the other in Memphis which represented the native Egyptian population.[1] Those of Greek and Macedonian origin made up his central administration in Alexandria and the key elements of the army. This pattern barely expanded over the succeeding centuries.

These criticisms are likely too harsh. After all, Ptolemy was not living in some utopian universe, but in the reality of his own. His successes in this light in the political sphere were impressive. He imposed his rule on the foreign land of Egypt, a land with a history of rebellion against just such foreign rulers. During Ptolemy's time there were no serious revolts and, in fact, none during the reigns of the first three Ptolemaic rulers. Ptolemy succeeded in gaining the trust and support of the local power structure, especially that of the priestly establishments. He did this through a policy based on patronage and non-interference in their affairs. In short, he gave the native elites reason to trust him. He also changed the nature of Egypt by exploiting Alexander's foundation of Alexandria, turning what had only barely begun by the time of the Conqueror's death into the capital and nerve center of Ptolemaic Egypt and the cultural center of the entire Hellenistic world. He also transfigured Egypt from an insular society into a major commercial and naval power in the eastern Mediterranean. As noted in the text, unlike his competitors, he was not interested in fighting to unite Alexander's empire. He clearly had seen that it could not survive, for the forces of disintegration were too great. After a failed attempt to create a ruling council to govern the empire, it was clear to Ptolemy that his colleagues were not ready, willing, or able to cooperate but that what Alexander had apocryphally predicted would come to pass: there would be a free-for-all amongst Alexander's former lieutenants and governors. With this realization Ptolemy took what he believed to be the jewel of Alexander's conquests, Egypt, and concentrated on maintaining his hold on that land and establishing his dynasty to rule it. What is seen by so many modern historians as Ptolemy's deliberate imperialism with the ultimate goal of winning out as Alexander's ultimate Successor is a misinterpretation of Ptolemy's foreign policy. In short, Polybius got it right. With the exception of Coelê Syria, Phoenicia, and Cyprus, areas critical for any attempt to invade Egypt, other acquisitions and alliances were in the main to hinder the growth in others' power. This was especially the case with respect to Antigonus, the one Successor with both the desire and ability to become the new Alexander. Ptolemy's foray into Greece was part of a program to recreate Philip's League of Corinth. Much like his later use of the Nesiotic League, he was not interested in expanding his holdings in the Greek world as a means to secure the throne of Macedonia, rather he was creating allies to resist the ambitions of his rivals. What was a very aggressive and dangerous early career as satrap of Egypt became the cautious Ptolemy of the later Successor Wars. When his attempt to organize Greece along the lines of Philip's League or, even more likely, those of the renewal proposed by Polyperchon came to nothing, he went back to Egypt. Those cities he had garrisoned in Greece eventually are found in the hands of others. Ptolemy made no attempt to reacquire them. Moreover, during those periods of chaos in Macedonia proper he made no effort to secure that throne. Those lands and territories that came into his hands outside of Cyprus, Coelê Syria, and Phoenicia, he was unwilling to run much risk in their defense. At the Battle of Ipsus, Ptolemy failed to participate. Once he had secured his goal of Egypt he devoted his further energies to protecting his prize by way of a defensive and cautious policy. For Egypt and Polybius' protective fence, he was willing to run risks, not elsewhere. Ptolemy created a stable state that was both a naval and a commercial power. His dynasty would survive for almost three centuries—not a bad run. Moreover, it was a state truly created by Ptolemy, the son of that otherwise obscure aristocrat Lagus.

Notes

Chapter 1

1. Unless otherwise noted, all dates henceforward are to be considered BC.
2. Anson 2013: 188.
3. See Anson 2020.
4. See for example Seibert 1969: 64–83; Landucci Gattinoni 1987: 37–42; 2008: 149–50; Bosworth 2002: 26; cf Rathmann 2014: 85–7.
5. Arrian's work survives in the fragments of other histories. Photius, a ninth-century author, whose work is variously called the *Bibliotheca* or the *Myrobiblion*, records 279 summaries of various works including that of Arrian's *Successors* (noted in the text as *Succ.* 1a). Three additional fragments of Arrian's original work are in the so-called Vatican Palimpsest which contains two brief fragments from Book Seven of Arrian's ten-book original (listed here as Arr. *Succ.* 24–5), and a papyrus fragment, *PSI* 12 1284, and the Gothenburg Palimpsest which contains excerpts from Book Ten. Photius also summarized the work of Dexippus' *History of the Events after Alexander the Great's Death*, which in turn was closely based on Arrian's Book One (designated *Succ.* 1b).
6. Nepos' *De viris illustribus* included lives of "foreign and Roman kings, generals, lawyers, orators, poets, historians, and philosophers." Only his *Excellentium imperatorum vitae* (*Lives of Excellent Commanders*) has survived.
7. Not generally believed.

Chapter 2

1. Walter Ellis (1994: 86n. 36) states that Arrian, *Anabasis* 3. 6. 6. might imply that Ptolemy had been made a *somatophylax* in 336. "On Philip's death those who had been banished on Alexander's account returned. Ptolemy σωματοφύλακα κατέστησεν." Ellis suggests that this means since he is appointed again in 330 that he must have been demoted. The author further sees this as being responsible for the lack of Ptolemy's participation in the the campaign in its early stages. Brian Bosworth's opinion (1980: 283) is much more likely. Arrian is anticipating how Alexander will ultimately reward those who were banished after the Pixodarus affair. According to this same passage in Arrian, Nearchus is made satrap of Lycia,

which is unlikely to have occurred until this area had been taken, or not until 334 (Arr. *Anab.* 1. 24. 3–4).
2. At the time of the accession of Alexander to the throne, in total the Companions numbered roughly 1,800 elite heavy cavalry men (Heckel 2016: 261).
3. It is likely that while the cavalry guards dated from much earlier, the institutions of the pages and *somatophylaces* are creations of Philip II. Prior to Philip the kings of Macedonia, while ostensibly autocrats with few checks on their authority, in practice were reliant on the Macedonian land-holding aristocracy. These individuals interpreted their standing as *hetairoi* as placing them almost on a par with the king, who in their estimation was simply the first among equals. That such individuals would condescend to become bodyguards of a sleeping king or permit their sons to become for all intents and purposes hostages to their fathers' good behavior while serving at court would appear unlikely. These were institutions copied from the Persian court and represent the change in the king's relationship with his aristocratic *hetairoi*. The balance under Philip II had shifted strongly in the king's favor. While there was likely an infantry guard for Philip's predecessors, the expansion of such a body into 3,000 soldiers with 1,000 men from this number being the *agema* was also one of his innovations. See Anson 2013: 55–62; 2020: 26–9, 55.
4. See the brief discussion with references in Heckel 2021: 428.
5. Bouché-Leclercq 2007 [1903]: 1. 3; Bevan 1968 [1927]: 21, but see Heckel 2021: 428.
6. The year is not in question, but the month is. Plutarch gives a date in July and Aristobulus, quoted by Arrian, says October. See Hamilton 1969: 7.
7. See Heckel 2021: 428.
8. Contra van Oppen de Ruiter 2013: 81.
9. Heckel also makes the claim that Laomedon, Nearchus, and Harpalus were also older, but this is not that certain. Laomedon is generally considered the younger brother of Ergyrius, but how much younger is unknown. Nearchus is an advisor to Demetrius, the son of Antigonus, in 314 and maybe dead in 306, but none of this means much. Antigonus, the son of Philip, and a contemporary of King Philip II, died in 301 at the age of almost eighty or eighty-six (Heckel 2021: 56). Heckel (1985: 289) hints that Harpalus may have been unsuited to military service because of his age, but there is no real evidence to judge him either older or roughly the same age as Alexander.
10. For example, Diodorus uses the terms interchangeably (17. 83. 7, 100. 1, 114. 1–2).
11. See Anson 2020: 94–5; 2015: 54–6
12. Even though the earliest reference to a Macedonian *hetairos* dates from the reign of Archelaus I (413–399) (Ael. *VH* 13. 4) and it has been claimed that the institution derives from Persian antecedents (Kienast 1973: 248–67), the relationship likely dates back to the Bronze Age (Hammond and Griffith 1979: 158–9).
13. In general, see Pownall 2010: 55–65.

14 For the many differences in the literary Homeric kingship and real Macedonian one, see Carlier 2000: 259–68.
15 Anson 2020: 173–83
16 Cf. Athen. 13. 572D.
17 Philip had created the Macedonian heavy infantry through converting many of the traditional Macedonian peasant population dependent on their aristocratic landlords into independent land holders. This companionship with his foot soldiers was less social and far more economic. See Anson 2009: 88–98.
18 For what we do know, see Stagakis 1962: 53–67.
19 The king was literally the first to engage and the last to leave the battle. Philip himself was wounded at least four times. He lost an eye at the siege of Methone (Didymus *In Dem.* 11. 22. col. 12. 43–64; Scholia *In Dem.* 18. 67; Dem. 18. 67; Diod. 16. 34. 5), had his right collarbone broken by an Illyrian lance (Dem. 18. 67; Didymus *In Dem.* 11. 22. col. 12. 64–13. 2), his hand damaged (Dem. 18. 67), and his right leg received a wound that left him thereafter lame (Didymus *In Dem.*11. 22, col. 13. 3–7; Dem. 18. 67). Philip's son Alexander received a head wound on the Granicus (Arr. *Anab.* 1. 15. 7–8; Diod. 17. 20. 6; Plut. *Mor.* 327a), one in the thigh at Issus (Arr. *Anab.* 2. 12. 1; Curt. 3. 12. 2; Plut. *Mor.* 327a), the shoulder and leg at the siege of Gaza (Arr. *Anab.* 2. 27. 2; Curt. 4. 6. 17, 23; Plut. *Mor.* 327a). He suffered a leg wound near Samarkand (Curt. 7. 6. 1–9; Arr. *Anab.* 3. 30. 10–11; Plut. *Mor.* 327a), was struck in the head and neck in Bactria (Arr. *Anab.* 4. 3. 3; Curt. 7. 6. 22), and had his lung pierced by an arrow in India (Arr. *Anab.* 6. 10. 1; Curt. 9. 5. 9–10).
20 For a detailed discussion of Philip's military and social reforms and their effect on the power of this king, see Anson 2020: 47–60, 79–81, 86–7.
21 While Plutarch refers to these individuals as *hetairoi*, he is using the term in the general sense of companions.
22 Generally, this was how *hetairos* was translated into Latin (Anson 2015: 49n. 19). *Philos* is often used in our late sources where *hetairos* would be more appropriate, and often the reverse is also true..
23 See Heckel 2021: 405; Anson 2020: 158–60, 180–1.
24 See Heckel 2021: 383–4.
25 On this episode and what it meant both for Alexander's position at court and for Philip's ambitions, see Anson 2020: 158–61.
26 Nicholas Hammond (1978: 336; cf. Antikas and Wynn-Antikas 2015: 682–92) believes there was an additional wife.
27 Little is known concerning Stephanus of Byzantium other than that in the sixth century AD he wrote a work titled *Ethnika*, a sort of geographical dictionary, but one where the author is primarily interested as a grammarian in proper adjective usage ("Stephanus of Byzantium," *OCD*). From the little that is known, he appears to have accurately used his sources.

28 See Heckel 2021: 174.
29 See Ellis, 1976: 34; Billows: 1995, 9–11; Hammond 1993B: 19–20.
30 Dell 1970: 121–2; Hammond: 1979: 654.
31 Methone was destroyed and its land given out to "Macedonians" (Diod. 16. 34. 5; Dem. 4. 35; Justin 7. 6. 14–16; Griffith 1965: 136); these recipients were ordinary Macedonians, not aristocrats. This was probably also the case with Apollonia, Olynthus, and thirty-two other communities in or near Thrace (Dem. 9. 26; Diod. 16. 53. 2–3; Just. 8. 3. 14–15; Hatzopoulos 1996A: 190–2, 195–6). An inscription tentatively dated to 335/334 records Alexander's gifts to individual "Macedonians" of lands associated with the Bottiaean towns of Calindoea, Thamiscia, Camacaea, and Tripoatis (Hammond 1988B: 383, 385–6; Hatzopoulos 1996A: 121–2; 1996B: 84–5).
32 See Anson 2020: 45–71.
33 It was this transformation of much of Macedonia's dependent population from tenants and dependent pastoralists into landowners that also in part was responsible for an explosion in the Macedonian economy. New lands were brought under cultivation and significant improvements were made in the lands already under cultivation. Non-landowning agricultural workers are not likely to make significant improvements to the land they work (Hanson 1995: 35). They tend to plant annual crops, avoiding those that require years of nurture before they become productive for fear that the ultimate profits will go to benefit others (Barlett 1980: 555). These new Macedonian landowners had a vested interest in improving their lands.
34 At Chaeronea Philip's army contained "not less than 2,000 cavalry" and 30,000 infantry (Diod. 16. 85. 5). Alexander took 1,800 Macedonian cavalry and 12,000 Macedonian infantry with him to Asia (Diod. 17. 17. 3–4), leaving behind in Macedonia 1,500 cavalry and 12,000 infantry with his regent Antipater (Diod. 17. 17. 5). There was also an advance force in Asia, but its size and composition are unknown (Diod. 16. 91. 2; Just. 9. 5. 8; Polyaen. 5. 44. 4).
35 Lagus, the son of Ptolemy, was a child of Thaïs (Plut. *Alex.* 38. 2; Athen. 13. 576E) who was either the concubine or the wife of Ptolemy. In Athenaeus (13. 576E) it is stated that Ptolemy married her after the death of Alexander.
36 This fourth-century AD statement regarding Seleucus is not referenced earlier in our surviving sources.
37 Hölbl 2001: 14.
38 Diodorus does not mention the succession of Alexander IV, but later refers to the "Kings" (19. 18. 6, 23. 2, 28. 5, 29. 1, 36. 6, 7, 39. 1, 7, 41 5, 42. 2, 47. 4).
39 Amyntas III, the father of Philip II, had two wives each of which presented him with three sons (Just. 7. 4. 5). Philip's full brothers, Alexander II and Perdiccas III, had preceded him on the throne and were dead.
40 Pausanias had earlier contended for the throne but had been repulsed through the aid of the Athenians in 368/367 (Aeschin. 2. 27–9).

41 Justin (11. 2. 3) states that Alexander had killed a step-brother, Caranus. This brother's existence has been questioned (Heckel 1979: 385–93). Another possible brother is Amphimachus. He is later called the "brother of the king [Arrhidaeus]" (Arr. *Succ.* 1a. 35), Alexander's half-brother and part of the dual monarchy after Alexander the Great's death. This designation might indicate an additional half-brother for Alexander. However, scholars typically believe that, if the statement is accurate and not a mistaken reference to that Arrhidaeus, the satrap of Hellespontine Phrygia (Heckel 2006: 22, following earlier scholars), Amphimachus is a son by Arrhidaeus' mother Philina, but from a earlier marriage, and not the son of Philip II (Bosworth 2002: 113; Carney 2000: 61, 276n. 45).
42 See Bagnall and Derow 240–1; on Menelaus, see Heckel 2021: 305.
43 Aelian in his *Varia Historia* includes in book 12, chapter 43 a number of these rags-to-riches stories. King Archelaus of Macedonia's mother was a slave, as was Darius III's.
44 The general consensus today is that, while the poverty of Lysimachus is to be doubted, the description of Lysimachus as a Thessalian is correct, even though both Pausanias (1. 9. 5) and Justin (15. 3. 1) describe him as Macedonian by birth, and Plutarch implies the same (cf. Plut. *Demetr.* 44. 6). Theopompus (*BNJ* 115 F-81=Athen. 6. 259F-261A) in a general account of the depravity of Philip II's "friends" states that a certain Agathocles who commanded troops under Philip was formerly a Thessalian slave. The name of Lysimachus' father and one of his sons was Agathocles (Arr. *Anab.* 6. 28. 4; *Ind.* 18. 3; Plut. *Demetr.* 31. 4. 46. 9). However, neither Theopompus nor any other author makes a connection between this former Thessalian slave and Agathocles, the father of Lysimachus. Further, Lysimachus in his struggle against Pyrrhus described the latter as a "foreigner, whose ancestors had always been subject to Macedonia" (Plut. *Pyrrh.* 12. 6). On identifying Lysimachus' ancestors as noble Macedonians, see I. L. Merker 1979: 31–5, whose arguments I still find persuasive.
45 Advancement within class is common. Demetrius, the son of Athaimenes, was promoted from ilarch (commander of a squadron) to hipparch (commander of 500).
46 Bosworth 1996: 116 and n. 84. Bosworth interprets Diodorus 17. 100. 2 (ἐν γὰρ τοῖς ἑταίροις παραληφθείς τις Μακεδών, ὄνομα Κόραγος) as "he was admitted among the Companions."
47 Anson 2020: 16–18.
48 On the prejudice of the aristocrats towards all those not of their class, see Anson 2015; esp. 241–61.
49 Philip had introduced the sarissa, or pike, into Macedonian warfare and, as a result, had transformed Macedonian from an often invaded and routinely exploited region into the greatest military power in the Western ancient world (see Anson 2020).
50 Stagakis 1962: 53–67; 1970: 86–102; Anson 2013: 24–5.

51 See Anson 2008: 17–30.
52 Pownall 2010: 55–65; Anson 2022: 22–8.

Chapter 3

1 Alexander suffered a head wound on the Granicus (Arr. *Anab.* 1. 15. 7–8; Diod. 17. 20. 6; Plut. *Mor.* 327A), one in the thigh at Issus (Arr. *Anab.* 2.12.1; Curt. 3. 12. 2; Plut. *Mor.* 327A), wounds in the shoulder and leg at Gaza (Arr. *Anab.* 2. 27. 2; Curt. 4. 6. 17, 23; Plut. *Mor.* 327A), and in the head and neck in Bactria (Arr. *Anab.* 4. 3. 3; Curt. 7. 6. 22), and a pierced lung in India (Arr. *Anab.* 6. 10. 1; Curt. 9. 5. 9–10). He likely contracted malaria in Cilicia or in Babylon on his return from India (Engels 1978: 224–8; Borza 1987: 36–8) or in both, relapsing later in Babylon from his earlier bout. He may also have suffered from West Nile disease (Marr and Calisher 2003).
2 Minor may rest in the eye of the beholder. Astaspes, the satrap of Carmania, was accused of plotting rebellion (Curt. 9. 10. 21, 29); Cleander, Heracon, Agathon, and Sitalces were all accused of plundering temples, tombs, and individuals (Arr. Anab. 6. 27. 4; Curt. 10. 1. 2–5); Autophradates, the satrap of the Tapurians and the Mardians, was accused of aspiring to the kingship of these regions (Curt. 19. 1. 39). While Curtius (10. 1. 22–38) declares that Oxines was innocent of the charges levelled against him, Arrian (*Anab.* 6. 30. 2) says he was guilty.
3 What if there was a grand conspiracy to kill John F. Kennedy? For those who are not familiar with the body of Oliver Stone's work, he also put forth in his film *JFK* an unabashed conspiracy tale.
4 In 310, he was seventeen (Diod. 20. 20. 1) or fifteen (Just. 15. 2. 3).
5 Greenwalt 1985: 75–6; Carney 2001: 78–82.
6 The *Alexander Romance* (3. 33 "Will of Alexander") and the anonymous *Liber de Morte Testamentoque Alexandri Magni* (115) present the alleged last will of Alexander with designating his unborn child, if a boy, as heir to the throne or, if a girl, leaving the decision to his companions.
7 He was still in Cilicia at the time of Alexander's death more than a year after he had left Babylon with a body of retired veterans returning to Macedonia. Travel time to Cilicia would have taken approximately three months (Engels 1978: 154–5; Anson 1986: 214). The delay in returning to Macedonia clearly was not unknown to Alexander who apparently expressed no concern, implying that there were legitimate reasons for the delay. Present in Cilicia was a major treasury which Craterus may have been using to prepare a fleet either to counter the growing unrest in Greece, which would ultimately lead to the Lamian War against Macedonian rule, or, perhaps, in preparation for Alexander's move to the West in search of

further conquests (Bosworth 1988B: 208–10; 2002: 31; Ashton 1993: 128–9). On Craterus' actions during this period, see Anson 2015: 51.

8 While Curtius is our most detailed source, his description of events has been called into serious question, with one commentator stating that his problems as a source are sufficient "almost to preclude belief in anything Curtius says about events after Alexander's death, except items confirmed by another source" (McKechnie 1999: 49).

9 Justin (13. 1. 8) only refers to them as *"principes,"* leaders, and he includes in this group Meleager who is not one of the *somatophylaces* (13. 2. 6).

10 McKechnie 1999: 49–56.

11 See Anson 2013: 33.

12 From Justin's context it is clear that the group that met was at least the *somatophylaces*. He speaks of these as "distinguished men" all capable of succeeding to the throne and all contenders in the aftermath of Alexander's death.

13 See Anson 1985: 311; 2013: 32–3.

14 Pat Wheatley and Waldemar Heckel (2011: 72; cf. Bosworth 2000: 241) believe that Ptolemy at this point in the discussion may indeed have had himself in mind.

15 Translation is from Yardley 1994: 124–5.

16 The location is confirmed by the presence of a throne (Curt. 10. 6. 4).

17 On the position of chiliarch, see Collins 2001: 259–83; Meeus 2009: 302–10.

18 According to Curtius (10. 6. 9) Roxane was at this time five months pregnant, but Justin (13. 2. 5) declares that she was in her ninth month.

19 Everyone present appears to have been armed, which is curious and suggestive that many came prepared for problems. Curtius here uses the Latin *hasta* for spear. These spears were traditionally in the Roman tradition thrusting spears, thus implying that in this meeting *sarissai* were present. Later, Curtius (10. 7. 18) refers to the presence of *tela* (javelins). In what must have been a crowded area, the presence of *sarissai* would appear doubtful and perhaps there is a bit of added color here in Curtius' account.

20 Alexander included Persians in his personal entourage, began to adopt Persian dress, court procedure, and advisors. He had married three eastern princesses, two of whom were Persian (Plut. *Alex.* 47. 7–8; Diod. 17. 107. 6; Arr. *Anab.* 7. 4. 4), and had overseen the mixed marriages of 10,000 Macedonian officers and soldiers and Asian women (Arr. *Anab.* 7. 4. 4–8). After his destruction of part of the palace in Persepolis in 331, which, except for mopping-up operations, gave Alexander control of the Persian Empire, the king began to change the campaign from one of vengeance against the Persians to one where the previously hated Persians were to become comrades-in-arms (Anson 2013: 153–79).

21 In Justin (13. 2. 7–10), this position is attributed to Meleager, but then so is his statement that if the *principes* want to place a boy on the throne, then Heracles is available whose mother is Asiatic.

22 On the power and loyalty of the garrison commanders as well as treasury officials to who or whatever was the central government, see Anson 2014: 219–20; 2015: 166–7.
23 See Chapter 4.
24 This alternative is very doubtful. After the creation of the two kings, Leonnatus, who had been passed over for a share in the regency, planned in 322 to usurp power in Macedonia, marry Alexander's sister, and declare himself king (Anson 2015: 83). Perdiccas in 321 was planning to do the same (Anson 2015: 96–101).
25 There is even a report that it was Alexander's wish that Perdiccas marry Roxane (*LM* 118; cf. Heckel 1988: 26). This last is associated by the *Liber de Morte* with the well-attested giving to Perdiccas by Alexander of his seal ring (*LM* 112). This was in all probability misinterpreted, with Alexander simply attempting to ensure the continuation of official state functions and the oversight of the succession (Rathmann 2005: 26).
26 Two at least of the three were Greeks: Pasas, a Thessalian, and Damis, a Megalopolitan. This suggests that Greek mercenaries joined with their Macedonian counterparts in the city (Anson 2015: 248). It is also reasonable to assume that the bulk of the non-European forces joined with the more cosmopolitan-minded *principes*. Present in Babylon at the time of Alexander's death was a force of more than 50,000 Persian infantry plus units of Cossaeans and Tapurians (Arr. *Anab.* 7. 23. 1–4). These troops had become part of Alexander's army. In Susa, Alexander had been joined by the *Epigoni*, 30,000 young Persians trained and equipped in the Macedonian fashion (Arr. *Anab.* 7. 6. 1; Curt. 8. 5. 1; Diod. 17. 108. 1–2; Plut. *Alex.* 47. 3, 71. 1). Later in the year, at Opis, the king created Persian units bearing Macedonian titles and Macedonian equipment (Arr. *Anab.* 7. 11. 3; Diod. 17. 110. 1–2; Just. 12. 12. 3–4). It was also at Opis that Alexander had dismissed roughly 10,000 of his Macedonian veterans (Arr. *Anab.* 7. 12. 1; Diod. 17. 109. 2; 18. 4. 1), retaining only 2,000 cavalry and 13,000 infantry (Curt. 10. 2. 8).
27 Justin (13. 4. 4) has Meleager and Perdiccas sharing responsibilities.
28 Curtius says 300.
29 In Justin, Meleager simply disappears from the narrative.
30 He did assign Cleomenes as Ptolemy's lieutenant to keep tabs on him (Arr. *Succ.* 1a. 5; Just. 13. 4. 11). He was soon assassinated by command of the new satrap (Paus. 1. 6. 3).

Chapter 4

1 In fact, Polybius claims that this was the goal of the first three Ptolemaic rulers of Egypt.
2 Diod. 18. 23. 3, 33. 3, 41. 4–5, 47. 5, 50. 2, 54. 4, 62. 3, 6–7; 19. 55. 4; 20. 106. 2, 4; 21. 1. 4a.

3   Diod. 18. 14. 1, 28. 4–6, 33. 3, 34. 2–4, 36. 1, 39. 5, 86. 3; 19. 55. 5, 56. 1, 86. 2–3; Plut. *Demetr.* 5. 4; 38. 1; Just. 15. 1. 7.
4   Gruen 1985: 253–71; Billows 1990: 156–60, 351–2; Bosworth 2000: 238–9; Hauben 2014: 260–1; Strootman 2014: 314–15; Worthington 2016: 4, 150–5, 210. For the more traditional Polybian view, see Bevan 1968 [1927]: 23; Will 1964: 332; Ellis 1994: ix, 33.
5   There is a reference to a treaty during this time between Demetrius and Ptolemy (*Suda*. s.v. "Demetrios Antigonou"). Seibert (1969: 180–3) has shown that this reference has conflated a number of items together out of chronological context. Given Ptolemy's overtures to one of Antigonus' rebellious nephews and Demetrius' subsequent operation in Cyprus, this alliance would appear to be unlikely. Demetrius' later unsuccessful attempt to bribe the Ptolemaic garrison commander of Corinth and Sicyon also tells against such an alliance (Plut. *Demetr.* 15. 1).
6   For the chronology, see Anson 2014: 150, 161–2.
7   This proposal is remarkably close to what Eumenes employed in 318. Eumenes was plagued with a divided command and sought some way to unify it. His solution may very well have been suggested by Ptolemy's earlier attempt at creating a ruling council. He declared that in future the commanders' meetings would be held in a tent in the presence of a throne, with replicas of Alexander's diadem and scepter and armor. Before each meeting the commanders would offer incense and do obeisance before the shrine of the god Alexander. After this ritual, the meeting would be held as if in the presence of Alexander (see Anson 2015: 165–7). In Curtius' description of Ptolemy's proposal (10. 6. 15) the meeting of his proposed council would take place before Alexander's throne.
8   It would appear likely from his description of the journey to and from Siwah that Ptolemy was present (Arr. *Anab.* 3. 3. 5, 4. 5), but the presence of Perdiccas is assumed since there is no evidence one way or the other. He was one of Alexander's chief commanders and advisors, so it is likely.
9   The exact chronology is unclear. Pausanias (1. 6. 3) dates the murder prior to the seizure of Alexander's body. Ian Worthington (2016: 20) argues that Ptolemy did not leave for Egypt until 322. and did not execute Cleomenes until his relationship with Perdiccas began to deteriorate. It is doubtful that Ptolemy would have waited to secure his satrapy, or to leave in place someone clearly present to spy on the satrap's activities. However, the fact that Perdiccas then did not send out a replacement strengthens Worthington's argument.
10 Perdiccas had sought her hand soon after his selection as regent (cf. Diod. 18. 23. 2). He, like Ptolemy, recognized the power Antipater possessed in Europe.
11 Justin (13. 6. 6–7) inaccurately says they were never married.
12 The actual status of Cyrene is unclear. Envoys from the city met with Alexander during his expedition to Siwah and a treaty of friendship and alliance was created

with them (Diod. 17. 49. 2–3). Arrian (*Anab*. 7. 9. 8) records Alexander as listing Cyrene with Egypt as areas acquired without striking a blow. They are in his speech listed separately.

13 Diodorus (18. 21. 9) says Cyrene, surrounding country and communities, was annexed to the "kingdom of Ptolemy." Ptolemy was not officially a king until 304 (Diod. 20. 53. 4; [Parian Marble] *FGrH* 239 B 23).

14 The Cyrenaeans in the midst of a civil war had previously received assistance from "their allies," neighboring Libyans and Carthaginians (Diod. 18. 21. 4). If Cyrene was part of this satrapy, the Cyrenaeans would not have gone elsewhere for help, nor would Ptolemy have needed an invitation.

15 Accepted by Badian 1967: 187–8.

16 On the death of a monarch his successor carried out a lustration of the army (cf. Just. 13. 4. 7; Curt. 10. 9. 11–13), held funeral games in honor of, and sacrifices were performed for, the dead king (Diod. 18. 28. 4, 19. 52. 5; Just. 9. 7. 11, 11. 2. 1; Athen. 4. 155A). The body would then be formally laid to rest in the royal tombs at Aegae (Borza 1990: 167, 256–60).

17 See Anson 2014: 52–8.

18 According to Cassius Dio, when Octavian touched Alexander part of the Conqueror's nose fell off.

19 As Schubert 1914: 180–1; Erskine 2002: 171; Schäfer 2002: 59–60.

20 See Anson 2014: 53–6.

21 On his career, see Heckel 2021: 100.

22 For the chronology see Boiy 2000; 2007: 44–50; Anson 2002/2003: 373–90; 2014: 58–9.

23 Archon was subsequently removed by Perdiccas (Arr. *Succ*. 24. 3–5), suggesting that he may have, at least in the mind of the regent, known of the plot and supported it.

24 In the summer of 322, Craterus finally arrived in Macedonia, no longer to replace Antipater, nor to share power with him, but in response to Antipater's call for aid against a Greek revolt that had broken out in what became known as the Lamian War. He arrived with 6,000 Macedonian veterans, 4,000 mercenaries, 1,000 Persian bowmen and slingers, and 1,500 cavalry, and willingly placed himself under Antipater's command (Diod. 18. 16. 4–5). On Craterus' career post-Alexander, see Anson 2012: 49–58; for the Lamian War, see Anson 2014: 28–41.

25 While this is not definitely known, later actions by Menander make it appear likely (Anson 2014: 56).

26 While the troops could have journeyed by ship, the rendezvous occurred during the time of Aegean storms and still would have taken at least a couple of weeks.

27 The Greek colonists who had been left in Alexander's new city foundations in the east on the news of Alexander's death attempted to return to Greece, but were crushed and annihilated on the orders of Perdiccas (Diod. 18. 7. 3–9), and the

Lamian War that broke out on the Greek mainland in an attempt by a coalition of Greek cities to escape Macedonian hegemony had been defeated (Diod. 18. 8. 1–18. 6; Just. 13. 5; Plu. *Phoc.* 23–6; Paus. 1. 25. 3–5; Hyp. 6. 1–20). On the campaigns in the East, see Schober 1981: 28–37; Holt 1988.

28 On Craterus' reluctance to seize power, see Anson 2012: 49–58; 2014; see also Pitt and Richardson 2017: 77–87.

29 Antipater was already dying when Demades arrived on a mission from Athens (Diod. 18. 48. 1; Plut. *Phoc.* 30. 4–6; *Dem.* 30. 3–4). Demades did not leave Athens earlier than mid-June 319 (see Errington 1977: 488 and n. 35 [*IG* II.² 383b]). Antipater's death then occurred in the summer, with the news reaching Antigonus in the late summer (Billows 1990: 80; Bosworth 1992: 80; Boiy 2007: 148). This dating corresponds to the Parian Marble's date of 319/318 for the death of Antipater ([Parian Marble] *FGrH* 239 B F-12).

30 Meadows and Thonemann (2013: 223–6), however, believe that Pamphylia was acquired by Ptolemy II.

31 On Egyptian and Cyrenaean relations, see Mitchell 1966; Lloyd 2000: 374.

32 See Anson 2015: 171–2.

33 On the League, see Merker 1970.

34 One consequence of the failed attack was that Demetrius rather ironically received the epithet "Poliorcetes," or city-sacker (Diod. 20. 92. 2, 103. 3).

35 This was the organization created by Philip II, the father of Alexander the Great, which formed a federation of Greek states under the leadership of the Macedonian king, but guaranteeing the autonomy of all members.

36 Bosworth 2000: 238–9. A similar suggestion was made by Hammond (Hammond and Walbank 1988: 166–9), but included the assumption that Alexander IV was still alive. Walter Ellis (1994: 46) believes that this ambition, if true, must have been "a short-lived aberration."

37 It has been suggested that Ptolemy himself was the source of the rumor, because he did not want to risk his forces in a pitched battle against Antigonus (Wheatley and Dunn 2020: 244).

38 For a full survey of Ptolemy's currency reforms, see Lorber 2018: 60–83.

Chapter 5

1 This is a rather fanciful tale. See later in this chapter.
2 See Chapter 2.
3 That Cleitus is referring to officers is made clear by his example. Cleitus exclaims, "You scorn the soldiers of Philip, forgetting that if old Atarrhias here had not called back the younger men when they shrank from battle, we should be lingering around

Halicarnansus" (Curt. 8. 1. 36). Atarrhias was a commander of the hypaspists, not a common soldier (Heckel 2021: 113).

4 Unfortunately, Diodorus (19. 82–84. 7) refers to all strategic and tactical plans as from both Ptolemy and Seleucus. While Appian (*Syr.* 54), Justin (15. 1. 6–7), and Pausanias (1. 6. 5) all attribute the victory solely to Ptolemy, however, none of them mentions that Seleucus even participated. It also appears that in the battle there was no division of command. Both commanders were stationed on the right wing (Diod. 19. 83. 4). Ptolemy's only clear independent action occurred in the aftermath of the battle when the fleeing troops were entering Gaza, Ptolemy and his accompanying force burst in with them and secured the city (Diod. 19. 84. 8).

5 See Anson 2015: 202–4.

6 Alexander led the Companion Cavalry at Chaeronea and his Successors also typically led cavalry forces in battle. Philip II, however, at Chaeronea led his infantry, likely the hypaspists (Anson 2020: 68–71).

7 On this campaign at the Persian Gates, see Heckel 1980; Bosworth 1980: 328–9; Speck 2002: 180–9.

8 See Speck 2002: 186–7.

9 Diodorus (17. 68. 1) says 300 cavalry, which would appear too small a force. This was to be the defense of the homeland. One would think that every available Persian soldier would be involved.

10 No other source mentions Ptolemy's activities at the Persian Gates.

11 Alexander left Babylon after a stay of thirty-four days (Curt. 5. 1. 39). Following Engels (1978: 71n. 1, 73n. 4), Alexander and his army then traveled the twenty-day journey to Susa (Arr. *Anab.* 3. 16. 7), likely arriving about the middle of December, where they remained for some time. Alexander held sacrifices, a relay torch race, and other athletic contests (Arr. *Anab.* 3. 16. 9). Engels suggests that Alexander then left Susa in the fourth week of December. He arrived in Persepolis in late January or early February. Given that the distance is about 400 miles, this would have taken an army marching optimistically at an average rate of between twenty to twenty-five miles about twenty days (Engels says thirty days). Some time would have been expended against the Uxians as well.

12 Justin (12. 10. 3) only refers to Ptolemy once in his entire account of Alexander's expedition and this occurs during the Mallian campaign when he is hit by a poisoned arrow. This is related more fully in Curtius (9. 8. 20–7).

13 On the battle in general, see Arr. *Anab.* 5. 8. 4–18. 3; Curt. 8. 13. 2–14. 46; Diod. 17. 87. 1–89. 3; Just. 12. 8. 1–7.

14 Arrian (*Anab.* 4. 30. 3) states that Alexander attacked with "700 *somatophylaces* and hypaspists." Even allowing for Arrian playing fast and loose with the terminology, this is a very confusing statement. Bosworth (1995: 192) suggests that the reference can be explained by assuming that the mention of the *somatophylaces* referred to the

agema of the hypaspists and an additional pentacosiarchy (unit of 500) of the hypaspists.

15 Diodorus (17. 85) also fails to mention Ptolemy and only notes Alexander in this context.
16 While a religious designation, in the eyes of our sources it became a "quasi-national" designation for all those living in this region (Bosworth 1996: 94).
17 On the nature of the Macedonian government before Philip and Alexander, see Anson 2020: 15–44.
18 The treasuries and many garrison commanders throughout the empire were independent of satrapal authority and answerable only to the central government (Anson 2015: 142–3, 208–9).
19 The specific charges are never specified. Diodorus (18. 23. 4) only states that they were false and unjust, and Arrian (*Succ.* 1a 20) gives no specifics either. However, the only possible charge must relate to Antigonus' failure to aid Eumenes.
20 On this entire period, see Anson 2015: 93–102.
21 See previous chapter.
22 On this campaign see Anson 2015: 97–124.
23 The Scythian invasion of Egypt in the seventh century BC was stopped by the marshes (Just. 2. 3. 14).
24 Isocrates (11. 12) describes the Egypt as defended by the immortal ramparts of the Nile.
25 Alexander's invasion came at a most opportune time in the history of Egypt. The enhanced defenses of Egypt, the fortresses, moles, etc., had been destroyed by the Persians in 343, and the most recent revolt of 338 had been suppressed by the Persians, but complete Persian control had not been established. Alexander came to Egypt as a liberator in the eyes of the Egyptians and the Persian satrap had insufficient forces to withstand him (Arr. *Anab.* 3. 1. 2); additionally, the Egyptians apparently on the news of the Persian defeat at Issus were again in revolt (Curt. 4. 7. 3–4).
26 This river is the northern border of modern Lebanon.
27 This typically happened in this new age where soldiers were primarily mercenaries. Over time Antigonus' army had grown with each of his victories (Diod. 18. 45. 4).
28 On these activities in Macedonia, the deaths of Philip III, his wife Eurydice, the invasion of Macedonia by Cassander, the death of Olympias, and the subsequent treatment of the remaining members of the royal family, see Carney 2006: 73–87.
29 On the war: Diod. 18. 8. 1–18. 6; Just. 13. 5; Plu. *Phoc.* 23–26; Paus. 1. 25.3–5; Hyp. 6. 1–20.
30 Diodorus describes these actions as taking place after the issuance of the Proclamation of Tyre by Antigonus.
31 Ophellas, who was primarily responsible for the annexation of the city for Ptolemy, had remained overseer for him since 322. He is not mentioned with respect to this

rebellion but is later found in charge and so must have been reinstated. In 308, he was approached by Agathocles, the tyrant of Syracuse, concerning a joint operation against the Carthaginians in North Africa (Diod. 20. 40. 1–2; Just. 22. 7. 4). The Syracusan claimed that he only wished to have a fellow Greek in charge of North Africa and that he was fully content with Sicily. Ophellas quickly consented and through a family connection in Athens began to assemble a large force for the campaign. He had married Euthydice, an Athenian descendant of the famous victor at Marathon, Miltiades (Diod. 20. 45. 5; Plut. *Demetr.* 14. 1). He set off against the Carthaginians with 10,000 infantry, 600 cavalry, 100 chariots, and many light-armed troops (Diod. 20. 40. 3–41. 1). Not long after his arrival, Agathocles betrayed him, killing the commander and taking control of his army (Diod. 20. 42. 3–5; Just. 22. 7. 5–6; *Suda* s. v. "Demetrius"; s. v. "Ophellas"). For a time, Cyrene remained independent, but in 300 Ptolemy's stepson Magas, the son of Berenice, retook the city for Ptolemy and remained as its governor (Paus. 1. 6. 8). The date of the rebellion is unclear. It would appear to have occurred with the death of Ophellas, but its end according to Pausanias was after Antigonus' death in 301, in the fifth year of the rebellion.

32 Gorre (2018: 140) has doubts about the presence of armed Egyptian troops because they do not appear again until 266 (Paus. 3. 6. 5) when Egyptian naval troops were being pressed into action as infantry. It should be noted that by the time of Ptolemy's death, with the large influx of Greeks into Egypt, many as military cleruchs, the need for Egyptian infantry was likely severely reduced, but in the early days of Ptolemy's time in Egypt such troops would have filled the ranks with needed bodies, especially as light-armed soldiers.

33 For detailed accounts of this battle, see Devine 1984: 31–40, 1989: 29–38; Billows 1990: 125–8; Sabin 2009: 151–3.

34 Plutarch (*Demetr.* 5. 2) lists 5,000 as slain. Since Demetrius only had in total 17,500 troops, and 8,000 were captured, only 4,500 troops would have escaped with Demetrius and yet he was able later to defeat a Ptolemaic general in northern Syria (Plut. *Demetr.* 6. 2–3). While Diodorus' report does appear low, the 5,000 appears too great.

35 With Wesseling's correction, as in the Loeb addition.

36 Demetrius had forty-three elephants (Diod. 19. 82. 3–4) and those not killed were all captured by Ptolemy (Diod. 19. 84. 4).

37 Pausanias (1. 6. 5) remarks that in this victory Demetrius killed "a few Egytpians."

38 Appian (*Syr.* 9. 54) says 1,000 infantry and 300 horse.

39 In addition to Polemaeus, Telesphorus (Diod. 19. 87. 1) also revolted against his uncle.

40 On the battle, see Diod. 20. 46. 5–47. 4, 7–53. 1; Plut. *Demetr.* 15–17. 1; Just. 15. 2. 6–9; Polyaen. 4. 7. 7; Paus. 1. 6. 6; App. *Syr.* 54; for the date: [Parian Marble] *FGrH* 239 B 21; Wheatley 2001: 133–56).

41 Plut. *Demetr.* 18. 1; [Parian Marble] *FGrH* 239 B 23; Just. 15. 2. 11; App. *Syr.* 54; Yardley, Wheatley, and Heckel 2011: 244–5; Gruen 1985: 258; cf. Diod. 20. 53. 3. See Chapter 6, note 50.
42 On this aspect of traditional Macedonian royal informality, see Errington 1974: 20; Anson 2013: 20; Introduction (this volume).
43 Demetrius maintained this alliance until 286 BC (Merker 1970: 142).
44 See Champion 2012: 11–16.
45 Four if you accept Athenaeus' claim that Thaïs was also his wife (13. 576E). Plutarch (*Alex.* 38. 3; cf. Diod. 17. 72. 2; Curt. 5. 7. 3) calls her his mistress (*hetaira*).
46 Ptolemy even came to address his correspondence to Pyrrhus as "the father to the son, greeting" (Plut. *Pyrrh.* 6. 8).
47 For the events that led to this accession, see Anson 2014: 177–8; Wheatley and Dunn 2020: 321–7.
48 While no source speaks of such a division, later events suggest it. When Alexander later requested help from Pyrrhus and Demetrius against his brother, he was apparently located in the western part of Macedonia, and Antipater, forming an alliance with Lysimachus, in the east (Plut. *Pyrrh.* 6. 4–5).
49 While the chronographers make Demetrius' first year as king 293/292 (*FGrH* 260 F-3.4), Habicht (1979: 21; cf. Wheatley 1997: 22) uses the evidence of Athenian decrees to arrive at the correct date of 294.
50 Tyre had been captured by Antigonus in 314 after a fifteen-month siege (Diod. 19. 61. 5).
51 On Arsinoe's career, see Carney 2013.
52 See Anson 2014: 184.
53 According to Nepos (*Reg.* 3. 4), his son and heir murdered him, but this is generally rejected (see Heckel 2021: 434).

Chapter 6

1 In his description of Alexander's use of ad hoc judicial assemblies, Errington (1978: 87–90) argues that Alexander in the latter stages of his campaign had to test his *auctoritas* before exercising his *potestas*. His power was there, but on occasion exercising it could cause complications. The more authority meant the less necessity of making use of one's power.
2 Just. 16. 2. 9, however, inaccurately says that Ptolemy the son of Lagus resigned and served his son as a member of his "*satellites*." In truth, he shared the rule with his son during the last two years of his reign.
3 Ptolemy had a fourth wife, Atacama (Apame), a Persian princess, the daughter of Artabazus, at one point Alexander's satrap of Bactria (Arr. *Anab.* 7. 4. 6). Plutarch

calls her Apame (*Eum.* 1). As Sabine Müller (2013: 204–6) has suggested, after Alexander's death and likely before Ptolemy's arrival in Egypt she was repudiated, since she was Persian and there was a good deal of Egyptian resentment toward the former rulers of Egypt. In general, with respect to the families of Ptolemy, see Ager 2018: 36–59.

4 Nepos (*Reg.* 21. 4) reports that Ceraunus was exiled by his father. This was likely the case with his brother.

5 On his epithet, he married his sister Arsinoe and they both together were the *philadelphoi*. While a common practice in pharaonic history, it was seen by many Greeks as obscene. Sotades of Maroneia is quoted as having "said many bitter things against Ptolemy the king, and especially this, after he had heard that he had married his sister Arsinoe, He pierced forbidden fruit with deadly sting." Philadelphus had his revenge. When Sotades had sailed from Alexandria and thought that he had escaped all danger, Ptolemy's general Patroclus caught him and shut him up in a leaden vessel, carried him into the open sea and drowned him (Athen. 14. 621A).

6 The report is the older king fell in love with a young Macedonian woman ([Satyrus] *BNJ* 631 F-21=Athen. 13. 557B-E; Plut. *Alex.* 9. 6–7; Anson 2020: 105–7).

7 His marriage to Atacama was part of Alexander's planned alliance with the Persians, not an alliance initiated by Ptolemy.

8 Arsinoe had an interesting career as a wife. After the death of Lysimachus, she married her half-brother Ptolemy Ceraunus, followed by her marriage to her full brother, Ptolemy II Philadelphus (Heckel 2021: 102–4).

9 The fleet accompanying Perdiccas to Egypt consisted of as many as ninety warships and a great number of merchant vessels (Anson 2015: 110). However, a sizable number of these combat vessels were diverted to Cyprus to deal with a rebellion there (Arr. *Succ.* 24. 6).

10 On these campaigns, see Anson 2015: 106–26.

11 While the sources are silent with respect to Cleitus' desertion, there is no evidence that he ever contested the crossing by the Europeans. Moreover, after Perdiccas' death, Cleitus is rewarded with the satrapy of Lydia (Diod. 18. 39. 6).

12 See also Walbank 1984: 80, and Préaux 1978; Rostovtzeff 1941.

13 As noted previously, Macedonian political tradition was amorphous at best. In terms of institutions there was the king. There was no formal assembly with constitutional rights. There was, however, a tradition of a powerful aristocracy that during most of the Argead period had to be placated, but outside of Macedonia these individuals saw their freedom of action and influence restricted by the new world created by Alexander. Unlike in the tradition of Macedonia prior to Philip II and Alexander III where aristocrats controlled entire regions beginning with Philip and accelerated in particular in Asia by Alexander, cities became the centers of administration and power, and land was often given out viritane to individuals.

Philip in the process of creating his new model army also created a growing middle class, a new third wheel in Macedonian political life and one tied closely to the monarchy (see Anson 2020: 73–92).

14 On the flooding cycle, see Manning 2007: 437.
15 On the Ptolemaic tax system, see Vandorpe 2007: 165–71.
16 In the Satrap Stele (ll. 19–21), an inscription dated to 311, Ptolemy's residence is called "the Fortress of the King of Upper and Lower Egypt Merikaamon-Setepenre, the Son of Re [Ra] Alexander, whose former name was Rakotis, on the shore of the great green sea of the Greeks." Racotis was the name of the Egyptian outpost located roughly on the same site as Alexandria. The inscription was created November 311 BC, while Egypt was officially ruled by Alexander the Great's infant son (Alexander II of Egypt, IV of Macedon), after victories in 312/311 secured the extension of Ptolemy's control into Syria/Palestine. Here, the satrap Ptolemy celebrated a thanksgiving festival that culminated in a royal donation to the native gods of Pe and Dep, precincts of the sacred city of Buto. The text of this donation is known as the Satrap Stele. For a copy translated into English, see http://philipharland.com/Courses/Readings/3106/Hellenistic%20Royal%20Inscriptions.pdf.
17 See McGing 1997: 273–99.
18 In Susa, Alexander arranged for himself and approximately eighty of his Macedonian and Greek *hetairoi* to marry Persian princesses (Arr. *Anab.* 7. 4. 4–7). Additionally, 10,000 other Macedonians who had married Asian women had their marriages registered and Alexander gave them large cash gifts (Arr. *Anab.* 7. 4. 8). This was part of Alexander's rapprochement with the Persians.
19 Alexander gave a massive banquet of reconciliation where he prayed for "harmony and fellowship between the Macedonians and the Persians" (Arr. *Anab.* 7. 11. 9).
20 On the initiation of these institutions by Philip, see Anson 2020: 26–9. Both of these institutions speak to a time when the traditional relationship of the king and the Macedonian aristocrats as that of companions where the king was the first among equals had been replaced by one where the king enjoyed much greater prominence. In both cases either the sons of aristocrats (pages) were to serve the king or the aristocrats themselves were to do the same.
21 Waldemar Heckel (1978: 226) suggests that this institution predated Philip and "developed from the machinery of the heroic monarchy." One of the duties of these elite bodyguards was to guard the king in his bedchamber (Heckel 1986: 285). The very nature of the relationship of these aristocrats with the monarch prior to Philip II was that between near equals. In a warrior world where the king is simply the first among equals, guarding the king's bedchamber would not be esteemed an honor, but rather would be seen as beneath the dignity of such individuals. The institution may have, following Heckel, existed previously as a purely military and advisory role until the reign of Philip II.

22 See Stanley Burstein (1977: 223–5) for the correct interpretation of the inscription.
23 See Leon Mooren 1983: 205–40.
24 The title *hetairos* disappears entirely in Ptolemaic designations. This indicates the change from the concept of companions wherein the king is the first among equals to those who were creatures of the court, serving at the king's pleasure.
25 On guest friendship and city-state politics, see Mitchell 2002; Herman 1987.
26 On *Proxenia* in general, see Perlman 1958: 185–91.
27 See Anson 2015: 49.
28 For an argument that these relationships were true *xenia*, see Polyb. 18. 14.
29 The *oikonomoi* were in origin Egyptian nome financial officials (on their duties, see Papadopoulou 2010: 1).
30 Translation: http://www.attalus.org/docs/seg/s28_60.html. For a full commentary on the inscription, see Shear 1978.
31 This was the common practice throughout the various Hellenistic kingdoms. Demetrius Poliocetes kept an Athenian embassy waiting for two years (Diod. 17. 113. 1–4. Plut. Dem. 42. 1–2).
32 Philip during his reign had acquired much "spear-won land," which he gave out to his *hetairoi* as was customary in Macedonia, but he also gave it out to individual soldiers who then became obligated to the king and served him as his newly created infantry army. See Anson 2008: 17–30.
33 See Chapter 2.
34 In 673 BC, the Assyrians were defeated (*ABC* 1. 4. 16); in 459/458, the Persians (Diod. 11. 74. 1–4) and again in 351 (Isoc. 5. 101; Dem. 15. 11–12; cf. Diod. 16. 48. 1).
35 In this passage Diodorus emphasizes that soldiers enrolled with the Egyptian satrap because of his "graciousness and nobility" but the financial reserves did not hurt.
36 On this organizational system, see Bagnall 1976B: 3–4.
37 On Jewish settlement in Ptolemaic Egypt, see Kasher 1978: 57–67.
38 See Kasher 1978: 57.
39 For Philip II, see Anson 2020: 77–83; for Alexander, see Anson 2013: 134–40.
40 However, this last power was likely done at the insistence of the Macedonian king, for Diodorus (16. 8. 2) reports that after capturing the city Philip exiled those who were disaffected by his acquisition. It is likely that Philip simply chose to have the people of Amphipolis do his bidding.
41 On these officials in Egypt, see Bagnall 1976A: 198–200.
42 On *Xenia*, *Proxenia*, and Philip II, see earlier in this chapter and in Anson 2020: 93–101.
43 On the inscription, see Cary 1928: 222–38; Larsen 1929: 351–68.
44 See also Green 1990: 191.
45 Manning 2012: 44.
46 On Cleomenes' career, see Seibert 1969: 39–51; Heckel 2021: 249.

47 See Anson 2021: 1–23.
48 Agnieszka Wojciechowska (2016: 87–91) argues that Alexander was fully coronated.
49 C. J. Johnson (1995) believes the Egyptian religious epithets were at the insistence of the priests. By and large Ptolemy remained at the core a Macedonian but also catered to the priests who were responsible for his acceptance by the native Egyptians.
50 Antigonus and Demetrius assumed the title of king in 306 after Demetrius' victory at Salamis (Plut. *Demetr.* 16. 3, 17. 2–18. 1, 27; Diod. 20. 53. 2; Just. 15. 2. 10; [Heidelberg Epitome] *FGrH* 155 F-1.7). Ptolemy held off until 304 (Plut. *Demetr.* 18. 1; [Parian Marble] *FGrH* 239 B 23; Just. 15. 2. 11; App. *Syr.* 54). The last document dated to Alexander IV is a payment-related papyrus from Thebes (P. Louvre 2440) of the month of Athyr, thirteenth year of Alexander (January 304). This document, as does the Satrap Stele, dates the beginning of Alexander IV's reign to 317 with the death of Philip III. These documents do not then acknowledge a dual monarchy. Demotic dating ends for Alexander IV in 305/304. While Tolley (2019: 259–75) suggests that this dating puts Alexander IV's actual death in 305/304, I would suggest it is in truth testimony to the year Ptolemy assumed the royal title. That then would be 304. The year 306 concluded with the failed invasion of Egypt by Antigonus and Demetrius in the late fall. The new campaign year began with the start of Demetrius' epic siege of Rhodes (Diod. 20.81.1–2). Given the context in Diodorus, it is clear that the siege began in the spring of 305. This siege is dated by the Parian Marble (*FGrH* 239 B 23) in the archon year 305/304, as is Ptolemy's assumption of a diadem. It is likely, however, that the siege began in the previous archon year, or in the spring of 305, and is only being noted as continuing in this year. All of the previous year's activities cannot be read on the stone. Since the siege lasted a year (Diod. 20. 100. 1), and Ptolemy only took the diadem after the siege's end (Gruen 1985: 257–8), 304 was the year of the siege's end and the assumption of a crown by Ptolemy. Eusebius' *Chronica* (*BNJ* 260 F-2) also places Ptolemy's regnal proclamation in 305/304. The year 304 is noted as an Olympic year (Diod. 20. 91. 1) and begins with Demetrius still besieging Rhodes. This year ended with the relief of Cassander's siege of Athens (Plut. *Demetr.* 23. 1) and Demetrius' campaigning in northern Greece (Diod. 20. 100. 5–6). That Diodorus' year 304/303 is in actuality 304 is confirmed by that author's listing of the death of Eumelus, the king of Bosporus, in his sixth year of rule (20. 100. 7). He came to the throne in 310 (Diod. 20. 24. 4–5). Moreover, Diodorus includes in this year Demetrius' acquisition of Chalcis, dated by the Parian Marble in 304/3 (*FGrH* 239 B 24).
51 Some Babylonian documents, however, date by regal years for Philip III after he is dead and also include regal years for Antigonus during the lifetime of Alexander IV (Boiy 2000: 115–21). See Habicht (2006: 75–84; cf. Bosworth 1971: 127) on the confusion concerning the dual monarchy.

52 See Tolley 2019: 262.
53 "Great chief" is another translation (Ockinga 2018: 167–8).
54 From the translation of Ritner 2003: 392–7 with modifications from Ockinga.
55 Nekhbet, patroness of Upper Egypt; Wadjet, patroness of Lower Egypt.
56 Or Selê, the fortress leading to Canaan.
57 See note 50.
58 It is suggested that these incidents may not have happened or have been exaggerated (Olmstead 1959: 89–92; Kienitz 1953: 108; Thompson 2012: 99n.3), but it would appear Egyptians believed that they did and that given the testimony of Herodotus, this belief goes back at least to the fifth century BC.
59 His choosing as his heir the younger Philadelphus over Ceraunus had much to do with family issues, but it is also true Ceraunus was more adventurous and consequently more of a danger to the dynasty's rule in Egypt.

Chapter 7

1 Initially, when Alexander was declared the son of Zeus (Amun) at Siwah, the soldiers did not seem to be concerned. At least there is no reference to any discontent, and they may have seen this as a positive. That their commander was the son of the greatest of the Greek gods might prove helpful in the coming campaigns. Over time, however, as Alexander began to take on more of the attributes of a Persian king, these changes became associated with his claim of divine sonship. These complaints came to a head in an argument he had with Cleitus which resulted in that friend and commander being killed by a drunken Alexander (Arr. *Anab*. 4. 8. 4–9) and later in the so-called mutiny at Opis where the soldiers ridiculed his claim of divine descent by declaring that he should continue the war with his father, he did not need them (Arr. *Anab*. 7. 8. 2–3). Many of these same Macedonians had no trouble worshipping the dead Alexander (Diod. 18. 60. 5–61. 3; Plut. *Eum*. 13. 5–8; Polyaen. 4. 8. 2). Ptolemy was neither Alexander, nor dead.
2 See Thucydides 1. 20. 2.
3 This was apparently just one of many explanations offered to Diodorus when he was in Egypt to explain the ritual. Diodorus (1. 85. 5) himself comments that "many other stories are told about the Apis, but we feel that it would be a long task to recount all the details regarding them."
4 In general, see Turner 1974: 239–42.
5 Translation by Turner 1974: 241.
6 Both the Egyptian priests and Ptolemy created quite an anti-Persian dialogue (in general, see Klintott 2007; Caneva 2016: 146–51). It was in the interest of both. It strengthened Ptolemy's position as the righter of Persian wrongs and

enabled the Egyptian priest to bring forward all such claimed wrongs to Ptolemy for correction.
7   Perhaps, only in the sense "of the mortal bearer of a divine office during his lifetime" (Höbl 2001: 92), or only in the sense of his ka, which for Francisco Bosch-Puche (2014: 82) in the context of a pharaoh is "the divine aspect of kingship that linked the living ruler with the gods and with all his royal predecessors."
8   Gustave Droysen (1877/78: 3. 23) saw the introduction of the Cult of Serapis as the first step to religious universalism. In this particular respect, I believe he is correct; that this would lead inexorably to Christianity (3. 7), not so much.
9   Even suggesting that it might have been the brainchild of Manetho, the Egyptian priest closely associated with Ptolemy (Stambaugh 1972: 63).
10 For example, Stambaugh 1972: 36; Kahil 1996: 77; Höbl 2001: 99; Lloyd 2000: 408; Wellendorf 2008: 34–5.
11 On the *Ephemerides*, see Bearzot 2017 "Alexander's Ephemerides" *BNJ* 117 T-1; Anson 1996: 501–4). It is possible that the reference to Serapeum was meant to indicate a connection to Tammuz, the rough Babylonian equivalent to Osiris, although Tammuz apparently did not have a temple in Babylon of his own (Barton 1915: 213–14).
12 The tale told to Tacitus (also found in Plut. *Mor.* 361F-362B) is, however, farfetched. "When King Ptolemy ... was giving the new city of Alexandria walls, temples, and religious rites, there appeared to him in his sleep a vision of a young man of extraordinary beauty and of more than human stature, who warned him to send his most faithful friends to Pontus and bring his statue here; the vision said that this act would be a happy thing for the kingdom and that the city that received the god would be great and famous: after these words the youth seemed to be carried to heaven in a blaze of fire. Ptolemy, moved by this miraculous omen, disclosed this nocturnal vision to the Egyptian priests, whose business it is to interpret such things. When they proved to know little of Pontus and foreign countries, he questioned Timotheus, an Athenian of the clan of the Eumolpidae, whom he had called from Eleusis to preside over the sacred rites, and asked him what this religion was and what the divinity meant. Timotheus learned by questioning men who had travelled to Pontus that there was a city there called Sinope, and that not far from it there was a temple of Jupiter Dis, long famous among the natives: for there sits beside the god a female figure which most call Proserpina. But Ptolemy, although prone to superstitious fears after the nature of kings, when he once more felt secure, being more eager for pleasures than religious rites, began gradually to neglect the matter and to turn his attention to other things, until the same vision, now more terrible and insistent, threatened ruin upon the king himself and his kingdom unless his orders were carried out. Then Ptolemy directed that ambassadors and gifts should be despatched to King Scydrothemis—he ruled over the people of Sinope at that time

—and when the embassy was about to sail he instructed them to visit Pythian Apollo... Apollo bade them go on and bring back the image of his father, but leave that of his sister. When the ambassadors reached Sinope, they delivered the gifts, requests, and messages of their king to Scydrothemis. He was all uncertainty, now fearing the god and again being terrified by the threats and opposition of his people; often he was tempted by the gifts and promises of the ambassadors. In the meantime three years passed during which Ptolemy did not lessen his zeal or his appeals; he increased the dignity of his ambassadors, the number of his ships, and the quantity of gold offered. Then a terrifying vision appeared to Scydrothemis, warning him not to hinder longer the purposes of the god: as he still hesitated, various disasters, diseases, and the evident anger of the gods, growing heavier from day to day, beset the king. He called an assembly of his people and made known to them the god's orders, the visions that had appeared to him and to Ptolemy, and the misfortunes that were multiplying upon them: the people opposed their king; they were jealous of Egypt, afraid for themselves, and so gathered about the temple of the god. At this point the tale becomes stranger, for tradition says that the god himself, voluntarily embarking on the fleet that was lying on the shore, miraculously crossed the wide stretch of sea and reached Alexandria in two days. A temple, befitting the size of the city, was erected in the quarter called Rhacotis; there had previously been on that spot an ancient shrine dedicated to Serapis and Isis. Such is the most popular account of the origin and arrival of the god... others claim that the same Ptolemy introduced the god, but that the place from which he came was Memphis, once a famous city and the bulwark of ancient Egypt. Many regard the god himself as identical with Aesculapius, because he cures the sick; some as Osiris, the oldest god among these peoples; still more identify him with Jupiter as the supreme lord of all things; the majority, however, arguing from the attributes of the god that are seen on his statue or from their own conjectures, hold him to be Father Dis [Hades]."

13 The connection between the Cult of Serapis and its Memphian origin is made conclusively by Ulrich Wilcken (1927: 77–8, 97–104).
14 A Greek form of Apis (Hdt. 2. 153).
15 For the embalming ritual, see Vos 1993.
16 Certainly, later the identification of Osiris and Isis with various Greek gods was common. "In fact, men assert that Pluto is none other than Serapis and that Persephonê is Isis" (Plut. *Mor.* 361E); "it is better to identify Osiris with Dionysus and Serapis with Osiris" (Plut. *Mor.* 362B). See Stambaugh 1972: 27–35.
17 See Bosch-Puche 2014B: 55–83 for a full discussion of Alexander's status as a legitimate pharaoh.
18 He had a number of variant Horus names as well: "Brave Ruler," "Brave Ruler who attacked foreign lands," "The Ruler of the rulers of the entire land," and "The Sturdy-Armed One" (von Beckerath 1999: 232–3).

19 See Anson 2003: 117–30; 2013: 97–109.
20 On Alexander's worship as Alexandria's founder, see Lianou 2010: 126–7.
21 Not the actual regalia that had accompanied the kings to Macedonia, but that fashioned for the occasion (Anson 2015: 165–6).
22 See Stambaugh 1972: 75–8.
23 For Plutarch (*Mor.* 78. 383A), "when these souls are set free and migrate into the realm of the invisible and the unseen, the dispassionate and the pure, then this god becomes their leader and king, since it is on him that they are bound to be dependent in their insatiate contemplation and yearning for that beauty which is for men unutterable and indescribable."
24 This particular text was found on the walls of Unas' pyramid.
25 Pfeiffer sees this association with ruler cult as very important because he insists the pharaoh was never a god and that only the office was divine. He points to the lack of specific cult associate with particular pharaohs. Again, I wonder at this concept being clearly understood by the majority of the Egyptian population. Moreover, there was the merging of pharaoh with various of the gods of Egypt. Their cult was then his cult.
26 See below. While there are examples of Osiris and Serapis as seeming to be separate deities, the association of both with Isis suggests their identification (*SEG* XVIII 657; P.Eleph. 23,8-12; P.Tebt. Ill 1, 815, col. IV 21–3). Of course, Serapis as opposed to the purely Egyptian god Osiris was associated with many more attributes. The Greek god was becoming in many respects a universal god.
27 Bernard 2001: no. 1.
28 Bernard 2001: no. 2.
29 According to Plutarch, Thales proclaimed that Osiris was Oceanus (*Mor.* 364D.
30 Apollonius did a couple of years later see to the founding of a temple of Serapis in Philadelphis, a town he himself had created (*P.Cair.Zen.* II 59168).
31 On the papyrus and its interpretation, see Rigsby (2001: 119–24) and Renberg and Bubelis (2011: 169–200).
32 Herodotus identifies Isis with the Greek goddess Demeter (2. 59. 2).
33 Echoed in Plutarch (*Mor.* 53. 372E).
34 Again, as in Plutarch (*Mor.* 62. 376B).

Chapter 8

1 At one time, Ptolemy was hailed as a second Thucydides (Strasburger 1934: 15–16; Seibert 1969: 1–26; Pearson 1983: 183, 211), Pearson (1983: 194) even claiming that Ptolemy used documents in constructing his history in his "scrupulous regard for

the truth," but his reputation as an historian has been challenged in more recent years.
2 As identified by Timothy Howe 2018A: "Ptolemy" *BNJ* 138.
3 Earlier arguments that Arrian did not use Ptolemy directly (e.g. Levi 1977: 277–330), but rather an intermediary source, are now generally ignored as without foundation (see Stadter 1980: 60–76).
4 Stadter (1980: 72) states that there is no such evidence that with respect to military matters Arrian preferred Ptolemy over Aristobulus, but see 6. 4. 2 where Arrian states, "ᾧ μάλιστα ἐγὼ ἕπομαι"; cf. Bosworth 1980: 16.
5 See the general discussion in Stadter 1980: 69–72.
6 Seibert 1969: 19; Worthington 2016: 214–15.
7 For the best current discussion with secondary citations of Ptolemy as an historical source, see Howe 2018A "Ptolemy" *BNJ* 138.
8 On the primacy of Ptolemy as Arrian's source, see Bosworth 1980: 16–33.
9 [Ptolemy] *BNJ* 138 T-2=Pliny *NH* 1. 12. 13. This consists of a list of authorities only.
10 An interesting comment, since it would be disgraceful for kings to lie. Alexander himself is supposed to have said that kings must always speak the truth to their subjects (Arr. *Anab.* 7. 5. 2).
11 However, Ian Worthington (2015: 215) suggests that the omission could be an attempt by Ptolemy to "mask the fact that he had not given the king sufficient protection as a bodyguard."
12 See Fraser 1972: 1. 312–22.
13 Eusebius (*BNJ* 260. F-3) places Cassander's death in 298/297 and Diogenes Laertius relates that Demetrius went to Egypt only after Cassander's death.
14 Errington 1969: 235–6, 241–2.
15 This passage will be discussed later. It is often held up as an attempt by Ptolemy to attack his rival in the First Diadoch War, Perdiccas (Errington 1969: 237–40; Müller 2011: 443–4, 2013: 75–92).
16 There is a Ptolemaeus mentioned, but it is not our historian king (Bosworth 1980: 148; Heckel 2021 [2006]: 427).
17 Executed on Alexander's orders (Arr. *Anab.* 3. 26. 3–4; Curt. 7. 2. 25–7, 31–2).
18 After a show trial executed on Alexander's orders (Arr. *Anab.* 3. 26. 1–3; Curt. 6. 11. 10–38; Plut. *Alex.* 49. 13; Just. 12. 5. 3).
19 Died of illness (Arr. *Anab.* 3. 25. 4; Curt. 6. 6. 18).
20 Likely killed on Alexander's orders for being the nephew of the Lyncestian Alexander who was executed after a show trial (see Heckel 2021: 42).
21 He disappears after the capture of Miletus (Heckel 2021: 464).
22 Killed in 330 (Arr. *Anab.* 3. 27. 3).
23 Disappears from the record after the battle on the Granicus.
24 Put to death with the conspirators connected to the trial and execution of Philotas (Curt. 6. 11. 36–8).

25 Disappears from the Alexander record in Bactria, but may have survived and served the Antigonids (Heckel 2021: 385).
26 Perdiccas also in this battle serves as a *somatophylax* with Alexander and the cavalry.
27 The son of Seleucus (Bosworth 1980: 207; Heckel 2021: 427).
28 Bosworth 1995: 40–1; Heckel 2021: 427.
29 Like Caesar after him.
30 See Heckel 2006: 23–6.
31 This is also the case in Heckel's most recent *Who's Who in the Age of Alexander the Great and his Successors,* an expanded edition of his *Who's Who in the Age of Alexander the Great.* Ptolemy the son of Philip, having appeared previously as a separate entry in the 2006 edition (#2, 234), is no longer listed in the new edition. Heckel in his 2006 edition does relate that this Ptolemy may in fact be a mistake for Polemaeus, the brother of Antigonus Monophthalmus (234). The disappearance is solved. By 2021, this son of Philip is identified likely correctly as Polemaeus, the brother of Antigonus (408 [#967]).
32 On this campaign at the Persian Gates, see Heckel 1980; Bosworth 1980: 328–9; Speck 2002: 180–9.
33 Speck (2002: 188–9) declares Ptolemy's actions to be exaggerated.
34 Bosworth (1980: 328) merely comments that any argument based on the lack of the patronymic "presupposes too much scrupulous accuracy in Arrian."
35 A similar situation appears in Curtius. Curtius (8. 13. 18–19, 23, 27, 14. 15) is the only source who mentions Ptolemy in an important role in the campaign against the Indian prince Porus. There is no such reference in Arrian. Here, as at the Persian Gates, what was being done by a number of different commanders becomes centered on the activities of one, namely Ptolemy.
36 This is clearly the case in India in the campaign against the Mallians, which Bosworth (1996: 133–42) describes as a campaign with no other purpose than to kill as many of them, men, women, and children, as possible, in order to forestall further resistance in the area.
37 Arrian reports that Alexander was to signal Craterus, while Curtius says Craterus was to attack when he heard the commotion caused by Alexander's attack.
38 Bosworth (1980: 329) believes that Ptolemy has usurped in his narrative the role actually carried out by Philotas. Curtius (5. 4. 30) makes no reference to any role played by Ptolemy, but does state, "Philotas, with Amyntas, Polyperchon and Coenus, who were ordered to take a different route, struck the barbarians with another fear." The bridging of the Araxes was then an invention. I don't think there is any need for such a radical interpretation of Arrian's account. Clearly Ptolemy's mission was secondary to all the others and its success exaggerated, but what is described in Arrian makes sense.
39 Diodorus (17. 68. 4) says 300 stades, but this is obviously a scribal error.

40 Curtius (5. 3. 17) says only 25,000 and most regard Arrian's figure as an exaggeration, but it may not be. It is associated with the number of 700 cavalry (Diodorus 17. 68. 1 says 300), which would appear small. This was to be the defense of the homeland. One would think that every available Persian soldier would be involved.
41 Howe 2015: 166–90.
42 This is similar to the case of Eumenes of Cardia's career serving Alexander. In our sources, it would appear that out of the blue, Alexander decided to make Eumenes one of the two commanders of the Companion Cavalry (Arr. *Anab.* 7. 14. 1; Plut. *Eum.* 2. 9–10). Prior to this appointment Eumenes is mentioned only once in command of cavalry. After the capture of the Indian city of Sangala in 326, he was sent in command of 300 horsemen to announce the fall of this city to other cities then in rebellion—in short, more a diplomatic mission than a military one (Arr. *Anab.* 5. 24. 6–7; Plut. *Eum.* 1.5; Curt. 9. 1. 19). Yet, after Alexander's death Eumenes is a standout cavalry commander (Plut. *Eum.* 4. 3–4, 5. 5; Diod. 18. 30. 6–32. 1; 19. 28. 3–4, 40. 2). In general, see Anson 2015: 36–7.
43 Related more fully in Curtius (9. 8. 20–7). This, in fact, is the only reference to Ptolemy in Justin from this time to Alexander's death.
44 Erigyius killed Satibarzanes in single combat, but the description is not as elaborate as Arrian's description of Ptolemy's struggle (Arr. *Anab.* 3. 28. 3; cf. Diod. 18. 83. 5–6; Curt. 7. 4. 33–8).
45 A number of scholars believe that Diodorus has used in conjunction with Hieronymus an additional source for the Diadochi favorable to Ptolemy (Seibert 1969: 64–83; Landucci Gattinoni 1987: 37–42; Bosworth 2002: 26), but see Anson 2015: 31.
46 Bosworth (1995: 141), however, suggests that Nearchus may also be a source for this section.
47 Curtius relates that on this campaign Ptolemy captured the most cities.
48 Curtius (7. 11. 5) ascribes Ptolemy's actions to a Myllinas, the "king's secretary." Heckel believes this is a real individual, the son of Asander (2021: 318). I think this is doubtful and this is an error of unknown origin.
49 Seibert (1969: 122) interprets Arrian (*Anab.* 4. 29. 4) as reproving Ptolemy for his lack of success. Bosworth (1995: 187–8) believes that if that had been the case, then Ptolemy would have omitted the entire section. Of course, another explanation is that he is reporting the incident honestly.
50 The last, Heckel (2018: 13) suggests, is "the most gratuitous example of Ptolemy's self-praise."
51 See Errington 1969: 236, 241.
52 Perdiccas is not mentioned in Plutarch's account of the fall of Thebes (*Alex.* 11. 5). Moreover, in Diodorus' account the incident occurs near the end of the siege.

53 See Anson 2015: 213–32.
54 Diodorus (17. 98. 4) alludes to the delay caused by the lack of "military equipment."
55 A similar situation occurred at the beginning of the siege of Halicarnassus. Alexander assumed that the city was going to be betrayed to him and consequently did not have scaling ladders with him at the beginning of the siege (Arr. *Anab.* 1. 20. 6). Alexander took the problem in his stride and retreated to organize a proper siege. He was more easily agitated during the Indian campaign. Perdiccas plays a major role in Arrian's account of the siege of Halicarnassus.
56 Of course, it could be claimed to be Alexander's fault because he ignored the "the portends of great danger which would come to the king from a wound in the course of the operation" (Diod. 17. 98. 3–4).
57 Later, however, Arrian only notes Hephaestion as the bridge builder (*Anab.* 5. 3. 5). There is no way of distinguishing the source of either comment, but it would appear both references were from his two commonly relied-on sources. Arrian only relates that neither Aristobulus nor Ptolemy says how the bridge was built (*Anab.* 5. 7. 1).
58 On the level of military literacy, see Harris 1989: 118, 255, 145–6, 166–7, 328–9. He notes that even junior officers may have been literate in a practical way, but not that many of the rank-and-file. They could read contracts and other documents. It is doubtful that even such literate individuals would curl up before the campfire with a good history to read. In the current United States military, attempts to promote those from bare literacy to high literacy have been disappointing, with the conclusion reached that the process "requires many thousands of wide-ranging reading and learning" (Sucht 1995: 70)—clearly a bit pessimistic, but indicative of the need for literacy that transcends the barest of essentials to be able to read a work of literature such as a history of Alexander's expedition.
59 Aristonous, in the chaotic assembly that arose after Alexander's death, suggested that Perdiccas be chosen as Alexander's successor (Curt. 10. 6. 16).
60 He is also mentioned just once in the *Indica* (18. 5).
61 Arrian (*Anab.* 6. 11. 7) states that there was disagreement about Leonnatus' actions, but this is a reference to the *legomena*, for earlier, as noted, he does list him as one of three, and in Book Seven he receives a golden crown. These last two passages are likely both from Ptolemy and Aristobulus, since these accounts are given without any hint of other traditions. It is not until 6. 11. 1 that Arrian refers to other sources.
62 On the later importance of snakes in the subsequent cult of Agathos Daimon, see Ogden 2015: 129–47.
63 My reservations with regard to Ptolemy's history as a piece of propaganda to enhance his power and authority and diminish that of his opponents also apply to a surviving document titled the "Last Days and Testament of Alexander the Great." This is a pamphlet that describes a poison plot to kill the king. To me this was a work that did not create or even enhance the rumors concerning Alexander's death

as the result of poison. This is clearly a work that derives from the rumors. After the fact, the author(s) will have given their own take on the rumors and associated various individuals in the plot, but this was to be a literary work meant for posterity. Waldemar Heckel's *The Last Days and Testament of Alexander the Great: A Prosopographic Study* remains the standard examination. Heckel's argument for Holcias being its author is strong and would explain the author's take on who was involved in the plot. I do not, however, accept that this was created as a propaganda piece meant to influence Macedonian opinion against Cassander in the struggles between him and Polyperchon. As Heckel has demonstrated, the idea of a poison plot and its primary perpetrators being the sons of Antipater was widely believed soon after Alexander's death. The "Testament" was meant, as was Ptolemy's history, as a work for posterity. That Holcias—if he was, indeed, its author—did not advertise his authorship is likely the result that it was written after Cassander was entrenched in power (see Chapter 4).

64 Hamilton 1969.
65 See Anson 2015: 164, 258; Roisman 2012: 242–3.
66 A point made by Errington (2015: 217).

Chapter 9

1 As noted in the text there was a further dichotomy in the native Egyptian world with the presence of Thebes as the capital of Upper Egypt.

Bibliography

Adams, W. L. 1986. "Macedonian Kingship and the Right of Petition." In *Ancient Macedonia IV. Papers read at the Fourth International Symposium held in Thessaloniki, September 21–25, 1983.* Institute of Balkan Studies. Thessaloniki.

Ager, S. 2018. "Building a Dynasty: The Families of Ptolemy I Soter." In *Ptolemy I Soter: A Self-Made Man.* Howe, T. (ed.). Oxbow. Oxford and Havertown, PA: 36–59.

Anson, E. M. 1986. "Diodorus and the Date of Triparadeisus." *American Journal of Philology* 107: 208–17.

Anson, E. M. 1996. "The Ephemerides of Alexander the Great." *Historia: Zeitschrift für alte Geschichte* 45: 50–4.

Anson, E. M. 2002/2003. "The Dating of the Death of Perdiccas and the Assembly at Triparadeisus." *Greek, Roman and Byzantine Studies* 43: 373–90.

Anson, E. M. 2003. "Alexander and Siwah." *Ancient World* 34: 117–30.

Anson, E. M. 2008. "Philip II and the Transformation of Macedonia: A Reappraisal." In *Macedonian Legacies: Studies in Ancient Macedonian History and Culture in Honor of Eugene N. Borza.* Howe, T., and Reames, J. (eds). Regina Books. Claremont, CA: 17–30.

Anson, E. M. 2009. "Philip II, Amyntas Perdicca, and Macedonian Royal Succession." *Historia: Zeitschrift für alte Geschichte* 58: 276–86.

Anson, E. M. 2012. "The Macedonians Patriot: The Diadoch Craterus." *The Ancient History Bulletin* 26: 49–58.

Anson, E. M. 2013. *Alexander the Great: Themes and Issues.* Bloomsbury. London, New Delhi, New York, and Sydney.

Anson, E. M. 2014. *Alexander's Heirs: The Age of the Successors.* Wiley/Blackwell. Malden, MA and Oxford.

Anson, E. M. 2015. *Eumenes of Cardia: A Greek Among Macedonians.* 2nd ed. Brill. Leiden and Boston.

Anson, E. M. 2016. "Fortress Egypt: The Abortive Invasions of 320 and 306 B.C." In *Alexander's Legacy.* Bearzot, C., and Landucci, F. (eds). L'erma di Bretschneider. Rome: 85–96.

Anson, E. M. 2020. *Philip II, The Father of Alexander the Great: Themes and Issues.* Bloomsbury Academic. London and New York.

Anson, E. M. 2021A. "The Foundation of Alexandria." *International Journal of Military History and Historiography.* Advance online publication: 1–23.

Anson, E. M. 2021B. "Alexander the Great. A life lived as Legend." In *Alexander the Great and Propaganda.* Walsh, J., and Baynham, E. (eds). Routledge. London and New York: 14–32.

Anson, E. M. 2022. "Philip and Alexander and the Nature of Their Personal Kingship." In *The Courts of Philip II and Alexander the Great: Monarchy and Power in Ancient Macedonia.* Pownall, F., Sulochana, and Müller, S. (eds). De Gruyter. Berlin and Boston: 17–31.

Antikas, T. G., and Wynn-Antikas, L. K. 2015. "New Finds from the Cremains in Tomb II at Aegae Point to Philip II and a Scythian Princess." *International Journal of Osteoarchaeology* 26: 682–92.

Asheri, D. 2007. "Book III." In *A Commentary on Herodotus Books I–IV.* Murray, O., and Moreno, A. (eds). Oxford University Press. Oxford and New York: 381–542.

Ashton, N. G. 1993. "Craterus from 324 to 321 B.C." in *Ancient Macedonia V. Papers read at the Fifth International Symposium held in Thessaloniki, October 10–15, 1989.* Institute for Balkan Studies. Thessaloniki: 125–31.

Austin, M. M. 1981. *The Hellenistic World from Alexander to the Roman Conquest. A Selection of Ancient Sources in Translation.* Cambridge University Press. Cambridge.

Badian, E. 1967. "A King's Notebooks," *Harvard Studies in Classical Philology* 72: 183–204.

Bagnall, R. S. 1976A. "Archagathos Son of Agathocles, Epistates of Libya." *Philologus. Zeitschrift fur klassiche Philologie* 120: 195–209.

Bagnall, R. S. 1976B. *The Administration of the Ptolemaic Possessions Outside Egypt.* Brill. Leiden.

Bagnall, R. S. 1984. "The Origin of Ptolemaic Cleruchs." *The Bulletin of the American Society of Papyrologists* 21: 7–20.

Bagnall, R. S. 1993. *Egypt in Late Antiquity.* Princeton University Press. Princeton.

Bagnall, R. S. 2002. "Alexandria: Library of Dreams." *Proceedings of the American Philosophical Society* 146: 348–62.

Bagnall, R. S., and Derow, P. 1981. *The Hellenistic Period: Historical Sources in Translation.* Blackwell. Malden, MA, and Oxford.

Balandier, C. 2007. "Les ouvrages fortifies et la défense de Chypre à la transition des époques classique et hellénistique: une évolution du réseau défensif aux IVe et IIIesiècles avant J.-C.?" In *Proceedings of the International Archaeological Conference: From Evagoras I to the Ptolemies. The Transition from the Classical to the Hellenistic Period in Cyprus, Nicosia, 29–30 November 2002.* Flourentzos, P. (ed.). Department of Antiquities, Nicosia, Cyprus: 145–59.

Barlett, P. 1980. "Adaptive Strategies in Peasant Agricultural Production." *Annual Review of Anthropology* 9: 545–73.

Barta, W. 1980. "Thronbesteigung und Krönungsfeier als unterschiedliche Zeugnisse königlicher Herrschaftsübernahme." *Studien zur altägyptischen Kultur* 8: 33–53.

Barton, G. A. 1915. "Tammuz and Osiris." *Journal of the American Oriental Society* 35: 213–23.

Baynham, E. 2004. *Alexander the Great. The Unique History of Quintus Curtius.* University of Michigan Press. Ann Arbor.

Bernard, E. 2001. *Inscriptiones grecques d'Alexandrie ptolémaïque.* Institut français d'archéologie orientale. Cairo.

Berthold, R. M. 1984. *Rhodes in the Hellenistic Age.* Cornell University Press. Ithaca, New York.

Berve, H. 1973. *Das Alexanderreich auf Prosopographischer Grundlage.* Vol. 2. Arno Press. New York.

Bevan, E. 1968 [1927]. *The House of Ptolemy: A History of Egypt.* Ares Press. Chicago.

Billows, R. 1990. *Antigonos the One-Eyed and the Creation of the Hellenistic State.* University of California Press.

Billows, R. 1995. *Kings and Colonists: Aspects of Macedonian Imperialism.* E. J. Brill. Leiden and New York.

Boast, J. 2006. "An Analysis of Egypt's Foreign Policy during the Saite Period." A thesis submitted to The University of Birmingham for the degree of MPHIL(B) in Egyptology.

Boiy, T. 2000. "Dating Methods during the Early Hellenistic Period." *Journal of Cuneiform Studies* 52: 115–21.

Boiy, T. 2007. *Between High and Low: A Chronology of the Early Hellenistic Period.* Verlag Antike. Frankfurt am Main.

Bommas, M. 2005. *Heiligtum und Mysterium: Die Verbreitung der Isiskulte in der Ägäis.* Zabern. Mainz.

Borza, E. 1990. *In the Shadow of Olympus: The Emergence of Macedon.* Princeton University Press. Princeton.

Bosch-Puche, F. 2013. "The Egyptian Royal Titulary of Alexander the Great. I. Horus, Two Ladies Golden Horus, and Throne Names." *Journal of Egyptian Archaeology* 99: 131–54.

Bosch-Puche, F. 2014A. "The Egyptian Royal Titulary of Alexander the Great, II: Personal Name, Empty Cartouches, Final Remarks, and Appendix." *Journal of Egyptian Archaeology* 100: 89–109.

Bosch-Puche, F. 2014B. "Alexander's Egyptian Names in the Barque Shrine at Luxor Temple." In *Alexander the Great and Egypt: History, Art, Tradition.* Grieb, V., Nawotka, K., and Wojciechowska, A. (eds). Harrassowitz Verlag. Wiesbaden.

Bosworth, A. B. 1971. "The Death of Alexander the Great: Rumour and Propaganda." *Classical Quarterly* 21: 112–36.

Bosworth, A. B. 1988A. *From Arrian to Alexander: Studies in Historical Interpretation.* Clarendon Press. Oxford.

Bosworth, A. B. 1988B. *Conquest and Empire: The Reign of Alexander the Great.* Cambridge University Press. Cambridge and New York.

Bosworth, A. B. 1992. "Philip III Arrhidaeus and the Chronology of the Successors." *Chiron* 22: 55–81.

Bosworth, A. B. 1996. *Alexander and the East: The Tragedy of Triumph.* Clarendon Press. Oxford.

Bosworth, A. B. 2000. "Ptolemy and the Will of Alexander." In *Alexander the Great in Fact and Fiction.* Bosworth, A. B., and Baynham, E. J. (eds). Oxford University Press. Oxford and New York: 207–41.

Bosworth, A. B. 2002. *The Legacy of Alexander: Politics, Warfare, and Propaganda under the Successors.* Oxford University Press. Oxford and New York.

Bouché-Leclercq, A. 2007 [1903]. *Histoire des Lagides.* Vol. 1. *Les cinq premiers Ptolémées (323–181 avant J.-C.).* Adamant Media Corporation. Brookline, MA.

Bowman, A. K., and Rathbone, D. 1992. "Cities and Administration in Roman Egypt." *Journal of Roman Studies* 82: 107–27.

Bowman, A. K., and Rathbone, D. 2002. *The Legacy of Alexander: Politics, Warfare, and Propaganda under the Successors.* Oxford University Press. Oxford and New York.

Briant, P. 1973. *Antigone le Borgne: Les débuts de sa carrière et les problèmes de l'assemblée macédonienne.* 2nd ed. Belles Lettres. Paris.

Briant, P. 2002. *From Cyrus to Alexander: A History of the Persian Empire.* Daniel, P. T. (trans.). Eisenbruns. Winona Lake, IN.

Burstein, S. M. 1977. "I. G. II^2 561 and the Court of Alexander IV." *Zeitschrift für Papyrologie und Epigraphik* 24: 223–5.

Burstein, S. M. 1991. "Pharaoh Alexander: A Scholarly Myth." *Ancient Society* 22: 139–45.

Caneva, S. C. 2018. "Ptolemy I: Politics, Religion and the Transition to Hellenistic Egypt." In *Ptolemy I Soter: A Self-Made Man.* Howe, T. (ed.). Oxbow. Oxford and Havertown, PA: 88–127.

Carlier, P. 2000. "Homeric and Macedonian Kingship." In *Alternatives to Athens: Varieties of Political Organization and Community in Ancient Greece.* Brock, R., and Hodkinson, S. (eds). Oxford University Press. Oxford and New York: 259–68.

Carney, E. D. 1992. "The Politics of Polygamy: Alexander and the Murder of Philip." *Historia: Zeitschrift für alte Geschichte* 41: 160–89.

Carney, E. D. 2000. *Women and Monarchy in Macedonia.* University of Oklahoma Press. Norman, OK.

Carney, E. D. 2006. *Olympias.* Routledge. New York.

Carney, E. D. 2007. "Symposia and the Macedonian Elite: The Unmixed Life." *Syllecta Classica* 18: 129–80.

Cary, M. 1928. "A Constitutional Inscription from Cyrene." *Journal of Hellenic Studies* 48: 222–38.

Casson, L. 1995. *Ships and Seamanship in the Ancient World.* Johns Hopkins University Press. Baltimore and London.

Classen, C. J. 1959. "The Libyan god Ammon in Greece before 331 B.C." *Historia: Zeitschrift für alte Geschichte* 8: 349–55.

Colburn, H. P. 2007: "The Role of Coinage in the Political Economy of Fourth Century Egypt." In *Ptolemy I and the Transformation of Egypt, 404–282 BCE.* McKechnie, P., and Cromwell, J. A. (eds). Brill. Leiden and Boston: 70–119.

Collins, A. W. 2009. "The Divinity of Alexander in Egypt. A Reassessment." In *Alexander & His Successors. Essays from the Antipodes.* Wheatley, P., and Hannah, R. (eds). Regina Books. Claremont, CA: 179–205.

Collins, A. W. 2012. "Cleomenes of Naucratis, Heroonpolis, and the Revenue from Red Sea Trade under Alexander the Great." *Zeitschrift für Papyrologie und Epigraphik* 180: 237–42.

Collins, N. L. 1997. "The Various Fathers of Ptolemy I." *Mnemosyne. A Journal of Classical Studies* 50: 436–76.

Corcella, A. 2007. "Book IV." In *A Commentary on Herodotus Books I–IV*. Murray, O., and Moreno, A. (eds). Oxford University Press. Oxford and New York: 543–721.

Crawford, D. J. 1980. "Ptolemy, Ptah and Apis in Hellenistic Egypt." In *Studies on Ptolemaic Memphis*. Crawford, D. J., Quaegebeur, J., and Clarysse, W. (eds). *Studia Hellenistica* 24: 1–42.

Dell, H. J. 1970. "The Western Frontier of the Macedonian Monarchy." In *Ancient Macedonia I. Papers read at the first international symposium held in Thessaloniki, August 26–29, 1968*. Laourdas, B. and Makaronas, Ch. (eds), Institute for Balkan Studies. Thessaloniki: 115–26.

Depuydt, L. 1997. "The Time of Death of Alexander the Great: 11 June 323 BC (–322), ca. 4:00–5:00 PM." *Die Welt des Orients* 28: 117–35.

Dever, W. G. 1997. "Ashdod." In *The Oxford Encyclopedia of Archaeology in the Near East*. Meyers, E. M. (ed.). Oxford: 219–20.

Devine, A. M. 1984. "Diodorus' Account of the Battle of Gaza." *Acta Classica* 27: 31–40.

Dillery, J. 1999. "The First Egyptian Narrative History: Manetho and Greek Historiography," *Zeitschrift für Papyrologie und Ep igraphik* 127: 93–116.

Dixon, M. 2007. "Corinth, Greek Freedom, and the Diadochoi, 323–301 B.C." In *Alexander's Empire: Formulation to Decay*. Heckle, W., Tritle, L., and Wheatley, P. (eds). Regina Books. Claremont, CA: 151–78.

Droysen, J. G. 1877–78. *Geschichte des Hellenismus*. 3 vols. F.A. Berthes. Gotha.

Ellis, J. R. 1976. *Philip II and Macedonian Imperialism*. Thames and Hudson: London.

Ellis, W. M. 1994. *Ptolemy of Egypt*. Routledge. London and New York.

Engels, D. W. 1978. *Alexander the Great and the Logistics of the Macedonian Army*. University of California Press. Berkeley, Los Angeles, London.

Errington, R. M. 1969. "Bias in Ptolemy's History of Alexander," *Classical Quarterly* 19: 233–42.

Errington, R. M. 1977. "Diodorus Siculus and the Chronology of the Early Diadochoi, 320–311 B.C." *Hermes* 105: 478–504.

Errington, R. M. 1978. "The Nature of the Macedonian State under the Monarchy." *Chiron* 8: 77–133.

Erskine, A. 2002. "Life after Death: Alexandria and the Body of Alexander," *Greece & Rome* 49: 163–79.

Fischer-Bovet, C. 2014. *Army and Society in Ptolemaic Egypt*. Cambridge University Press. Cambridge and New York.

Frankfort, H. 1948. *Ancient Egyptian Religion: An Interpretation*. Dover Press. Mineola, NY.

Fraser, P. 1972. *Ptolemaic Alexandria*. 3 vols. Clarendon Press. Oxford.

Fredricksmeyer, E. A. 2000. "Alexander the Great and the Kingship of Asia." In A. B. Bosworth and E. J. Baynham (eds). *Alexander the Great in Fact and Fiction*. Oxford University Press. Oxford and New York: 136–66.

Fuller, J. F. C. 1960. *The Generalship of Alexander the Great*. Da Capo Press. New Brunswick, NJ.

Gorre, G. 2018. "Ptolemy Son of Lagos and the Egyptian Elite." In *Ptolemy I Soter: A Self-Made Man*. Howe, T. (ed.). Oxbow. Oxford and Philadelphia: 128–48.

Grabowski, T. 2013. "Ptolemaic Foundations in Asia Minor and the Aegean as the Lagids' Political Tool." *Electrum* 20: 57–76.

Greenwalt, W. 1985. "The Search for Arrhidaeus." *Ancient World* 10: 69–77.

Greenwalt, W. 1989. "Polygamy and Succession in Argead Macedonia." *Arethusa* 22: 19–45.

Griffith, G. T. 1965. "The Macedonian Background." *Greece & Rome* 12: 125–39.

Gruen, E. 1985. "The Coronation of the Diadochoi." In *The Craft of the Ancient Historian: Essays in Honor of Chester G. Starr*. J. Eadie and J. Ober (eds). University Press of America. Lanham, MD, and London: 253–71.

Habicht, C. 1958. "Die herrschende Gesellschaft in den hellenistischen Monarchen." *Sozial- und Wirtschaftsgeschichte* 45: 1–16.

Habicht, C. 2006. "The Literary and Epigraphic Evidence for the History of Alexander and His First Successors." In *The Hellenistic Monarchies: Selected Papers*. Habicht, C. (ed.). University of Michigan Press. Ann Arbor.

Hamilton, J. R. 1969. *Plutarch Alexander: A Commentary*. Clarendon Press. Oxford.

Hammond, N. G. L. 1978. "'Philip's Tomb' in Historical Context." *Greek, Roman and Byzantine Studies* 18: 331–50.

Hammond, N. G. L. 1986. "The Kingdom of Asia and the Persian Throne," *Antichthon* 20: 73–85.

Hammond, N. G. L. 1988A. "The King and the Land in the Macedonian Kingdom." *Classical Quarterly* 38: 382–91.

Hammond, N. G. L. 1988B. "The Royal Journal of Alexander." *Historia: Zeitschrift für alte Geschichte* 37: 129–50.

Hammond, N. G. L. 1993A. *Sources for Alexander the Great: An Analysis of Plutarch's "Life" and Arrianos' "Anabasis Alexandrou*," Cambridge University Press. Cambridge.

Hammond, N. G. L. 1993B. "The Macedonian imprint on the Hellenistic world." In *Hellenistic History and Culture*. Green, P. (ed.). University of California Press. Berkeley: 12–23.

Hammond, N. G. L., and Griffith, G. T. 1979. *A History of Macedonia*, Vol. 2 550–336 B.C. Clarendon Press. Oxford.

Hammond, N. G. L., and Walbank, F. W. 1988. *A History of Macedonia*. Vol. 3. 336–167 B.C. Clarendon Press. Oxford.

Hanson, V. D. 1995. *The Other Greeks: The Family Farm and the Agrarian Roots of Western Civilization*. Free Press. New York.

Harris, W. V. 1989. *Ancient Literacy*. Harvard University Press. Cambridge, MA, and London.

Hatzopoulos, M. 1996A. *Macedonian Institutions under the Kings*. Vol. 1: *A Historical and Epigraphic Study*. Diffusion de Boccard. Paris.

Hatzopoulos, M. 1996B. *Macedonian Institutions under the Kings*. Vol. 2: *Epigraphic Appendix*. Diffusion de Boccard. Paris.

Hauben, H. 2013. "Callicrates of Samos and Patrochos of Macedon. Champions of Ptolemaic thalassocracy." In *The Ptolemies, the Sea and the Nile: Studies in Waterborne Power*. Buraselis, K., Stefanou, M., and Thompson, D. J. Cambridge University Press. Cambridge and New York: 39–65.

Hauben, H. 2014. "Ptolemy's Grand Tour." In *The Age of the Successors and the Creation of the Hellenistic Kingdoms (323–276 B.C.)*. H. Hauben and A. Meeus (eds). Peeters. Leuven: 235–61.

Head, B. V. 1879. *"A" Catalogue of the Greek Coins in the British Museum: Macedonia, etc.* Vol. 5. Trustees of the British Museum. London.

Heckel, W. 1977. "The Conspiracy Against Philotas." *Phoenix* 31: 9–21.

Heckel, W. 1978. "'Somatophylakes' of Alexander the Great: Some Thoughts." *Historia: Zeitschrift für alte Geschichte* 27: 224–8.

Heckel, W. 1979. "Philip II, Kleopatra and Karanos," *Rivista di filologia e di istruzione classica* 107: 385–93.

Heckel, W. 1980. "Alexander at the Persian Gates." *Athenaeum* 58: 168–74.

Heckel, W. 1985. "The 'Boyhood Friends' of Alexander the Great." *Emerita* 53: 285–9.

Heckel, W. 1986. "'Somatophylakia': A Macedonian 'cursus Honorum'." *Phoenix* 40: 279–94.

Heckel, W. 1988. *The Last Days and Testament of Alexander the Great*. Franz Steiner. Stuttgart.

Heckel, W. 1992. *The Marshals of Alexander's Empire*. Routledge. London and New York.

Heckel, W. 2003. "Alexander and the 'Limits of the Civilised World'." In *Crossroads of History: The Age of Alexander*. Heckel, W., and Tritle, L. A. (eds). Regina Books. Claremont, CA: 147–74.

Heckel, W. 2016. *Alexander's Marshals: A Study of the Makedonian Aristocracy and the Politics of Military Leadership*. 2nd ed. Routledge. Abingdon and New York.

Heckel, W. 2018. "Ptolemy: A Man of His Own Making." In *Ptolemy I Soter: A Self-Made Man*. Howe, T. (ed.). Oxbow. Oxford and Havertown, PA: 1–19.

Heckel, W. 2021. *Who's Who in the Age of Alexander and his Successors from Chaironeia to Ipsos (338–301 BC)*. Greenhill Books. Barnsley.

Herman, G. 1987. *Ritualised Friendship and the Greek City*. Cambridge University Press. Cambridge.

Hölbl, G. 2001. *A History of the Ptolemaic Empire*. Saavedra, T. (trans.). Routledge. London and New York.

Holt, F. L. 1988. *Alexander the Great and Bactria: The Formation of a Greek Frontier in Central Asia*. E. J. Brill. Leiden and New York.

Howe, T. 2008. "Alexander in India: Ptolemy as Near Eastern Historiographer." In *Macedonian Legacies: Studies in Ancient Macedonian History and Culture in Honor of Eugene N. Borza*. Howe, T., and Reames, J. (eds). Regina Books. Claremont, CA: 215–33.

Howe, T. 2015. "Introducing Ptolemy: Alexander and the Persian Gates." In *The Many Faces of War in the Ancient World*. Heckel, W., Müller, S., and Wrightson, G. (eds). Cambridge Scholars Publishing. Newcastle upon Tyne: 166–95.

Howe, T. 2018A. "Ptolemy, the Son of Lagus." In *Brill's New Jacoby*.

Howe, T. 2018B. "Kings Don't Lie: Truthtelling, Historiography and Ptolemy I Soter." In *Ptolemy I Soter: A Self-Made Man*. Howe, T. (ed.). Oxbow. Oxford and Havertown, PA: 155–84.

Howe, T. 2021. "The 'Pursuit' of Kings: *imitatio Alexandri* in Arrian's Darius and Bessus 'Chase Scenes.'" In *Alexander the Great and Propaganda*. Walsh, J., and Baynham, E. (eds). Routledge. Oxford and New York: 54–70.

Johnson, C. J. 1995. "Ptolemy V and the Rosetta Decree: The Egyptianization of the Ptolemaic Kingship." *Ancient Society* 26 : 145–55.

Kahn, D., and Tammuz, O. 2008. "Egypt is Difficult to Enter: Invading Egypt—A Game Plan (seventh–fourth centuries BCE)." *Journal of the Society for the Study of Egyptian Antiquities* 35: 37–66.

Kasher, A. 1978. "First Jewish Military Units in Ptolemaic Egypt." *Journal for the Study of Judaism in the Persian, Hellenistic, and Roman Period* 9: 57–67.

Khalil, E. 2012. "The *ploion hellenikon* of Roman Egypt: What Was Greek about It?" *British Museum Studies in Ancient Egypt and Sudan* 19: 71–82.

Kienast, D. 1973. *Philipp II. von Makedonien und das Reich der Achamieniden*. Wilhelm-Fink. Munich.

Kienitz, F. 1953. *Die politische Geschichte Agyptens vom 7. bis zum 4. Jahrhundert vor der Zeitwende*. Akademie-Verlag. Berlin.

Klinkott, H. 2007. "Xerxes in Ägypten. Gadanken zum negativen Perserbild in der Satrapenstele." In *Ägypten unter fremden Herrschern zwischen persischer Satrapie und romischer Provinz*. Pfeiffer, S. (ed.). Antike. Frankfurt: 34–53.

Koenen, L. 1994. "The Ptolemaic King as a Religious Figure." In *Images and ideologies: Self-definition in the Hellenistic World*. Bulloch, A., Gruen, E. S., Long, A. A., and Stewart, A. (eds). University of California Press. Berkeley, Los Angeles, Oxford: 26–115.

Krentz, P., and Wheeler, E. L. 1994. *Polyaenus Stratagems of War*. 2 vols. Ares. Chicago.

Landucci Gattinoni, F. 1987. "La figura di Tolomeo nei libri XVIII–XX di Diodoro." *Aevum antiquum* 61: 37–42.

Landucci Gattinoni, F. 2003. *L'arte del potere: Vita e opera di Cassandro di Macedonia*. Franz Steiner. Stuttgart.

Landucci Gattinoni, F. 2010. "Cassander and the Legacy of Philip II and Alexander III in Diodorus' Library." In *Philip II and Alexander the Great: Father and Son, Lives and Afterlives*. Carney, E., and Ogden, D. (eds). Oxford University Press. Oxford and New York: 113–21, 275–80.

Larsen, J. A. O. 1929. "Notes on the Constitutional Inscription from Cyrene." *Classical Philology* 24: 351–68.

Levi, M. A. 1977. *Introduzione ad Alessandro Magno*. Rusconi. Milan.

Lewis, N. 1986. *Greeks in Ptolemaic Egypt: Case Studies in the Social History of the Hellenistic World*. Clarendon Press. Oxford.

Lianou, M. 2010. "The Role of the Argeadai in the Legitimation of the Ptolemaic Dynasty: Rhetoric and Practice." In *Philip II and Alexander the Great: Father and Son, Lives and Afterlives*. Carney, E., and Ogden, D. (eds). Oxford University Press. Oxford and New York: 123–33, 280–4.

Lloyd, A. B. 2000. "The Late Period (664–332 BC)." In *The Oxford History of Ancient Egypt*. Shaw, I. (ed.): 364–87.

Lloyd, A. B. 2002. "The Egyptian Elite in the Early Ptolemaic Period: Some Hieroglyphic Evidence." In *The Hellenistic World: New Perspectives*. Ogden, D. (ed.). The Classical Press of Wales. Swansea: 117–36.

Lorber, C. C. 2012. "Dating the portrait coinage of Ptolemy I." *American Journal of Numismatics* 24: 33–44.

Lorber, C. C. 2018. In *Ptolemy I Soter: A Self-Made Man*. Howe, T. (ed.). Oxbow. Oxford and Havertown, PA: 60–87.

Lund, H. S. 1992. *Lysimachus: A Study in Early Hellenistic Kingship*. Routledge. London and New York.

Ma, J. 2013. "Alexander's Decision-Making as a Historical Problem." *Revue des Études Militaires Anciennes* 6: 1–13.

Mahaffy, J. P. 1895. *The Empire of the Ptolemies*. Macmillan. London and New York.

Malamat, A. 1974. "Megiddo, 609 B.C.: The Conflict Re-examined." *Acta Antiqua* 22: 445–9.

Malek, J. 1997. "Review of O'Connor and Silverman 1995." *Journal of Egyptian Archaeology* 83: 227–8.

Manning, J. G. 2010. *The Last Pharaohs. Egypt Under the Ptolemies, 305–30 BC*. Princeton University Press. Princeton.

McGing, B. C. 1997. "Revolt Egyptian Style: Internal Opposition to Ptolemaic Rule." *Archiv für Papyrusforschung und verwandte Gebiete* 43: 273–314.

McKechnie, P. 1999. "Manipulation of Themes in Quintus Curtius Rufus Book 10." *Historia: Zeitschrift für alte Geschichte* 48: 44–60.

Meadows, A. 2006. "The Ptolemaic Annexation of Lycia: SEG 27.929." In *Symposium Proceedings: The IIIrd Symposium on Lycia 07–10 November 2005 Antalya*. Vol II. Dörtlük, K., Varkivanc, B., Kahya, T., des Courtils, J., Dogan Alparslam, M., and Boyraz, R. (eds). Suna & Inan Kıraç Research Institute on Mediterranean Civilizations. Antalya: 459–70.

Meadows, A. 2013. "The Ptolemaic League of Islanders." In *The Ptolemies, the Sea and the Nile: Studies in Waterborne Power*. Buraselis, K., Stefanou, M., and Thompson, D. J. (eds). Cambridge University Press. Cambridge and New York: 19–38.

Meadows, A., and Thonemann, P. 2013. "The Ptolemaic Administration of Pamphylia." *Zeitschrift für Papyrologie und Epigraphik* 186: 223–6.

Meeus, A. 2008. "The Power Struggle of the Diadochoi in Babylon, 323 BC," *Ancient Society* 38: 39–82.

Meeus, A. 2014. "The Territorial Ambitions of Ptolemy I." In *The Age of the Successors and the Creation of the Hellenistic Kingdoms (323–276 B.C.)*. Hauben, H., and Meeus, A. (eds). Peeters. Leuven: 263–306.

Merker, I. L. 1970. "The Ptolemaic Officials and the League of Islanders." *Historia: Zeitschrift fur Alte Geschichte* 19: 141–60.

Merker, I. L. 1974. "Demetrios Poliorketes and Tyre." *Ancient Society* 5: 119–26.

Metcalf, W. E. 2012. *The Oxford Handbook of Greek and Roman Coinage*. Oxford University Press. Oxford.

Mitchell, B. M. 1966. "Cyrene and Persia." *Journal of Hellenic Studies* 86: 99–113.

Mitchell, L. 2002. *Greeks Bearing Gifts: The Public Us of Private Relationships in the Greek World, 435–323 BC*. Cambridge University Press. Cambridge.

Mooren, L. 1975. *The Aulic Titulature in Ptolemaic Egypt: Introduction and Prosopography*. Verhandelingen van de Koninklijke Academie voor Wetenschappen, Letteren en Schone Kunsten van België, Klasse der Letteren, XXXVII 78. Paleis der Academiën. Brussels.

Mooren, L. 1981. "Ptolemaic Families." In *Proceedings of the Sixteenth International Congress of Papyrology, New York, 24–31 July 1980*. (*American Studies in Papyrology* 23). Bagnall, R. S., Browne, G. M., Hansen, A. E., Koenen, L. (eds). Scholars Press. Chico, CA: 289–301.

Mooren, L. 1983. "The Nature of the Hellenistic Monarchy." In *Egypt and the Hellenistic World: Proceedings of the Internatinal Colloquium Leuven, 24–26 May 1982*. E. van T Dack, P. van Dessel, and W. van Gucht (eds). *Studia Hellenistica* 27: 205–40.

Moyer, I. S. 2011. *Egypt and the Limits of Hellenism*. Cambridge University Press. Cambridge.

Mueller, K. 2004. "Dating the Ptolemaic City-Foundations in Cyrenaica: A Brief Note." *Libyan Studies* 35: 1–10.

Mueller, K. 2006. *Settlements of the Ptolemies: City Foundations and New Settlement in the Hellenistic World*. Peeters. Leuven.

Müller. S. 2009. *Das hellenistische Königspaar in der medialen Repräsentation*. Walter de Gruyter. Berlin and New York

Müller. S. 2011. "In Abhängigkeit von Alexander? Hephaistion bei den Alexanderhistoriographen." *Gymnasium* 118: 429–56.

Müller. S. 2013. "Ptolemaios und die Erinnerung an Hephaistion." *Anabasis* 3: 75–91.

Oates, J. 1986. *Babylon*. Revised edition. Thames and Hudson. New York.

Ockinga, B. G. 2018. "The Satrap Stele of Ptolemy: A Reassessment." In *Ptolemy I and the Transformation of Egypt 404–282 BCE*. McKechnie, P., and Cromwell, J. A. (eds). Brill. Leiden and Boston.

Ogden, D. 2015. "Alexander, Agathos Daimon, and Ptolemy: The Alexandrian Foundation Myth in Dialogue." In *Foundations Myths in Ancient Societies: Dialogues and Discourses*. Sweeney, N. M. (ed.). Pennsylvania State University Press. State College, PA: 129–50.

Olmstead, A. T. 1959. *History of the Persian Empire*. University of Chicago Press. Chicago and London.

O'Neil, J. L. 2000. "The Creation of New Dynasties after the Death of Alexander the Great." *Prudentia* 32: 118–37.

O'Neil, J. L. 2006. "Places and Origin of the Officials of Ptolemaic Egypt." *Historia: Zeitschrift für Alte Geschichte* 55: 16–25.

O'Sullivan, L. 1997. "Asander, Athens and IG II² 450." *Zeitschrift für Papyrologie und Epigraphik* 119: 107–16.

Papadopoulou, D. 2010. "The administration of Egypt in Hellenistic Times. The Rise and Fall of the *oikonomos*." *Anistoriton Journal* 12: 1–8.

Papantoniou, G. 2012. *Religion and Social Transformations in Cyprus: From the Cypriot Basileis to the Hellenistic Strategos*. Leiden: Brill.

Parke, H. W. 1967. *Greek Oracles*. Hutchinson. London.

Pearson, L. 1955. "The Diary and the Correspondence of Alexander the Great." *Historia: Zeitschrift für alte Geschichte* 3: 429–55.

Perlman, S. 1958. "A Note on the Political Implications of Proxenia in the Fourth Century B.C." *Classical Quarterly* 8: 185–91.

Pfeiffer, S. 2008. "The God Serapis, His Cult and the Beginnings of the Ruler Cult in Ptolemaic Egypt." In *Ptolemy II Philadelphus and His World*. McKechnie, P., and Guillame, P. (eds). Brill. Leiden and Boston.

Pfeiffer, S. 1983. *The Lost Histories of Alexander the Great*. Scholars Press. Chico, CA.

Piejko, E. 1985. "'Second Letter' of Alexander the Great to Chios." *Phoenix* 39: 238–49.

Pitt, E. M., and Richardson, W. P. 2017. "Hostile Inaction? Antipater, Craterus and the Macedonian Regency." *Classical Quarterly* 67: 77–87.

Poddighe, E. 2002. *Nel segno di Antipatro: l'eclissa della democrazia ateniese dal 323/2 al 319/8 a.C.* Carocci. Rome.

Pownall, F. 2010. "The Symposia of Philip II and Alexander III of Macedon: The View from Greece." In *Philip II and Alexander the Great: Father and Son, Lives and Afterlives*. Carney, E., and Ogden, D. (eds). Oxford University Press. Oxford and New York: 55–65, 256–60.

Préaux, C. 1978. *Le Monde hellénistique: la Grèce et l'Orient (323–146 av. J.-C.* Vol. 1. Presses Universitaires de France. Paris.

Rathmann, M. 2005. *Perdikkas zwischen 323 und 320: Nachlassverwalter des Alexanderreiches oder Autokrat?* Der Österreichischen Akademie des Wissenschaften. Vienna.

Renberg, G. H., and Bubelis, W. S. 2011. "The Epistolary Rhetoric of Zoilos of Aspendos and the Early Cult of Sarapis: Re-reading P. Cair.Zen. I 59034." *Zeitschrift für Papyrologie und Epigraphik* 177: 169–200.

Rigsby, K. J. 1988. "An Edict of Ptolemy I." *Zeitschrift für Papyrologie und Epigraphik* 72: 273–4.

Rigsby, K. J. 2001. "Founding a Sarapeum." *Greek, Roman and Byzantine Studies* 42: 117–21.

Ritner, R. K. 2003. "The Satrap Stela (Cairo JdE 22182)." In *The Literature of Ancient Egypt: An Anthology of Stories, Instructions, Stelae, Autobiographies, and Poetry*, 3rd ed. Simpson, W. K. (ed.). Yale University Press. New Haven: 392–7.

Roisman, J. 1984. "Ptolemy and His Rivals in His History of Alexander." *Classical Quarterly* 34: 373–85.

Roisman, J. 2012. *Alexander's Veterans and the Early Wars of the Successors*. University of Texas Press. Austin.

Roisman, J. 2014. "Perdikkas' Invasion of Egypt." In *The Age of the Successors and the Creation of the Hellenistic Kingdoms (323–276)*. Brill. Leiden: 455–74.

Rostovtzeff, M. 1941. *The Social and Economic History of the Hellenistic World*. Vol. 1. Clarendon Press. Oxford.

Rowlandson, J. 2007. "The character of Ptolemaic aristocracy: problems of definition and evidence." In *Jewish Perspectives on Hellenistic Rulers*. Rajak, T., Pearce, S., Aitken, J., and Dines, J. (eds). University of California Press. Berkeley, Los Angeles, London.

Ruzicka, S. 2012. *Trouble in the West: Egypt and the Persian Empire, 525–332 BC*. Oxford University Press. Oxford and New York.

Sabin, P. 2009. *Lost Battles: Reconstructing the Great Clashes of the Ancient World*. Hambledon Continuum. London and New York.

Samuel, A. E. 1988. "Philip and Alexander as Kings: Macedonian and Merovingian Parallels." *American Historical Review* 93: 1270–86.

Samuel, A. E. 1993. "The Ptolemies and the Ideology of Kingship." In *Hellenistic History and Culture*. Green, P. (ed.). University of California Press. Berkeley, Los Angeles, London: 168–210.

Sawada, N. 2010. "Social Customs and Institutions: Aspects of Macedonian Elite Society." In *A Companion to Ancient Macedonia*. Roisman, J., and Worthington, I. (eds). Wiley-Blackwell. Oxford and Malden, MD: 392–408.

Schäfer, C. 2002. *Eumenes von Kardia und der Kampf um die Macht imj Alexanderreich*. Marthe Clauss. Frankfort.

Schäfer D. 2011. *Makedonische Pharaonen und hieroglyphische Stelen. Historische Untersuchungen zur Satrapenstele und verwandten Denkmäten*. Peters. Leuven.

Schep, L. 2009. "The Death of Alexander the Great: Reconsidering Poison." In *Alexander & His Successors. Essays from the Antipodes*. Wheatley, P., and Hannah, R. (eds). Regina Books. Claremont, CA: 227–36.

Schober, L. 1981. *Untersuchungen zur Geschichte Babyloniens und der Oberen Satrapien von 323–303 v. Chr.* Peter D. Lang. Frankfurt and Bern.

Schubert, R. 1914. *Die Quellen zur Geschichte der Diadochenzeit*. Dietrich. Leipzig.

Seibert, J. 1969. *Untersuchungen zur Geschichte Ptolemaios' I*. C. H. Beck. Munich.

Shaw, I. 2000. "Egypt and the Outside World." In *The Oxford History of Ancient Egypt.* Shaw, I. (ed.). Oxford University Press. Oxford and New York: 308–23.

Shear, T. L. 1978. *Kallias of Sphettos and the Revolt of Athens in 286 B.C. (Hesperia: Supplement XVII).* American School of Classical Studies at Athens. Princeton.

Speck, H. 2002. "Alexander at the Persian Gates. A Study in Historiography and Topography." *American Journal of Ancient History* 1: 5–234.

Stadter, P. A. 1980. *Arrian of Nicomedia.* University of North Carolina Press. Chapel Hill.

Stagakis, G. J. 1962. "Institutional Aspects of the Hetairos Relation." Unpub. Diss. University of Wisconsin. Madison.

Stambaugh, J. 1972. *Sarapis under the Early Ptolemies.* Brill. Leiden.

Stefanou, M. 2013. "Waterborne recruits: the military settlers of Ptolemaic Egypt." In *The Ptolemies, the Sea, and the Nile. Studies in Waterborne Power.* Buraselis, K., Stefanou, M., and Thompson, D. J. (eds). Cambridge University Press. Cambridge.

Stewart, A. 1993. *Faces of Power: Alexander's Image and Hellenistic Politics.* University of California Press. Berkeley 1993.

Stambaugh, J. E. 1972. *Sarapis under the Early Ptolemies.* Brill. Leiden.

Strasburger, H. 1934. *Ptolemaios und Alexander.* Dieterich'sche Verlagsbuchhandlung. Leipzig.

Strootman, R. 2011. "Kings and cities in the Hellenistic Age." In *Political Culture in the Greek City After the Classical Age.* Alston, R., van Nijf, O., Williamson, C. (eds). Peeters. Leuven: 141–53.

Sucht, T. G. 1995. *The Military Experience and Workplace Literacy: A Review and Synthesis for Policy and Practice.* National Center on Adult Literacy. University of Pennsylvania. Philadelphia.

Sucht, T. G. 2014. "'Men to Whose Rapacity Neither Sea Nor Mountain Sets a Limit': The Aims of the Diadochs." In *The Age of the Successors and the Creation of the Hellenistic Kingdoms (323–276 B.C.).* H. Hauben and A. Meeus (eds). Peeters. Leuven: 307–22.

Tarn, W. W. 1950. *Alexander the Great.* Vol. 2. *Sources and Studies.* Cambridge University Press. Cambridge.

Thompson, D. J. 2012. *Memphis Under the Ptolemies.* 2nd ed. Princeton University Press. Princeton.

Tolley, H. 2019. "The End of the Satrapies: The Date of Alexander IV's Death." *Athens Journal of History* 5: 259–78.

Trigger, B. G, Kemp, B. J., O'Connor, D., and Lloyd, A. B. 1983. *Ancient Egypt: A Social History.* Cambridge University Press. Cambridge.

Trigger, B. G, Kemp, B. J., O'Connor, D., and Lloyd, A. B. 2003. *Understanding Early Civilizations.* Cambridge University Press. Cambridge.

Turner, E. 1974. "A Commander-in-Chief's Order from Saqqâra." *Journal of Egyptian Archaeology* 60: 239–42.

Turner, E. 1984. "Ptolemaic Egypt." In *The Cambridge Ancient History.* Vol. 7, Part 1. Walbank, F. W., Astin, A. E., Frederiksen, M. W., and Ogilvie, R. M. (eds). Cambridge University Press. Cambridge: 118–74.

van der Spek, R. J. 2009. "Multi-Ethnicity and Ethnic Segregation in Hellenistic Babylon." In *Ethnic Constructs in Antiquity: The Role of Power and Tradition.* Derks, T., and Roymans, N. (eds). Amsterdam University Press. Amsterdam: 101–15.

Vandorpe, K. 2007. "Agriculture, Temples and Tax Law in Ptolemaic Egypt." In *L'agriculture institutionnelle en Égypte ancienne: État de la question et perspectives interdisciplinaires.* Moreno Garcia, J. C. (ed.). Villeneuve-d'Ascq: Université Charles-de-Gaulle. Lille: 165–71.

Van Dessel, P., and Hauben, H. 1977. "Rhodes, Alexander, and the Diadochi." *Historia: Zeitschrift für alte Geschichte* 26: 307–39.

Van Oppen de Ruiter, B. F. 2013. "Lagus and Arsinoe: An Exploration of Legendary Royal Bastardy." *Historia: Zeitschrift für alte Geschichte* 62: 80–107.

Von Beckerath, J. 1999. *Handbuch der ägyptischen Köonigsnamen.* P. von Zabern. Mainz.

Von Reden, S. 2007. *Money in Ptolemaic Egypt: From the Macedonian Conquest to the End of the Third Century BC.* Cambridge University Press. Cambridge.

Vos, R. L. 1993. *The Apis Embalming Ritual: P.Vindob. 3873.* Peeters. Leiden.

Voss. R. L. 1993. *The Apis Embalming Ritual.* Peeters. Leiden.

Walbank, F. W. 1984. "Monarchies and monarchic ideas." In *The Cambridge Ancient History.* Vol. 7, Part 1. *The Hellenistic World.* Walbank, F. W., Astin, A. E., Frederiksen, M. W, Ogilvie, R. M. (eds). Cambridge University Press. Cambridge: 62–100.

Wallis Budge, E. A. 1967 [1895]. *The Egyptian Book of the Dead (The Papyrus of Ani) Egyptian Text, Transliteration and Translation.* Dover Publications. New York.

Wellendorf, H. 2008. "Ptolemy's Political Tool: Religion." *Studia Antiqua* 6: 33–8.

Wheatley, P. 2002. "Antigonus Monophthalmus in Babylonia, 310–308 B.C." *Journal of Near Eastern Studies* 61: 39–47.

Wheatley, P. 2013. "The *Heidelberg Epitome*: A Neglected Diadoch Source." In *After Alexander: The Time of the Diadochi (323–281 BC).* Alonso-Troncoso, V., and Anson, E. M. (eds). Oxbow Books and The David Brown Book Company. Oxford and Oakville: 17–29.

Wheatley, P., and Dunn, C. 2020. *Demetrius the Besieger.* Oxford University Press. Oxford.

Wilcken, U. 1927. *Urkunden der Ptolemäerzeit (Ältere Funde).* Vol. 1. Papyri aus Unterägypten. Walter de Gruyter. Berlin.

Will, É. 1964. "Ophellas, Ptolémée, Cassandre et la chronologie." *Revue des études anciennes* 66: 320–33.

Willekes, C. Forthcoming. "Cavalry Battle in Greece and in the Hellenistic East." In *A Companion to Greek Warfare.* Garvin, E., Howe, T., and Heckel, W. (eds). Wiley-Blackwell. Oxford.

Wojciechowska, A. 2016. "From the Macedonian Conquest to the Coronation of Ptolemy I." In *From Amyrtaeus to Ptolemy: Egypt in the Fourth Century B.C.* Wojciechowska, A. (ed.). Harrassovitz Verlag. Wiesbaden.

Wörrle, M. 1977. "Epigraphische Forschungen zur Geschichte Lykiens, I. Ptolemaios I. und Limyra." *Chiron* 7: 43–66.

Worthington, I. 2016. *Ptolemy I, King and Pharaoh of Egypt.* Oxford University Press. Oxford and New York.

Yardley, J. C., Wheatley, P., and Heckel, W. 2011. *Justin. Epitome of The Philippic History of Pompeius Trogus. Volume II, Books 13–15: The Successors to Alexander the Great.* Oxford University Press. Oxford and New York.

Youtie, H. C. 1948. "The Kline of Sarapis." *The Harvard Theological Review* 41: 9–29.

Index

Abreas 167
Actium, battle of 168
Adea (*also* Eurydice) 53, 87, 183
Aegae 52, 54, 78, 180
Aëropus 17, 33
Aetolia, Aetolians 54, 56, 77, 159
Agathocles, father of Lysimachus 175
Agathocles, son of Lysimachus 97, 100, 104, 175
Agathocles, tyrant of Syracuse 175, 184
Agathon 176
Agema 13, 172, 183
Agis, Ptolemaic general 89
Agis, Spartan king 160
Agrianes 71, 155
Alcetas 53, 69, 105
Alexander II 174
Alexander III, the Great *passim*
　administration 1, 2–4, 5, 167, 177, 186
　ambition 3, 4
　army 5, 6–7, 37, 68, 167, 178
　"Brotherhood of Man" 4–5, 187
　death 1, 3, 7, 8, 29–31, 197–8
　divinity 130–1, 135, 136, 140, 179, 190
　nature of empire 1–4, 8
　Persianization 2, 5–6, 39, 163, 172, 177, 178
　romance 1, 46, 148, 162, 176
　wounds 173, 176
Alexander IV 4, 23, 34, 43, 62, 87, 92, 95, 109, 122–3, 174, 181, 189
Alexander V 104
Alexander, son of Aëropus 16, 33
"Alexander Tent" 40, 179
Alexandria, capital of Ptolemaic Egypt 24, 52, 78, 107, 108, 114, 115, 117, 118, 120, 132, 138, 149, 167, 168, 169, 186
　cultural center of Hellenistic world 114, 132, 149
　foundation 49, 115, 117, 121, 129, 132, 136, 140, 149, 164–5, 167, 168, 169, 187, 191–2

Alcimachus 116
Amathus 83
Amphipolis 20, 116, 137, 168
Amun(-Ra) 107, 123, 124, 130, 135, 136, 165, 190
Amyntas, brother of Peucestas 109
Amyntas, father of Philip II 10, 174
Amnytas, father of Philip, a Macedonian commander 151
Amyntas, son of Andromenes 27, 151, 195
Amyntas, son of Arrhabaeus 150
Amyntas, son of Euthon 111
Amyntas Perdicca, son of Perdiccas III 2, 3, 23, 33, 48, 53
Amyntor 17
Androsthenes 20
Anteas 1, 19
Anticyra 127
Antigone, daughter of Berenice 98
Antigonus Monophthalmus 1, 4, 7, 8, 9, 10, 24, 45, 46, 47, 54, 55, 56, 57–8, 60–2, 63–4, 65, 67, 68, 69, 77, 78, 82–3, 84–9, 91–2, 93–6, 97, 101, 108, 110, 127–8, 131, 158, 160, 163–4, 166, 170, 172, 179, 181, 183, 184, 185, 189, 195
Antipater, regent 33, 38, 42, 49–51, 52, 53, 54, 55–8, 68, 77–8, 82, 84, 88, 97–8, 99, 100, 103, 104, 105, 109, 160, 174, 179, 180, 181, 185, 198
Antonius, Marcus 168
Aornus, Rock of 74–5, 158
Apame (*see also* Atacama) 185–6
Apis 107, 120, 121, 124, 128–9, 131–2, 133, 134–5, 138, 139, 140, 142, 167, 190, 192
Apollonides of Cardia 20
Apollonius 141–2, 193
Archelaus 172
archisomatophylaces 108
Archon, satrap 53, 180

Argead (dynasty) 2, 3, 4, 22, 23–4, 31, 32, 33, 40, 47, 48, 63, 76, 92, 93, 95, 103, 109, 112, 128, 139, 186
Argaeus, Macedonian pretender to the throne 23
Argaeus, son of Ptolemy I 104
Argyraspids 80, 163, 166
Ariobarzenes 71, 153–4
Aristeas 114, 116
Aristeia 70, 74, 156–7
Aristobulus 72, 145–8, 151, 155–7, 161–3, 164, 172, 194, 197
Aristonous 19, 36, 40, 161–2, 197
Aristotle 15, 108, 120
Arrhabaeus, nephew of Lycestian Alexander 150, 194
Arrhabaeus, son of Aëropus 33
Arrhidaeus, Macedonian commander and later regent 53, 54–5, 57
Arrhidaeus (*see also* Philip III) 3, 4, 18, 23, 32, 34, 35, 36, 37–8, 40, 41–2, 43, 175
Arrian, Flavius Arrianus 10, 17, 22, 23, 31, 33, 42, 48, 49, 50, 55, 69, 70, 71–2, 73–4, 75, 120, 145–65, 166, 171, 172, 176, 180, 182, 183, 184, 195, 196, 197
Arsinoe, daughter of Ptolemy I and wife of Ptolemy II 97, 100, 104, 140, 185, 186
Arsinoe, mother of Ptolemy I 22, 23, 24, 27
Artabazus 32, 185
Artaxerxes III Ochus 32, 79, 124
Artaxerxes V (Bessus) 71
Asander 30, 88, 196
Aspasians 74, 157
Assyrians 80, 120, 188
Astaspes 176
Atacama, second wife of Ptolemy I 185, 186
Atarrhias 181–2
Attalus, Macedonian battalion commander 41, 42, 84
Attalus, father of Cleopatra, Philip II's seventh wife 19
Augustus 41
Autophradates 176

Babylon, Babylonia 5, 7, 29, 31, 33, 36, 38, 42, 43, 44, 47, 48, 49, 50, 51, 52, 53, 54, 55, 58, 59, 63, 64, 76, 77, 80, 84, 86, 91, 92, 122, 133, 161, 165, 176, 178, 182, 189, 191
Bactria, Bactrians 32, 155, 173, 176, 185, 195
Balacrus 77
Barsine, mother of Heracles 3, 23, 31–2, 37, 39
Berenice, fourth wife of Ptolemy I 23, 97, 98, 104, 184
Bessus (Artaxerxes V) 71–2, 154–6
Beqaa Valley 83, 114
Biblus 86
Brahmans 75
Brasidas, Spartan commander 137
"Brotherhood of all Mankind" 4–6, 107–8

Caesar, Julius 168, 195
Callias 112
Callicrates 112
Caltrops 90
Calybe 20
Canopic branch of the Nile 78
Canopus 115
Cappadocia 63, 77, 84
Caria 7, 17, 18, 40, 59, 60, 62, 63, 80, 88, 89, 93
Carthaginians 184
Cassander, king of Macedonia 4, 47, 57, 58, 61, 62, 63–4, 84, 86, 87, 88, 91–9, 104, 127, 163, 183, 189, 194, 198
Cassandreia 87
Celaenae 91
Cenchreae 89
Chaeronea, battle of 28, 32, 70, 174, 182
Chalcidice 117
chiliarch, official 32, 39, 58
chiliarchy, unit of 1,000 men 155, 157, 158
Chios, Chians 116
Chorienses, Rock of 73
Chrysis 128
Cilicia 58, 59, 60, 62, 77, 80, 86, 89, 90, 91, 92, 97, 98, 104, 176
Cilles 91, 112
Cleander 176
Cleitus, son of Dropidas 31, 56, 67–8, 146–7, 181, 190

Cleitus, fleet commander 85, 105, 186
Cleomenes 49, 50, 55, 76, 119–20, 178, 179
Cleopatra, Alexander the Great's sister 9, 22, 45, 47, 52, 53–4, 63, 78, 94, 104, 163
Cleopatra, seventh wife of Philip II 18–19
Cleopatra VII 107, 168
cleruchy, cleruchs 69, 91, 113, 114, 119, 184
Coelê Syria 59, 60, 61, 64, 68, 83, 114, 129, 170
Coenus 153, 157, 160, 195
Companion Cavalry 13, 17, 25, 26, 28, 34, 36, 41, 42, 70, 71, 150, 155, 172, 182, 196
Concilium Plebis 35
contio, contiones 35
Corinth 17, 62, 63, 87, 89, 93, 101, 170, 179
Corinth, League of 47, 50, 63, 88, 93
Corragus 16, 25
Corupedium, battle of 100
Cossaeans 7, 75, 80, 178
Craterus 33, 38, 42, 50, 54, 55, 57, 58, 68, 71, 75, 77, 78, 80, 104, 150, 153, 161, 163, 176, 177, 180, 181, 195
Cratesipolis 62–3, 93
Curtius, Curtius Rufus 7, 22, 31, 33, 34–8, 39, 40, 41–2, 44, 46, 50, 68, 70, 71, 72, 73–5, 120, 147, 149, 152, 153–7, 160, 161–2, 176, 177, 178, 179, 182, 195, 196
Cybele 143
Cynnane 3, 53–4
Cyprus 4, 22, 24, 30, 59, 60, 61, 62, 64, 68, 69, 83, 85, 86, 88, 89, 92, 94, 95, 96, 99, 100, 112, 142, 143, 160, 170, 179, 186
Cyrene 49, 50–2, 55, 60, 69, 76–7, 83, 89, 113, 114, 117–18, 142, 179, 180, 184
Cyrus the Great 1

Damascus 32, 55
Darius I, king of Persia 2
Darius III, king of Persia 17, 32, 69–70, 71, 134, 162, 175
Dataphernes 71, 72, 155
Deidamia 97
Delos 88, 141
Demades 77, 130, 181

Demetrius Poliorcetes 24, 45–7, 60–1, 63, 64, 67, 68, 131, 132, 172, 179, 181, 184, 185, 186, 189
Demetrius of Phalerum 149
Demetrius, son of Athaimenes 175
Demo 128
Demosthenes 111
Diodorus Siculus 9, 10, 33, 34, 35, 36, 42, 44, 45, 49, 50, 52, 54, 56, 59, 63, 72, 81, 82, 84, 86, 88, 122, 131, 137, 155, 158, 160–1, 164, 172, 174, 175, 180, 182, 183, 184, 188, 189, 190, 195, 196, 197
Dioicetes 113
Dion 116
Dionysus 23, 107, 135, 138, 139, 192
Dioxippus 16, 25
Drongilus 20

Egypt, Egyptians 4, 6, 8, 9, 22, 45, 46, 47, 48–9, 50, 52, 53, 55, 56, 59–60, 61–2, 63, 64–5, 68, 69, 70, 76, 78, 82, 83, 84, 85, 86, 89, 90, 91, 92, 95, 97, 100, 104, 105–8, 112–13, 114–25, 127–41, 167–70, 179, 180, 184, 186, 187, 188, 189, 190–1, 193, 198
"Fortress Egypt" 78–80, 82–3, 96, 183
Eirene, daughter of Ptolemy I 104
Eordaea 19, 21
Ephemerides 133–4, 191
Epigoni 7, 10, 104, 176
Epirus 97–8, 99
Epistates 116
Erigyius 14, 18, 196
Erythrae 86
Eumelus 189
Eumenes of Cardia 7, 10, 24, 25–6, 30, 40, 52, 55, 57, 58, 60, 67, 68, 69, 77, 84–5, 86, 89, 104, 105, 137, 163–4, 165, 179, 183, 196
Eunostus 104
Eurydice, daughter of Antipater 49, 97, 98, 103, 104
Eurydice, wife of Philip III (*also* Adea) 53, 87, 183
Euthydice 184

Fayum 117
Fort of Camels 70, 81

Gabene, battle of 69, 85
Gaugamela, battle of 37, 67, 70, 71, 101, 150, 160
Gaza, battle of 45–6, 61, 64, 68, 82, 83, 91, 101, 112, 114, 182, 184
Gaza, city 86, 90, 91, 173, 182
Gaza, siege of 173, 176
Gedrosian Desert 7, 31, 75
Glaucias, king of Illyria 97
Golden Horus, an official name of pharaoh 121, 123, 136
Granicus, battle of 67, 70, 101, 136, 150, 151, 152, 171, 176, 194

Hades 107, 138, 143, 192
Hannibal 169
Harpalus 18, 31, 51, 172
Hellenistic Age 3–4, 6, 10, 11, 21, 68, 69, 100–1, 103, 105, 107, 108–10, 115, 116–17, 119, 132, 142, 147, 149, 166–7, 168–9, 188
Hellespontine Phrgyria 9, 84, 175
Helots 6
Hephaestion 17, 73, 75, 150, 151, 157, 160, 161, 197
Hephaestus 134
Heracleitus 67
Heracles, god 22, 23, 74, 130
Heracles, son of Alexander the Great 3, 23, 31–2, 36, 37, 39, 93, 177
Heracles-Thonis 115
Heracon 176
Hermolaus 27
Heromenes, son of Aëropus 33
hetaireia 109
hetairoi 5, 13–16, 17, 18–22, 25–6, 27, 31, 32, 33, 34, 36, 38, 109–11, 112, 172, 173, 185, 187, 188
Hieronymus of Cardia 10, 82, 157, 196
hipparch, leader of a hipparchy 25, 175
hipparchy, a division of the Companion Cavalry 155
Holcias 30
Hopkins, A. 30
hoplite 15
Horus 121, 123, 139
Horus Nebty, an official name of pharaoh 121, 123, 136, 192
Hydaspies, battle of 28, 73, 151, 155

hypaspist 13, 26, 71, 74, 75, 80, 155, 157, 163, 166, 182, 183
Hyphasis 30, 37, 38–9

Ilê Basilikê 13, 17
Illyria, Illyrians 16, 19, 21, 97, 173
India, Indians 1, 2, 7, 13, 31, 69, 70, 73, 74, 75, 146, 149, 150, 151, 153, 155, 156–9, 173, 176, 195, 196, 197
Indus River 7, 18, 29, 30, 46, 74, 75, 106, 110, 120, 161, 162, 168
Iollas, son of Antipater 30
Ipsus, battle of 10, 60, 61, 64, 68, 97, 98, 101, 158, 170
Isaurians 77
Isis 140, 142–3, 192, 193
Islanders, League of (also Nesiotic League) 61, 63, 96, 100, 170
Isocrates 6, 183
Issus, battle of 17, 31, 51, 67, 69, 70, 101, 150, 151, 152, 160, 171, 176, 183, 190

Joppa 86
Justin, Justinus Frontinus 10, 23, 33–4, 35–8, 41–2, 46, 49, 155, 160, 161, 174, 175, 177, 178, 182

Kennedy, J. F. 176

Lachares 98
Lagus, father of Ptolemy I 21–4, 27
 as a patronymic *passim*
Lagus, son of Ptolemy I 20
Lamia 128
Lamian War 9, 51, 57, 77, 88, 176, 180, 181
Laomedon 18, 20, 60, 84, 85, 172
Larandians 77
League of Corinth 88, 170, 181
Leaina 128
Legomena 146, 147, 197
Lemnos 88
Leonnatus 1, 9, 19, 21, 36, 38, 42, 43, 55, 56, 74, 75, 94, 150, 151, 157, 161, 162, 178, 197
Liber de Morte Testamentumque Alexandri Magni 30–1, 176, 178, 197–8

Limyra 111
Library, in Alexandria 114, 132, 149, 166, 168
Lord of Asia 76, 84
Luciano, "Lucky" 39
Lucian of Samosota 14
Lycia, Lycians 7, 18, 60, 62, 84, 89, 90, 93, 100, 111, 171
Lydia 7, 54, 63, 80, 160, 186
Lyncestis 1, 19, 33
Lysandra, daughter of Ptolemy I 97, 100, 104
Lysimachus 10–11, 24, 25, 30, 36, 47, 57, 61, 64, 73, 84–5, 91–2, 93, 94, 95, 96–7, 98, 99–100, 104, 109, 165, 175, 186

Magas 184
magistoi (*see also* principes) 33
malaria 29, 176
Mallians 146, 148, 153, 159, 161, 162, 182, 195
Manitho 112, 138, 191
Malus 89
Mastira 20
Medius 31
Megara 63
Meleager 35–7, 40, 41–2, 43, 53, 104, 153, 177, 178
Memphis 132–41, 164–5, 169, 192
Menander, satrap 54, 180
Menander, playwright 132
Menelaus, brother of Ptolemy I 24, 88, 89, 92, 94, 175
Menelaus, father of Philip cavalry commander 151
Menidas 160
Metamorphosis 142–3
Methone 117, 173, 174
Miltiades 184
Myllinas 74–5, 196

Napoleon 169
Naucratis 115, 117
Nearchus 18, 19, 20, 36, 39, 40, 171, 172, 196
Nebuchadrezzar, palace of 38
Neoptolemus, king of Epirus 98
Neoptolemus, commander of the hypaspists 163

Nepos, Cornelius Nepos 10, 171, 185, 186
Nesiotic League (*see also* League of Islanders) 61, 63, 96, 100, 170
Nicaea, daughter of Antipater 50, 52, 53, 54
Nicaea, wife of Lysimachus 100
Nicanor, Ptolemaic general 83–4
Nicanor, son of Antipater 30
Nicanor, son of Parmenion 150, 194
Nicocles 92
Nicocreon 85, 89
Nile River 60, 78–9, 80, 81, 83, 89, 105, 113, 117, 120–1, 122, 141, 183
Nilopolis 134
Nomes 24, 106, 113, 115, 117, 119, 140, 188

Octavian 52, 180
oikonomoi 111, 188
Olympias 18, 19, 30, 53, 54, 78, 87, 164, 183
Olynthus, Olynthians 15, 87, 117
Ophellas 51–2, 83, 183–4
Opis 5, 39, 107, 178, 190
Oreitai 75
Orestis 19, 21, 28
Osiris 107, 128, 131–2, 134, 135, 138–40, 142, 191, 192, 193
Osorapis 135

pages 13, 14, 27, 28, 42, 108–9, 162, 172, 187
Pamphylia, Pamphylians 7, 18, 60, 90, 181
Paphos 83, 92
Paraetacene, battle of 7
Parmenion 17, 31, 32, 70, 150, 154
Parysatis, wife of Alexander the Great 32–3
Patrae 87
Patroclus 186
Pausanias, assassin 33
Pausanias, geographer 23, 44, 175, 182, 184
Pausanias, pretender to Macedonian throne 174
Pella 19
Pelops 112
Pelusiac branch of the Nile 78, 83
Pelusium 79, 80, 81, 82
Perdiccas III, king of Macedonia 33, 46
Perdiccas, son of Orontes 1, 9, 21, 30, 32, 33, 34, 36–43, 44, 45, 46–55, 56, 57,

58–9, 60, 64, 65, 67, 68, 70, 72, 73, 74, 75–8, 80–2, 83, 84, 94, 95, 101, 104–5, 109, 113, 123, 131, 147, 149, 150, 156, 157, 158–60, 161, 163, 164, 165, 166, 174, 178, 179, 180, 186, 194, 195, 196, 197
Perpelaus 96
Persephonê 192
Persepolis 70–1, 153–4, 177, 182
Perilaus 89
Persia, Persians 1–5, 6, 7, 17, 18, 29, 31, 32, 38, 50, 51, 70–1, 78, 80, 84, 86, 88, 91, 101, 103, 108, 120, 124, 129, 134, 136, 160, 165, 169, 172, 177, 178, 180, 182, 183, 185, 186, 187, 188, 190, 195, 196
Persian Gates 70–1, 73, 150, 151–5, 182, 195
Peucestas, son of Alexander 6, 36, 86, 91, 109, 159, 161, 162
Peucestas, son of Macartatus 129
pezehetairoi, foot companions 15, 17, 25, 27, 173
Phaselis 93
Phila 50, 97
Philadelphoi 186
Philip II, king of Macedonia 2, 3, 6, 8, 11, 13, 18, 24, 25, 27, 29, 32, 33, 44, 48, 50, 53, 67, 68, 70, 76, 87, 88, 104, 108, 111, 113–15, 116, 120, 181, 182, 183
  army reforms 15–17, 25, 112, 173
  father of Ptolemy I? 21–3, 156
  nation building 19–21, 25, 26–7, 172, 175, 186, 187, 189
Philip III, king of Macedonia (*see also* Arrhidaeus) 4, 23, 34, 42–3, 53, 77, 81, 87, 109, 122, 123, 128, 183, 189
Philip IV, king of Macedonia 92, 99
Philip, father of Antigonus Monophthalmus 172, 195
Philip, son of Menelaus 151
Philippopolis 20
philos, philoi, philia 14, 17–18, 28, 70, 109–10, 112, 116, 173
Philotas, son of Parmenion 17, 18, 31, 150, 152, 153, 154, 194, 195
philoxenos 116
Phoenicia 59, 60, 61, 64, 83, 84, 85–6, 89, 90, 91, 96, 114, 129, 170

Photius 171
Phrygia, Phrygians 9, 54, 77, 108, 142, 158, 160
Pisidia, Pisidians 77
Pithon 36, 41, 56, 57, 84, 86
Pixodarus 17–19, 67, 84, 171
Plato 111
Plutarch 10–11, 17, 18, 20, 21, 24, 29, 30, 33, 98, 132–4, 147, 161, 162, 172, 173, 175, 184, 185–6, 191, 193, 196
Pluto 192
Polemaeus, Antigonus' nephew 92–3, 94, 184,
Polemaeus, brother of Antigonus 195
polis, poleis 2, 107, 111, 112, 115, 117
Polyaenus 10, 67, 81
Polybius 8, 14, 45, 101, 170, 178
Polycleitus 88–9
Polyperchon 24, 58, 62, 84, 86, 87–9, 92, 93, 109, 164, 170, 195, 198
Pompeius Trogus 10, 33, 37, 41–3, 44, 52
Porus 73, 155, 195
principes (*magistoi*) 33, 34–5, 36, 37, 177, 178
propaganda 52, 56, 59, 63, 147–50, 163–6, 197–8
proxenos, proxenoi, proxenia 110–11, 112, 116, 188
Ptah 107, 128, 134
Ptolemais, daughter of Ptolemy I 97
Ptolemais Hermiou 115, 117
Ptolemy I Soter *passim*
  administration 4, 6, 103, 105–25, 167, 169, 187, 188
  religious policy 128–42
Ptolemy II Philadelphus 47, 100, 104, 106, 114, 122, 127, 128, 131, 186, 190, 193
Ptolemy III 23, 133, 139
Ptolemy Ceraunus 11, 47, 100, 186, 190
Pydna 87
Pyrrhus 10, 97–100, 175, 185

Racotis 187
Raphia, battle of 107
Rhodes, Rhodians 4, 31, 61–2, 86, 88, 95–6, 127, 131, 189
Rome, Romans 3–4, 10, 33, 35, 94, 118, 132, 133, 138, 140, 142, 147, 167, 168–9, 171, 176, 177

Roxane 32, 37, 39, 41, 43, 44, 87, 92, 95, 177, 178

Salamis, battle of 4, 24, 60, 62, 68, 85, 94–5
Salamis, city on Cyprus 83, 85, 89, 94, 189
Samos 49, 50, 51, 77, 112
sarissa, pike 16, 175, 177
Satibarzanes 196
satrap 2, 5, 6, 9, 18, 43, 44, 48, 49, 50, 54, 60, 76–7, 80, 81, 84, 86, 117, 119, 122, 128, 164, 171, 179, 180, 183
Satrap Stele 122–3, 124, 129, 187, 189
Savior gods 61, 95, 162, 127–8, 130–1, 137
Scepsis 92
Schep, L. 30
Seleucus 1, 6, 10–11, 22, 24, 47, 57, 61, 64, 67, 68, 73, 83, 84, 86, 89, 90, 91, 92, 94, 95, 96, 97, 98, 100, 101, 112, 152, 174, 182, 195
Serapis, cult of 107, 131–3, 135, 137–42, 149, 167–8, 191–2, 193
Sicyon 62, 63, 87, 93, 101, 179
Sidon 60, 61, 86, 90, 96, 98, 100
Sinai 78, 82, 90
Sindh 75
Sisimithres, fortress of 73
Sitalces 176
Siwah, oracle 52, 53, 62, 127, 130, 135–6, 162–3, 164–5, 179–80, 190
Socrates, squadron commander 151
Soli 83, 104
Somatophylaces 1, 13, 16, 18, 34–9, 44, 45, 108, 109, 147, 151, 161, 162, 172, 177, 182–3, 187, 195
Sosigenes 111
Sotades of Maroneia 186
Spitamenes 71, 72, 155
Stateira, wife of Alexander 32
Stephanus of Byzantium 173
Stone, O. 30
Suda 57, 63, 179
Susa 5, 18, 98, 107, 160, 163, 178, 182, 187
Swat valley 74

Syria, Syrians 54, 55, 57, 60, 64, 83, 84, 85, 89, 91, 95, 96, 114, 123, 184, 187

Tacitus 133, 138, 191–2
Tammuz 191
Tapurians 7, 80, 176, 178
tax farming 106
Telesphorus 184
Temenus, king of Macedonia 22
Thaïs, wife of Ptolemy I 103, 104, 174, 185
Thebes, capital of Upper Egypt 107, 115, 135, 136, 189, 198
Thebes, Greek city 70, 87, 98, 150, 158–9, 196
Theocritus 113
Theodotus 89
Theopompus 25, 175
Thessalonice, daughter of Philip II 87, 99, 163
Thessalus 17, 18
Thibron 51–2
Thucydides 193
Tiberius 41
Timaeus 161
Triparadeisus 57, 84, 109
Tripolis 86, 90, 160
Tropheus 108
Tyre 60, 61, 85, 86, 88, 90, 96, 98, 100, 103, 185
Tyre Proclamation 86–7, 183

Upper Macedonia 19, 22, 28, 33
Uxians 153, 182

West Nile disease 176

Xanthus 93
xenos, xenoi, xenia 14, 110–11, 112, 116, 188

Zeus 14, 22, 46, 62, 130, 138
Zeus Amun 135–6, 165, 190
Zeus Hetaereius 15